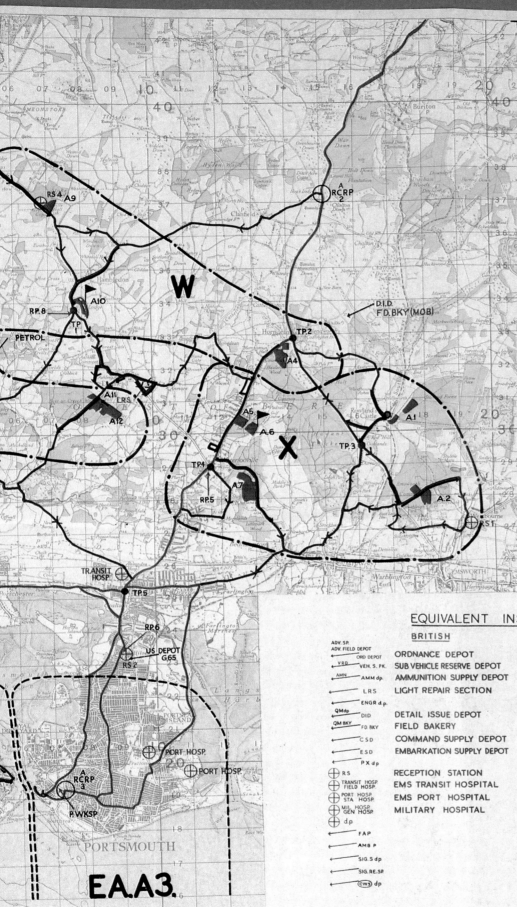

AREA 'A'
OVERLORD GENERAL INFORMATION MAP
1. MAY 1944.

SHEET ONE OF FIVE

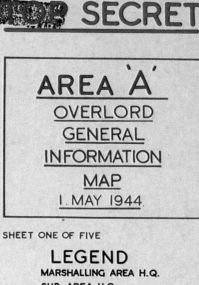

LEGEND

	MARSHALLING AREA H.Q.
	SUB-AREA H.Q.
	CAMPS (Nº Shown – eg. A.I.)
○ RCRP	ROAD CONVOY REGULATING POINT
● TP	TRAFFIC POST
	VEHICLE PARK or STANDINGS
	ONE-WAY ROUTE
	ONE-WAY OPERATIONAL – TWO-WAY ADM. & CIVILIAN
	TWO-WAY ROUTE
	SUB-AREA BOUNDARY
	EMBARKATION AREA BOUNDARY
PETROL	PETROL OIL & LUBRICANT DUMP
RP	RECOVERY POST (VEHICLE)
P. WKSP	PORT WORKSHOP
	DETRAINING STATION
PW	PRISONERS of WAR CAGE

EQUIVALENT INSTALLATIONS

	BRITISH	U.S.
ADV. SP. / ADV. FIELD DEPOT		
ORD DEPOT	ORDNANCE DEPOT	ADVANCE FIELD DEPOT & ADVANCE SHOP
VRD / VEH. S. PK.	SUB VEHICLE RESERVE DEPOT	VEHICLE SUPPLY PARK
AMN / AMM dp.	AMMUNITION SUPPLY DEPOT	AMMUNITION DISTRIBUTING POINT
LRS	LIGHT REPAIR SECTION	
ENGR d.p.		ENGINEER DUMP
QMdp / DID	DETAIL ISSUE DEPOT	QUARTER-MASTER DISTRIBUTING POINT
QM BKY / FD BKY	FIELD BAKERY	QUARTER-MASTER BAKERY
CSD	COMMAND SUPPLY DEPOT	
ESD	EMBARKATION SUPPLY DEPOT	
PX dp		POST EXCHANGE DUMP
RS	RECEPTION STATION	
TRANSIT HOSP / FIELD HOSP	EMS TRANSIT HOSPITAL	FIELD HOSPITAL
PORT HOSP / STA. HOSP	EMS PORT HOSPITAL	STATION HOSPITAL
MIL. HOSP / GEN HOSP	MILITARY HOSPITAL	GENERAL HOSPITAL
d.p		MEDICAL DISTRIBUTING POINT
FAP		FIRST AID POST
AMB P		AMBULANCE POST
SIG. S dp		SIGNAL SUPPLY DUMP
SIG. RE. SP		SIGNAL REPAIR SHOP
(CWS) dp		CHEMICAL WARFARE DUMP

APPROVED BY CENTRE
ZONE SUB COMMITTEE
18 APRIL 1944

(SIGNED) P.W. KEMP WELCH
LT. COL. AQMG (OPS)

(SIGNED) G.M. BOSTOCK COL FA
PLANNING DIVISION SBS

PT. OF 1" SHEET 132 OF G.S.G.S. SERIES Nº 3907.

Produced from Model Supplied

5 Miles
9,000 Yards

D-DAY

OPERATION OVERLORD

**From the Landing
at Normandy to the
Liberation of Paris**

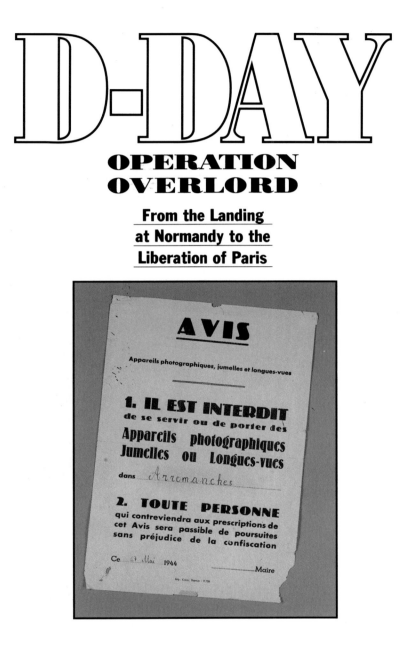

D-DAY

OPERATION OVERLORD
From the Landing at Normandy to the Liberation of Paris
Foreword by WINSTON S. CHURCHILL

SMITHMARK

A Salamander Book

This edition published in 1993 by
SMITHMARK Publishers Inc.,
16 East 32nd Street, New York, NY 10016

SMITHMARK books are available for bulk
purchase for sales promotion and
premium use.
For details write or telephone the
Manager of Special Sales,
SMITHMARK Publishers Inc.,
16 East 32nd Street, New York, NY 10016
(212) 532-6600

©Salamander Books Ltd

10 9 8 7 6 5 4 3 2 1

Library of Congress Cataloging-in-
Publication Data
D-Day : Operation Overlord : from the
   landing at Normandy to the liberation
   of Paris / Foreword by Winston S.
   Churchill.
         p.   cm.
   Includes bibliographical references
   and index.
   ISBN 0-8317-2188-X: $24.98
   1. World War. 1939-1945—Campaigns
   —France—Normandy.
   2. Operation Overlord. 3. Normandy
   (France)—History, Military.
   4. World War. 1939-1945—Campaigns
   —France.
   D756.5.N6D46   1993
   940.54'2142—dc20   93-1883
                                  CIP

All correspondence concerning the
content of this volume should be
addressed to
Salamander Books Ltd,
129-137 York Way,
London N7 9LG, England

CREDITS

Editor: Tony Hall

Designer: Paul Johnson

Indexer: David Linton

Captions: Tony Hall, Chris Chant

Translations: First Edition Translations,
Cambridge

Picture researcher: Tony Moore

Color Artwork: Stephen Seymour
22-23; 138-139; 142-143
©Salamander Books Ltd

Map artwork: Geoff Denney Associates
©Salamander Books Ltd

Diagram artwork: Kevin Jones Associates
©Salamander Books Ltd

Commissioned color photographs:
Don Eiler, Richmond, Virginia
10-11; 16-17; 19; 24-25; 26; 28; 38 (bottom);
42-43; 44-45; 47; 52-53; 55; 56; 58
(bottom); 61; 72; 81 (bottom) 86-87; 90-91;
92 (top); 94; 124-125; 126; 127 (both); 137;
141; 146-147 (all); 149; 151; 168-169;
174-175; 190-191; 194-195; 200-201; 205
(both); 206-207; 209; 213; 221

Michael Dyer Associates, London
Endpapers; Halftitle; Title; 4-5; 8; 20;
30-31; 32-33; 35; 37; 38 (top); 39; 40; 46;
50-51; 58 (top); 60; 62-63; 66; 73; 76-77;
78; 79; 80; 81 (top); 84; 92 (bottom, both);
95; 98 (all); 99 (all); 100-101; 102; 104-105;
106; 113; 114; 115; 120-121; 130; 132-133;
134 (all); 150; 152-153; 156-157; 158-159;
161; 162-163; 165; 167; 172; 173; 178-179;
184-185; 187; 188; 192 (both); 193; 204;
213; 216-217; 219; 220; 222; 224
©Salamander Books Ltd

Retouched photographs Janos Marffy
26; 35; 36; 58; 92 (top); 96; 102; 115; 165;
167; 173
©Salamander Books Ltd

Filmsetting and Calendars:
The Old Mill, London

Color reproductions:
Scantrans Pte Ltd, Singapore

Printed in Italy

PUBLISHER'S ACKNOWLEDGMENTS

In the preparation of this volume, we have
been extremely fortunate to have
received the advice and support of
militaria collectors, museum directors and
their staffs, and photographic archives
both public and private. We would also
like to thank in particular: Mr. Winston
Churchill; Dr. Jean-Pierre Benamou;
M. Phillipe Jutras; M. Henri G. Levaufre;
M. Marc Jacquinot; Mme. Catherine
Horel; Mr Krzysztof Barbarski; Lt. Gen. Sir
Michael Gray, Chairman, Airborne
Assault Normandy Trust; Stephen Brooks;
Ed Bartholomew; John Frost; Lt. Col.
George Forty, David Fletcher of The Tank
Museum; Jack McDevitt, Hugh
Heffelfinger, George Whittington of the
Ranger Battalion Association of World
War II; Doon Campbell; Virginia Hewitt of
the British Museum; Graham Bartlett of
the National Meteorological Library. Staffs
of the stills photographic departments of:
The National Archives, Washington DC;
Imperial War Museum, London;
Bundesarchiv, Koblenz, Germany; the
authors of the G-2 reports; Christine
Delaborde, and Britta Martins. We would
also like to extend a special thanks to
Bernard Nalty, Don Eiler, and the staff of
Michael Dyer Associates for their
invaluable contributions. A very special
thank you is extended to Russ Pritchard,
whose knowledge and enthusiasm helped
get the project off the beaches.

Publisher's Notes:
The calendars which head each chapter
run in day order from Sunday to Saturday.
While many individual units are named in
this book, because of the restrictions of
space, many, many more are not. We hope
readers excuse any notable absences.
   For details of the contributing museums
see "Acknowledgments" on page 221.

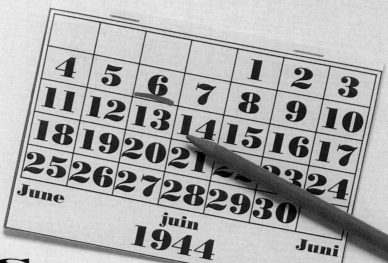

Contents

Foreword

This was the greatest amphibious operation ever undertaken in the history of warfare. The scale was majestic; 5,000 ships, together with thousands of lesser craft, backed by 11,000 aircraft were, in the space of 48 hours, to hurl nearly 200,000 men against Hitler's much vaunted Atlantic Wall, behind which Field Marshal von Rundstedt's 60 Divisions were lying in wait, half of them concentrated on the coast from Holland to Normandy under the command of Field Marshal Rommel. All told, the *Overlord* plan conceived by General Eisenhower and the Combined Chiefs of Staff, called for an army of 2,000,000 men — half American and half British & Commonwealth — being deployed to Europe across the Normandy beachhead.

If the scale of this military undertaking was heroic, so too was its objective: nothing less than the defeat of Nazi Germany and the Liberation of Europe. The story is an epic of heroism and sacrifice, but also of victory and success. I am delighted that this volume addressing the subject afresh 50 years on from these dramatic events, places before the public the fruits of the researches and viewpoints of many and diverse military experts and historians, drawn from Britain, the United States and Germany. It is a worthy contribution to the already large body of histories, biographies and autobiographies that have illuminated and recorded for posterity those fateful hours and days that followed the dawning of June 6, 1944, that will forever be known as D-Day.

From the vantage point of half a century's hindsight, the success of the enterprise and its ultimate victorious conclusion seems predestined and inevitable. That was certainly not how it appeared either to General Eisenhower or Prime Minister Churchill on the eve of the invasion. Indeed the latter, before turning in for the night, told his wife: "Do you realise that by the time you wake up in the morning, 20,000 men may have been killed?"

The responsibility and risks of launching so many men on such an enterprise were enormous. Much could go wrong, as none knew better than Winston Churchill. Twenty-nine years before, thousands of British and Empire soldiers had perished under withering machinegun fire as they sought to land on the beaches of Gallipoli — an enterprise with which Churchill had been closely associated in his capacity as First Lord of the Admiralty, and for which he had been made the scapegoat.

Perhaps it was for that reason that he fought so tenaciously to postpone D-Day from 1943 to 1944 — despite enormous pressure for the earlier date from Marshal Stalin, and indeed the Americans. Rather than risk all, as a gambler, on a single throw of the dice in a premature and potentially disastrous assault against Hitler's "Fortress Europe," Churchill believed in the need for an approach-march to victory. This was to be provided by the campaigns in North Africa, Sicily and Italy — all theatres where, without control of sea or air, Hitler was unable to deploy ground forces on a scale decisive enough to avoid defeat. Far from being irrelevant side-shows, as some have suggested, they proved indispensable steps in the transformation of raw recruits fresh out of civilian life, into armies of battle-hardened veterans with the expertise and self-confidence that can only be developed in action and under the fire of the battlefield.

In consequence of postponing the opening of the Second Front by a year, the balance of advantage turned heavily in favour of the Allies. The scale of the American military buildup in Britain was much greater; indeed all of southern Britain was turned into an armed camp of British, Commonwealth and American soldiers. Many more landing ships were available, and new weird and wonderful devices for dealing with underwater defences and for breaching the Atlantic Wall had been developed.

Meanwhile the Nazi forces had suffered severe attrition and blows to their morale. The Red Army had inflicted a decisive defeat on the German Army at Stalingrad early in 1943. British and American forces had routed Rommel's German-Italian army in North Africa; Sicily had been taken, southern Italy invaded and, as the D-Day forces were already embarking for their great assault, word came from General Alexander that Rome had been liberated. In addition, a further year of the Allied Bombing Offensive, that alone carried the war to the enemy heartland, had undoubtedly taken its toll, not just of the Luftwaffe — which was to be conspicuous by its absence at the critical phase of the landings (putting up a mere 100 sorties compared to the Allies' 14,600 in the 24 hours of June 6) but on the enemy's war-production and communications network.

Deception undoubtedly played a key role in the success of the landings, Rommel being firmly convinced that they would take place in the Pas de Calais area around Calais and Boulogne, where he had concentrated his forces and where the defences were strongest. Furthermore the fact that British cypher-breakers at Bletchley had cracked the German code and were able to provide daily *Ultra* decrypts of German radio traffic, including signals sent by Hitler and German High Command to their armies in the field, proved an inestimable advantage.

Of course the *sine qua non* for the Normandy invasion and the ultimate Liberation of Europe was that in those critical days of May/June 1940 when Hitler launched his "Blitzkrieg" against France, Belgium and the Low Countries, and all of Europe surrendered before his onslaught, was that Britain alone had stood firm, refusing — against all the odds — to surrender or to parley. Given recent criticism levelled against Churchill by latter-day 'Revisionist' historians, that he failed to negotiate 'terms' with Hitler in the summer of 1940 or the spring of 1941 — which of course would have led to the establishment of a "Quisling" Government in Britain, together with all the Nazi apparatus of the Gestapo and Death Camps — it is perhaps worth making the point that without Britain as an unsinkable "aircraft-carrier" anchored off the shores of Northern Europe, the D-Day landings — which would have been impossible to mount from more than 3,000 miles (4,800km) away across the Atlantic — could never have taken place. The Liberation of Europe would have been indefinitely postponed and it is no exaggeration to say that it is entirely possible that, even to this day, the Nazi swastika might still be flying over the capital cities of Europe.

My Grandfather came to office on May 10, 1940 — the very day Hitler unleashed his Western "Blitzkrieg" — with two innermost convictions. First, that in our Island the British nation was unconquerable. Secondly, that only with the combined might of the English-speaking peoples, including pre-eminently the "Great Republic across the Seas" (as he was wont to call America), could Hitler be defeated and Europe Liberated. D-Day and what flowed from it, marked the fulfilment of that final conviction.

Winston S. Churchill
April 1993

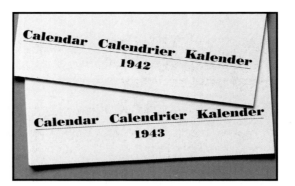

The Second Front Debate

1

Charles Kirkpatrick

In an address to students at the US Army War College in the mid-1920s, Brig. Gen. Fox Conner harshly characterized the business of fighting as part of an alliance. While serving in France as an operations officer on Gen. John J. Pershing's staff, he had witnessed the perpetual inability of the Allied and Associated powers to settle on a common strategy against the Germans or even to agree on allocation of resources. The incessant pursuit of purely national interests, in his opinion, prevented the Allies from bringing the full weight of their military and economic power efficiently to bear against their common enemy. Thus, as he pondered the problem for the benefit of the Army's future stategists, Conner concluded that, if he had to go to war again, he would prefer to go to war against an alliance, rather than against a single power.

Conner was a considerable scholar of the military art, but his strictures on the perils of alliances had already been voiced centuries before by Sun Tzu, the ancient Chinese philosopher of war, who warned against entering into alliances without being entirely certain of the war aims of the potential ally. Hastily conceived agreements, Sun Tzu suggested, could easily founder because two powers fighting a common foe might themselves have conflicting intentions. His was sound advice, for whenever two or more nations combined their efforts in war during the succeeding centuries, bitter disagreements, rather than concord, were often the rule. In fact, one of the peculiarities of alliances is that successful ones have always tended to disintegrate in discord as fast as unsuccessful ones. That certainly was the American experience of World War I, the first major occasion since the Revolution when

the United States had waged war in concert with allies. As isolationism and the depression jointly spiraled through the 1930s, a residuum of suspicion was directed even against the United Kingdom. There were those, both in the Army and out, who believed American naivety had been cold-bloodedly exploited in 1917 in a war to preserve the British Empire.

The Anglo-American alliance of World War II stood in contrast to the experience of 1917-18 as perhaps the most successful coalition in the history of modern warfare. From

the very beginning, the United States and the United Kingdom adopted the defeat of Germany as their common goal. Agreement on ultimate aims nonetheless did not imply agreement in detail, and the progress of the war was marked by periodic disputes. Among the most famous was the occasionally

Below: German forces, such as this column of Erwin Rommel's 7th Panzer Division seen in May 1940, had been in Belgium and France for four years and had developed a full appreciation of the tactical difficulties posed by operations close to the Channel coast.

acrimonious debate between Generals Dwight D. Eisenhower and Sir Bernard L. Montgomery about the proper strategy to be employed on the European continent: the "broad front" or the "knife-like thrust." The springs of such disagreements arose from the gradually evolving leadership of the coalition. Until 1943, Britain was the dominant partner and consequently more powerfully influenced the course of the alliance. After 1943, however, the United States, by virtue of its contribution of the greater mass of manpower and economic power, became senior partner. The Second Front debate, more than any other, was emblematic of that shift in coalition leadership. It was, furthermore, the most significant difference of opinion that arose between the United States and Britain during the war. Both nations agreed that Germany had to be assaulted, but the specific agreement that the assault would be launched from England, across the English Channel, to the coast of France, was reached only after extended discussion. At its root, the Second Front debate was the question of whether the alliance would adhere to a long-term plan for a cross-channel attack, or would retain the flexibility to take advantage of the military situation at the time of attack to strike where Germany was weakest. Economic, political, and military differences, as well as differences in national styles of waging war, complicated the debate.

The American Position

Even before the fall of France in May 1940, the United States was slipping away from the dubious neutrality that it had proclaimed at the start of the European war. President Franklin D. Roosevelt declared a national emergency and ordered the Navy into the Atlantic, ostensibly on "neutrality patrols," but in fact to help the British by convoying ships at least part of the way across the danger zone. Against the possibility that the United States would eventually enter the war, American naval and military staffs began a series of unofficial, unrecognized, but nonetheless crucial discussions in Washington between January and March, 1941. The most important single decision the military leaders reached in these American-British Conversations, or ABC talks for short, was that Germany would be the number one enemy of any future Anglo-American partnership. Such a decision was contrary to long-standing assumptions of Army and Navy war planning. Plan *Orange*, meticulously refined

Above: American troops land in Iceland during July 1941. The USA was not yet involved in the war, but this move signaled the importance attached by Roosevelt's administration of this mid-Atlantic bastion, and the relief of British troops for combat.

over more than two decades, outlined the strategy to be employed when the United States and Japan eventually went to war, as many naval and military officers assumed would eventually happen. Tension in the Pacific increased throughout 1941, and thoughtful observers of the Far East warned of Japanese aggressive designs that would almost certainly involve American interests and possessions. Despite this, American leaders agreed that any war that might begin with Japan would have to take second place; primacy of effort would go to defeating Germany.

Much of this reflected President Roosevelt's conviction that the fate of the United States was indissolubly linked with that of the United Kingdom. The continued existence of the latter was in the best interests of the United States, not only because of the commonality of language and culture, but also because Britain stood as a bulwark against any possible Axis aggression in the Americas. American armed forces in 1941

Below: The signature of the Franco-German armistice at Compiègne on June 21, 1940 sealed an enormous German success that had been gained relatively cheaply. Hitler, seen here with senior political and military leaders on this occasion, knew that Britain was isolated and that any invasion to wrest Europe from Germany would be an undertaking of immense difficulty.

were frankly unready for global war, and it was the British fleet, guaranteeing control of the Atlantic, that provided security during the period of national mobilization that the President was attempting to hurry. The President and his principal advisors were likewise convinced that the United States should do that which was morally right, rather than just that which was politically expedient. The conclusion Roosevelt drew was that American energies should be focused in support of the British to defeat the greatest threat to the free world. That threat, he concluded, was Germany. Prime Minister Winston Churchill's delight with the agreement, however, was soon to be tempered by the American view on how it should be carried out. American plans for the impending war were conditioned by an interplay of military philosophy and economic and geographic constraints that did not affect the United Kingdom.

One aspect of European military thought that had fallen on fertile ground in the United States came from one of the most profound military thinkers of the century, Maj. Gen. J. F. C. Fuller, a highly experienced British officer whom many regarded as the foremost exponent in the world of armored warfare. Fuller's enumeration of the "principles of war" appealed greatly to Americans. A listing of the most important considerations in military operations naturally appealed to the mechanically-minded. Yet the principles of war were more than just a check-list for military commanders. They were, rather, an organized way of thinking about war, and most officers saw the "principle of the objective" as far and away the most important of all considerations. Their military ideal was a legacy of the American Civil War and the style of Gen. U. S. Grant, who tenaciously maintained contact with Gen. R. E. Lee's

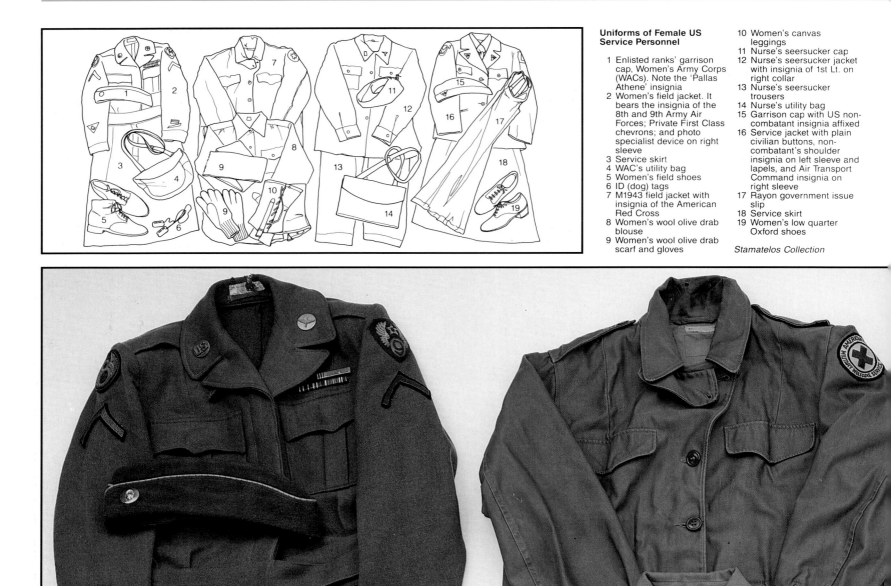

Uniforms of Female US Service Personnel

1 Enlisted ranks' garrison cap, Women's Army Corps (WACs). Note the 'Pallas Athene' insignia
2 Women's field jacket. It bears the insignia of the 8th and 9th Army Air Forces; Private First Class chevrons; and photo specialist device on right sleeve
3 Service skirt
4 WAC's utility bag
5 Women's field shoes
6 ID (dog) tags
7 M1943 field jacket with insignia of the American Red Cross
8 Women's wool olive drab blouse
9 Women's wool olive drab scarf and gloves
10 Women's canvas leggings
11 Nurse's seersucker cap
12 Nurse's seersucker jacket with insignia of 1st Lt. on right collar
13 Nurse's seersucker trousers
14 Nurse's utility bag
15 Garrison cap with US non-combatant insignia affixed
16 Service jacket with plain civilian buttons, non-combatant's shoulder insignia on left sleeve and lapels, and Air Transport Command insignia on right sleeve
17 Rayon government issue slip
18 Service skirt
19 Women's low quarter Oxford shoes

Stamatelos Collection

Army of Northern Virginia until he achieved victory. Americans preferred a short, extremely violent war, with all possible resources brought to bear in continuous combat until the enemy was defeated. The principle of attacking a clearly defined and attainable military objective, almost always the main body of the enemy's army, accorded well with the limitations under which American officers perceived they would have to fight.

Geography was equally important. Broad oceans offered the Americas great physical security from attack, but they also isolated the continent from European and Asiatic battlefields. In the event of war, as planners at the Army War College clearly foresaw during the 1920s and 1930s, the United States would have to erect and maintain a large and sophisticated logistical structure to send substantial forces across the oceans, sustain them in foreign theaters, and employ them against powerful enemies on other continents. If war came in Asia as well as in Europe, as some officers expected, the problem of allocating scarce resources would be even more acute. Those essential demands on manpower and materiel would certainly detract from the total fighting power the United States could muster. These geopolitical factors were expressed in the American planning document for World War II.

In the spring and summer of 1941, during the last months of peace for the United States, the War Department was superintending the sale of surplus war materiel to Britain and other nations arrayed against Hitler, and considering how to meet the demands imposed by the recently passed Lend-Lease Bill, under the terms of which the United States would transfer massive amounts of military equipment to the countries fighting the Axis. At the same time, the Army was involved in a limited expansion, virtually a peace-time mobilization, that threw mobilization plans out of joint. In the work of military supply and procurement, chaos reigned. In an attempt to develop a manageable production plan,

the Assistant Secretary of War and President Roosevelt asked the general staff for an estimate of what would be needed to defeat the Axis if the United States became involved in the war.

Gen. George C. Marshall, Army Chief of Staff, handed that question to Albert C. Wedemeyer, an infantry major assigned to the War Plans Division of the general staff, and Wedemeyer's staff estimate, later known as the Victory Plan, succinctly delineated the steps necessary to win a European war. Wedemeyer reasoned that he could not estimate the nation's total military production requirements unless he had some idea of the size and missions of the Army in the event of war. He immediately drew on the substance of the ABC talks to define the Army's mission in the event of war. The chief task, he assumed, was the defeat of Germany, to which all other missions would be subordinate.

Military logic, as embodied in the principles of war, demanded that the Army strictly keep its eye on the objective, and not fritter its limited energies away in attractive, but indecisive, side issues. If the defeat of Germany was the objective, then the mission was to attack the heart of German power as early and as forcefully as possible. That meant massing the Army for a direct invasion of the continent of Europe at the earliest possible date. Determining that date relied on three interrelated factors: the date by which enough men could be trained and equipped for war, the date by which the necessary shipping would be available to move them to Europe and sustain them there, and the date by which the necessary military preconditions for attack could be completed.

Careful consideration of Army mobilization and training, military construction, and naval and merchant shipbuilding revealed that the Army could expect to go over to the offensive no earlier than July 1, 1943. Achieving the necessary military conditions for attack, though simple to state, was a more uncertain proposition. Wedemeyer suggested in his plan that no invasion of Europe could succeed until the navies defeated the Axis fleets and secured the Atlantic lines of communication; the Allies established air superiority over Europe; air bombardment had disrupted the German economy and industry, thus decreasing that country's warmaking potential; German military forces

had been weakened; and adequate bases had been established. Although he did not specify it in the Victory Plan, Wedemeyer assumed, and fellow war-planners explicitly stated, that the only useful European bases that would still be available to the United States in 1943 would be those situated in the British Isles.

Thus, before war even began for the United States, there existed a conceptual plan for the ultimate defeat of Germany. That plan relied on an invasion of the continent of Europe to strike into the heart of Germany, to the exclusion of all other military designs. Implicit in the plan were fighting and winning the Battle of the Atlantic; what became known as the combined bomber offensive that sought to destroy German industry and economic life; continued attacks on the Germans wherever they could be found, to decrease their military strength; and the creation of a major American buildup in Britain. The climactic battle, because of the practicalities of production and military preparations, could not start before July 1943, two years hence.

Below: Convoy escort in the Atlantic was a constant drain on Allied naval resources. Heavier warships such as battleships and cruisers were needed so long as there was a threat of German surface raiders, but smaller escorts later sufficed against the U-boats.

Above: Photographed from a Boeing Fortress maritime reconnaissance aircraft of RAF Coastal Command, this convoy is making a port turn as it approaches a British harbor after its hazardous journey across the Atlantic with weapons, materiel and food for Britain.

American war planners accordingly had to figure on deploying a large army and air force, as well as a powerful navy, to Europe; sustaining it there while maintaining long and easily attacked lines of communications across the oceans; allotting enough military power at least to contain the Japanese in the meantime; and producing enough materiel to support not only American forces, but also the armies of the Allies. This, they felt, could never be done without a master plan, adjustable in fine detail, but not in its major points. Such massive industrial production demanded careful timing, and Americans wanted a corresponding military timetable.

The choice of Britain as a base for the attack on Europe, made while Eisenhower was chief of War Plans Division in early 1942, was equally crucial. Early, planners dismissed fanciful ideas of landings in Liberia and subsequent campaigns through North Africa, across the Mediterranean, and into southern Europe. A concept to deliver American troops to Russia was scrapped because shipping routes to Murmansk or through the Persian Gulf, both for troops and for supplies, were simply too long. Attacks through Portugal, Norway, and Spain were all dismissed as too roundabout.

For a time, there was serious thought about an attack from the Mediterranean, where the British were already doing well against German forces. Despite Prime Minister Winston Churchill's later enthusiasm for the "soft underbelly" of Europe, Americans rejected the Mediterranean avenue of approach because long supply lines made it impossible to concentrate full Allied strength there, and because of the distance to the heart of Germany from North American bases when the attack had to pass through southern Europe. More serious opposition to an attack through the south of France, or through Italy, or through the Balkans, arose because of the

extremely difficult terrain, favorable for defense, that stood between the Mediterranean shores and Germany.

The choice settled on Britain for all of the reasons that made the other options impractical. The most important single consideration was that Britain lay on the shortest of all possible transatlantic routes from the United States. A perennial problem for war planners, regardless of the proposed operation, was the perpetual Allied shortage of merchant ships. The Battle of the Atlantic had consumed too many ships, both merchant and naval; losses that were made up by new construction at the cost of accumulating the tonnage needed to increase the pace of offensive operations. Many convoys had to be dedicated to feeding and supplying the British Isles, while others tried to sustain the Soviet ally, whose continued resistance was an essential element in all American war planning. Once war began, other vessels had to be diverted to maintain American and Commonwealth military strength in the Pacific, even at minimal levels. Economy of supply was therefore a foremost consideration. A short route meant a shorter travel time. An easy route facilitated large convoys. Good ports in Britain meant a shorter turnaround time for the ships. Placing the American buildup in the British Isles was the most efficient use of scarce shipping.

Secondly, the British Isles were a logical point of departure for military operations against the continent. Big enough to support the buildup, the islands were also the best place from which to use the relatively short-ranged fighters of the Royal Air Force to support landings, and an unsinkable aircraft carrier for the American Army Air Forces. The short distance across the English Channel offered for the Allies the chance to give the attacking infantry continuous and effective air support. The Royal Navy, major units of which were already concentrated around the North Sea to bottle up the German surface fleet, could most easily be used to support landings against the Channel coast. Most important, however, was the geographical fact that the most direct route into the center of Germany was the one from the French coast opposite England, and thence across northwest Europe. That route also offered the minimum in natural, and therefore defensible, obstacles. Militarily, it was the most logical choice.

For the Americans, the decision to use the United Kingdom was axiomatic. When compared with the other possible avenues of approach, it was superior in almost every way, offering the possibility of the quickest buildup and concentration of force. The intention to concentrate rapidly in Britain meant that the United States would enforce rigorous economies of manpower and materiel in other theaters, while intensifying the campaign of aerial attack on Germany and blockade of Europe, and the naval war in the Atlantic. Industrial mobilization plans began to structure American industry to support such a plan, and the military enthusiastically began to organize itself around the requirements for just such a major attack. American planning for what became Operation *Overlord* actually began before the

Above: US troops embark for Europe at the Hampton Roads Port of Embarkation at Newport News, Virginia. Such transports generally carried up to 1,500 men, but larger vessels such as the liners *Queen Elizabeth* and *Queen Mary* could each carry 15,000 men.

United States entered the war, and it was always the essence of American war policy. Literally everything the United States did was aimed at that decisive invasion of the continent, and military operations were judged in terms of how well they contributed to that end. *Overlord* was far more than just D-Day, and far more than just one important battle. It was the culmination of the entire American strategy.

The British Position

Geographical location and a different philosophy of waging war gave the British a different outlook on the nature, timing, and location of the Second Front against Germany. At the time of the initial staff talks, the United Kingdom had already been at war for some two years and had suffered grievous losses during the Battle of France, the Battle of Britain, and the Battle of the Atlantic. Even as the famous Eighth Army began its successful march across North Africa after the battle of El Alamein, it was clear that the British lived in a world of ever-declining resources. Certainly from 1943 onward, their forces would never be as strong tomorrow as they were today, because the limits of British and Commonwealth manpower had been reached. It was also true that the British were forever confronted with the specter of the Somme. Politically, militarily, practically, and in humanitarian terms, it was unthinkable that Britain should again suffer the enormous casualties that she had borne in the 1914-18

war. The notion of attacking carefully prepared fortifications along the French coast struck many conscientious soldiers as being potentially as costly as any of the great assaults of World War I.

British political and military leaders were therefore inclined to be extremely cautious. They certainly were in favor of an invasion of Europe, but only when the time was right; when circumstances were in the Allies' favor. They could not, many held, afford to be repulsed. If the invasion failed for any of the many possible dangers inherent in such a risky operation, then, at least from the British point of view, there could be no second try. Churchill and his commanders accordingly had the tendency to define favorable circumstances very precisely.

The British were also historically a maritime power, and their entire experience in dealing with a hostile continental military power — chiefly the wars of the French Revolution and of Napoleon — inclined them to a sea power solution. The result was that many preferred to draw a blockade, a net of steel, around the Axis and gradually pull it tighter and tighter, nibbling away with the army at exposed bits of Axis military strength. At the end, following the successful naval battles of the Atlantic and the bombing campaign which British leaders agreed were necessary preconditions for the assault, Germany would be debilitated and weak. A single, powerful blow would then be enough.

The British further counseled caution because they had a more recent, more extensive, and generally more sobering understanding of amphibious operations than the American allies, whose last important landing had been during their civil war, and who, it was possible to argue, had never conducted an *opposed* amphibious landing at all. British planners well understood that the English Channel, however narrow at various points, was a formidable barrier that had stopped Napoleon and, more recently, the technically sophisticated Germans. More to the point was their own World War I landing at Gallipoli, which warned of the high costs of attacking a hostile shore, and appeared to show that well-organized defenses could contain even successful landings.

Carefully studied between the two world wars, Gallipoli convinced thoughtful soldiers that the defender would always be able to bring up reinforcements faster than the attack could build up his forces on the invasion beaches, and would likewise be better able to supply and support those forces than the attacker. Amphibious landings were by nature always frontal assaults, very much like those that characterized fighting on the Western Front; although without the advantages of extensive artillery support, the availability of reserves, and attacks launched from prepared positions. The British experience on the Western Front had been grim; how much worse, then, a frontal attack that arose from the waves? It was the lessons learned from the 1942 attack on the French port of Dieppe (Operation *Jubilee*), however, that worried invasion planners most.

British forces had launched minor raids on the French coast almost from the moment of the evacuation of the army from Dunkirk. In August 1942, Lord Louis Mountbatten's Combined Operations headquarters passed from mere raids to a deliberate, large-scale invasion of Dieppe. The intention was never to hold the beachhead, but to test military and naval cooperation; the use of combined arms in large-scale landings of infantry and armored troops; and the organization of air forces in obtaining and maintaining control of the air over invasion beaches. Mountbatten's operation was also to test a new piece

Below: One of the few commanders to shine at Dieppe was Lt. Col. Lord Lovat, whose No. 4 Commando captured the Varangeville battery. On D-Day, Lovat, by then a brigadier, led his 1st Special Service Brigade on the eastern flank of the *Sword* beach landings.

Above: The Dieppe raid of August 1942 provided invaluable lessons about amphibious tactics, and confirmed the utility of two items seen here: the new Churchill tank (with extended exhausts for deep wading) and the Landing Craft, Tank, of which 24 were used.

of equipment, the Landing Craft, Tank (LCT), to see whether it could place tanks directly on the beaches, thus enabling assault forces to take a port by direct frontal assault.

The August 19 landings, conducted largely with soldiers of Canadian 2nd Division, although about one thousand British troops and some fifty US Rangers also took part, were an unmitigated tactical failure. German resistance was unexpectedly fierce. Within nine hours of the assault, British commanders were forced to withdraw the survivors under heavy pressure from the defenders. Almost one thousand soldiers died in the attack and around two thousand were left on the battlefield as prisoners of war. Of the 6,100 men in the assault force, only 2,500 returned to England. If Dieppe was a dry run for the eventual invasion of France, its high casualty lists made British planners' blood run cold. Ordinary German garrison troops, it turned out, and not elite formations, had repulsed the Canadian attack. One of the chief lessons of Dieppe was thus that a large naval bombardment force was essential to crack the prepared defenses of any hostile shore, and the accumulation of that force awaited the winning of critical naval battles in the Atlantic and elsewhere. Clearly, the lessons of Gallipoli still applied. There was not much subtlety to amphibious assaults, and overwhelming force was essential if there was to be any hope of success.

The consequence of all these considerations was that the British always appeared willing to explore alternate strategies and points of attack that would enable the alliance to hit the enemy where circumstances offered, rather than adhering strictly to a carefully conceived and, as they saw it, excessively rigid, plan. Senior American officers and their staff planners tended to see Churchill's perpetual willingness to entertain other objectives than the cross-channel attack as an unwillingness to conduct that operation at all. Even as the

English-speaking nations marshaled their forces for their joint war against Germany, the suspicions of which Sun Tzu had written so many centuries before began whisperingly to penetrate the structure of an alliance both Churchill and Roosevelt regarded as unshakable.

The Progress of the Debate

When Roosevelt, Churchill, and their chiefs of staff met at the *Arcadia* Conference in Washington, DC, immediately after Pearl Harbor, they endorsed the earlier and informal agreement to defeat Germany first, while containing the Japanese. They further agreed to wear down Axis strength by tightening a ring around those nations and to use aid to the Russians, naval blockade, strategic bombing, and limited offensives at points of Allied superiority as their principal means. While American staff studies envisioned a major attack into the heart of Germany, such a proposal formed no part of the *Arcadia* agreement because it did not seem, at that moment, to be possible.

First principles occasioned no disagreement. "The only thing that ever really frightened me during the whole war," Winston Churchill wrote, "was the U-boat

peril." In the early years, German submarines threatened to starve Britain out of the war. Later, winning the Battle of the Atlantic was essential to concentrating ground, naval and air forces for an invasion of the continent. By the time the United States Navy entered the battle, the Royal Canadian Navy and the Royal Navy had established convoy routes and an effective system to escort the vital merchantmen across the ocean. Despite

Above: The Boeing B-17s of the US 8th Bomber Command played a decisive part in the preparations for D-Day by wrecking Germany's war-making industries and by helping to isolate northwestern France by attacks on all types of transport facilities.

these efforts, sinkings spiraled until the introduction of escort aircraft carriers and effective radar coverage gave the Allies the upper hand. Losses reached a crescendo in December 1943, after which German successes dropped off sharply. At the same time, the rate of construction overtook the rate of ships destroyed. As of January 1944 the Allies could say that the Battle of the Atlantic had been won. Rapidly, delivered tonnages of supplies and equipment increased. The secure line of communication across the ocean guaranteed that the invasion, once started, could be sustained with replacements, supplies, and new weapons.

The other major precondition for invasion was also attained by 1944. When the US Army Air Forces arrived in England, the Bomber Command of the Royal Air Force was already busily attacking German cities by night. Following a profound disagreement about techniques, the two air forces each followed their own doctrines: the British bombed at night and the Americans by day. While the air war over Europe did not precisely prove the strategic bombing theories, propounded between the wars by Italian general Guilio Douhet, or realize the predictions of its American prophets — German industry was still functioning at the time of the surrender in 1945 — it did have a profound impact on the ground war. Possibly the most important result of the bombing campaign over Germany was that it drew increasing numbers of Luftwaffe fighters away from the fighting fronts and dedicated them to home air defense. The day bombing campaign was decisive in this regard, for the 8th Bomber Command became the anvil on which the 8th Fighter Command, the hammer, literally pounded the life out of the German air force. As Luftwaffe losses increased, a second consequence was the German shift in production from bombers to fighters, thereby decreasing

Below: Typical of the success of the strategic bombing effort in support of the ground forces is the damage caused by 8th Bomber Command to this German factory, previously a major element in the supply of tanks to the German army.

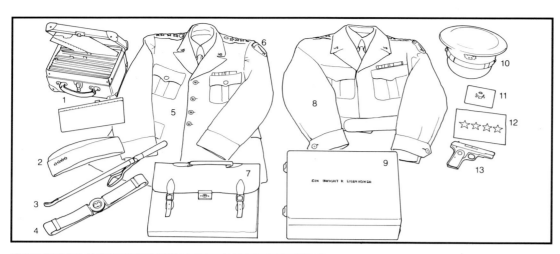

Uniforms and Personal Memorabilia of Gen. Dwight D. Eisenhower

1 Leather map case containing linen-mounted maps of NW Europe. Inscribed on the lid: "Gen D. Eisenhower"
2 General's garrison cap with four star insignia
3 Leather riding crop with inscribed silver band
4 General officer's pistol belt
5 General's summer service jacket with four star insignia, together with cotton khaki shirt and olive drab wool tie
6 SHAEF shoulder patch
7 Leather brief case. Interior marked: "Eisenhower, United States Army"
8 Field jacket, known as the "Ike jacket," with four star and SHAEF insignia. Shown with shirt and olive drab tie
9 Dispatch case used by Gen. Eisenhower and staff at SHAEF
10 Officer's service cap with general officer's insignia
11 Cartier silver cigarette case
12 General's vehicle pennant
13 Colt M 380 auto pistol, SN 135171 carried by Gen. Eisenhower

Eisenhower Library and Museum: 1-12; West Point Museum: 13

the capability of the remaining tactical air force to support the German army. The Allies had to have aerial superiority, at least over the invasion beaches, to hope for success in the amphibious landings. The combined bomber offensive achieved that goal. By D-Day, German fighter forces were largely stripped out of France, and only two German sorties appeared over the invasion beaches. The first round of the landings was therefore won in what turned out to be very costly battles that the Allied air forces fought in the skies over Germany in the long months of 1943 and early 1944.

Simultaneously, the bombing campaign enormously increased the difficulties the Germans had to overcome in keeping their war machine running. While the factories survived, and production in some cases actually increased, the bombers crippled the German transportation network and systematically attacked the fuel supplies essential not only to the armed forces, but also to the lines of communications. German army units in France, among other places, accordingly became somewhat anaemic with respect to supplies. They were also deficient in armament, and part of that may also be attributed to the bombing campaign. That German army units, both on the eastern and on the western fronts, did not have a large artillery and anti-tank reserve may in part be attributed to the voracious demands of the anti-aircraft organization within Germany for high velocity guns and skilled gunners.

Finally, air power offered a partial solution to the manpower problem. In sheer numbers, the Germans in France could always muster more men than the Allies could put on the beaches at one time. The trick was to strike the Germans, as far as possible, at a place they did not expect, and to keep them from concentrating their divisions to repel the assault. Planning for the landings assumed that Allied air forces, freed from aerial combat missions because they had already won the air battle over France, could perform the tactical mission of isolating the Normandy

GEN. DWIGHT D. EISENHOWER.

The uniforms and car pennant of Gen. Eisenhower seen here, all carry the insignia of four star general. Eisenhower was promoted to this rank in February 1943 during the Tunisian campaign.

The engraved inscription on the riding crop *3* reads: "General D.D. Eisenhower, Supreme Allied Commander, E.T.O. (European Theater of Operations) 1944." The Cartier cigarette case, *11*, carries the Great Seal of the United States. On the gold-washed interior is engraved: "To Victorious General Ike Eisenhower, Xmas 1943, Selma and Maxine."

battlefields from the Reich, destroying rail lines, bridges, and centers of communication. Particularly by the time of the landings, Allied fighter bombers, operating almost without opposition from the Luftwaffe, made it impossible for the Germans to move in daylight. Roads became deathtraps, and German mobility — together with German capacity to mass forces to deal with the invasion — was hobbled.

British and American planners correctly foresaw all of these necessities and, as time revealed the impact of the great air battles over the continent, laid plans to exploit the advantages that were gained. From the American point of view, Maj. Albert Wedemeyer's sketch of the essential military tasks to be performed before the final attack on Germany was proceeding well, and seemed to be fulfilling the terms of reference laid down in the *Arcadia* agreement. British staffs agreed that, whatever the future plans of the alliance, these battles had to be won. When the Allies met again at Casablanca in January 1943, they agreed the plan toward entering the continent of Europe in 1944, to set up a planning staff to work out the details of such an operation, and to push the buildup of forces in the United Kingdom while continuing operations in the Mediterranean. Disagreements arose from other sources, at once perceptual and practical.

The essential point is that both Allies agreed that the ultimate attack on the German-occupied continent had to be made in northwestern Europe. While, however, the Americans were anxious to make that attack as soon as possible, the British were concerned that the time should be right. In the end, the decision to launch the invasion across the English Channel was not made final until both Allies were persuaded that it made military sense. Because of their practical concerns, that time came later for the British than for the Americans who, in part conditioned by residual suspicions from the previous war, worried that the British delays portended a refusal to make such landings at all.

The Anglo-American landings in North Africa (Operation *Torch*) exacerbated the debate, because they diverted troops already earmarked for the attack Americans saw as

Above: There was considerable British emphasis on the importance of the Soviet effort against the Germans, in events such as this "Salute to the Red Army" pageant in the Albert Hall, London. Political leaders were well aware of the high cost of the Eastern Front.

decisive. Gen. Marshall and his staff had already devised a plan (*Bolero*) to concentrate American troops in the United Kingdom for a massive attack on France in the spring of 1943. This attack, dubbed *Roundup*, envisioned using 48 divisions, 30 of which would be American, on a six-division front between Le Havre and Boulogne, supported by a powerful air force. An attractive aspect of *Roundup* was that the Germans had only begun to fortify the coast in 1942, and the bulk of their army was critically engaged in Russia. To exploit the unlikely collapse of the German army as a result of that fighting or, more likely, to create a diversion in case the Russians found themselves in serious trouble, Marshall's staff devised a contingency plan that used only three and a half divisions, to be launched across the Channel as early

as September 1942. This plan, *Sledgehammer*, was always unlikely, but still made British planners uneasy because it suggested that the Americans did not have any realistic understanding of the difficulties involved.

Regardless of the invasion plan under discussion, President Roosevelt's agreement to divert American troops to North Africa, and the subsequent agreement to use those troops in assaults on Sicily and on the coast of Italy, made it impossible to concentrate the forces and materiel to invade northwestern Europe in 1943. Americans suspected that Prime Minister Churchill intended to continue to postpone operations in northwestern Europe indefinitely, in favor of those in the Mediterranean that would serve long-range British political interests. In fact, that possibility seems to have existed only in the minds of the American joint chiefs, who had a different and more optimistic definition of favorable military conditions for the final attacks in France than did the British.

In fact, while Americans insisted that final plans for the landings in France go forward,

THE STATISTICAL PROGRESS OF OPERATION *BOLERO* FROM 1942 TO MAY 1944
The arrival of the first American troops and materiel in Britain came quickly after Germany and Italy declared war on the US on December 11, 1941. The buildup, however, was to be quite slow until the beginning of 1944. This was due in part to the initial lack of shipping and speed of war production, the U-boat threat in the Atlantic, and the diversion of US troops into North Africa and the Mediterranean in 1942-43. These figures show that initial American plans to launch a European invasion in 1942 or 1943 would have been logistically impractical.

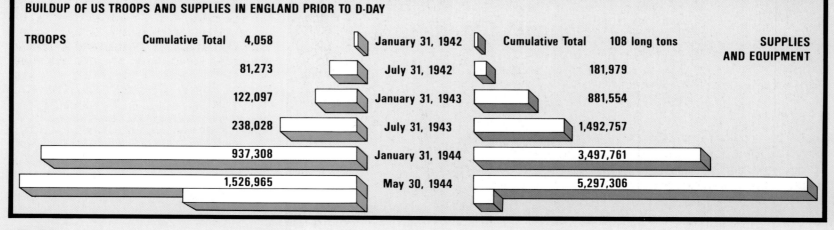

BUILDUP OF US TROOPS AND SUPPLIES IN ENGLAND PRIOR TO D-DAY			
TROOPS Cumulative Total	4,058	January 31, 1942	Cumulative Total 108 long tons **SUPPLIES AND EQUIPMENT**
	81,273	July 31, 1942	181,979
	122,097	January 31, 1943	881,554
	238,028	July 31, 1943	1,492,757
	937,308	January 31, 1944	3,497,761
	1,526,965	May 30, 1944	5,297,306

and that a final date be set, it was the British who pointed out the critical shortage of LSTs (Landing Ship, Tank) and other landing craft to make the assault powerful enough to succeed. Until production of LSTs could catch up with demand, no assault on the coast of France could be powerful enough to counter the expected German riposte. Such a landing would, as far as Churchill and his advisors could see, be a repetition of Dieppe, where a single, well-entrenched German company had halted three battalions and the overall losses had been proportionate to those of the first day on the Somme in 1916. It is in that context that the Prime Minister's often-quoted remark about French beaches being choked with the bodies of British and American youth must be understood.

Instead of wishing to cancel *Overlord*, Churchill and his military advisors argued through 1943 that the assault had to be made stronger. Finally, only after a high-level conference at Norfolk House in February 1944, in which more tank landing ships were promised from the United States and reallocated from other theaters, did the means appear more nearly to suit the demands.

Marshall and his staff in particular, and the American joint chiefs in general, rightly complained that the landings in North Africa could have no meaningful impact on the course of the war, and that the subsequent assaults on Sicily and Italy frittered away precious resources in an aimless strategy of opportunism that formed no part of a coherent plan for the defeat of Germany. To that extent, their criticism of peripheral warfare, especially when contrasted to the ideal of maintenance of the objective, was on the mark. But that point of view overlooked important practical considerations. President Roosevelt knew that it was politically important for American troops to come to grips with the Germans some time in 1942. Forces certainly had to be accumulated in the United Kingdom for the invasion of the continent, but to hold those soldiers idle there only encouraged critics — Gen. Douglas MacArthur and senior naval commanders among them — who wanted to concentrate American strength on fighting the Japanese, a war in which Americans in general had vested far more emotion. Practically, it turned out that Mediterranean operations were militarily expedient, giving the US Army time to shake down for war and to learn the difficult lessons that the British had already had three years to assimilate. Landings and warfare in the Mediterranean hardened the soldiers, brought the most capable commanders to the fore, and gave both nations experience in conducting amphibious warfare, experience that was almost certainly crucial to the subsequent success of *Overlord*.

It was in this context that the Allies agreed at the *Trident* Conference in Washington, in May 1943, to use forces already in the Mediterranean to invade Italy, but also to set May 1, 1944, as the date for the cross-channel invasion and to that end to concentrate the buildup of their forces in Britain. Later in August 1943, at the *Quadrant* Conference in Quebec City, they reaffirmed that intention. Finally, at the Tehran-Cairo Conferences of November-December 1943, the long and anxious debates ended with the appointment of Eisenhower as supreme commander for the invasion, the principal Anglo-American effort in 1944. An impatient Generalissimo Josef Stalin was responsible, in part, for the final decisions of the

Above: A copy of the note sent to Stalin from President Roosevelt confirming Gen. Eisenhower as commander of *Overlord*. The note was written at the end of the Tehran Conference. Eisenhower was personally told of his appointment by Roosevelt in Tunis on the president's journey back to America. The news was not made public until a presidential radio broadcast on December 24.
"From the President to Marshal Stalin
The — immediate — appointment of General Eisenhower to command of Overlord operation has been decided upon."
— Roosevelt
Eisenhower Library and Museum

Below: At the *Eureka* Conference held at Tehran in Persia during December 1943, President Roosevelt and Prime Minister Churchill informed Premier Stalin that the cross-channel invasion would be launched in May or June 1944. Stalin agreed to launch a Soviet general offensive at the same time.

conference. He had long been pressing the Western Allies to open a Second Front that would take some of the pressure off of his forces, and it was at his insistence that Roosevelt and Churchill finally named a supreme commander. If no commander were named, Stalin believed, then there was also no prospect that plans for a Second Front would be translated into reality any time in the near future.

The final date was set, as Prime Minister Churchill had earlier suggested, by the moon and the weather. The decision for *Overlord* was finally a compromise and an artful merging of the two nations' conceptions of how to wage the war. At the end, however, it was more a reflection of the realism of the British proposal at the *Arcadia* Conference of December 1941 than of the optimism that colored the American estimates of the art of the possible through 1942 and 1943.

That the alliance stood firm throughout the Second Front debate was the result of several related and indispensable facts. One key to that success was that, from the very beginning of the most preliminary discussions between the two powers, British and American leaders agreed on their common objective. A second was the utter determination of Prime Minister Churchill and President Roosevelt that the solidity of the Anglo-American alliance had absolute primacy over every other question. A third was that Gen. Dwight D. Eisenhower, military leader of the coalition and a protégé and student of Conner came to his task as supreme commander determined to make the coalition a success, and built a staff that mirrored his determination.

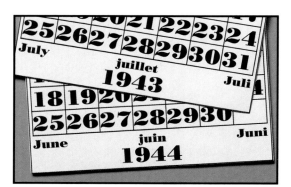

Preparations for Overlord

2

Stephen Badsey

Almost from the fall of France in 1940, British plans and preparations began for its liberation. Churchill organized or sponsored a number of "private armies" to carry out raids or encourage resistance in France and other occupied countries, and in fact the first Commando raid on German positions in France took place only 20 days after Dunkirk. The Commandos, the Special Operations Executive (SOE), and the Airborne Forces all grew from raiding forces like these, into sizeable organizations that played a major role in the British effort on D-Day. Despite debates over strategy and the perilous British strategic position until the middle of the war, it was always clear to Churchill and his military staffs that only the liberation of France could secure the defeat of Germany.

Operation *Bolero*
The entry of the United States into the war made it possible to draw up realistic plans for the invasion, starting with Operation *Sledgehammer*, a possible small landing at Cherbourg in 1942, and developing to Operation *Roundup*, a major invasion of the Pas de Calais planned for 1943. In July 1942, in order to provide the American forces for *Roundup*, the Allies began Operation *Bolero*, the movement of troops and weapons to Britain on a massive scale. *Bolero* continued for nearly two years as *Roundup* was postponed until 1944, and eventually modified into Operation *Overlord*. Meanwhile the British continued to train and organize their own

troops for the invasion, increasingly supplemented by forces from the Commonwealth, and from Allied "governments in exile" in London, whose forces were equipped by the British and Americans.

The United States began to build up its armed forces immediately after the collapse of France, in anticipation of its involvement in the war, and thereafter its military industrial achievement was little short of phenomenal. Although in many cases the factories themselves had to be built before they could produce the tanks or aircraft, American war production tripled in 1941, increased over fourfold in 1942, and fourfold again in 1943. The United States by itself out-produced Germany by four to one in tanks during the war,

and more than two to one in total munitions. In addition to equipping their own forces, the Americans supplied the British with about a quarter of their weapons and equipment, paid for largely by Lend-Lease. In return, the British provided the Americans with some of their own specialist weapons, and with most of their barracks, airfields and training grounds for *Overlord*.

The American "Invasion"
Nothing had quite prepared the British public, however, for the scale of the American arrival. The first American troops to reach the UK landed in Belfast harbor in January 1942, and Americans were stationed in Northern Ireland throughout the war.

Right: Officers and diplomats from many of the Allied nations (France and Poland among them) gather in London during the summer of 1943 to celebrate "United Nations Day" and the signing of the Atlantic Charter by Roosevelt and Churchill in August 1941.

THE CHOICE OF NORMANDY

A large number of practical considerations governed the choice of the invasion's location. An area somewhere along the French/Belgian coast had won tacit approval from planners as far back as 1942, because of its distance from the English coast and German border. The assault area itself would need to be close enough for fighter cover from Britain, large and flat enough to get the divisions ashore and keep them supplied, have a hinterland that allowed the swift development of a beachhead, but at the same time was not heavily defended. The proximity of major ports was essential, but the Dieppe raid in 1942 had proved that a direct attack on a defended port wasn't an option. In 1943, when the COSSAC planners began to look at these problems, it was the Bay of Seine area and the Calvados coast of Normandy which seemed to fulfill the requirements. Critics, however, said that it did not contain a major port, was too far from Britain, too far from the bulk of the German army and that (prophetically) the Norman bocage country inland would cause major difficulties. Nevertheless, by the end of 1943 the choice of the Calvados coast had been agreed on, despite the fact that almost everything else in the COSSAC plan was to be either rejected or revised. (See page 27.)

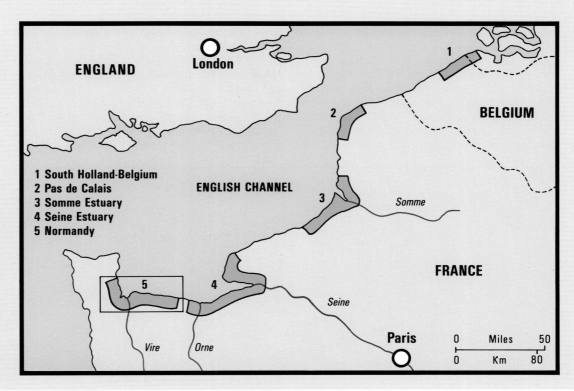

1 South Holland-Belgium
2 Pas de Calais
3 Somme Estuary
4 Seine Estuary
5 Normandy

Because of the threat of German invasion in 1940, most of the British forces had been based in southeast and eastern England. This left the western half of Britain for the arriving American armies. The final decisions to land American forces on the western invasion beaches of Normandy, and the British on the eastern beaches, had its origins in this purely practical solution to the problem of accommodating the Americans.

By spring 1944, as the plans for *Overlord* were finalized, the British civilian population was playing host to the largest invasion force ever assembled in one place, of which about half was American. To make *Bolero* possible, the United States produced over 2,500 Liberty ships of 7,000 tons each as troop transports. The British contribution included the

Below: Surrounded by the impedimenta of the forthcoming invasion, US troops "stand in line for chow" somewhere in southern England during late May 1944. Racial segregation was still the order of the day, so the black troops queue separately from the white soldiers.

transport of 425,000 men in the ocean liners *Queen Mary* and *Queen Elizabeth*, adapted to each hold 15,000 men per trip. By 1944 the Allied domination of the sea and air was so complete that the transfer of American and Canadian troops to Britain across the Atlantic was completed virtually without loss.

The Britain to which the GIs came was a gloomy and depressing country, and this had little to do with the weather. In order to defeat Germany, Britain had organized itself for war to a greater degree than any other member of the Allies, conscripting even women after 1941. Over half the working population was either in uniform or in civilian war employment, and half the national income was devoted to war expenditure. Strict rationing, an average working week of 50 hours, and some 295,000 civilian dead and injured in air raids all contributed to an air of war-weariness in a country which had little to cheer about in its fifth year at war.

A nation traditionally wary of foreigners accepted its army of friendly occupation with remarkably good grace, although some suspicion and trouble on both sides was inevitable. The arrival of American troops far from home in a remote Cornish or Scottish village usually meant a sudden increase in prices, and a corresponding shortage of alcohol and dancing partners for the local men. Compensations ranged from razor blades and candy to American charm and the music of Glenn Miller.

The United States armed forces were still segregated, with black troops mainly used in non-combat roles. Britain had for centuries had its own small black communities, but these existed only in the major ports, while Indian, West Indian and African troops of the British Empire were usually stationed overseas, and none were intended to fight in Normandy. Most people in Britain had simply never seen black soldiers before, and probably many believed the story that American blacks were specialist night-fighting troops with artificially darkened skins. Generally, as in all their dealings with their Allies, the British accepted the American practice of segregating their troops, while reacting with angry disbelief to American behavior outside their own experience, such as the racist attitude of many white American officers or the rare cases of serious violence between white and black troops.

By D-Day, some British people seemed to be getting almost as weary of the Americans as of the war, and both governments were acting to encourage better relations and understanding between their peoples. But as with all news, the bad was being reported more readily than the good, and the predominant American memory of Britain was of friendly people. Just as the Anglo-American alliance coped with its strains surprisingly well, so over 70,000 British girls married GIs immediately after the war and returned home with them.

By June 1944, *Bolero* had done its work. The Allied forces assembled for D-Day numbered over 1,700,000 British troops, 1,500,000 Americans, 175,000 Dominion troops (chiefly Canadians) and 44,000 from other allies. Over 1,300 warships, 1,600 merchant ships, and 4,000 landing ships and craft were available for the liberation campaign, together with 13,000 aircraft (including 5,000 fighters and 4,000 bombers) and 3,500 gliders. In terms of fighting troops, the British had three armored divisions, eight infantry divisions, two airborne divisions and ten independent brigades ready for Normandy, plus one Canadian armored division, two infantry divisions and one independent brigade. There was also a single Polish armored division and a parachute brigade, both equipped by the British. The Americans with their much greater resources had six armored divisions (out of 16 which would fight in Europe before the end of the war), 13 infantry divisions and two airborne divisions waiting in Britain, and more still training in the United States.

The tactical air forces for direct support of these armies numbered some 100 RAF or Commonwealth squadrons (1,200 aircraft) and 165 USAAF squadrons (2,000 aircraft). Simply to assemble such a force had been a colossal undertaking.

The High Command

At the *Arcadia* Conference of December 1941, the Americans and British established a command system enabling them to plan and fight the war jointly. This began at the top with the close personal relationship between President Roosevelt, who was also commander-in-chief of all American forces, and Prime Minister Churchill, who created the title of Minister of Defence for himself in 1940 to fulfil a similar function. Although a lawyer by profession, Roosevelt had been Secretary of the Navy in World War I, and had a good practical understanding of warfare, but tended to leave the planning to his military staffs. Churchill, whose military and naval experience stretched back to the Malakand Expedition of 1897, took a far

MARTIN B-26B MARAUDER
Flying out of Stansted airfield, Essex, bound for France, "Shopworn Angel" of the 495th Bomb Squadron, 344th Bomb Group, was laden with 8,500lb (225kg) bombs, 3,950 rounds of machine gun ammunition and just over 900 US gallons (3,330l) of high-octane aviation fuel. On an order issued on June 4, all invasion aircraft and gliders were painted on wings and fuselage with invasion markings: five alternate black and white bands.

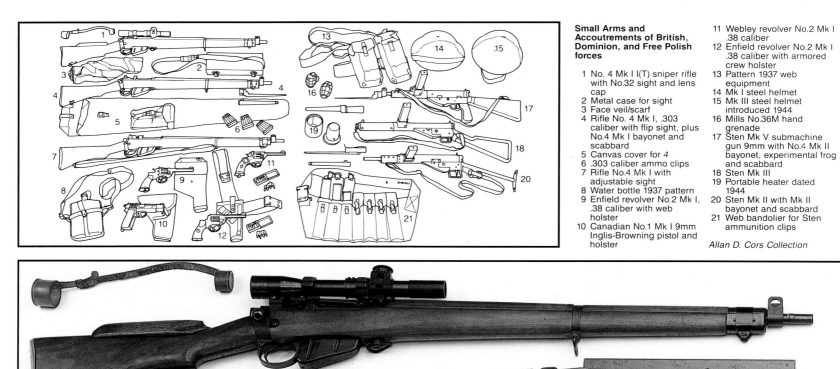

Small Arms and Accoutrements of British, Dominion, and Free Polish forces

1 No. 4 Mk I I(T) sniper rifle with No.32 sight and lens cap
2 Metal case for sight
3 Face veil/scarf
4 Rifle No. 4 Mk I, .303 caliber with flip sight, plus No.4 Mk I bayonet and scabbard
5 Canvas cover for 4
6 .303 caliber ammo clips
7 Rifle No.4 Mk I with adjustable sight
8 Water bottle 1937 pattern
9 Enfield revolver No.2 Mk I, .38 caliber with web holster
10 Canadian No.1 Mk I 9mm Inglis-Browning pistol and holster
11 Webley revolver No.2 Mk I .38 caliber
12 Enfield revolver No.2 Mk I .38 caliber with armored crew holster
13 Pattern 1937 web equipment
14 Mk I steel helmet
15 Mk III steel helmet introduced 1944
16 Mills No.36M hand grenade
17 Sten Mk V submachine gun 9mm with No.4 Mk II bayonet, experimental frog and scabbard
18 Sten Mk III
19 Portable heater dated 1944
20 Sten Mk II with Mk II bayonet and scabbard
21 Web bandolier for Sten ammunition clips

Allan D. Cors Collection

more active role once the invasion of France had been agreed, and was only narrowly prevented from sailing with the forces on D-Day itself.

The formula established at the *Arcadia* Conference, with Roosevelt, Churchill and their staffs meeting at intervals to decide strategy, continued throughout the war. An important part of planning was that the Supreme Allied Commander for a designated theater of war must have control over all forces in it, regardless of nationality. In December 1943 Gen. Dwight D. Eisenhower was named as Supreme Allied Commander Europe, and his command as the Supreme Headquarters Allied Expeditionary Forces,

or SHAEF. Given the greater American contribution to the liberation forces, there was little doubt that an American officer should be appointed, and Eisenhower was the natural choice. Born in 1890, he had served in the army since 1911 and had considerable staff experience, but had never seen combat of commanded as much as a battalion. Eisenhower had risen rapidly from brigadier-general in 1942 to full general and Supreme Allied Commander in the Mediterranean a year later through his remarkable skill in handling the complex political problems of coalition warfare. His relaxed style and ability to find a compromise often won him only grudging admiration from his subordinate

commanders, but his insistence on co-operation and coordination at all levels gave him the respect of political leaders, and was to be decisive for the outcome of the liberation battle.

The appointment of subordinate commanders for Operation *Overlord* reflected the importance of integrating British and American forces; the fact that Britain was the host nation; and the need to coordinate air forces with land operations. The Deputy Supreme Allied Commander was Air Chief Marshal Sir Arthur Tedder. The same age as Eisenhower, Tedder had originally joined the Army in World War I, transferring into the Royal Flying Corps and so into the RAF.

Basic small arms for British, Dominion, and those Polish units reequipped in Britain, were the Enfield No.4 rifle, .303 caliber, Sten gun variations, 9mm, and Webley or Enfield revolvers, .38 caliber. Different variations were made in the United States, Canada, Australia and New Zealand to supply demand. For example *10* is Canadian and *20* was made in New Zealand.

As Air Officer Commander-in-Chief Middle East Air Force in 1941, he had pioneered the use of ground attack aircraft, developing the "Tedder carpet" of bombs laid in front of the advancing troops. A sometimes prickly figure, Tedder made little secret of his belief that air power was chiefly responsible for winning the war. Despite this, he worked extremely well with Eisenhower.

Rather than place an American in charge of the British naval and air forces which were also used to defend Britain itself, Eisenhower's remaining senior commanders were also British. The Allied Naval Commander-in-Chief Expeditionary Force was Adm. Sir Bertram Ramsay. Born in 1883, Ramsay was old for his command, but had proved his considerable abilities in amphibious warfare, first as one of the principal organizers of the Dunkirk evacuation in 1940, then of the *Torch* landings in 1943, and finally as commander of the naval forces for the Sicily landings later the same year. Command of the Allied Expeditionary Air Force (AEAF) as given to Air Chief Marshal Sir Trafford Leigh-Mallory. Born in 1892, Leigh-Mallory was a controversial choice with an erratic reputation stretching back to his command of RAF 12 Group during the Battle of Britain. His relations with Tedder in particular were often difficult, although they agreed on the importance of air power. The AEAF itself consisted of British 2nd Tactical Air Force and US 9th Air Force, which between them averaged over 3,000 sorties a day during the Battle of Normandy, but through his AEAF Headquarters in London, Leigh-Mallory could also coordinate air support from virtually the whole RAF and USAAF in Britain.

Shortly after his appointment, Eisenhower faced and overcame his first major test on the issue of command of the air. Leigh-Mallory, with Tedder's support, wanted the heavy

Below: Air Chief Marshal Sir Arthur Harris believed it a great mistake to divert the effort of his Bomber Command from the strategic role to support of the armies for D-Day, but the tactical success of his heavy bombers proved to be better than expected.

Above: D-Day planning table and chairs. These were used from October 1943 to May 1944 for the deliberations of Gen. Eisenhower and his staff. They were later used by Gen. Marshall and the Joint Chiefs of Staff during May and June 1944. *Eisenhower Library and Museum*

four-engined long-range bomber forces in Britain, which did not come directly under Eisenhower, switched to attack the French railway system as a crucial component of AEAF strategy. The aim was to secure control of the air over France and restrict German movement on the ground; the so-called "Transportation Plan." Instead, RAF Bomber Command under Air Chief Marshal Sir Arthur Harris and United States Strategic Air Forces in Europe under Gen. Carl Spaatz (known together as "the Bomber Barons") insisted that the best support which they could give *Overlord* would be to continue their strategic attacks on German industrial cities. Their resistance was so great that Eisenhower, despite his preference for compromise, had to threaten resignation before securing control of the heavy bombers in April. They were to play a leading part in the eventual Allied victory in Normandy.

Even with SHAEF's great resources, limitations in the number of landing craft, the number of suitable beaches, and the rate of transport across the English Channel meant that only a fraction of its forces could land on D-Day itself. The initial landing forces would be from 21st Army Group, commanded by Gen. Sir Bernard Montgomery, who would act as the ground forces commander directing the battle for Eisenhower, while SHAEF headquarters remained in Britain. Born in 1887, Montgomery was an immensely controversial figure who inspired extremes either of admiration or scorn from his colleagues for his arrogant manner, made even more infuriating by his consistent ability to win. Even the tolerant Eisenhower came to threaten Montgomery's dismissal on more than one occasion during the war. The placing of increasing numbers of American troops and resources under this difficult foreigner would cause considerable friction as the Battle of Normandy progressed.

From D-Day onwards, 21st Army Group would consist of US First Army under Lt. Gen. Omar Bradley, an old colleague of Eisenhower, and British Second Army under Lt. Gen. Miles Dempsey. When enough troops

had crossed to Normandy, two new armies would be created and Eisenhower with SHAEF headquarters would take over the battle from Montgomery. Bradley would take command of 12th US Army Group, consisting of US First Army and US Third Army (an additional US Ninth Army was added in August), while Montgomery would remain in command only of his 21st Army Group, by then consisting of British Second Army and Canadian First Army. Meanwhile a second amphibious landing, Operation *Dragoon*, was to take place in the south of France in August with forces of 6th Army Group under Lt. Gen. Jacob Devers, composed of US Seventh Army and French First Army. The SHAEF liberation forces under Eisenhower would finally number seven armies, four of which would be American. Although *Overlord* would start with a predominantly British high command, gradually the Americans with their much greater resources would take over.

Montgomery's Master Plan

Both during and after the war, Montgomery claimed that all his battles were fought according to a precise "master plan" drawn up beforehand, from which he never deviated, and which the enemy was never able to affect. This attitude earned Montgomery many critics, particularly Tedder and Bradley who regarded him as a highly suspect figure, and led to much argument after the war. The first military plans for *Overlord* and Normandy were drawn up between March and July 1943 by a joint Anglo-American staff in London under the British Lt. Gen. Frederick Morgan, known as COSSAC (Chief of Staff to the Supreme Allied Commander). Although in theory the Allies could land anywhere from Norway to the south of France, Morgan and his staff rapidly narrowed the choice of landing beaches down to two areas, the

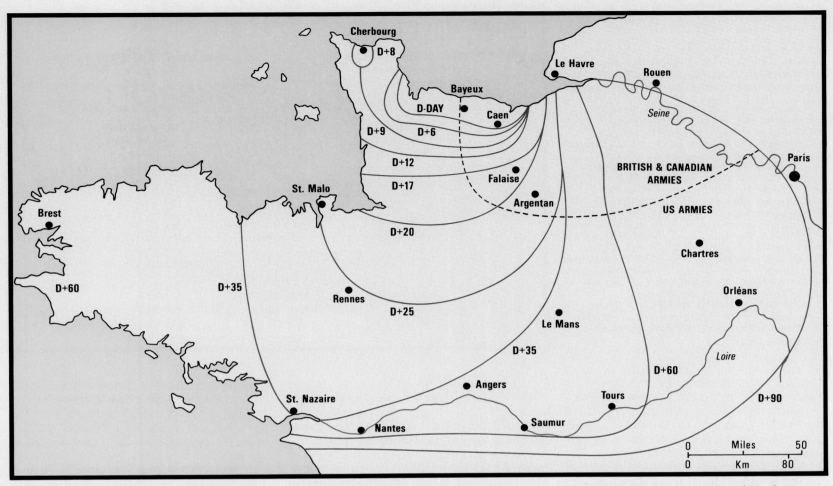

THE PROJECTED *OVERLORD* "PHASE LINES" This was the intended advance from D-Day to D+90, drawn up by Montgomery's staff at 21st Army Group. They were first revealed at a presentation by 'Monty' of his plan of campaign which was given to the commanders and staff of SHAEF on April 7, 1944. Whether these objectives were planned targets or theoretical forecasts were questions that were to cause much heated debate when *Overlord* seemed to stall in the bitter fighting around Caen and in the bocage later in the year.

shortest route across the Straits of Dover to the Pas de Calais or a landing in the Bay of the Seine in Normandy. Regarding the Pas de Calais landing as too obvious, and likely to meet the heaviest German defences, Morgan chose Normandy.

When SHAEF took over from COSSAC in January 1944, Montgomery inherited and modified Morgan's plan. With more troops and landing craft available than COSSAC had expected, Montgomery extended the landing area from three beaches to five, including a site on the Cotentin Peninsula.

Montgomery's plan called for five divisions (instead of COSSAC's three) to land with the first wave on a 61-mile (98km) front, supported by four more divisions and divisional airborne landings on both flanks. The Americans would take the westernmost beaches, codenamed *Utah* and *Omaha*, and the British and Canadians the eastern beaches, codenamed *Gold*, *Juno*, and *Sword*. As with every major military operation there were two key dates. For planning purposes everything had to be ready for Y-Day, or "ready day," set for June 1. But the operation would not actually start until D-Day, a date shortly after Y-Day to be chosen by Eisenhower. Every military operation had its own "D-Day," but this would become the most famous one of all.

Montgomery rightly guessed that the Germans would put their greatest effort into stopping the invasion on the beaches on D-Day

Right: The SHAEF Chiefs of Staff. Back row: Gen. Bradley, Adm. Ramsay, Air Chief Marshal Leigh-Mallory, Gen. Walter B. Smith. Front row: Air Chief Marshal Tedder, Gen. Eisenhower, Gen. Montgomery. Below: Beret of Gen. Sir Bernard Montgomery. 'Monty' began wearing the beret and insignia of the Royal Tank Regiment (RTR) in North Africa. This beret is of the early 1944 period bearing the cap badges of the RTR (1922 version) left, and that of a British general, right.
Memorial Museum, Bayeux

THE ALLIED CHAIN OF COMMAND
Between January and March 1941, talks between British and American military and naval staffs had taken place in Washington. Known as the ABC talks, they were unofficial, but were to form the basis of the strategic agreement between the two Allies — Germany first.

Within two days of Germany's declaration of war against the United States (December 11) Prime Minister Churchill had set sail for Washington and the first inter-Allied strategic conference. Code-named *Arcadia*, it took place between December 22 and January 13, and set the seal on the Western Alliance. One of the most important decisions reached at *Arcadia* was the creation of a Combined Chiefs of Staff.

Based in Washington it would report to the Chiefs of Staff of Britain and the United States and from there to the President and Prime Minister. It was from the Combined Chiefs that Gen. Eisenhower received his directive for the invasion of Nazi occupied Europe: "You will enter the continent of Europe, and in conjunction with the other Allied [United] Nations, undertake operations aimed at the heart of Germany and the destruction of her Armed Forces."

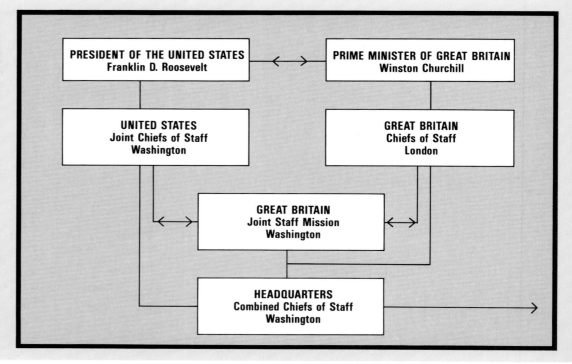

itself, rather than allowing the Allies to get ashore. Once D-Day was successfully over, Montgomery's plan depended on Ramsay's sea-borne supply-line to reinforce his position in Normandy, for which the early capture of a major port and harbor was vital. The lesson of Dieppe was that a port could not easily be captured on D-Day from the sea, and the plan was to supply 21st Army Group over the Normandy beaches for the first few days before securing the nearby port of Cherbourg. While building up its own forces and supplies, 21st Army Group would rely on Leigh-Mallory's AEAF to control the air and prevent the Germans reinforcing their line by attacking troops and transports moving towards Normandy. The most important factors restricting the choice to Normandy or the Pas de Calais was that both lay within fighter range of southern England, and that the sea lanes could be easily protected.

In broad terms, Montgomery's "master plan" depended on surviving D-Day, holding enough territory to prevent his forces being pushed into the sea, winning the buildup battle, and so breaking out of the beachhead. But at planning conferences for SHAEF and 21st Army Group commanders in April and May, Montgomery outlined his expectations for the battle in greater detail. Coming straight off the beaches, British Second Army would capture the regional capital of Caen, the only major city in the landing area, on D-Day itself, and carry on deep inland. At the same time, US First Army would move across the Cotentin and capture Cherbourg as a supply port within a week. Montgomery anticipated a fairly steady Allied advance as the Germans retreated before him, giving up most of Normandy. From a strong position between Caen and Falaise, Montgomery would then threaten a direct advance east-

ward towards the River Seine with his British forces. There is little doubt (except for that created by Montgomery himself after the war) that he would have carried out this threat if the Germans had failed to defend against it, but it was largely a feint to draw the bulk of German forces in against the British.

Montgomery's preferred option, instead, was for the whole of the 21st Army Group to pivot on Falaise as the Americans pushed southwards out of Normandy as far as St. Malo and Rennes by the end of June. At this point there would be a pause, as with enough troops ashore and space to deploy them, Eisenhower would take over the battle from Montgomery. With 6th Army Group arriving from the south but much hard fighting still to come, the Allies expected to reach the River Seine at Paris about three months after D-Day.

For planning purposes, in April and May Montgomery's staff drew up a series of maps showing phase lines and options on how he expected the battle to develop. Although no battle ever runs according to a timetable (or a "master plan") it was quite clear after the invasion that what was happening bore little resemblance to these detailed plans. Montgomery's insistence that everything was going perfectly, and that his "master plan" was still intact, only served to increase suspicion of him during the battle, and to tarnish his reputation afterwards. By the time France was liberated, many were arguing that the battle had been won in spite of Montgomery, and not because of him.

The Free French
On June 6, 1940, as the French armies collapsed under the German attack, Maj. Gen. Charles de Gaulle was called from command of his armored division to become Under-Secretary for National Defense and War. Twelve days later, as the French government also collapsed, de Gaulle fled to London, where he announced his intention to fight on, denouncing the armistice with Germany and the Pétain government, and appointing himself as leader of a National Committee of

Below: Weapons such as these were supplied and used by the OSS and SOE for silent killing. *1.* The Welrod: 9mm single shot silenced pistol. Accurate at 15-30 yds (13-27m). *2.* The Liberator: .45 single shot smoothbore designed for partisans. It is shown with packing case, visual instructions and wooden ejector rod. *3.* High Standard Model H-D .22 semi-automatic pistol. *4.* High Standard Model B .22 semi-automatic pistol. *Eisenhower Library and Museum*

THE SHAEF CHAIN OF COMMAND
Appointed to command Operation *Overlord* at the end of 1943, Gen. Eisenhower became Supreme Allied Commander Europe, and his command, the Supreme Headquarters Allied Expeditionary Force (SHAEF). Eisenhower arrived in London on January 14, 1944. To begin with, SHAEF moved into 20, Grosvenor Square while also having quarters in the old COSSAC HQ at Norfolk House, St. James's Square. However, SHAEF soon moved to Bushy Park, west of the city. As the time for the invasion drew closer, operational personnel, together with the headquarters of 21st Army Group moved down to Portsmouth where the communications and command center for Operation *Neptune* had already been established at Southwick House.

SHAEF HEADQUARTERS

BUSHY PARK

April 1944

Southampton

Poole

SOUTHWICK HOUSE

Portsmouth

Boulogne

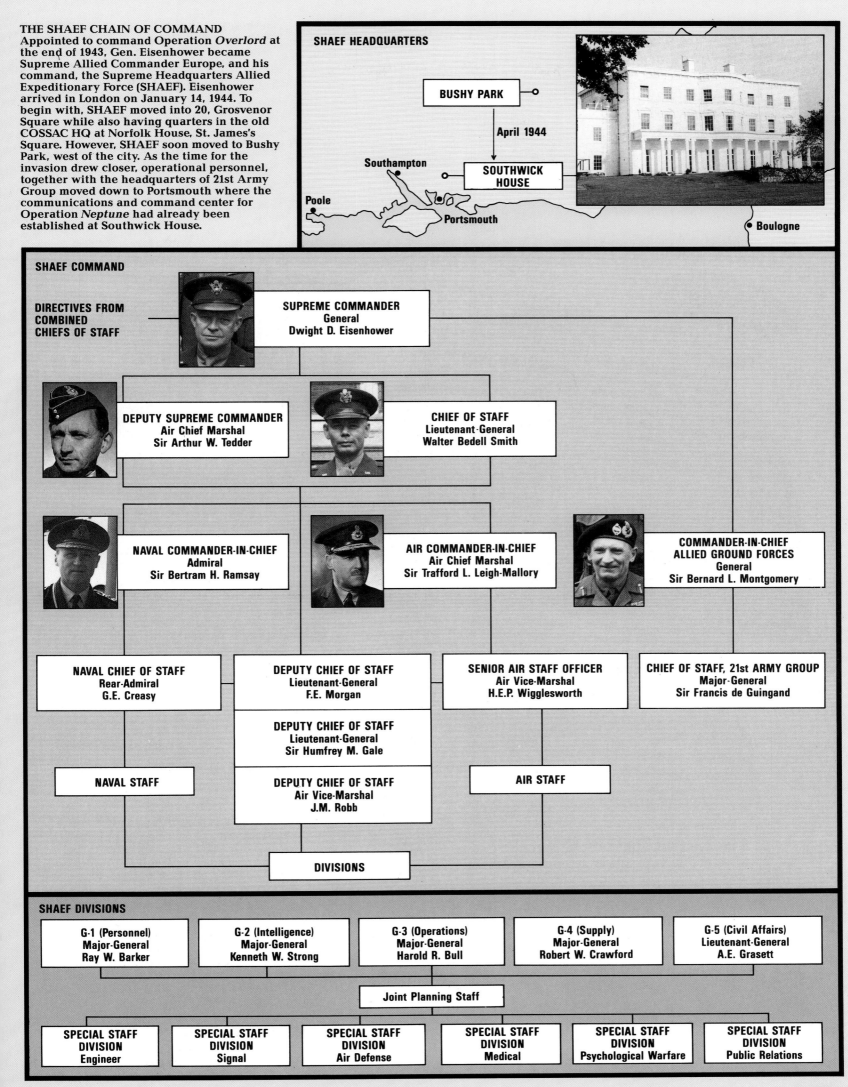

SHAEF COMMAND

DIRECTIVES FROM COMBINED CHIEFS OF STAFF

SUPREME COMMANDER
General
Dwight D. Eisenhower

DEPUTY SUPREME COMMANDER
Air Chief Marshal
Sir Arthur W. Tedder

CHIEF OF STAFF
Lieutenant-General
Walter Bedell Smith

NAVAL COMMANDER-IN-CHIEF
Admiral
Sir Bertram H. Ramsay

AIR COMMANDER-IN-CHIEF
Air Chief Marshal
Sir Trafford L. Leigh-Mallory

COMMANDER-IN-CHIEF ALLIED GROUND FORCES
General
Sir Bernard L. Montgomery

NAVAL CHIEF OF STAFF
Rear-Admiral
G.E. Creasy

DEPUTY CHIEF OF STAFF
Lieutenant-General
F.E. Morgan

SENIOR AIR STAFF OFFICER
Air Vice-Marshal
H.E.P. Wigglesworth

CHIEF OF STAFF, 21st ARMY GROUP
Major-General
Sir Francis de Guingand

DEPUTY CHIEF OF STAFF
Lieutenant-General
Sir Humfrey M. Gale

NAVAL STAFF

DEPUTY CHIEF OF STAFF
Air Vice-Marshal
J.M. Robb

AIR STAFF

DIVISIONS

SHAEF DIVISIONS

G-1 (Personnel) Major-General Ray W. Barker	G-2 (Intelligence) Major-General Kenneth W. Strong	G-3 (Operations) Major-General Harold R. Bull	G-4 (Supply) Major-General Robert W. Crawford	G-5 (Civil Affairs) Lieutenant-General A.E. Grasett

Joint Planning Staff

SPECIAL STAFF DIVISION Engineer	SPECIAL STAFF DIVISION Signal	SPECIAL STAFF DIVISION Air Defense	SPECIAL STAFF DIVISION Medical	SPECIAL STAFF DIVISION Psychological Warfare	SPECIAL STAFF DIVISION Public Relations

Uniforms and Equipment of Free French Forces

1 Pattern 1934 Air Force cap of flying officer captain
2 Air Force service dress, captain's coat and trousers, pattern 1934 "Louis Blue"
3 Shearling B-2 type light winter flying jacket
4 British flying goggles
5 Captain's kepi, Foreign Legion
6 Grenadier captain's 1935 pattern service dress jacket and trousers
7 Belt and holster for Unique 17 7.65 semi-automatic pistol
8 Beret of No.4 Commando 1st Special Service Brigade
9 British Pattern 1940 battle dress. Note No.4 Commando, Free French and Combined Operations insignia
10 British Pattern 1937 webbing with pouches for 50 round drums of Thompson .45 submachine gun ammo
11 Toggle rope
12 British Pattern 1908 water bottle
13 American Model 1928-A1 Thompson submachine gun
14 British Fairbairn-Sykes fighting knife
15 British Pattern 1937 gaiters
16 British hob-nailed boots
17 Army Service Dress Pattern 1939, of 2nd Lt. of artillery
18 Commando pack

Memorial Museum, Bayeux

Liberation. By November 1942, when the Germans occupied Vichy France, de Gaulle's position as leader of the Free French — renamed the Fighting French in August 1943 — was reasonably secure, but his utterly uncompromising approach meant that for the rest of the war his relations with the British and Americans were difficult. The central problem, as the date of the invasion drew closer, was that de Gaulle claimed the right to assume the government of France upon liberation, whereas the Americans and British insisted on some form of election being held before recognizing that government. To de Gaulle, this was insulting and presumptuous, as was the Allies' issuing of "liberation

money" to their troops without his authorization. A private understanding with Eisenhower helped ease the situation.

In 1944 most of de Gaulle's forces were in Italy or being prepared for the *Dragoon* landings as the French First Army, but it was obviously politically important for French troops to take part on D-Day. The French cruisers *Montcalm* and *Georges Leygues* and the destroyer *La Combattante* formed part of Adm. Ramsay's command on D-Day, while 2nd Tactical Air Force included five RAF Fighting French squadrons. Two French parachute battalions were serving with the British Special Air Service Brigade (SAS), and dropped three nine-man combat teams into

Brittany on the night before D-Day. In order to have French troops land with the first wave on D-Day itself, a token force of 176 French commandos from No. 10 (Inter-Allied) Commando under Commandant Phillippe de Vaisseau Kieffer was transferred to No. 4 Commando to land at *Sword* Beach. De Gaulle also provided 2nd French Armored Division (armed and equipped by the Americans) as part of the SHAEF forces intended for Normandy, with the specific role of liberating Paris. Its commander, Maj. Gen. Jacques-Philippe Leclerc, had escaped from a German prisoner of war camp in 1940 to join de Gaulle. Described as "a modern d'Artagnan," he was actually the Vicomte de Hautecloque, but

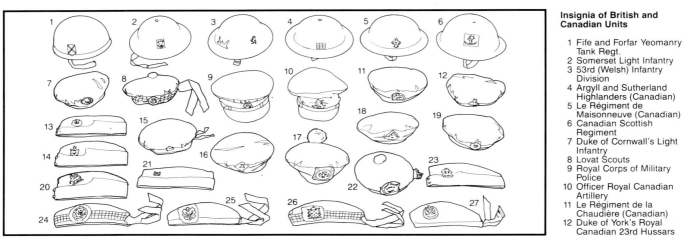

Insignia of British and Canadian Units

1 Fife and Forfar Yeomanry Tank Regt.
2 Somerset Light Infantry
3 53rd (Welsh) Infantry Division
4 Argyll and Sutherland Highlanders (Canadian)
5 Le Régiment de Maisonneuve (Canadian)
6 Canadian Scottish Regiment
7 Duke of Cornwall's Light Infantry
8 Lovat Scouts
9 Royal Corps of Military Police
10 Officer Royal Canadian Artillery
11 Le Régiment de la Chaudière (Canadian)
12 Duke of York's Royal Canadian 23rd Hussars
13 Officer Royal Engineers
14 Officer Intelligence Corps
15 4th County of London Yeomanry (Sharpshooters)
16 Green Howards
17 North Nova Scotia Regiment (Canadian)
18 Royal Canadian Artillery
19 Royal Regiment of Canada
20 2nd (Queen's Royal) Regiment of Foot
21 Staffordshire Yeomanry
22 Argyll and Sutherland Highlanders (Canadian)
23 Royal Regt. of Canada
24 Argyll and Sutherland Highlanders
25 Highland Light Infantry
26 Canadian Scottish Regiment
27 Queen's Own Cameron Highlanders of Canada

Memorial Museum, Bayeux

had taken the name "Leclerc" to protect his family, still living in France.

As part of the D-Day plans, attempts were made to coordinate the various French resistance groups, known as the "Secret Army." Although the main function of the Resistance was to provide information for the landings, some groups were also given specific sabotage targets to slow the Germans down. In December 1943 the British SOE and the American Office of Strategic Services (OSS) created a single Special Forces Headquarters as part of SHAEF, and in May 1944 de Gaulle's chief of staff, Gen. Joseph Pierre Koenig, was appointed commander of the French Forces of the Interior (FFI) under

which all resistance groups were placed, giving them some official status as soldiers rather than irregulars (or, as the Germans insisted, "terrorists"). The various factions of the Resistance were by no means all automatically loyal to de Gaulle, who in turn was prepared to take British and American arms and supplies for his own resistance groups, but not to recognise the work of the SOE and OSS. Neither de Gaulle nor Koenig was involved in the strategic planning for *Overlord*, and in April the British government blocked the movement of all diplomats or diplomatic correspondence into or out of the United Kingdom, making exception only for the Americans and Russians. As a result,

de Gaulle — increasingly angry over the Anglo-American refusal to recognize his government — refused to take part in joint radio broadcasts with the other Allied leaders on D-Day, insisting on his own broadcast in which he mentioned only French Forces.

Ruperts, Whales and Great Panjandrums
For centuries before the Allied landings in 1944, the approved way to take a sea fortress had been to land elsewhere and capture it from the landward side, as the Americans planned to do with Cherbourg. But for D-Day itself the Allies would have to assault a heavily defended position, the German Atlantic Wall, from the seaward side. Dieppe had

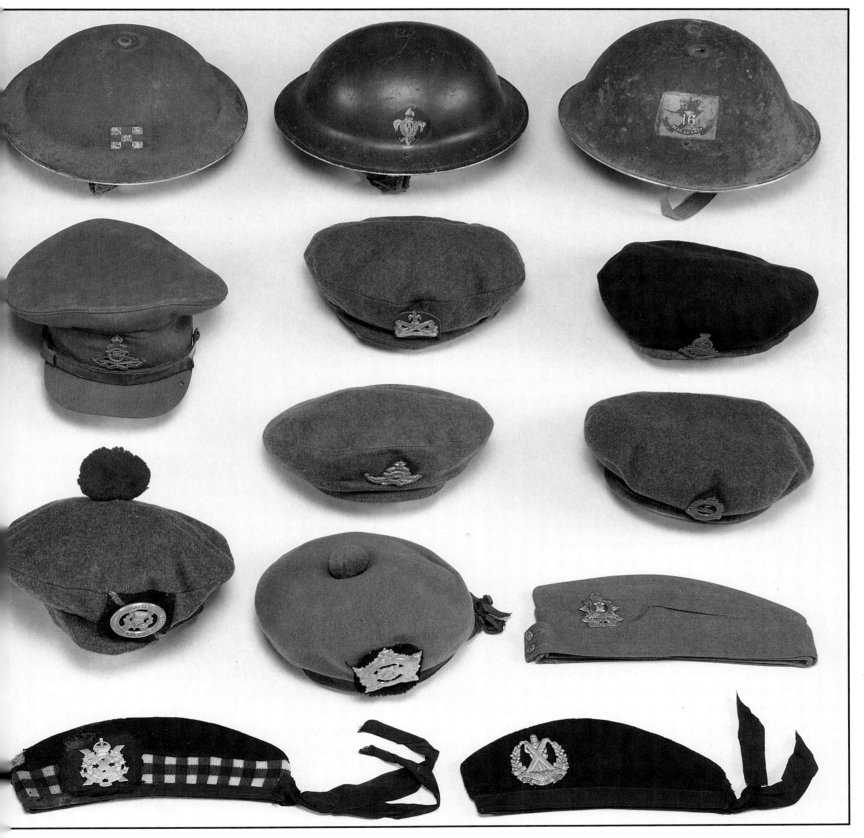

TECHNICAL SKETCHES OF "HOBART'S FUNNIES"
1. Sherman Crab Mk II flail tank. The flail was driven by the tank's engine. The Crab would cross a minefield at about 1½mph (2.4km/h) clearing a path 9ft (2.7m) wide. *2.* Churchill Mk VII Crocodile flamethrowing tank. It could shoot a liquid flame to a range of over 80 yards (72m). Note the fuel link at the rear. This connected to the armored fuel tank (No. *3*) which had a capacity of 400 gallons (1,800l) of pressurized fuel *4.* Churchill Bridgelayer, front view. The bridge weighing 4.8 tons was operated hydraulically by the tank's crew of two. Churchill Engineer Tank (AVRE). Designed as an armored carrier for assault engineers, the AVRE carried a crew of six including a demolition engineer. It was armed with a 290mm petard spigot mortar (or "Flying Dustbin"). This fired a 40lb (18kg) charge up to 80 yards (72m). The mortar was reloaded through a hatch in the top of the hull. *6.* Churchill Armored Ramp Carrier ARK Mk II. This was designed to bridge defense ditches and sea walls. *7.* Sherman DD tank with float screen folded. *Bovington Tank Museum*

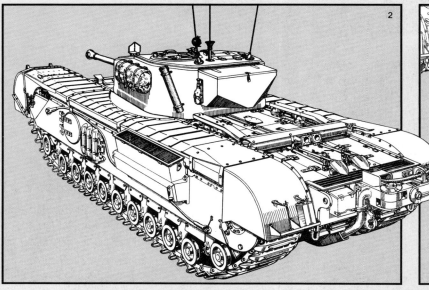

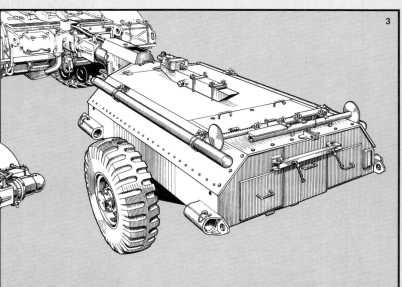

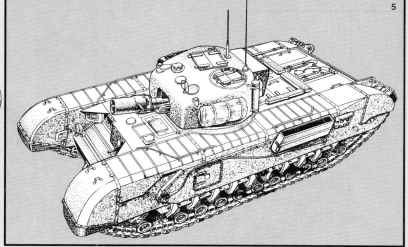

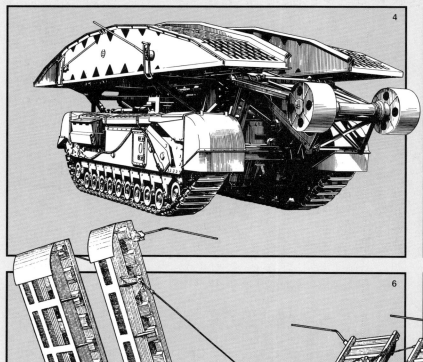

shown the need for special equipment in order to overcome beach defenses, clear minefields, and press inland rapidly. For D-Day a host of inventions was tried out with greater or lesser success, from specialist landing craft to folding bicycles. Among the most simple was the soldier's "invasion wader," a cumbersome garment meant to keep the wearer dry from the landing craft to firm ground. For their assault on the sheer cliffs of the Pointe du Hoc, the US Rangers developed rocket-propelled grappling hooks and ropes, and borrowed extension ladders from the London Fire Brigade. The airborne forces produced a variety of gadgets, including the British-designed but American-manufactured "Eureka" radar beacon, carried by paratroop pathfinders and activated to guide aircraft approaching the drop zone. Far cheaper, and of doubtful value, was the metal toy "cricket" issued to American airborne troops as a recognition aid for their night drop into Normandy. In the fighting, the signal of a cricket clicking turned out to be too similar to the sound of a rifle being cocked. The most bizarre, if most engaging, airborne contribution to surprise

Below: A renovated Churchill Crocodile and (bottom) the Crocodile in action. The fire projector can be seen located in place of the bow machine gun. The fuel trailer (not visible) could be jettisoned either in an emergency or when empty. Crocodiles were not delivered into service until April 1944. Amongst other actions, they supported the US Army in its attack on Brest. *D-Day Museum, Portsmouth*

Top: A renovated Sherman Crab flail tank. Note the insignia of the British 79th Armoured Division on the flail arm. Above: the flail in operation. Because of its very slow operating speed, the Crab was not used in the vanguard of an advance; it cleared identified minefields rather than found them. In combat, the Crab was used in teams, one flailing while others gave fire support. *Bovington Tank Museum*

on D-Day was *Rupert*, quarter-sized dummy parachutists dropped in their thousands across northern France to coincide with the real airborne drop.

From past experience, the Allies knew that landing infantry from the sea was comparatively straightforward, but to overcome enemy strongpoints they would need to get tanks and artillery ashore and inland quickly, past beach defenses, over soft sand and sea walls. A variety of specialist vehicles were built, put through trials and either adopted or discarded. A British specialist design unit, Department MD1 (sometimes known as "Winston Churchill's Toyshop"), which had already provided the PIAT anti-tank gun, developed the "beehive" demolition charge for clearing obstacles in large numbers for D-Day, together with a bridgelaying tank known as the "Great Eastern." Among other methods of clearing beach obstacles tested by the British was "The Great Panjandrum," a giant rocket-driven catherine wheel which was meant to roll along the beach exploding mines, but which proved a signal failure. However, the "tankdozer" or armored bulldozer, and the flail tank or Crab to explode mines were both successes, and were employed on D-Day. Other successful tank

Left: The DD (Duplex Drive) amphibious tank offered only marginal fields of vision in the water, but was tactically important for the swimming ability provided by its combination of propeller, and detachable flotation screen that was pneumatically raised.

the codename *Mulberry*, to be towed across the English Channel on D + 1 and assembled over the next two weeks. From July 1943 onwards, 37,000 British laborers worked on the two *Mulberry* harbors, one for the British and one for the Americans, and more than a million tons of concrete, ballast and steel were used in their construction, including the blockships sunk to provide breakwaters for them. Although their aircraft photographed the components of *Mulberry* being built in British harbors and estuaries, the Germans failed to work out its purpose. Floating breakwaters called "bombardons" protected an inner ring of giant concrete boxes known as *Phoenix*, towed across and then sunk in position, with a final line of blockships called *Corncob* to form *Gooseberry* or safe anchorages, and the great *Whales* or floating piers at which the ships were to dock, with flexible floating metal roadways leading to the shore. Other *Gooseberry* anchorages were to be formed off the remaining invasion beaches by *Corncob* blockships. The great advantage of *Mulberry* was that it gave the Allies an insurance policy against failing to take a port soon after D-Day.

designs adopted for D-Day by the British included the "bobbin" tank, the flame-thrower tank or Crocodile, the fascine tank, the Churchill ARK (armoured ramp carrier) and the AVRE (Armoured Vehicle Royal Engineers) with a 290mm petard mortar, known along with the other specialist armor as "Hobart's Funnies" with reference to Maj. Gen. Percy Hobart, the former pioneer of armored warfare entrusted with their development. In the British forces, this specialist armor was grouped together in the 79th Armoured Division.

The most successful specialist tank used on D-Day was a joint Anglo-American development, the swimming or amphibious Sherman tank fitted with its own propellers for use at sea. Known as the DD-Sherman (for "Duplex

Drive") these were to be launched from landing craft and swim into the beach ahead of the first lines of infantry. Each DD-Sherman was fitted with a "flotation screen," a large canvas skirt which hid most of the tank when erected and was meant to keep the sea out, and special exhaust vents to prevent water flooding the engine. They worked well, but could easily swamp in heavy seas.

At the other end of the scale from the two-cent "cricket," Allied planning for Normandy included one project described as "probably the greatest military engineering achievement since the Persian crossing of the Dardanelles by a bridge of boats in 480BC." In order to provide a safe anchorage until the capture of Cherbourg, two giant prefabricated harbors were built in Britain under

Below: A DD-Sherman tank tows a "porpoise" raft. Half-loaded with ammunition or other essential beach-head supplies, the raft floated nicely and could be towed without undue difficulty even though this further slowed the already sluggish DD tank.

Below: Two of the key figures in *Overlord* were Lt. Gen. Sir Miles Dempsey (left), commanding the British Second Army, and Maj. Gen. Sir Percy Hobart, whose 79th Armoured Division supplied the vehicles that played so major a part in the invasion.

Below: The low freeboard of their vehicles made many DD tank crewmen worry about the threat of being swamped and then sinking, so a modified version of the Davis Submarine Escape Apparatus was developed to provide them with a means of escape.

Mulberry

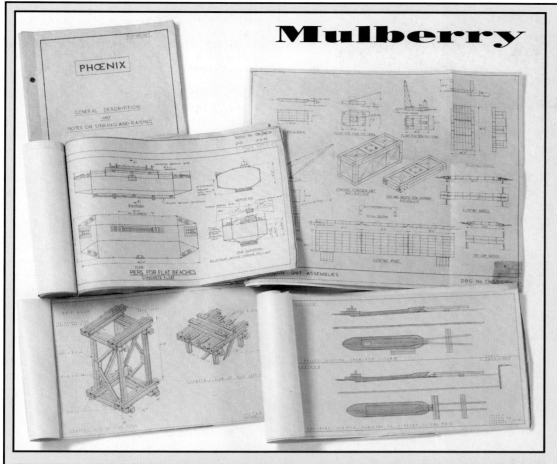

CONSTRUCTION BLUEPRINTS OF *MULBERRY*
This small selection of the original technical plans for the *Mulberry* harbors includes details on the *Phoenix* caisson breakwaters, concrete floats for the *Whale* pier roadways and construction plans for pontoon units. There were three major construction sites on the English coast: the Thames Estuary (*Phoenix*); Pegwell Bay between Ramsgate and Deal in Kent (*Whale*); and Southampton (*Phoenix*, *Whale* and the Bombardon breakwaters).

The original plan for *Mulberry* had been agreed at the *Quadrant* Conference in Quebec in 1943. It was based on the requirements of COSSAC's original plan for a three-division assault. The unloading capacity per day of each harbor was to be 5,000 tons for the American harbor (*Mulberry A*) and 7,000 tons for the British harbor (*Mulberry B*), together with 2,500 vehicles a day unloaded between the two. This planned capacity was not revised when the invasion plan was later extended to a five-division front. It was the logistics of this larger assault which created the need for the *Gooseberry* system of blockship breakwaters. These blockships (known as *Corncobs*) were assembled in the Firth of Lorn on the west coast of Scotland at D-10. At D-7 they began their long journey to the English Channel.
Below: *Whale* "Liebnitz" pierheads and *Phoenix* caissons are assembled off Selsey on D-1.
Inset: Two *Phoenix* caissons under construction. In all, 150 were built at varying sizes from 1,500 tons to 6,000 tons.
D-Day Museum, Portsmouth

Operation *Fortitude*

Throughout the war, one great Allied area of superiority over Germany was in political and military intelligence. The Germans had their successes, but although they were often highly proficient at gathering information, they seldom made the best use of it. German policies towards occupied countries, and even resistance to Hitler in Germany itself, made it much easier for the Allies to establish spy networks in Europe than for the Germans to build up such networks in Britain.

The most carefully guarded intelligence success on the Allied side during the war was the *Ultra* secret, which played a major part in providing the Allies with a picture of German defenses in Normandy. Before the war the Germans had adopted for encoding secret radio signals a typewriter-like machine named *Enigma*, based on a set of coded wheels which was meant to produce unbreakable ciphers. Building on work already done by the Poles before 1939, British mathematicians and cryptanalysts based at Bletchley Park, Buckinghamshire, built what amounted to a primitive computer to break the *Enigma* ciphers, and in the months before D-Day used German radio traffic together with more conventional intelligence methods to create a very accurate picture of their dispositions in Normandy. Expecting

Below: The English-made Gestetner duplicator which was used at Allied Supreme Headquarters to print Eisenhower's original one-page message which was later issued to all invasion participants (see page 71). *Eisenhower Library and Museum*

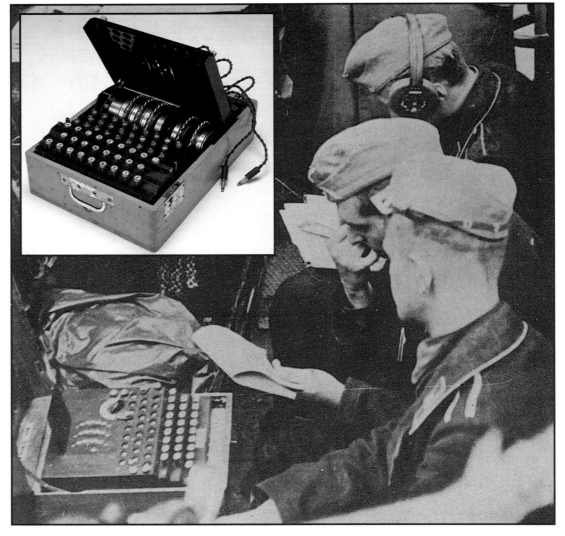

Above inset: A German *Enigma* enciphering machine. Invented in the early 1920s it was originally used commercially. Main picture: An *Enigma* machine in use in Gen. Guderian's command vehicle, France 1940. *The Sikorski Museum*

Below: The Allies made extensive use of inflatable tank and truck dummies to deceive the Germans about dispositions and strengths, and more limited use of rigid dummies such as this LCT2, which was 160ft (48m) long and could be assembled in six hours.

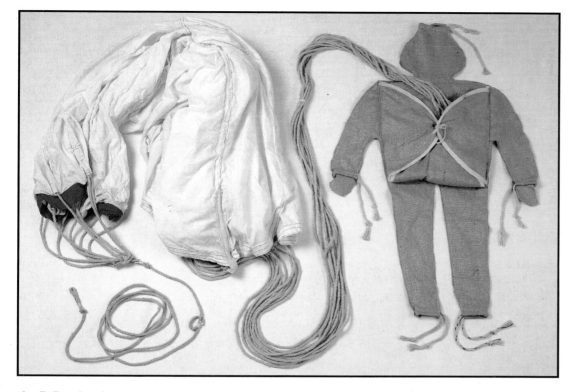

some kind of real existence, and many were fighting formations intended for another purpose. Troops training in Scotland were exaggerated by *Fortitude North* into the non-existent British Fourth Army poised to invade Norway, a threat which kept 27 German divisions waiting in Scandinavia almost until July. Even more impressive was *Fortitude South*, which created in southern England the US 1st Army Group or FUSAG to rival 21st Army Group and threaten the Pas de Calais, as the Germans expected. Allied cover plans encouraged the Germans to believe that command of FUSAG had been given to the Allied general they most feared, Lt. Gen. George S. Patton. In fact Patton was marked to command US Third Army, but even after D-Day the threat of FUSAG kept most of Fifteenth Army in the Pas de Calais, waiting for an invasion that never came. When Third Army did appear in Normandy, Twenty Committee agents passed to the Germans the story that Patton had been demoted from command of FUSAG after a blazing row with Eisenhower, and had been replaced by the head of US Army Ground Forces, Lt. Gen. Lesley McNair.

In an enterprise like *Overlord*, involving millions of men and women and months of detailed planning, complete security was at the same time vital and almost impossible to achieve. If the Germans could establish the date and place of D-Day then they could meet the invasion on the beaches with overwhelming force. A separate codename, Operation *Neptune*, was used to cover all Allied plans regarding information from embarkation to invasion, and a new security classification of *Bigot*, higher even than Top Secret, invented to cover it. Security scares in the last few days before D-Day ranged from the gruesome to the bizarre. More than one officer was sent home or demoted in April and May for indiscreet talk. When ten *Bigot* officers were lost in a German E-Boat attack on an American training exercise off Slapton Sands in Devon in April, divers had to search the sea bed to make sure that all their corpses were recovered. A major scare developed when a package burst open in an Army mail sorting office in Chicago, revealing a set of *Overlord* plans accidentally addressed by Sgt. Thomas Kane, working at SHAEF Headquarters, to his sister. Strangest of all, the compilers of the *Daily Telegraph* crossword puzzle, Sidney Dawe and Melville Jones, found themselves under investigation after several D-Day codenames, including *Overlord* itself, appeared in their puzzles during May and early June.

The result of *Fortitude* was that, although accepting the possibility of a landing in Normandy, most German assessments favored the Pas de Calais, and a landing in good weather. Through German penetration of French Resistance groups, Fifteenth Army knew some of the coded messages used to alert the Secret Army to the D-Day landings, and went on alert on June 5 in response. But the message was not passed on to the unsuspecting Seventh Army, nor to Rommel who was at home in Germany for his wife's birthday. Despite the immense preparations involved in *Overlord*, the surprise on D-Day would be complete.

the D-Day landings to take place in the Pas de Calais, the Germans placed their strongest forces there — 17 divisions of Fifteenth Army compared to 11 divisions of Seventh Army defending Normandy — and gave the Pas de Calais section of the Atlantic Wall the highest priority. A large part of the Allied success depended on Seventh Army not being reinforced before D-Day, and on Fifteenth Army remaining in position even after the first landings.

"In wartime," Churchill observed in October 1943, "truth is so precious that she should always be attended by a bodyguard of lies." Anglo-American strategic planning throughout the war was governed by the principle that every plan should be accompanied by a plausible deception plan, to face the Germans with a choice of possible threats against which to defend. For D-Day the overall deception and disinformation plan was codenamed Operation *Bodyguard*. Central to this was Operation *Fortitude*, an elaborate attempt to convince the Germans that the forces for *Overlord* were almost double their real size by the use of dummy encampments, faked radio signals, cover names and special detachments of troops. The Germans were particularly impressed by confirmation of troop movements and locations coming from their network of agents in Britain, built up painstakingly since 1940. However, in an operation almost as well-guarded as *Ultra*, British counter-intelligence had by

Right: The five *Daily Telegraph* crosswords which between May 2 and June 1, 1944 accidentally revealed five key codewords in their clues.
May 2, crossword 5,775, "17 Across: One of the US" (4). Answer *Utah*. May 22, crossword 5,792, "3 Down: Red Indian on the Missouri" (5). Answer *Omaha*. May 27, crossword 5,797, "11 Across: -but some big-wig like this has stolen some of it at times" (8). Answer *Overlord*. May 30, crossword 5,799, "11 Across: This bush is a centre of nursery revolutions" (8). Answer *Mulberry*. June 1, crossword 5,801, "15 Down: Britannia and he hold to the same thing" (7). Answer *Neptune*.

Above: A *Rupert*. When dropped over occupied France, these dummies carried with them two types of gunfire simulator. The rubber dummies featured later in the film *The Longest Day* are actually props.
Pegasus Bridge Museum, Bénouville

1943 tracked down and caught every German agent in the country. Several of these agents were kept under British control to transmit false information back to Germany as part of *Fortitude*, run by the top secret "Twenty Committee" (from the Roman numerals XX or double-cross), which told the Germans only what the British wanted them to believe. The deception was so complete that some German reports showed two Australian divisions in southern England, when the nearest was actually in Burma.

Some of the forces for *Fortitude* were completely fictitious, like the American infantry division in Iceland reported to the Germans by Twenty Committee agents. But most had

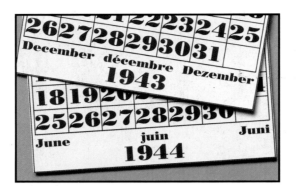

The German Defenses

Detlef Vogel

"Fortress Europe"

By the time the first Allied ships appeared off the coast of Normandy at dawn on June 6, 1944, and before a single Allied soldier had set foot on land, the German defenders had already lost three battles over "Fortress Europe:" for many months British and American aircraft had not only ruled the airspace over England and the Channel, but also dominated the skies over the mainland of western Europe; German surface vessels and U-boats had also failed even to interfere significantly with the vast flow of men and materiel from America to the UK, let alone bring it to a halt; last but not least, all attempts to obtain accurate intelligence about Allied intentions and options had proved fruitless. The Germans remained ignorant of the place, the time and the strength of the attack on "Hitler's Europe" until the actual moment of the landing.

Despite these important Allied successes, the Germans nevertheless attempted to arm themselves against the expected attack. First and foremost it was of critical importance as to how cooperation could be ensured with the countries of western and northern Europe, on whose territory a defensive network was to be established. Whether the French, Belgians, Dutch, Danes and later the Norwegians cooperated with the occupying forces, maintained a passive stance, or actively aided the Resistance, would inevitably have a significant effect on the efficiency of the defensive buildup.

Although the Germans never intended to treat the peoples of western Europe as harshly as those in the east and southeast of the continent, they still failed by a long way to establish a forward-looking policy of partnership. This failure was caused both by their

ideology and their lack of a cosmopolitan outlook: they established in the occupied countries only puppet governments, whose collaboration was assured, but which consequently enjoyed little popular support; they left them in ignorance about their future role in a "German League of Nations" or the "New European Order:" instead they set up an efficient régime of suppression everywhere and from the very beginning devoted their efforts to exploiting the manpower and material resources of the occupied countries to the full.

All these factors drove many people into an attitude of resignation, and not a few into active resistance, even though they may initially have nurtured positive expectations towards the Germans. With the waning military strength of the German Reich, their sympathies turned increasingly towards the Allies. The governments of collaboration, such as the Vichy régime in France for example, gradually lost credibility, and de Gaulle's "Comité Français de Libération Nationale" (French Committee of National Liberation) began to gather support in its native country. De Gaulle's uncompromising attitude towards the reclamation of French sovereignty and the expulsion of the invader came to represent a credible prospect for more and more French people. Similar movements were under way in the other occupied countries of western and northern Europe. Of the concept of a common European imperium, somewhat in the style of the Holy Roman

Empire as the Nazi leaders now and then liked to portray it, no trace was evident by the time of the Allied landings.

Collaboration and Resistance

Small wonder then that under these conditions, the German commanders in western Europe had from the start to discount any possibility of direct military participation by the occupied countries against an Allied invasion. The population and their representatives were only to comply with certain instructions to facilitate German defensive measures in the event of a landing: not to block up transport routes behind the front by unnecessary travel or movement; to hand over any vehicles or other logistic material required; and to hold the Resistance movements in check with their police forces.

Right: A PzKpfw V Panther tank in Paris. The German forces in France were comparatively large and made up of a large number of low- and medium-grade formations leavened by a fairly small number of high-grade infantry and armored formations.

DURANT 3 HIVERS

LA **L.V.F**
LEGION DES VOLONTAIRES FRANÇAIS
S'EST COUVERTE DE GLOIRE
POUR LA FRANCE ET POUR L'EUROPE

Above: The dark side of the French occupation. Firing squads faced those members of the Resistance brought to these execution posts, set up by the Germans in the shooting range at the Ministry of Aviation in Paris.

Above: Another side to occupation. A 1944 recruiting poster for the French collaborationist organization "LVF" (Legion of French Volunteers Against Bolshevism), advertizing their role on the Eastern Front since 1941. "For France and for Europe."

They would continue, however, to work hard for the occupying power: in the German-controlled armaments and supply industry, in administration and in the security forces, and above all on the still-unfinished fortifications on the coast and in the ports. In the event of a major British and American landing, the Commander-in-Chief West, Field Marshal von Rundstedt, was looking for the same "loyal" behavior from the French as during Operation *Jubilee* at Dieppe in 1942.

Even if German relations with the populations of the occupied countries were not overly friendly, they at least succeeded, by means of a series of flexible measures, in avoiding a repeat of the situation in the "real bandit countries" — by which they meant mainly the Soviet Union and Yugoslavia. The Chief of General Staff at C-in-C West, Gen. Blumentritt, estimated that 10 percent of the population might undertake active resistance following a landing — and the Germans could live with that.

In addition, the Germans in the west were in a position to carry out their defensive preparations in countries which possessed an excellent infrastructure (roads, railways, rivers, canals, workshops, and depots). Allied bombers together with the Resistance, however succeeded in destroying much of this network by D-Day. Thus at the end of May thousands of supply trains were stuck in Belgium and eastern France, unable to proceed further westwards because of the shattered railway system.

This was the situation as the Germans found it (or brought about themselves) in the occupied countries. The main question remained — when, in what strength and above all *where* would the Allies land? German leaders had been asking themselves this question off and on ever since the cancellation of Operation *Sealion*, the plan to invade England following the defeat of France in the summer of 1940. By mid-May 1941, according to officers of the Naval War Staff, Britain was already in a position to mount raids and small landings, and exactly a year later the Army High Command estimated the strength of enemy forces in the UK at 44 divisions.

The C-in-C West was prompted by these and similar indications to alert his units as early as February 1943 to the possibility of a landing: "The signs and the available information give growing evidence that we must very soon face the long-expected major landing by the Anglo-Americans."

In contrast to the Allies, the Germans had no central commanding authority where all information could be collated in the event of a landing. There existed instead a glorious profusion of intelligence agencies of all kinds, who not only worked solely for their own benefit, but also competed viciously against each other: besides the legendary "Abwehr" of Adm. Canaris, the "Foreign Armies West" department of the Army High Command was also responsible for intelligence-gathering. Similar departments with the same job were operated by the Foreign Office, C-in-C West, the Navy, the Luftwaffe and Himmler's Reich Central Security Office. The Reich SS Leader even succeeded in February 1944 in wrestling the "Abwehr" from the Armed Forces High Command. This process continued until June 1944, with a consequent fatal effect on intelligence-gathering and evaluation.

Invasion Targets

This plethora of secret service agencies and their lack of cooperation inevitably meant that information obtained was never collated thoroughly enough to evaluate exactly how true it was. It is no wonder therefore that in May 1944 the Germans believed Allied reports that there were approximately 80 divisions in Britain, making up five armies (British Second and Fifth, Canadian First and US First and Ninth) in two army groups, who were capable of launching 20 divisions across the Channel simultaneously. The defenders were also convinced at an early date that the main attack must come at the Pas de Calais, since the Allies would

without doubt want to advance by the shortest route on the Ruhr. At the same time their vast potential would enable them to carry out diversionary operations practically anywhere along the coastline of Europe, from Norway to the Balkans. Hitler, the Wehrmacht Operations Staff, von Rundstedt and Rommel (the commander of Army Group B) all persisted in this basic evaluation of the situation until well after the actual landing. It was only Naval Group West and Air Fleet (Luftflotte) 3 in Paris who preserved any doubts in this respect. At the beginning of 1944, the officers of the Navy could not believe that the Americans and British would attack across the narrowest part of the Channel — just where the Germans might expect them to. They also regarded with some scepticism the copious reports of an American group of forces (FUSAG) in southeastern England, since according to their intelligence there was no shipping assembled there for them. How were these FUSAG troops to get across the Channel? In their view a more likely landing site was between the Somme estuary and Cherbourg.

In May 1944, Luftflotte 3 also came to this conclusion, following the Allied bombing of the Seine and Loire bridges. When the Luftwaffe officers reported their findings to superior authority, Allied intelligence managed to intercept and decode the transmission. Although it caused some anxious moments at SHAEF, this was not the case in the German camp. Hitler, the Wehrmacht Operations Staff, von Rundstedt and Rommel, luckily for the Allies, all ignored it. They continued to anticipate an invasion further to the northeast where, according to experience, the enemy would land in the vicinity of large ports. Huge concrete caissons (sections of *Mulberry*) had of course been observed in British harbors, but they were thought to be merely embarkation aids.

Waffen-SS Uniforms and Equipment

1 Helmet with camouflage cover, 1st type, plane tree pattern
2 Camouflage smock, 2nd type. Note the reversible pattern variation
3 M1943 field cap, 2nd pattern
4 M1940 helmet, with double decal, rough paint finish
5 Field blouse, private, reconnaissance unit, 30th Waffen-SS Grenadier Div. (Russian No.2)
6 Non-regulation Panzer field jacket of Italian material, known as the Normandy pattern. Unit is Panzer Regt. 1, 1st SS Panzer Div., ''Lieben-standarte Adolf Hitler''

7 Binoculars 6x30 with bakelite case
8 Field blouse, reed green cotton fatigue pattern of Panzer Grenadier
9 M1942 helmet camouflaged with sand/paint mix
10 Shelter quarter (Zeltbahn), plane tree camouflage with spring and fall (autumn) patterns
11 Karabiner 98k, 7.92mm
12 Bayonet 98k with bakelite grips for 12
13 Mess kit M31
14 Web battle pack
15 Folding shovel
16 M1931 canteen and cup

Military History Shop, Inc., Kennett Square, PA: 5-6, 8; Milwaukee Public Museum, WI: 2; Pritchard Collection: 1, 3-4, 7, 9-16

The Waffen-SS were pioneers in the use of the camouflage uniform, introducing helmet covers and smocks as early as 1940. The various patterns became synonymous with these units, as were the SS runes on the collar and the distinctive sleeve eagle.

The sleeve and collar insignia of field blouse *5* is that of Ukrainian volunteers of the ''Ukrainian Liberation Army'' (see also page 55). The web battle pack *14*, served in lieu of a full field pack; the mess kit, Zeltbahn, and bag being attached to the webbing 'A' frame.

In addition to the site of the landing, the date and the time of the start of the invasion were naturally of critical importance for the defenders, if they wanted to avoid keeping their units on the coast at a permanent, wearying state of alert. According to the Germans, the invasion would have to be mounted after the winter storms, most probably in May, the earliest time by which at least five consecutive days of good weather could be guaranteed. The practice landing operations of the Allies in England and the recently-completed operations along the Italian coast, however, also gave various indications of the nature and date of the coming invasion. The Germans thus knew they must expect a

heavy air bombardment of their dèfenses and the early deployment of airborne forces and armored units, together with large-scale shelling from the enemy navy off the coast. All this would take place in the early dawn of the first day, about two to three hours after the low water.

If, with this background information, one studies the exact tables of Naval Group West, showing tides, phases of the moon and first and last light, the amazing conclusion becomes inescapable: in the area between Le Havre and Cherbourg — where many Navy officers indeed expected the landing to occur — the optimal conditions for a landing, should May slip by quietly, would prevail

only during the period from June 5-7. Similar favorable conditions would not recur until the 19th of the month — and even then without the moonlit nights so important to the Allied air forces. Yet Hitler, Jodl (Chief of the Wehrmacht Operations Staff), von Rundstedt and even Rommel still remained unmoved by this evidence. They steadfastly maintained the same attitude towards the enemy that they had held for years. It was only Hitler himself who briefly adopted the idea that Normandy offered good conditions for an airborne landing. The strengthening of defenses against this eventuality however made little difference to the overall German defense plan.

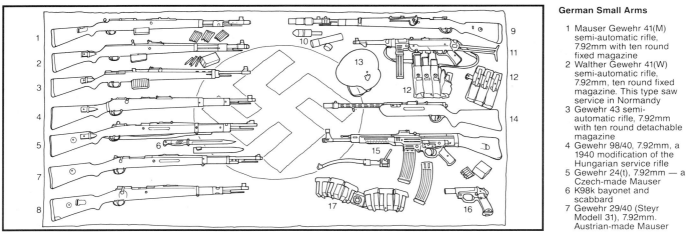

German Small Arms

1 Mauser Gewehr 41(M) semi-automatic rifle, 7.92mm with ten round fixed magazine
2 Walther Gewehr 41(W) semi-automatic rifle, 7.92mm, ten round fixed magazine. This type saw service in Normandy
3 Gewehr 43 semi-automatic rifle, 7.92mm with ten round detachable magazine
4 Gewehr 98/40, 7.92mm, a 1940 modification of the Hungarian service rifle
5 Gewehr 24(t), 7.92mm — a Czech-made Mauser
6 K98k bayonet and scabbard
7 Gewehr 29/40 (Steyr Modell 31), 7.92mm. Austrian-made Mauser

issued to Luftwaffe troops
8 Gewehr 33/40, 7.92mm. Modified Czech carbine used by mountain and airborne units
9 K98k, 7.92mm with grenade launcher and sight
10 Anti-tank rifle grenade (Gr.G.Pzgr.40)
11 Machine pistol 1940 (MP 40) Schmeisser, 9mm
12 Pair of canvas MP 40 magazine pouches
13 M1942 Army helmet
14 MP 35 Bergman 9mm
15 StG 44 (Sturmgewehr 44), 7.92mm kurz (short). The curved barrel (Krummlauf)
16 Flare pistol 42 (Leuchtpistole), 27mm
17 Waistbelt with ammunition pouches for K98k, G 43

Allan D. Cors Collection

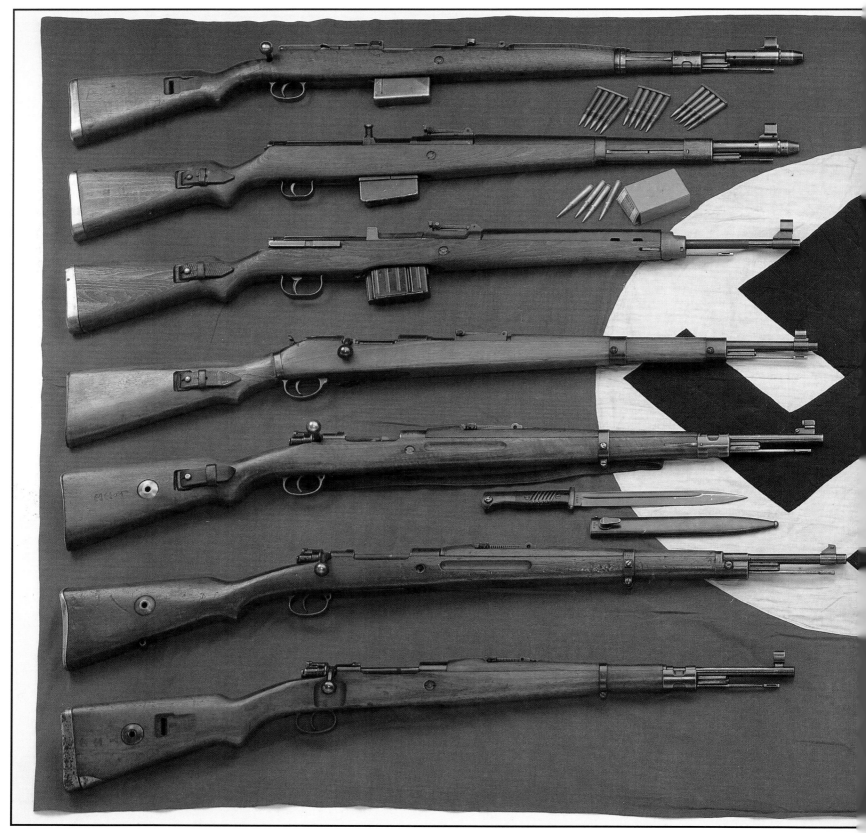

German Dispositions

The Allied strength in Britain as calculated by the Germans naturally forced them to maintain a presence along the entire coastline. It was impossible to set up a focal point for the defenses, since subsidiary operations at least could be mounted anywhere. The potential advantage of an "inner line," the rapid movement of German divisions from one coast to another, would also be nullified in Gen. Jodl's view by the large number of Allied troops surrounding Europe on all sides. Furthermore, Hitler and his generals still had to devote the major proportion of their military resources to the Eastern Front, to face the powerful onslaught

of the Red Army. In summer 1943 fresh forces were needed for the fighting in Italy. The Germans were also compelled to send many divisions to combat the uprisings in Yugoslavia and Greece. Taken together, these demands far outstripped the capabilities of Hitler's Germany. The German leader and his advisors therefore resolved to seek a strategic solution.

Until the late autumn of 1943 they still looked to the east for their salvation, hoping to achieve the first decisive victory there. With the aid of the huge potential released by a defeated Soviet Union, and with their rear no longer threatened, they would then do their utmost to put fear into the hearts of

the English and Americans. The Navy and the Luftwaffe would then get the lion's share of production of modern armaments instead of the Army. This plan however came to nothing as the fighting in the east became ever more bitter and prolonged.

Between October and November 1943 German strategy nevertheless underwent a fundamental change in emphasis. Hitler now ordained the struggle against the Red Army as no longer decisive to winning the war. The Germans might have to give up some territory, but they would be able to stop well before the borders of the Reich. In the west however matters were coming to a head. Should the Allies gain a foothold anywhere

Above: Flag of the German Labor Front (DAF). Labor unions in Germany were organized into one huge paramilitary organization. The DAF was the major source of skill and labor for the armaments industry and major defense projects. *Levaufre Collection*

on the west coast of Europe, Germany would have lost the war. In Hitler's view, an attempted invasion by the Allies would also represent a golden opportunity for the Reich. For if they could inflict a defeat on the British and Americans they would be incapable, for psychological reasons alone, of mounting another invasion in the foreseeable future. Then, Hitler's imagination ran on, following a decisive victory in the west, it would be possible to concentrate all his forces in the east and finally crush the Soviet Union. Everything thus depended on ensuring that all available resources were devoted to defeating the Allies in the west.

The Strategic Alternatives
Yet how was this to be achieved? There were basically two alternatives: the Germans must either try to defeat a landing during its very execution, entailing the defeat of the combined sea and air operations, or force the issue on the ground following the actual invasion. At first it seemed that the German leadership would decide on the former option, as Hitler himself declared in May 1943 that, "The Atlantic is my western perimeter, and even if I must fight a defensive battle there, that is still better than having to defend myself on the coast of Europe." In this he agreed with Grand-Adm. Doenitz, who was still convinced a sea power such as England could only properly be defeated at sea. Despite the great slaughter of the U-boats in the spring of 1943, Doenitz repeatedly tried to persuade Hitler to continue the war at sea. Although the Navy had been unable to discover the causes behind the loss of so many U-boats, Doenitz resumed the tonnage war against the Allied convoys in autumn 1943, only to be heavily defeated once again.

In the meantime matters had been firmly settled in favor of the second option — defeating the Allies on the European mainland. Doenitz's plan could anyway only have worked with the cooperation of a strong Luftwaffe. Unfortunately Goering, the Supreme Commander of the Luftwaffe lacked not only the means, but also the concep-

Above: Officers of an Organization Todt labor battalion under guard after the liberation of Cherbourg, June 1944. The Todt was a paramilitary construction organization originally set up by the Nazis in 1938 to build the Siegfried Line.

tual vision for such a campaign. The Army too was still very reserved about the concept of a combined defense: "The soldier is somehow anxious and nervous about having water in front of his own positions. He wants to get away from the coast," commented the Navy in August 1944, not entirely without justification.

It is hardly surprising then that Hitler's Order No. 51 of November 1943 allocated only minor operational tasks to the Luftwaffe and the Navy in the west. Essentially, they were only to act if a landing took place. Hardly any facet now remained of the idea of a comprehensive strategy to engage the enemy before he reached the coast. The only such means still available was the intended bombardment of England by the V-weapons. Their introduction was planned for June 1944. With these weapons Hitler

and his generals hoped to destroy the morale of the British population; delaying the invasion plans, if not putting an end to them entirely. Otherwise the main burden of the defense would fall on the Army.

The Atlantic Wall
Since there was also a shortage of manpower here, the German leadership made every effort to make good this lack with fortifications. Plans had been drawn up as early as the end of 1941 for an Atlantic Wall, which would consist of a vast number of fortified positions, bunkers, artillery pieces, anti-aircraft defenses, obstacles and barriers in the immediate vicinity of the coast. Following the model of similar installations already built in Norway, hundreds of thousands of foreign and German workers were employed in the ensuing months and years, under the

Below: Dating from early 1943, this photo of a major gun emplacement under construction in the Pas de Calais reveals the fact that the Germans were making a determined effort to create an impossibly powerful "Atlantic Wall" of impregnable defenses.

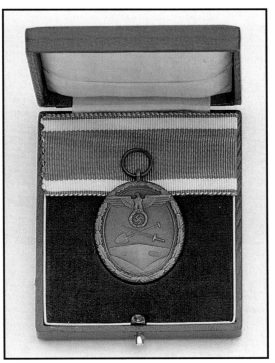

Above: Concealment was as important as raw strength in the lesser features of the Atlantic Wall, a fact indicated by the completion of this anti-tank bunker in the guise of a French farm house to lure targets within the emplaced gun's lethal range.

Above: The Defense Wall Honor Medal. First authorized by Hitler to commemorate the building of the Siegfried Line, it was reinstated in October 1944 for all personnel who had worked on fixed defensive positions since June 6, 1944. *Fistrovich Collection*

control of the Organization Todt, in fortifying first the Franco-Belgian coastline, and later all sectors of the coast along the Channel. From November 1942, following the landing of Allied troops in North Africa, fortifications also sprang up in the south of France. According to von Rundstedt and his staff, the sea was to serve as "the best anti-tank ditch" before the Atlantic Wall.

The German rate of construction was impressive: by the day of the invasion they had completed 12,247 of the 15,000 fortifications

Left: Another feature of the German defensive effort was mining, and huge fields of these potentially decisive weapons were laid in key areas. These German soldiers are carrying Teller mines, powerful and sophisticated anti-tank weapons that came in a number of sizes.

originally planned (with 943 more on the Mediterranean coast), built 500,000 beach obstacles, and laid 6.5 million mines. This was largely thanks to the energetic Field Marshal Rommel, who had made every possible effort to turn the coast into a fearful obstacle to the Allies. There was only one small problem however: like the other German leaders, Rommel's eyes were fixed on a landing at the Pas de Calais area, and the greatest resources were therefore devoted to the area held by Fifteenth Army. Where the Allies actually did land, opposite Seventh Army, the defenses were less thoroughly prepared. Although Army Headquarters had 74,000 Todt workers and 3,765 vehicles at its disposal, only about half the planned program had been completed by May 1944.

DEFENDING GERMAN DIVISIONS ON THE FRENCH/BELGIAN COAST, JUNE 6, 1944
The disposition of divisions prior to the invasion reflected not only German defensive strategy but also the state of the manpower availability.

Faced with an enormous Allied force across the Channel, but not knowing where the invasion would come, the German High Command made the decision to post divisions along the entire length of the coast. This would stretch the available manpower to its limit. They would, however, be behind the fortified Atlantic Wall, and the bulk of the forces would be positioned where logically the invasion would have to come, namely the Pas de Calais north of the Seine.

Most of the divisions along the coast were non-motorized and were to fight from fixed positions. The motorized divisions and Panzer divisions, which were vital to any counterstrike against the invader, were to be positioned behind these coastal units and the Atlantic Wall to form a mobile reserve to react *after* the Allies were ashore. Since the German Navy and Luftwaffe were too weak to oppose the invasion force at sea, this was seen to be the most logical strategy.

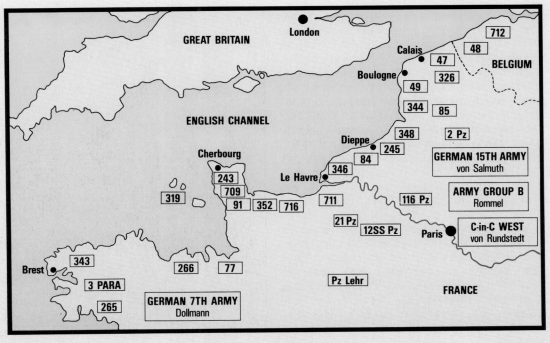

There were many problems, particularly with the naval guns which were to have ranged far out to sea. Of the planned second defense line 12.5-18.5 miles (20-30km) inland, only a small part had been completed. Furthermore the lion's share of the available material and manpower had been swallowed up in fortifying the ports of Cherbourg, St. Malo, Brest, Lorient and St. Nazaire, since the Germans assumed the Allies would land in the immediate vicinity of large ports.

Von Rundstedt and his staff knew of course that the chain of fortifications comprising the Atlantic Wall could only be as strong as its weakest link. He therefore made it clear to his commanders in the coastal fortifications again in February 1944: "There must be no retreat in the west!" In the event of an invasion, they would have to stand firm until motorized reserves arrived to throw the Allies back into the sea. Yet the German leaders, and especially Hitler himself, were not 100 percent convinced by their own plans, otherwise they would not, as early as autumn 1943, have reconnoitred a retrenchment line running from the River Somme via the Rivers Marne and Saone to the Swiss border. This was naturally carried out in strict secrecy, and only a few handpicked staff officers were told of it. After all, nobody wanted to demoralize the Army prematurely.

Still it is astounding that an army created for, and practised in mobility should suddenly decide to plant itself behind a wall. One reason for this may have been that the majority of the divisions under C-in-C West's control were "static," i.e. non-motorized divisions. His main objective up to November 1943 had been to form new mobile units. These divisions however were removed from the control of the C-in-C West as soon as they were brought up to strength in men and equipment. Hitler's Order No. 51 of the same month forbade any further transfers from the west to the south or east because of the new strategy. In reality however, many motorized units still left the west after this time because they were so urgently needed on other fronts.

Against this background it is easy to see why arguments raged for months in the German camp over the disposition of the few Panzer divisions available. Were they in fact the real linch-pin of the German defense system in the west? Should these divisions be positioned directly behind the Atlantic Wall, to be able to react rapidly to an Allied landing, as Rommel demanded for example, or should they be retained at more central points? After much wrangling a compromise was reached: some Panzer divisions were moved closer to the coast, while others formed a central reserve around Paris. This seemed to be the ideal solution, for now an enemy landing could be opposed immediately, and the reserve deployed when the main Allied thrust had been clearly identified.

Two factors soon become evident: the Germans were clearly hoping for a decisive result in the battle for the Allied bridgehead, since they knew from experience that the Allies would be at their weakest during this initial phase of the invasion. The "Panzer controversy", however, reveals that it was only Army officers who remained involved in the

Atlantic Wall: the Beach Obstacles

In building the Atlantic Wall, the Germans had to create a defensive position along nearly 3,000 miles (4,800km) of coastline from Holland to the Spanish border. Unable to build concrete fortifications everywhere, the Germans were forced to rely on mines and obstacles to fortify huge stretches of open beach, or other remote coastal areas reckoned to be assailable (photo G). In some cases obstacles were created from looted material taken from conquered countries. Right, (photo A): An Allied low-level air-reconnaissance photograph of the French coast, taken at low tide, showing a typical defensive layout.

Starting at the seaward side (far right) are a line of large wooden posts (detail photo D). These face out to sea and are armed with mines or other impact detonated explosives. Another line of wooden obstacles lies in the center (detail photo H). Also carrying mines, they face to shoreward and are designed to impale landing craft retreating before the outgoing tide. Along the shoreline (far left) are grouped steel obstacles known to the Allies as Hedgehogs (detail photo I). Standing about 5ft (1.5m) high they were designed to impede the progress of landing craft and tanks.

These obstacles would be supported by large minefields. Mines were also used on several types of mined raft (photos E and F). These ingenious devices were meant to strike landing craft far out from shore. See also the variety of German mines on pages 50-51.

Below, (photos B and C). The installation of obstacles by German labor units. Some 500,000 obstacles were emplaced on the coast by the time of the Allied invasion. Though crude, and evidently labor-intensive to install, these beach obstacles were cheap, easily manufactured and quite deadly. A major concern of the Allies on D-Day would be to clear these quickly and with as few casualties as possible.

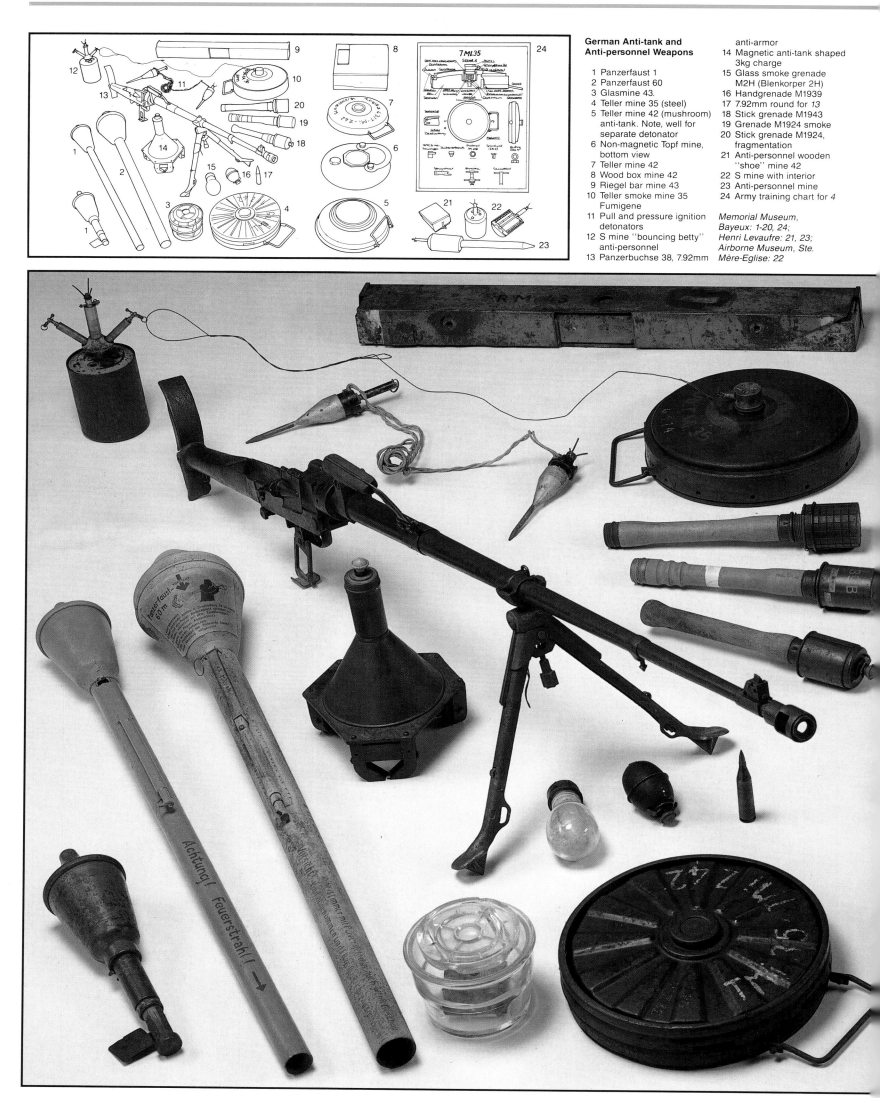

German Anti-tank and Anti-personnel Weapons

1 Panzerfaust 1
2 Panzerfaust 60
3 Glasmine 43.
4 Teller mine 35 (steel)
5 Teller mine 42 (mushroom) anti-tank. Note, well for separate detonator
6 Non-magnetic Topf mine, bottom view
7 Teller mine 42
8 Wood box mine 42
9 Riegel bar mine 43
10 Teller smoke mine 35 Fumigene
11 Pull and pressure ignition detonators
12 S mine ''bouncing betty'' anti-personnel
13 Panzerbuchse 38, 7.92mm anti-armor
14 Magnetic anti-tank shaped 3kg charge
15 Glass smoke grenade M2H (Blenkorper 2H)
16 Handgrenade M1939
17 7.92mm round for 13
18 Stick grenade M1943
19 Grenade M1924 smoke
20 Stick grenade M1924, fragmentation
21 Anti-personnel wooden ''shoe'' mine 42
22 S mine with interior
23 Anti-personnel mine
24 Army training chart for 4

Memorial Museum, Bayeux: 1-20, 24; Henri Levaufre: 21, 23; Airborne Museum, Ste. Mère-Eglise: 22

defense plan. They addressed themselves chiefly to the problem of what was to be done after an enemy landing. The crucial question of where and when the Allied attack would begin, however, received much less attention. It remained a purely hypothetical question as to whether the vast resources invested in the Atlantic Wall might not better serve the Luftwaffe and the Navy. Apart from the technical and organizational feasibility of such a redirection of effort, it must be remembered that Hitler and the majority of his senior officers still persisted in the tradition of being exclusively a land power. They thus developed a "fortress" mentality, out of which they seemed unable to escape.

Clash of Responsibilities

The defensive preparations in the west were considerably hindered by the complicated and intermingled areas of responsibility which prevailed there. The title C-in-C West represented a pious wish rather than reflecting the real situation. In contrast to Eisenhower's comprehensive powers, von Rundstedt had direct control of only a part of the armed forces in the west. It was understandable and tolerable that the flying units of Luftflotte 3 should still come under the command of the head of the Luftwaffe. When, on the other hand, paratroop units and Luftwaffe field divisions — nominally part of the Luftwaffe — were withdrawn from

the direct control of the C-in-C West, this naturally caused friction. A similar situation existed with the Naval security units and the coastal batteries. The fortress commandant in a port city was always an Army officer, and organized the defense with land operations in mind — a state of affairs which often came into conflict with the ideas of the Navy. Superior authorities such as the Armed Forces High Command or Navy High Command were often forced to intervene and settle the arguments which thus arose.

Waffen-SS and reserve units were also only von Rundstedt's to dispose of under certain conditions. He was often frustrated to find that only by chance had his staff come to

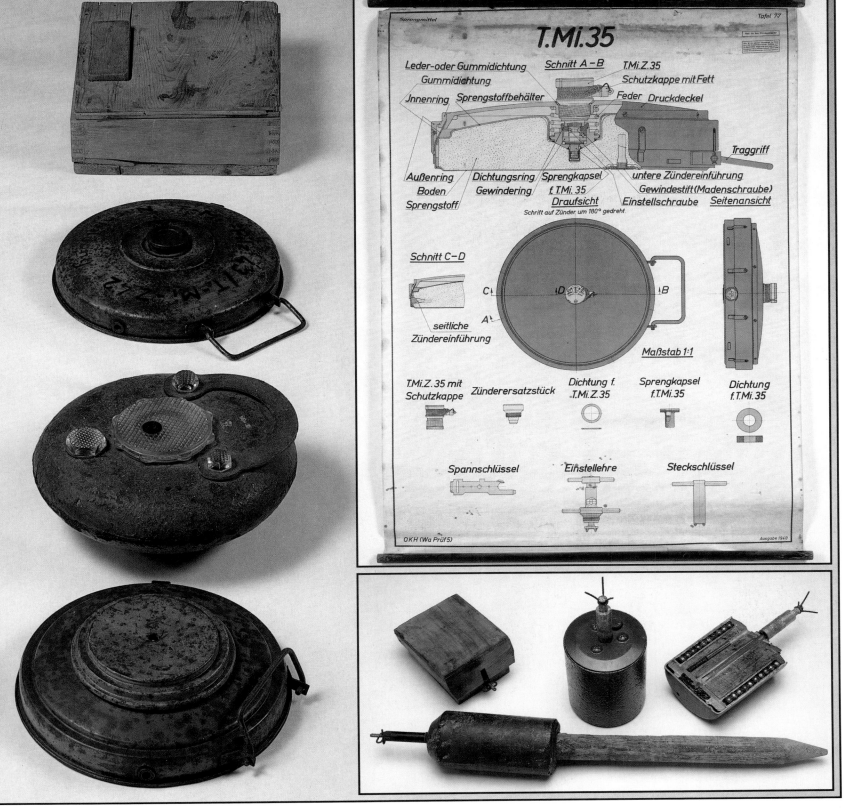

Axis Handguns

1 Mauser Model 1896, 7.63mm self-loading pistol with wooden holster/stock. Also seen are leather holster harness, cleaning rod, follower spring
2 Mauser HSc semi-automatic pocket pistol, 7.65mm
3 Mauser Model 1906 7.65mm
4 Walther PPK 7.65mm semi-automatic pistol
5 Walther Model 4 6.35mm semi-automatic pistol
6 Walther Model 8 6.35mm
7 Walther Model PP 7.65mm
8 P.38 semi-automatic pistol with private purchase shoulder holster
9 P.08 9mm semi-automatic pistol — with open toggle
10 P.08 9mm semi-automatic

pistol with private purchase shoulder holster
11 P.38 9mm semi-automatic pistol, slide open with Type 1 holster
12 Hungarian Femaru Model 1937 (P.37u) 7.65mm
13 Czech CZ 27 (P.M27) 7.65mm semi-automatic
14 Belgian FN Browning Model 1922 (P626b) 7.65mm semi-automatic
15 Belgian FN Browning Model 1935 (P640b) 9mm
16 Polish Radom VIS Model 1935 (P36p) 9mm
17 French Unique Kriegsmodel 7.65mm semi-automatic
18 Spanish Astra 600 (P.600/43) 9mm

Eugene Gibson: 1-2; Gordon Russell: 3-6; Russ Pritchard Collection: 7-18

learn of major manpower and equipment changes within such divisions. Military commanders in the west also had their own chains of command, which bypassed C-in-C West and ran direct to Army High Command in Berlin.

All of this could have been justified with the argument that different operational tasks required a different command structure. What remained completely incomprehensible however was the confused network of responsibilities within the Army itself. Even there the C-in-C West was not assured of complete powers of command. His most potent weapon, the motorized divisions, were partly removed from his control, in that they formed part of the Army High Command reserve. It was precisely this fact which was to have such dire consequences for the initial German reaction to the landings. The 2nd Panzer Division for example was by no means untypical, when thrown in at the crucial point of the assault, in having to give an ear to four different command authorities: in the order of battle it formed part of Panzer Group West, tactically it belonged to the I SS Panzer Corps, territorially it was under the control of the military commander for Belgium and Northern France, and for supply purposes it was still in Fifteenth Army. Nor was this by any means an exceptional case.

Even such an experienced officer as Gen. Blumentritt, the Chief of the General Staff at C-in-C West, was apt to get hot under the collar, and he gave vent to his feelings in a letter to Jodl in January 1944: "Everything here is in a complete mess, tangled and confused at every possible point."

Blumentritt may thereby have been thinking of the prolonged argument between Field Marshals von Rundstedt and Rommel, which had been going on since the end of 1943. Rommel's Army Group B Staff had originally been languishing in Italy. Perhaps Hitler saw in this a suitable opportunity to use the "Desert Fox" in the west, since nobody knew the western Allies as well as Rommel. His staff were therefore transferred to France in the

The Luger P.08 (9) and the Walther P.38 (8) were manufactured concurrently until 1942 when Luger production ceased. Military requirements later forced Walther to license P.38 production to Mauser and Speewerke.

This production was still insufficient to fill the handgun needs of the Axis, with the result that inferior or obsolete weapons were often used by rear area troops, while front line personnel were often issued with captured arms (including Russian) or those manufactured in conquered or allied countries. This resulted in the use of huge numbers of Belgian, Czech, French, Hungarian and Polish handguns, usually 9mm or 7.65mm. Very few revolvers were used by the Axis, as there was a strong preference for semi-automatic weapons.

New Year, in order to improve the defensive fortifications along the coast — technically a job which fell within the responsibility of the armies under C-in-C West. Rommel, who had a direct line to Hitler, then also managed to arrange things so that all troops from Holland to St. Nazaire (Army Commander Netherlands, Fifteenth Army, and Seventh Army) were placed under his command from January 15, 1944. Not satisfied with this, his hunger for power also soon gave him the veto on the use of motorized units, and he also tried to bring parts of the First and Nineteenth Armies in Southern France under his control. Von Rundstedt, seeing his own influence diminishing day by day, finally sent a note to the Armed Forces High Command in the spring of 1944, which he rounded off by saying that should his authority be restricted any further, there would seem to be little point to his continued service in the west. This had the desired effect. The dispute was terminated forthwith at the beginning of May with a victory for von Rundstedt: C-in-C West was placed in control not only of Rommel's Group B, but also of the newly-formed Army Group G (First and Nineteenth Armies) and Panzer Group West. This was only a formal arrangement, however, since the restrictions on his authority mentioned above still remained in effect. In other words, the situation now, after months of frustrating arguments, was virtually the same as at the end of 1943. To illustrate this in a little more detail: when C-in-C West laid out the new organisation for his command authorities on May 12, 1944, it took eight pages just to list his main areas of responsibility.

One may well enquire into the exact reasons for such a situation. In the author's opinion the following should be borne in mind: firstly the system of divided responsibility was deeply rooted in the traditions of German leadership, the tendency running through civil and military, private and public institutions ever since the foundation of the German Empire in 1871, irrespective of the ruling political system. Bismarck's "Lesser German Empire" did not grow organically, but was a conglomeration of varying mentalities and interests, which naturally gave rise to much rivalry. Nor did this situation change at all in the 20th century.

Above: As the war progressed, the Germans became increasingly short of oil fuels, and increasing reliance was once more placed on animal power. Here a German soldier controls a couple of horses dragging a "Belgian Gate" type of obstacle into position.

Secondly, Hitler was very careful to observe the principle of power sharing. Nobody was allowed to become powerful enough to threaten him. In this the German dictator was simply following the established tradition. This naturally proved to be a breeding ground for petty jealousies, self-seeking servility, and obsession with prestige at all levels in the power structure.

GERMAN DIVISIONS ON THE CALVADOS COAST, NORMANDY, TO JUNE 6, 1944, AND THE CHAIN OF COMMAND IN THE WEST
The confused nature of the German Army's High Command is graphically illustrated. Von Rundstedt may have had nominal control in the west, but Rommel and Army Group B had the direct line of command. To complicate matters further, it was Hitler who maintained direct control over the all-important Panzers, which also operated under their own command structure.

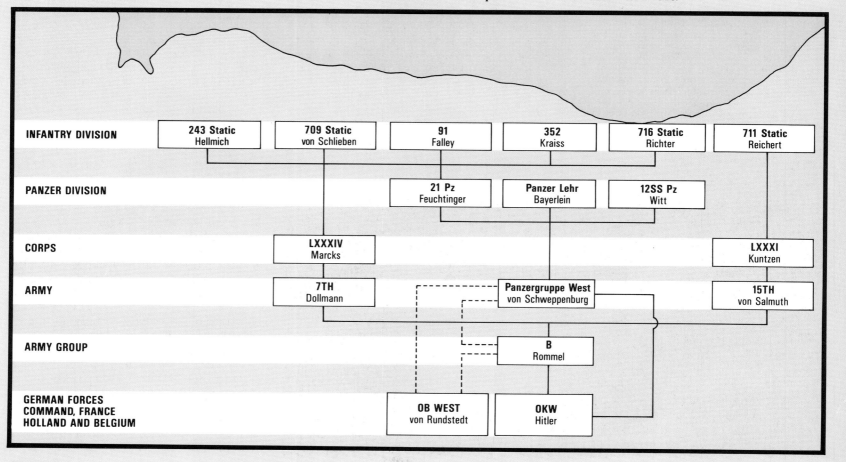

INFANTRY DIVISION	243 Static — Hellmich	709 Static — von Schlieben	91 — Falley	352 — Kraiss	716 Static — Richter	711 Static — Reichert
PANZER DIVISION			21 Pz — Feuchtinger	Panzer Lehr — Bayerlein	12SS Pz — Witt	
CORPS		LXXXIV — Marcks				LXXXI — Kuntzen
ARMY		7TH — Dollmann		Panzergruppe West — von Schweppenburg		15TH — von Salmuth
ARMY GROUP				B — Rommel		
GERMAN FORCES COMMAND, FRANCE HOLLAND AND BELGIUM		OB WEST — von Rundstedt		OKW — Hitler		

Yet although motorized units were still leaving the west up to the last moment, the Germans were still able to field about 1,600 tanks, all at least equal to those of the Allies in firepower and mobility.

Most of the 10 motorized units in the region were stationed close to the Channel, mainly in the central area between Holland and the Seine. South of the Seine, however, there was only the 21st Panzer Division around Caen and two further units (12th SS Panzer and Panzer Lehr) at least 62 miles (100km) from the Normandy coast. Here, where the Allies would soon land, the LXXXIV Army Corps would have to put up the best defense it could with six divisions and numerous independent anti-tank, tank, air landing, artillery and "Ost" battalions (battalions composed of eastern European nationalities).

Shortages of Materiel
The one factor which most reduced the combat readiness of the units in the west was the increasing shortage of fuel supplies. Allied bombing of the German fuel industry had had far-reaching consequences: training programmes had had to be curtailed, depots reduced in size and number, and transport in general slowed down. In many cases the Germans now had to make do with bicycles and horse transport.

The manpower state in the German camp was also gradually wearing thin. The huge losses, particularly in the east, increasingly forced Hitler and his followers to use foreign workers in the factories in order to release German workers for the Army. At the end of November 1943 the Army High Command initiated a so-called "combing out" drive to round up all surplus manpower from all walks of life for service at the front. C-in-C West even formed a special staff for this purpose in February 1944 under the command of a general. The result was pitiful. Despite the severest penalties for evasion, by April only 6,500 soldiers had been enlisted in the west (according to Jodl the available manpower in the region was 1,870,000, together with 310,000 in Norway and 170,000 in Denmark). Yet in Paris alone at this time there were 50,000 Germans engaged in innumerable occupations.

This abortive effort demonstrated once more how complicated and involved the command structure in the west had become. Nobody could even judge any more whether an organization had too many or too few personnel. It is little wonder therefore that the manpower needs of von Rundstedt's divisions underwent little improvement. In the SS divisions, more than 50 percent of the troops were often under 20 years of age, while the "static" divisions were made up with many over-age soldiers. The manpower shortage was considerably exacerbated by the Allied bombing of important transport and armaments centers in the occupied west. The Germans were forced to devote an ever-increasing number of men to repairing the damage caused. So far as the equipment of his units was concerned, von Rundstedt's divisions did not always receive the most up-to-date equipment from the factories, and often had to make do with obsolete, captured equipment to make up the numbers. This often

In relation to military matters one often has the impression that, for many high-ranking officers, the thing closest to their heart was not the military objective, but rather their careers or the reputation of their branch of the service or military unit. This was not an unknown motive in the Allied camp, and one has only to think of Patton, Montgomery and MacArthur in this respect. Amongst the German leadership, however, this situation and attitude was rather more the rule than the exception.

The Order of Battle
At the time of the landing, von Rundstedt's staff disposed altogether over 60 divisions. This represented an increase of 10 major units since mid-1943. What might at first sight seem an imposing array can easily be put

Above: German Army "volunteers" from Soviet Central Asia. The Allies in Normandy were surprised by the numbers of East Europeans and Soviets in German uniform. In fact the German Seventh Army west of the Seine had 13 "Ost" battalions made up of such troops. Inset: Arm shields of volunteer units from Soviet republics. Top, Georgia; Middle, Russian Army of Liberation; Bottom, Turkestan. *Fistrovich Collection*

into better perspective on closer examination. Over the same period, the proportion of still-incomplete divisions increased correspondingly. About 20 divisions were "static" units, and many of the Panzer divisions had only arrived in France and Belgium during the course of spring 1944. Their equipment and manpower states were particularly problematical for the C-in-C West, as was the transfer to the Eastern Front in March 1944 of the II SS Panzer Corps and its two combat-ready units. Even later, when all indications pointed to an imminent invasion, the German leadership continued to withdraw motorized units from the west, some units stationed northwest of Orléans leaving C-in-C West's control as late as June 4. They would have been particularly useful only two days later when they could have been employed in attacking Allied troops in Normandy. These events only go to show that Hitler's vision of an enemy airborne landing in the Normandy region was nothing more than a passing fancy.

Below: A meeting in Paris in early 1944 of the combined German High Command West. These were the men who were to meet the onslaught of Operation *Overlord*. Facing left to right, Gen. von Schweppenburg — commander Panzer Group West; Gen. von Blaskowitz — commander Army Group G (southern France); Field Marshal Sperrle (Luftwaffe) — commander Luftflotte 3; Field Marshal von Rundstedt — C-in-C West; Field Marshal Rommel — commander Army Group B; Adm. Krancke — commander Naval Group West. Backs to camera left to right, Gen. Plocher (Luftwaffe) — chief of staff Luftflotte 3; Gen. Blumentritt — chief of staff C-in-C West; Gen. Speidel — Rommel's deputy.

tried the technical know-how of the operators and severely complicated supply requirements.

The flying units of Luftflotte 3 and IX Air Corps had to contend with similar problems. At the end of May 1944, Luftflotte 3 had just over 900 aircraft on inventory, of which only 650 were operational (with a further 145 aircraft in Norway). The IX Air Corps, whose bombers had carried out sporadic attacks on British embarkation ports in the weeks before the landing, albeit without causing significant damage, reported only 100 combat-ready aircraft by the end of May. In the event of an invasion the Germans planned to transfer approximately 1,000 aircraft to the west from all parts of occupied Europe. Even with this number — should the transfer actually to take place — the Germans would still find themselves in an hopelessly inferior position. Although the Minister for Armaments, Albert Speer, had again succeeded in considerably increasing aircraft production in 1944, this output far outstripped the availability of properly trained pilots. It was for this reason for example that in May 1944, out of a total of 2,155 aircraft losses by the Luftwaffe, 847 were accidents not involving enemy action.

Below: Kriegsmarine (German Navy) badges. From the top, submarine war badge; torpedo/patrol boat badge, second pattern; torpedo/patrol boat badge, first pattern. Fistrovich Collection, center; Pritchard Collection, remainder

The Navy in the west also faced a similar sorry outlook. After most of the large surface units had been brought back to harbor in Norway or Germany, only 3 destroyers, 5 torpedo boats, 34 motor gun-boats, 163 mine-hunters and 34 U-boats were left in the west. Due to the weakness of the Luftwaffe even these units were unable to venture outside

Above: With its major surface vessels destroyed or bottled up in harbors round northern Europe, the German Navy had to rely almost exclusively on the efforts of its U-boats. This is the death of such a boat, just one of 41 U-boats sunk in May 1943.

the anti-aircraft protection of their harbors during daylight hours.

Yet Doenitz ordered these warships to be employed regardless of potential losses. According to the Grand-Admiral, they had only one job in the event of a landing: "Attack and sink." At the end of March 1944, Doenitz proposed using the U-boats in a style

Below: The task of the U-boats was made all the harder by the advent of escort carriers in convoy escort groups. This photograph records the approaching end of *U-118*, a "Type XB" class boat depth-charged and sunk by aircraft of the USS *Bogue* on June 12, 1943.

reminiscent of the Japanese kamikaze mentality: "The U-boat which causes losses to the enemy during a landing has fulfilled its ultimate aim and justifies its existence, even if it remains there." As it turned out, most of the U-boats intended for this purpose never had the opportunity, for Doenitz had ordered them back out into the mid-Atlantic at the end of May, when the threat of an invasion seemed to have receded.

The only effective weapon remaining to the Navy in the west to combat a landing seemed to be the use of mines. Naval Group West wanted to mine the whole sea around the Isle of Wight with the aid of the Luftwaffe. The latter however refused to have anything to do with this plan, leaving the Navy with the sole remaining option of laying so called "lightning barrages" along the coast at the last minute. In order for this to be feasible however, the enemy approach across the Channel would have to be detected in good time. The head of Naval Group West, Adm. Krancke, hoped to be able to do this with his few remaining patrol boats which patrolled the coastline, weather permitting, each night.

The Troops' Morale
The precarious situation of Hitler's Germany could not be kept secret from the ordinary soldier forever, in spite of all the Nazi propaganda which was showered on him. Allied air superiority over Germany and in the west was enough on its own to show the overwhelming materiel superiority already enjoyed by the Allies. The confidence in victory and the spirit of the earlier years were gone, as is revealed by the tenor of many soldiers' letters home. The troops could also notice the increasingly colder atmosphere in the occupied territories, where a passive attitude, changing to disdain and outright disobedience were encountered more frequently. Whether the fight against supposed or

Above: German sailors promenade along the sea front of a French coastal town. Note the fact that the buildings have been fortified to serve as extra strongpoints for the German defense, which was based on the concept of repulsing the invasion on the coast.

actual Resistance members, in which an ever-growing number of Wehrmacht troops were employed, served to raise morale, must remain undecided. In any event, the German measures against Allied "commando troops" (teams of national or Allied troops engaged in reconnaissance or sabotage) seemed likely to put their own side in the wrong: they must be granted no quarter, even if they surrendered without a fight, were the orders from above. Such orders were of course to be acknowledged, but the written record of the orders was to be immediately destroyed.

Many soldiers may have asked themselves how this was to be reconciled with the idea of the "ethical and moral superiority" and the "nobility" of German aims, as their leaders characterized them.

It appeared to be difficult, for many reasons, to turn the soldier in the west into such a fanatical fighter as his comrades on the Eastern Front. The long sojourn away from an active front had led here to typical "instances of malingering." Many troops adopted an increasingly careless and sloppy attitude: they lost their weapons and other equipment, became involved with local women and, especially in France, fell victim to a fascination with the country and the people. Rigorous punishments imposed by military courts and superior officers had little effect on these tendencies.

Another battle fought almost in vain, was that over the attitude towards the Allies in the coming conflict. In contrast to the Eastern Front, where many men believed they were engaged in a crusade against Bolshevism and the "sub-human" Slavs, the British and Americans were viewed much less negatively. The Army High Command summed up the feelings of many soldiers in the west by saying that they held the regrettable but appropriate "assumption of facing a more humane opponent." One event from the end of 1943 may serve as a good example of this attitude: an Allied "terror flier" parachuted from his shot-down aircraft over France and was soon taken prisoner by a troop of German soldiers. The NCO in charge offered the pilot a cigarette, in full view of some French civilians. Von Rundstedt practically foamed at the mouth with anger when he heard of this and ordered shortly afterwards that any similar cases of "completely misplaced sentimentality" must in future be punished. No less a figure than Goebbels, the Reich Propaganda Minister, strove to reverse this

Left: Each side's propaganda machine was keen about major weapons with personalized messages. Photographed in 1940, this German sailor is inscribing a sarcastic greeting message for Winston Churchill on a moored mine before its despatch into the water.

attitude and attacked the bombing of German cities as an uncultured act of barbarity.

Senior officers again emphasized that in the event of a landing, it would be a fight "to the death." Jodl made the following prognosis: "Then we shall see who fights harder and dies easier, the German soldier faced with the destruction of his homeland, or the Americans and English, who don't even know any longer what they are fighting for in Europe." At the end of 1943 he even invoked history in front of senior military men and officials in the hope of encouraging the more lethargic types: "We will be victorious, because we must be victorious, for otherwise there would be no sense anymore to world history."

It was on the "wonder weapons" that the Germans, at home and the front, now pinned their remaining hopes. Many letters home from the front show that they continued to have faith that these weapons would change the course of the war at the eleventh hour.

In view of the Allied superiority, this applied especially to the troops in the west. Where a cohesive group of soldiers with previous combat experience could be found, or where a unit with a tradition or a reputation still existed, the Allies could certainly count on stiff opposition. This was the case for most of the motorized divisions and also some of the infantry and paratroop divisions. Other units, however, had been cobbled together out of diverse groups from all branches of the service, of differing age groups and often varying degrees of fitness. Amongst this latter category were many of the "static", security and reserve divisions, from whom a lot less heroism could be expected.

Before the Invasion

At the highest level, the mood amongst Hitler and his generals shortly before the invasion was one of confidence. The Führer could hardly wait for the landing since he was completely convinced of a forthcoming victory of German arms, whilst Rommel above all gave a very optimistic impression. In his view he had done everything humanly possible in the right place to prepare a warm reception for the Allies.

A week before the landing at the latest, it must have been absolutely clear to SHAEF that they would achieve strategic surprise, for there were no indications at all that the enemy had changed his long standing idea of

Above: A Goliath wire controlled demolition device. Size: 5 x 2ft (1.5 x .6m), weight: 800lbs (369kg); speed: 5-10mph (8-16km/h); explosive charge: 83kg (182lbs). Some were found behind *Utah* beach but were ineffective.
Memorial Museum Bayeux

a main thrust aimed at the Pas de Calais. Even if the Germans were to learn the true Allied intentions now, it would be far too late for them to undertake any significant regroupings.

The question still remained as to whether the British and Americans could also achieve tactical surprise on the day of the invasion. At one moment it seemed they would not, when an error of potentially huge proportions occurred at Supreme Headquarters. When Eisenhower postponed the landing from June 5 to 6 due to bad weather, SHAEF ordered all ships already at sea back to the nearest harbor. One convoy of 135 vessels however failed to receive the order, and steamed on alone towards the Normandy coast. The Allies did not succeed in contacting and stopping the convoy until it was 25 nautical miles (46km) south of the Isle of Wight. Luckily for the invasion forces the Germans failed to suspect anything. Sea and

air reconnaissance in the Normandy area had been suspended due to the bad weather, a quite understandable step, for after several weeks of the most favorable weather conditions, the Allies would certainly not want to land now, in weather fit for neither man nor beast. At least so thought many senior officers in C-in-C West's area, and turned their

Below: German military awards. Top row from the left: Iron Cross First Class; Iron Cross Second Class; War Merit Cross with Swords First Class. Second row: Infantry Assault Badge; Army Flak Badge; War Badge for coastal artillery. Third row: War Merit Cross with Swords Second Class; General Assault Badge; Black Wound Badge, for one or two wounds in action; Silver Wound Badge, for three or four wounds; Gold Wound Badge, for five or more, or death. Fourth row: Gold Close Combat Bar; Tank Destruction Badge; Gold Tank Destruction Badge; Motor Vehicle Driver's Badge of Merit in Gold.
Fistrovich/Pritchard Collections

Below: The V-1 in flight. The V-1 (or Fieseler 103 flying bomb) was operated by crews of 50 Luftwaffe personnel. It had a range of up to 200 miles (320km) but was very inaccurate over long distances and was also prone to crash soon after launch.

minds to other things: they went to play war games in Rennes, took a few days' holiday or visited their French lady friends.

However, the weather forecast of the meteorologist at C-in-C West for June 5 was not so negative as this behavior might suggest. After a front of bad weather, went the report, periods of better weather could be expected on the following day. Strangely enough, this forecast was exactly the same as that of the Allies.

There had however already been much clearer signs of an impending invasion: in the middle of May, the German Security Service in France had reported that the "Secret Army" had gone to the highest state of alert and that consequently an invasion could be expected between the 20th of the month and June 10. On the first day of the same month, the Naval Intelligence Service noticed a further indicator of the approaching attack: the Allies had already changed the key code settings for their radio traffic after only 30 days, something which they normally only did after three months. They were also clearly trying to knock out by bombing all of the defenders' radio monitoring posts along the coast. Finally, on June 1 and 3 the German authorities received, quite openly, the clearest indication of all that the invasion was imminent: the BBC had been repeatedly broadcasting to the Resistance movements the first part of a stanza from one of Verlaine's poems which ran: "Les sanglots longs des

Above: Three Waffen-SS commanders — Fritz Witt, Sepp Dietrich and Kurt Meyer, accompany Field Marshal von Rundstedt, the C-in-C West, as he inspects the 12th SS Panzer Division "Hitler Jugend" on a Belgian training ground during March 1944.

violons de l'automne." If this was to be followed by the second part, the German Secret Service knew that the landing would follow within 48 hours. The British promptly broadcast the second part: "blessent mon coeur d'une langueur monotone," at 21:15, June 5.

A short while earlier the C-in-C West had given the following evaluation of the situation: "There are no definite signs that the invasion is imminent," since the result of Allied air attacks on the coastal fortifications certainly could not have come up to enemy expectations. Naval Group West expressed the same conclusion a day earlier, on June 4: the Allies, as they thought, had only enough landing craft for just over 10 divisions. They would therefore need more time to assemble

the shipping capacity for the 20 divisions estimated as necessary by the Germans.

On the basis of these judgements, the C-in-C West still took no concrete steps against a possible landing on the evening of June 5. In any case, the BBC had sent out many such alert messages in the past, without the expected invasion happening. The officers at C-in-C West simply assumed that this latest message was the signal for the start of widespread acts of sabotage.

The situation began to change however shortly after midnight when airborne landings were reported on the Orne and the Cotentin peninsula. LXXXIV Army Corps in Normandy now initiated Alert State II (highest alert); they were shortly followed by Fifteenth Army. Naval Group West and Luftflotte 3 also followed suit. Even now the High Command in the west did not think they were facing a major landing, and therefore deemed sea reconnaissance by surface vessels as unnecessary. The weather conditions and tides were hardly favorable anyway.

When a few ships were sighted off Port-en-Bessin towards 03:00 on the morning of June 6, Adm. Krancke nevertheless ordered sea reconnaissance by surface vessels. An hour and a half later the first torpedo boats put out from Le Havre.

Around 06:45 the situation seemed to have calmed down a little, when the Chief of Staff of Seventh Army reported that, contrary to earlier estimations, there was no evidence of any seaborne landing. At that moment in fact the coastal fortifications were already under fire from Allied warships. Nevertheless, the Seventh Army Headquarters, according to the Chief of Staff, were quite capable of handling the situation without any assistance.

At that very moment, landing craft were approaching the coast under the cover of naval and aerial bombardment. The invasion had begun and the Allies had succeeded in achieving complete tactical surprise.

Below: Occupying a bunker position apparently hit by shellfire or bombs, a German observer surveys the Allied invasion fleet off the Normandy coast. The ebb of the tide has exposed the mass of beach defenses, but these were known to the Allies.

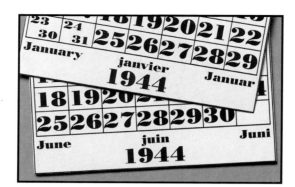

Operation Neptune

4

Edward Marolda

When daylight began to pierce the darkness on the morning of June 6, D-Day, German observers on France's Normandy coast saw spread out before them as far as the eye could see an armada of over 5,300 naval vessels, from the largest battleship to the smallest patrol boat. This invasion flotilla, the most powerful ever assembled, with warships, amphibious ships, auxiliaries, and landing craft from Great Britain, the United States, France, Canada, Poland, Norway, Greece, and the Netherlands, was poised to start the liberation of Europe.

Over two years before that momentous day, British and American military staffs had begun preparations for the invasion of the continent. The London-based staff of Lt. Gen. Frederick E. Morgan, the Chief of Staff to the Supreme Allied Commander (COSSAC), had begun planning for a landing in western Europe back in early 1943. Morgan's group developed the so-called "COSSAC" Plan for the invasion of France, from May 1943 on code-named *Overlord*. The naval aspect of that enormous undertaking would later be called *Neptune*.

The COSSAC plan called for an amphibious assault along a relatively narrow 30-mile (48km) front, with three infantry divisions seizing the beachhead and two others reinforcing them. Morgan unveiled the plan to Allied leaders at the first Quebec Conference in August 1943 and soon afterwards the US-British Combined Chiefs of Staff approved it in principle. Although the COSSAC planners would have preferred a stronger effort, they did not have the clout to get for *Overlord* the additional air, naval, and ground forces they felt essential. That year the Americans were focused on the war in the Pacific and the campaign against the U-boat menace in the

Atlantic, while the British, especially Prime Minister Churchill, were seriously considering alternative campaigns in Norway and the Mediterranean.

The appointments of Generals Eisenhower and Montgomery to *Overlord* at the end of

1943 finished the COSSAC plan. Neither was happy about its limited scope, either in number of divisions deployed or its narrow beachhead. By January 1944 the COSSAC plan was being completely revised to include an attack by five infantry divisions abreast on a 61-mile (98km) beach front. Unlike Morgan, these officers, who had the strong support of Roosevelt and Churchill, were able to re-emphasize the prior understanding that *Overlord* had first call on Allied resources worldwide.

An officer who shared the views of Eisenhower and Montgomery on the broad front approach was Adm. Sir Bertram Ramsay, selected by the British Admiralty to serve as Naval Commander Allied Expeditionary Force. Ramsay was an easygoing naval officer who possessed a brilliant intellect and the ability to address a problem clearly. This veteran of World War I, and more recent amphibious operations at Dunkirk and in the Mediterranean, was charged with planning and overseeing the naval aspects of the invasion program.

Planning *Neptune*

During the first half of 1944, Allied leaders, including Ramsay and Rear Adm. Alan G. Kirk, the ranking American naval officer in *Neptune*, feverishly worked to acquire additional assault divisions and a host of additional landing ships and craft, escorts,

Left: German and Allied military currency. Top, German Army scrip, five Reichsmarks, issued Berlin, September 1944. Below, Allied "invasion" francs, issued to all troops in France. Printed in America by the Forbes Lithograph Corp. of Chelsea, MA; from June 6, 1944, to June 15, 1945, over 680 million of these notes were delivered.
D-Day Museum, Portsmouth

minesweepers, and logistic support vessels. The change to the strategic plan meant that more embarkation ports and training grounds had to be set aside in southern England, already chock-a-block with troops, armored vehicles, motor transport, and supplies. Furthermore, the new invasion plan made it clear that the Allies would not have the wherewithal to support a simultaneous and complementary landing in the south of France, code-named *Anvil,* or to launch the Normandy assault in May, as originally planned. Eisenhower postponed *Anvil* to August and rescheduled the cross-channel operation for June 5, 1944.

It was soon clear that the Royal Navy could not by itself meet the new operational requirements for *Neptune.* The British felt compelled to maintain a strong Home Fleet in Scotland in case Hitler's pocket battleships, cruisers, and other major combatants based in Germany sortied into the North Sea or moved south into the English Channel to contest the Allied landing. The British also feared a foray by the German battleship *Tirpitz* deployed in Norway against Allied convoys steaming through Arctic waters to the Soviet Union. As a result, the British kept in reserve three fleet carriers, three modern battleships (which they also chose not to risk to the mines off the French coast), and 16 other major units. British intelligence, however, overestimated the operational ability of the German surface fleet, whose warships and bases had been the target of Allied bombers for many months and would have been hard pressed to mount a serious attack against the Allies in any area.

The British took drastic steps to provide the additional sailors, warships, and other vessels needed for *Neptune.* The Royal Navy laid up 49 old combatants and decommissioned a minelaying squadron so that their crews could man more combat-effective ships and craft. The British even transferred soldiers and airmen to the sea service. Finally, the Admiralty recalled ships from the Mediterranean theater, halted the dispatch of units to the Eastern Fleet in the Indian Ocean, and reduced the number of Atlantic convoy escorts.

Despite these measures, Eisenhower's naval staff was concerned they still lacked enough amphibious vessels and bombardment ships to carry out the expanded *Neptune* plan. Hence, they called on the US Navy to make up the deficit. This led to one of the few acrimonious exchanges between the British and the Americans during the preparations for *Neptune.* The British felt the Americans were employing too many amphibious vessels in their Pacific operations to the detriment of the European theater. Adm. Ernest J. King, the flinty C-in-C US Fleet and Chief of Naval Operations, disagreed, contending that he had been generous with the allocation to the European theater of Landing Ships, Tank (LST), Landing Craft, Infantry (LCI), Landing Craft, Tank (LCT), and other amphibious vessels.

The crux of the problem was that there were just not enough amphibious types in service to handle all of the Allies' global requirements. The high losses in the Atlantic and the Caribbean to German U-boats

during 1942 had mandated increased building in US shipyards of convoy escort ships rather than landing ships and craft. The postponement of a 1943 landing in Europe also diverted amphibious vessels to other theaters.

The whole issue became moot when the British shifted LSTs and LCIs from the Mediterranean and increased the troop and vehicle load capacities of their vessels, as the Americans had done. What is more, Adm. King began to send newly constructed amphibious vessels directly from the shipyards to England. Consequently, the Allied naval force had a sufficient number of amphibious vessels on D-Day.

The short-tempered but brilliant King also objected to the dispatch of major US warships to European waters. He felt that the British had an adequate number of these combatants to handle bombardment and naval gunfire support duties. He was persuaded otherwise when Rear Adm. John L. Hall, slated to head one of the two American amphibious task forces, strongly expressed his concern for the success of the operation. Finally in April 1944, King deployed to England three old battleships (*Arkansas, Nevada* and *Texas*) and a squadron of destroyers. Still, as the American

Above, from top left: US Navy uniforms and equipment. M1 steel helmet in Navy gray with added folk art. M1 helmet, M1936 pistol belt, USN M1 knife and sheath, M1910 canteen and cover, ID tags and M1938 leggings worn by a member of 28th Sea Bee Battalion at Cherbourg. Dungaree work uniform, M1943 service shoes. Earphones, microphone and steel talker's helmet used by guncrew chiefs. *Stamatelos Collection*

naval historian Samuel Elliot Morison has correctly observed, "the Royal Navy supplied the lion's share of gunfire support ships" and, he might have added, the majority of the other ships and craft involved in *Neptune.*

The Royal Navy (which included units of the Royal Canadian Navy) would put to sea on June 5 with a total of 3 battleships, 17 cruisers, 65 destroyers, 360 coastal craft, and 447 frigates, destroyer escorts, corvettes, minesweepers, and similar vessels. The US Navy contribution included three battleships, three cruisers, 34 destroyers, 111 coastal craft, and 49 frigates, destroyer escorts, minesweepers and patrol craft. Another 49 French, Polish, Greek, Dutch, and Norwegian-manned warships and combat craft would sail in the invasion fleet. The amphibious landing ships and craft totalled 4,126 vessels (3,261 British and 865 US.)

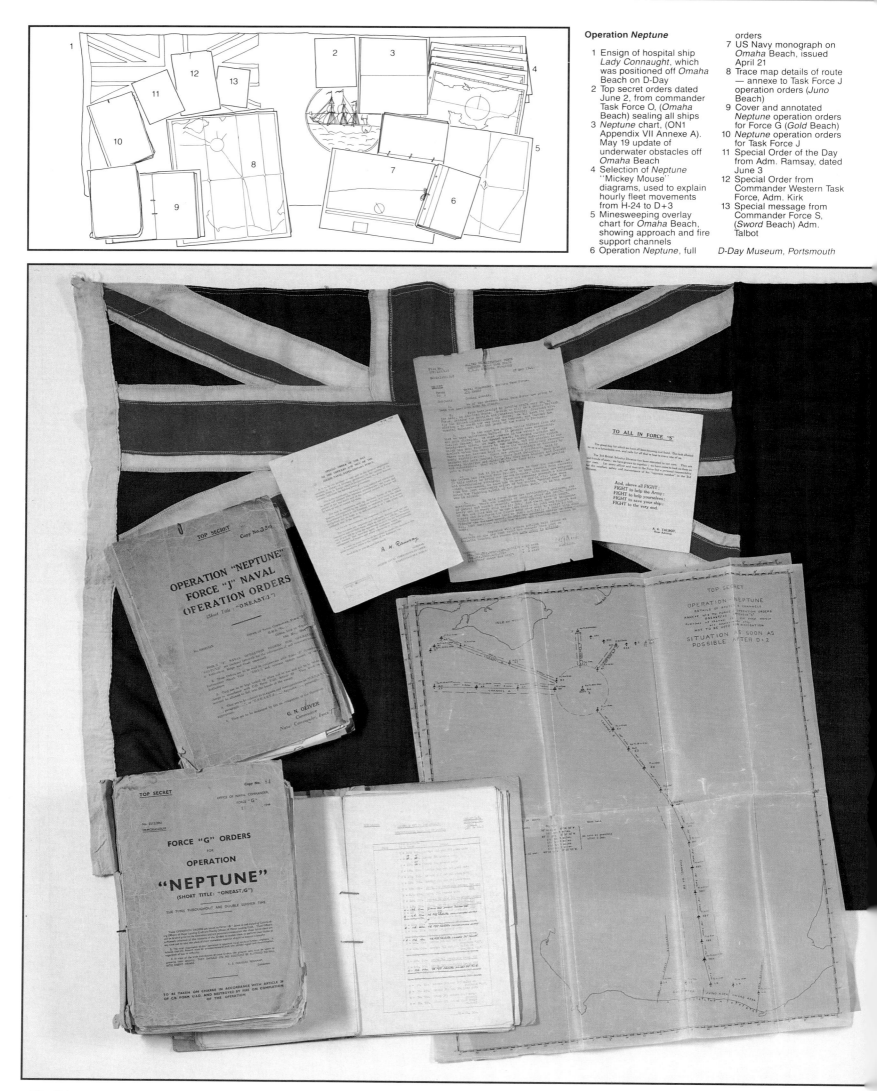

Operation *Neptune*

1 Ensign of hospital ship *Lady Connaught*, which was positioned off *Omaha* Beach on D-Day
2 Top secret orders dated June 2, from commander Task Force O, (*Omaha* Beach) sealing all ships
3 *Neptune* chart, (ON1 Appendix VII Annexe A). May 19 update of underwater obstacles off *Omaha* Beach
4 Selection of *Neptune* ''Mickey Mouse'' diagrams, used to explain hourly fleet movements from H-24 to D+3
5 Minesweeping overlay chart for *Omaha* Beach, showing approach and fire support channels
6 Operation *Neptune*, full orders
7 US Navy monograph on *Omaha* Beach, issued April 21
8 Trace map details of route — annexe to Task Force J operation orders (*Juno* Beach)
9 Cover and annotated *Neptune* operation orders for Force G (*Gold* Beach)
10 *Neptune* operation orders for Task Force J
11 Special Order of the Day from Adm. Ramsay, dated June 3
12 Special Order from Commander Western Task Force, Adm. Kirk
13 Special message from Commander Force S, (*Sword* Beach) Adm. Talbot

D-Day Museum, Portsmouth

"Operation Neptune Naval Operation Orders" (6) were issued from Adm. Ramsay's headquarters on April 10, 1944. The scale and detail of the orders was remarkable. Divided into 22 separate sections (ON1-22) with appendices, the complete orders came to 1100 pages. Every conceivable aspect of the operation was covered, from assembling the fleet (ON4); to minesweeping (ON6); to data on navigation and weather (ON18). Air defense was explained in ON12, and the command areas for the assault beaches was dealt with in ON19. The orders also covered the installation of *Mulberry* (ON16), and *Pluto*, the undersea pipeline (ON21).

Because the orders had to be understood by both Royal Navy and US Navy, as well as other Allies, great care was taken to ensure that all terms used were understandable to all.

All of the Allied leaders associated with *Neptune* were conscious of the British amphibious disasters at Gallipoli in World War I and at Dieppe in 1942, while the Americans knew that even though their recent landing at Tarawa Atoll in the Pacific by US Marines in November 1943 had succeeded, the cost in lives had been much too great. These military professionals knew that an amphibious landing operation, involving coordinated air, sea, and ground operations, was one of the most complex of military evolutions to achieve successfully.

To avoid a catastrophe in France, Allied soldiers, sailors, and airmen underwent thorough and continuous training. Rear Adm. John Wilkes, greatgrandson of Commodore Charles Wilkes, the 19th-century American explorer of the Pacific, was charged with preparing US forces for their part in *Neptune*. Beginning in December 1943, the energetic admiral put the Americans through demanding training exercises at Slapton Sands and Torquay in Devon. Full-scale rehearsals took place in which the troop units and ships that were slated to fight together also trained together. Much of this training occurred in late April and early May. The Germans helped make this training real. On April 28, nine fast German E-boats burst in on a night time training exercise in Lyme Bay off the Devon coast and sank two of the

precious LSTs before escaping in the confusion. That night off southern England, 600 American soldiers and sailors died, most of them by drowning. Despite this tragedy, the rigorous training régime prepared US and British amphibious forces well.

Furthermore, Allied maintenance and repair units were especially successful in keeping the ships and craft of the amphibious flotilla operational. On June 1, 99.3 percent of the US and 97.7 percent of the British amphibious vessels were seaworthy and prepared for action.

The Allied navies also emphasized training for the gunfire support mission. Separate teams of naval officers were assigned to the landing forces to help ensure naval gunfire accuracy. The British called these teams Forward Observers Bombardment and the Americans referred to them as Shore Fire Control Parties. These groups, which would go ashore with airborne and amphibious assault troops, trained intensively with the gun directors of their primary support ship. They were trained to call in fire from other

Allied ships as well. British and US Navy aircrew of Royal Air Force Spitfires and Mustangs and Royal Navy Seafires trained with the fire directors of the bombardment ships to adjust fire from the air.

Above: During one of the many rehearsals that helped to ensure the eventual success of the D-Day landings, three American amphibious vessels (Landing Craft, Tank, Nos 3, 474 and 526) disgorge trucks onto the beach at Slapton on the southeast coast of Devon.

THE GROUND FORCE UNITS AND CHAIN OF COMMAND FOR THE *OVERLORD* ASSAULT
The landings would run west to east, *Utah* to *Sword*. (*Band* was never used). They were timed to coincide with the incoming tide. Each of the five beaches was to have its own H-Hour (time of infantry assault). The H-Hours would begin at *Utah* at 06:30, 30 minutes after sunrise. (See the individual beach maps in Chapter 5.) It is important to note that the timing of the D-Day landings, and in fact the timings of all operations in Normandy, were based on a

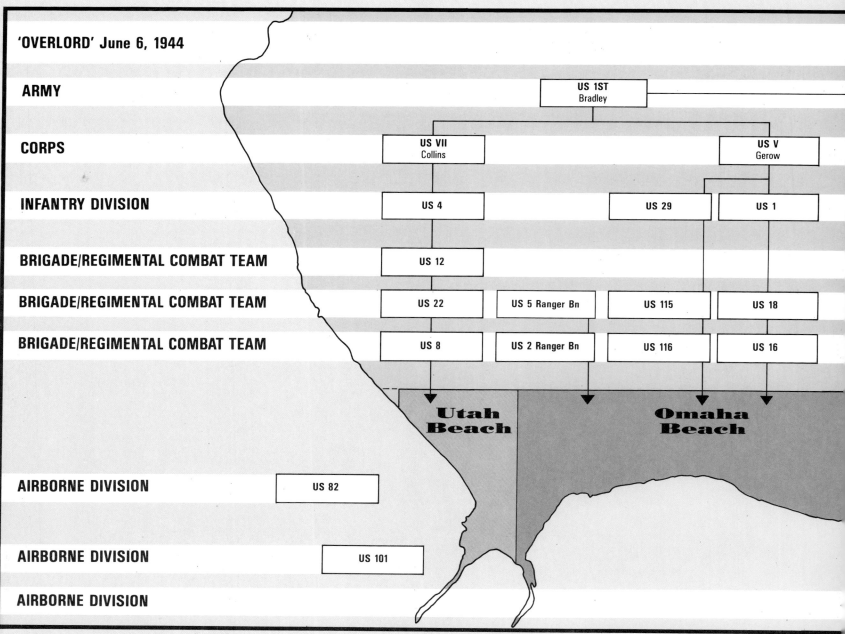

'OVERLORD' June 6, 1944

	Utah Beach		Omaha Beach	
ARMY			US 1ST Bradley	
CORPS	US VII Collins			US V Gerow
INFANTRY DIVISION	US 4		US 29	US 1
BRIGADE/REGIMENTAL COMBAT TEAM	US 12			
BRIGADE/REGIMENTAL COMBAT TEAM	US 22	US 5 Ranger Bn	US 115	US 18
BRIGADE/REGIMENTAL COMBAT TEAM	US 8	US 2 Ranger Bn	US 116	US 16
AIRBORNE DIVISION	US 82			
AIRBORNE DIVISION	US 101			
AIRBORNE DIVISION				

The success of the Normandy invasion hinged not only on sound and thorough training but on the preparations for the logistic support of the mammoth enterprise. Allied forces had to seize a beachhead and hold it against determined German counterattacks. But they also needed strength to break out into the interior of France. Thus, the flow of troops, tanks, guns, vehicles, food and fuel into the beachhead had to be heavy and uninterrupted. The Allied capture of Cherbourg, the only major port of the Cotentin Peninsula, would alleviate some of their logistic problems. But this could not be expected to happen early in the campaign ashore, and if the Germans feared losing Cherbourg, they would undoubtedly sabotage the port to render it unusable.

Consequently, the British developed two

Left: Under cover of barrage balloons, men of the US Army board amphibious vessels in an English port during May 1944. On the left is a Landing Craft, Infantry, and on the right is one of the Landing Craft, Vehicle Personnel, from the assault transport USS *Thurston*.

artificial harbors, code-named *Mulberry*, that would be emplaced off the invasion beaches. The design and construction of these pier and pontoon structures, which Morison characterized as a "tribute to British brains and energy," was handled by the British Admiralty and War Office. Through prodigious effort, British defense plants, shipyards, engineering firms, government agencies, and other sectors of the British warmaking establishment completed both *Mulberries* in time for D-Day. The Royal Navy was assigned the task of assembling the *Mulberry* components in four areas off Portland, Poole, Selsey and Dungeness; towing them across the Channel with over 150 US and British tugboats, and forming them into beachhead breakwaters and harbors. Within several days of the landing, the Allies hoped to have both *Mulberries* functioning, one off the British beaches and one off the American. Each *Mulberry* was designed to berth seven deep-draught ships, 20 coastal craft, 400 tugs and auxiliary vessels, and 1,000 smaller craft, and handle 7,000 tons of supplies daily.

double daylight saving time of GMT + 2 hours.

According to the plan, each beach assault was to be organized into separate phases, each carefully timed. Thus at H – 120 minutes the

first LSTs would be in position and unloading their DD tanks. At H – 60 minutes the bombardment of beach and defenses would begin. The DD tanks would hit the beach at

H – 10 minutes, and first infantrymen would land 10 minutes later — H-Hour. That was the plan — the reality on June 6 was in some cases to be very different.

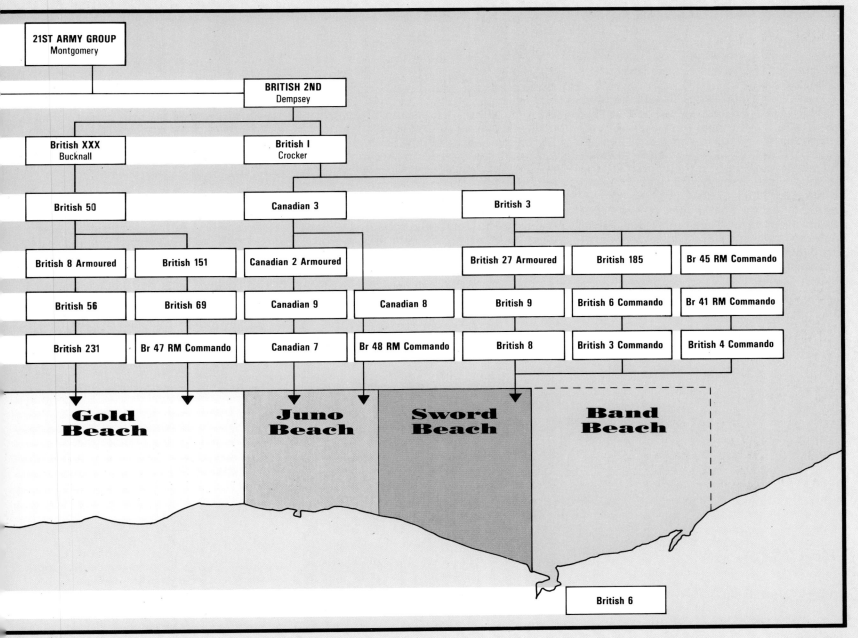

Allied naval planners, who understood the devastating power of spring storms in the Channel, also felt it prudent to develop five beachhead shelters, known as *Gooseberries*, for landing craft and other smaller vessels. The *Gooseberries* would be formed by the sinking of blockships, called *Corncobs*, just offshore. Once Adm. Ramsay approved the concept, the Allies gathered 69 surplus British and US ships in Scotland.

Other preparations involved operations in proximity to the enemy. Throughout early 1944, the Allies launched small boat forces on missions all along the French coast, not only to deceive the Germans about the true invasion site, but to gather essential intelligence for the landing. For instance, in January the Royal Navy deployed several trawlers and motor launches and midget submarine *X-20*, all under the command of Lt. Cdr. H.N.C. Willmott, off the proposed American beaches on the Normandy coast. Two British soldiers swam ashore from the submarine and after collecting vital information on the beach sand, shingle, and gradients returned safely to the boat.

Perhaps the most important information available to the Allies, however, was gleaned by codebreakers from intercepted enemy radio traffic. American intelligence units hit a bonanza when they picked up a series of transmissions from Berlin to Tokyo made by Gen. Oshima Hiroshi, Japanese Ambassador to Germany. Having just completed a personal inspection of Hitler's Atlantic Wall, Oshima sent his superiors detailed reports of German defenses.

Armed with intelligence such as this, in April 1944, Adm. Ramsay issued his final plan for *Neptune*. The mission of Allied naval forces was to transport the Allied Expeditionary Force across the sea, help secure and defend a beachhead on the continent, and develop logistic facilities to sustain the advance into France of 26-30 infantry and armored divisions. The admiral stressed that the naval operation was a "combined British and American undertaking by all services of both nations."

Eisenhower had not only assigned Ramsay overall responsibility for the naval forces

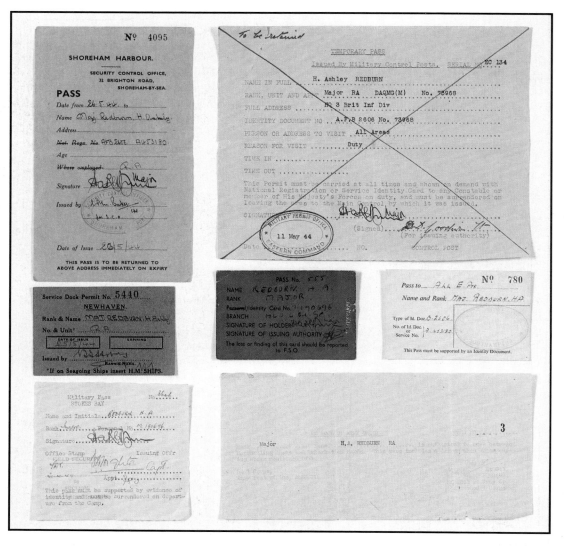

connected with *Overlord* but with control in battle of those naval forces deployed off the invasion coast. The admiral's chief combat commands comprised two task forces. The Western Task Force was led by calm, self-confident Adm. Kirk, a veteran of the Sicily landings and commander of the US Atlantic Fleet's amphibious forces. His contingent included two infantry divisions of Lt. Gen. Omar N. Bradley's US First Army, which would storm the *Utah* and *Omaha* beaches on the western flank of the invasion. Kirk's chief subordinates were Rear Adm. Don P. Moon

Above: Dockyard and security passes of Maj. H. O. Redburn, Royal Artillery. Maj. Redburn was assigned to the quartermaster's dept. of the 3rd British Division which was to land on *Sword* beach. The passes were issued in May 1944. *D-Day Museum, Portsmouth*

(Force U) and Rear Adm. John L. "Jimmie" Hall (Force O), who would direct the assaults at *Utah* and *Omaha*. The Eastern Task Force, under British Rear Adm. Sir Philip Vian, would land one Canadian and two British divisions of Lt. Gen. Miles C. Dempsey's British Second Army on 30 miles (50km) of coast between the River Orne and Port-en-Bessin. Responsible for the naval assault forces at the *Gold*, *Juno* and *Sword* beaches were Commodore Cyril E. Douglas-Pennant (Force G); Commodore Geoffrey N. Oliver (Force J); and Rear Adm. Arthur G. Talbot (Force S).

Force B, led by Commodore C.D. Edgar, and Force L, commanded by British Rear Adm. William E. Parry, had the critical responsibility of landing the seven support divisions on the second tide of D-Day, together with the assembly of the *Mulberry* artificial ports and *Gooseberry* boat shelters.

For the most part, British and American naval commanders directed the forces of their respective nations, but ships and craft from every national contingent steamed in

Left: A gun crew mans its 40mm Bofors gun to provide AA cover as LSTs are loaded in preparation for the *Overlord* operation. In the event, German aircraft achieved no effective opposition to the preparation or implementation of this vast undertaking.

The Landing Craft

1. Landing Craft, Gun (Large). Armament, two 4-inch guns, two 20mm or 2-pounder guns. 2. Landing Ship, Infantry (Large). Capacity, 12 LCAs, 697 troops. 3. Landing Craft, Infantry (Small). Capacity, 102 troops, 18 bicycles. 4. Landing Craft, Infantry (Large). Capacity, 188 troops or 75 tons of cargo. 5. Landing Barge, Kitchen. Capacity, provisions for 900 men for one week. 6. Landing Ship, Dock. Capacity, 3 LCTs or 14 Landing Craft, Assault (shown). LCA capacity 35 troops and 800lb (360kg) of equipment. 7. Landing Craft, Flak. Armament, four 2 pounder and eight 20mm guns. 8. Landing Craft, Tank. Capacity 4-6 40 ton tanks. 9. Landing Craft, Navigational. 10. Landing Craft, Tank (Rocket). Armament, up to 1,064 5-inch rockets.

each of the task forces. Thus British destroyers, French cruisers, and a Dutch gunboat operated in Adm. Kirk's command while US coastal craft, two Greek corvettes, and a Polish cruiser fought with Adm. Vian's forces.

Preparing the Ground

Allied superiority at sea and in the air over it made the Normandy invasion possible. The British and American navies and air forces were so successful against Grand-Adm. Doenitz's U-boats in 1943 that his fleet was unable to prevent the Allied buildup in Britain and early in 1944 was clearly on the defensive in the Atlantic Ocean. The battleships and cruisers of the German Navy, which once dared to operate from French ports and even to steam brazenly through the narrow English Channel, had either been sunk or penned into their ports.

Even for the less-easily detected German combatants such as destroyers, E-boats, and minelayers, it became foolhardy, except on moonless nights, to venture into the Channel.

The same applied to the Luftwaffe, whose fighters were already fully committed defending vital industrial plants, transportation links, and military resources ashore from the depredations of the Allied bomber fleets. In short, by June 1944, the Allies owned the Channel between England and France and the air over it.

To keep the enemy on the defensive, beginning on April 17, British minelayers, motor launches, motor torpedo boats, and aircraft laid almost 7,000 mines off the enemy's principal naval bases at Boulogne, Le Havre, Cherbourg, and Brest and along much of the Breton coastline. This operation was not without cost. German torpedo boats sank an escorting ship, the Canadian destroyer *Athabascan*, and a British motor torpedo boat (MTB) ran afoul of an enemy mine.

In spite of these Allied measures, the Germans still had lethal forces that they could throw into battle to defeat an Allied landing. The Allies expected their foe to spare no man or machine in their defense of the Atlantic Wall. The most immediate threat to the invasion armada would come from 50 U-boats based in Brittany and approximately 100 fast attack craft (E-boats and R-boats) and midget submarines concentrated in the French Atlantic ports. The Allies would also have to contend with German sea mines.

Protection of the invasion fleet's flanks in the waters between Cornwall and Brittany on the west and the Dover-Calais narrows on the east was provided by 24 destroyers and frigates and approximately 22 flotillas of motor torpedo boats, motor and steam gunboats, and motor launches.

The Allies took measures to combat the enemy's naval threats. The RAF Coastal

Command reinforced its air groups patrolling the waters between Ireland and the Brittany Peninsula and off Scotland. There were so many aircraft in 19 Group, responsible for the western approaches to Normandy, that each segment of the broad patrol area was overflown every half-hour, day and night (see page 130). Most of the U-boats, if they escaped attack, would be forced to proceed submerged and this would exhaust their batteries long before they reached the cross-channel invasion routes.

The Coastal Command units off Scotland drew first blood in the campaign against the U-boats. On May 16, Doenitz ordered many of the boats operating in Norway to deploy to the Bay of Biscay off France. For the next 18 days the submarines ran the gauntlet set up by the British in the North Atlantic. Coastal Command aircraft sank 7 of the 22 U-boats they spotted.

Other Allied air forces prepared to cover the passage of the naval armada across the Channel and to protect the vulnerable transport and glider aircraft ferrying the three US and British airborne divisions to Normandy. For this task, the Allies deployed almost 2,000 fighter aircraft organized in 171 squadrons. These units would be controlled from fighter direction stations located in England, on board three LSTs in the Channel, and eventually ashore in Normandy. Swarms

ALLIED BOMBARDMENT SHIPS AND THEIR D-DAY TARGETS
These warships, alongside over 60 destroyers, targeted German defenses and gun batteries in each of the five assault areas. Bombardment was to begin at dawn. Targets were to be fired at until return fire ceased or the position was taken by ground troops. Fire was to be targeted with the help of spotter aircraft and by forward observers (known as Forward Observer Bombardment — FOB by the British, and Shore Fire Control Party — SFCP by the Americans).

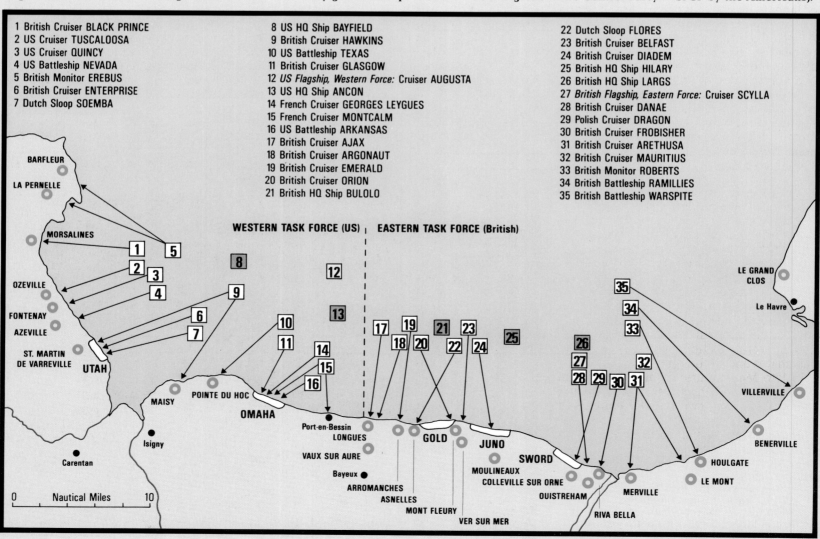

1 British Cruiser BLACK PRINCE
2 US Cruiser TUSCALOOSA
3 US Cruiser QUINCY
4 US Battleship NEVADA
5 British Monitor EREBUS
6 British Cruiser ENTERPRISE
7 Dutch Sloop SOEMBA
8 US HQ Ship BAYFIELD
9 British Cruiser HAWKINS
10 US Battleship TEXAS
11 British Cruiser GLASGOW
12 *US Flagship, Western Force:* Cruiser AUGUSTA
13 US HQ Ship ANCON
14 French Cruiser GEORGES LEYGUES
15 French Cruiser MONTCALM
16 US Battleship ARKANSAS
17 British Cruiser AJAX
18 British Cruiser ARGONAUT
19 British Cruiser EMERALD
20 British Cruiser ORION
21 British HQ Ship BULOLO
22 Dutch Sloop FLORES
23 British Cruiser BELFAST
24 British Cruiser DIADEM
25 British HQ Ship HILARY
26 British HQ Ship LARGS
27 *British Flagship, Eastern Force:* Cruiser SCYLLA
28 British Cruiser DANAE
29 Polish Cruiser DRAGON
30 British Cruiser FROBISHER
31 British Cruiser ARETHUSA
32 British Cruiser MAURITIUS
33 British Monitor ROBERTS
34 British Battleship RAMILLIES
35 British Battleship WARSPITE

WARSHIPS INVOLVED IN THE D-DAY LANDINGS

The largest contribution of warships was made by the Royal Navy (the total number of which also included ships of the Royal Canadian Navy). The number of US Navy ships, particularly those tasked with gunfire support, was increased in early 1944 after appeals to Adm. King in Washington from senior US Navy officers. The invasion fleet also included a small — but important — number of vessels from other Allied countries. These included two Greek corvettes, two Dutch sloops, and three Norwegian destroyers. The Polish supplied one cruiser and two destroyers, while a French force included two cruisers, one destroyer, four frigates, and two corvettes.

The total figure does not include those warships in the Western Approaches or the Royal Navy force of 2 battleships, 8 cruisers and 20 destroyers in the North Sea, keeping a watch on the remains of the German surface fleet in the Baltic.

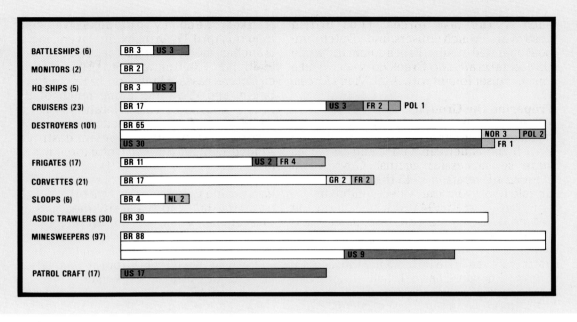

of fighters would also fly covering missions high above and all around the invasion site and maintain this presence, day and night, throughout *Neptune*.

To avoid Allied sailors mistaking paratroop-laden transports for German fighters and bombers and shooting them down, which occurred too frequently during the invasion of Sicily, the command established air corridors that would skirt the invasion armada to the east. In addition, sailors were schooled in aircraft recognition.

For the invasion armada to converge on assembly points off southern England, form into groups, and proceed through established lanes to the French coast without ships going off course or straying into German or Allied minefields, it was essential that there be navigation aids all along the route. These aids included motor launches and floating beacons situated at critical points.

The destruction of enemy coastal guns and beach defenses would begin with strikes by Allied bombers in the early hours of D-Day and reach a crescendo in the hour before the assault. Furthermore, each of the five assault forces was assigned a group of bombarding ships and these groups would concentrate their fire on the 24 enemy batteries emplaced around the landing beaches.

Each of the larger bombarding ships was assigned an enemy coastal gun site, normally containing four guns, as her first priority. The German batteries usually armed with the long-range, anti-ship 4.9-inch and 6.1-inch guns were protected by seven feet (2m) of reinforced concrete. Wheeled artillery pieces, smaller guns which could shift their fire from naval vessels to troops on the beach, were positioned both in concrete casemates and in the open.

In late May thousands of warships, amphibious landing ships, transports, and auxiliary ships and craft, and hundreds of thousands of Allied troops converged on the ports, rivers, and open roadsteads of southern England. Armored vehicles and trucks

Right: HMS *Bulolo* was converted in 1942 from an armed merchant cruiser to a Landing Ship, Headquarters with accommodation for 258 troops and six LCP(L)s but more importantly command facilities and the communication system to handle 2,300 messages per day.

boarded ships directly from the beach by way of newly built hard stands, appropriately called "hards." The British and American infantry assault divisions, and the naval forces that would enable the Allied host to cross the treacherous Channel, assembled in England in the same order in which they would storm the Normandy coast. The US 4th Infantry Division, slated to assault *Utah* Beach on the Cotentin Peninsula, gathered on the Devon coast at Salcombe, Dartmouth, and Brixham. To the east in Dorset at Portland, Weymouth, and Poole was the US 1st Infantry Division, which would seize *Omaha* Beach. Continuing on to the east in Hampshire was the British 50th (Northumbrian) Infantry Division at Southampton, the Canadian 3rd Infantry Division around Southampton and Portsmouth, and the British 3rd Infantry Division near Portsmouth and at Shoreham and Newhaven. The last three divisions would storm ashore on *Gold, Juno,* and *Sword* Beaches.

The reinforcing or follow-on divisions and their naval escorts were located on the wings of the Allied invasion assembly, with the US 29th Infantry Division to the west on the Devon and Cornish coasts at Plymouth and

Falmouth and the British 7th Armoured and 51st (Highland) Divisions around the Thames Estuary at Tilbury and Felixstowe. The battleships and other heavy units of the bombardment groups swayed at anchor in Belfast, Northern Ireland and in Scotland's Clyde Estuary.

One of the keys to a successful amphibious operation is to select the day and time of day when the weather and the tides are optimum. To increase the chances of surprise and to provide the invading forces with concealment from enemy guns, Allied army leaders advocated a night landing. Naval officers, however, made it clear that a landing during daylight hours was absolutely essential to ensure accurate naval gunfire support and to coordinate launching and reloading of landing craft. Moreover, Allied underwater demolition teams and beach engineers needed light to clear lanes to the beach through the German obstacles.

Allied planners wanted the assault to begin three or four hours before high tide and be preceded by a moonlit night that would ease the navigation problems of the thousands of vessels and aircraft making the Channel, and help the airborne troops maintain some

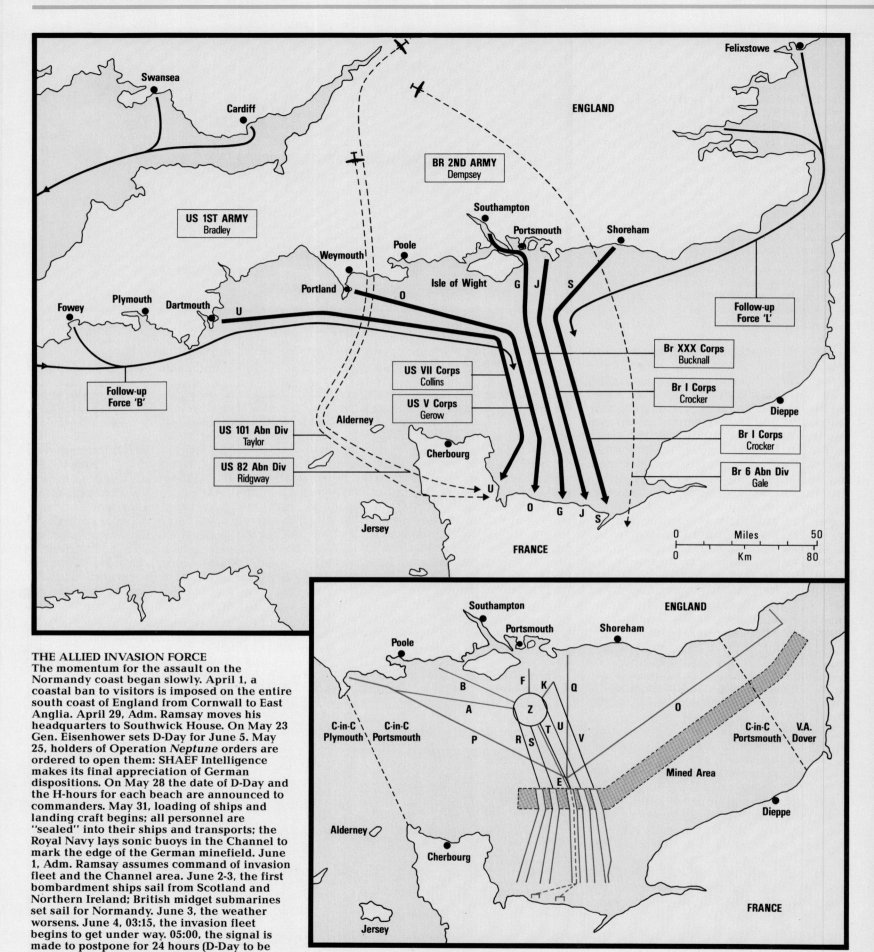

THE ALLIED INVASION FORCE

The momentum for the assault on the Normandy coast began slowly. April 1, a coastal ban to visitors is imposed on the entire south coast of England from Cornwall to East Anglia. April 29, Adm. Ramsay moves his headquarters to Southwick House. On May 23 Gen. Eisenhower sets D-Day for June 5. May 25, holders of Operation *Neptune* orders are ordered to open them: SHAEF Intelligence makes its final appreciation of German dispositions. On May 28 the date of D-Day and the H-hours for each beach are announced to commanders. May 31, loading of ships and landing craft begins; all personnel are "sealed" into their ships and transports; the Royal Navy lays sonic buoys in the Channel to mark the edge of the German minefield. June 1, Adm. Ramsay assumes command of invasion fleet and the Channel area. June 2-3, the first bombardment ships sail from Scotland and Northern Ireland; British midget submarines set sail for Normandy. June 3, the weather worsens. June 4, 03:15, the invasion fleet begins to get under way. 05:00, the signal is made to postpone for 24 hours (D-Day to be now June 6). All craft return to port except one LCT convoy. June 4, 23:00, to enable fleet to make the June 6 date, Ramsay issues order to sail. June 5, 04:15, the final decision is made to "go." June 5, from 23:00 onwards, aircraft bearing Allied airborne troops begin to take off for France.

CROSS-CHANNEL ROUTES

The assault fleet consisted of Force U (12 convoys), Force O (9 convoys), Force G (16 convoys), Force J (10 convoys), Force S (12 convoys), together with ancillary vessels. the immediate followup Task Forces B and L were also underway from ports in Wales and the east coast of England (see page 122 for details of the units carried.)

As laid out in *Neptune*'s meticulous plans, each convoy was to converge through routes A, B, F, and K to Point Z, 8 miles (12km) southeast of the Isle of Wight, the entire fleet would then assemble in an area 5 miles (8km) in radius, known as "Piccadilly Circus." From there, minesweepers sailed south sweeping five clear channels (R, S, T, U, V), one for each of the Task Forces. These lanes then divided in two, to provide clear passage for the faster and slower craft.

The chart also shows — in blue — the routes taken by the *Mulberry* harbors after D-Day; from their assembly areas off the English coast, across the Channel, to their final positions off *Omaha* beach and the town of *Arromanches* in the British sector.

order as they dropped behind the beach defenses. There were only three or four days each month in the spring when all these conditions prevailed in the Channel between England and Normandy. Taking all these factors into consideration, on May 23, Gen. Eisenhower established D-Day as June 5. Two days later, this critical information was passed to naval commanders when Adm. Ramsay ordered them to open their sealed operation orders. Simultaneously, he prohibited the crews of the invasion flotilla from sending out mail, using the telephone, or wiring telegrams. Then, on May 28, all crews and troops were "sealed" in their ships.

A few security breaches occurred anyway. Several communication transmissions connected D-Day with June 5, and tugs were inadvertently issued charts of the Bay of the Seine. Despite these lapses the Germans remained unaware of the invasion date.

On June 1, Adm. Ramsay, from his "battle headquarters" at Southwick House near Portsmouth, took command of Allied naval forces. The following evening two British midget submarines, X-20 and X-23 (markers for Forces J and S), proceeded out to sea from Portsmouth, and the bombardment ships sortied from the Clyde. In the words of Stephen W. Roskill, the British naval historian, "like the giant flywheel of a power plant its first movement was barely perceptible, but with every revolution it gained further momentum until it was running smoothly at the speed for which it had been designed."

Right: The weather forecast charts for June 4 and 6, 1944. Forecasts were made for the following 48 hours and were presented to the Supreme Commander at three daily meetings by Group Capt. J. M. Stagg, RAF, SHAEF's Chief Met Officer. Top, the chart for 18:00, June 4, on which the decision to invade was based. A cold front bringing high winds and low cloud have cleared the French coast bringing a period of more settled weather behind it. Below, the chart for D-Day, 07:00. At the beachhead the wind was west-north-west force 3 becoming force 4. There was 50-75 percent cloud cover at 3,000 to 7,000 feet (900 to 2,100m).

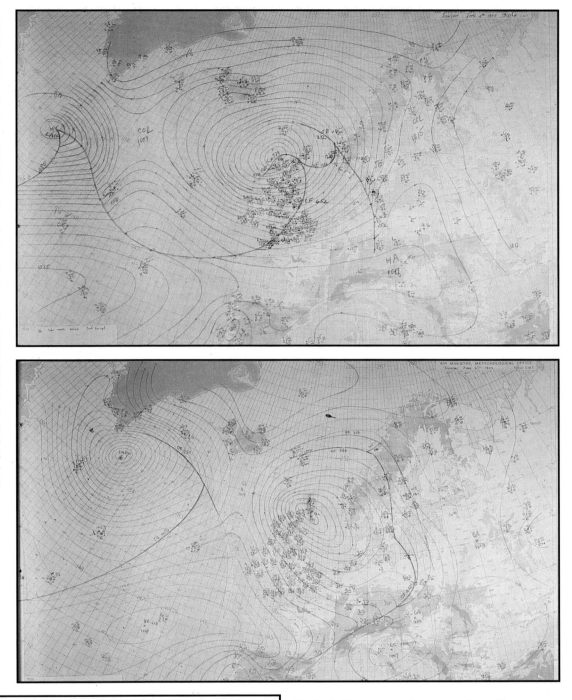

Far left: The personal message from the Supreme Commander Allied Expeditionary Force, Gen. Eisenhower, to all personnel taking part in the invasion. Left: Gen. Montgomery's personal message that was read out to all troops of the 21st Army Group before D-Day. D-Day Museum, Portsmouth

On Sunday, June 4, however, convinced by his meteorologists that the weather would be too rough the following day, Gen. Eisenhower postponed the operation for 24 hours. Convoys that had already set sail had to return to their anchorages; all except one large US convoy that only received the recall message when approaching French waters.

Time was running out for Gen. Eisenhower. If the invasion could not be launched on June 6, tide and moonlight conditions would not be suitable for another two weeks. The troops, many seasick, could not be confined too long on board crowded ships. To let them disembark would compromise security. Finally, at 04:15 on June 5, the Supreme Commander Allied Expeditionary Force started the monumental enterprise in motion with the simple words, "OK, we'll go."

That same morning Adm. Ramsay boarded a motor torpedo boat which proceeded to a vantage point off the coast of southern England. The most powerful invasion fleet the world had ever seen began steaming past him en route to the hostile shore of occupied France. Allied minesweepers cleared coastal waters along the coast of southern England and four channels leading to a general assembly area, nicknamed "Piccadilly Circus," eight miles (12km) southeast of the Isle of Wight. From this staging point, five miles (8km) in radius, the Allied naval units established five marked channels, altogether known as "the Spout," south toward France. The Germans had laid a mine barrier to the west of Dieppe and south of the 50th parallel, through which the Allied minesweepers cleared and marked ten channels with lighted buoys, each channel being 400 to 1,200 yards (360-1,080m) wide. The Western Task Force was allotted four lanes and the Eastern Task Force six.

Once the invasion convoys crossed into the assault area off Normandy, the minesweepers swept ahead of the task forces to clear areas from which warships would bombard coastal targets and amphibious ships would lower away landing craft for the run-in to the beach. During the operations, German mines damaged two British ships, the destroyer *Wrestler* and an LST. By skilfully clearing passages through the German minefield, however, Allied minesweepers made it possible for the thousands of other vessels in the armada to reach the far shore safely.

Equally important to the success of *Neptune* were the hundreds of buoy-laying vessels, salvage and rescue vessels, colliers, oilers, water tankers, telephone cable-laying vessels, despatch boats, smoke-making trawlers, and landing craft repair vessels.

Below: This photograph reveals a pair of LCTs against a background of loaded LSTs in an English harbor during late May or early June 1944. Visible on the nearer LCT are two M4 Sherman medium tanks with extended exhausts for deep wading capability.

Right: Eisenhower's "in case of failure" message. Just prior to the invasion, the general wrote out this draft of an announcement to be made should the landings fail. Note the incorrect date — July 5 — an indication of the stress the Supreme Commander, and all at SHAEF HQ must have felt at this time. The message reads: "Our landings in the Cherbourg-Havre area have failed to gain a satisfactory foothold and I have withdrawn the troops. My decision to attack at this time and place was based upon the best information available. The troops, the air and the Navy did all that bravery and devotion to duty could do. If any blame or fault attaches to the attempt it is mine alone." *Eisenhower Library and Museum*

Aside from mines, the elements, including a sea with large, foam-crested waves and a 16-to 20-knot wind from the west, posed the greatest hazard to the Allied naval force. A small number of light craft, most of which were being towed across the Channel, sank before reaching the far shore.

The heavy seas that caused thousands of seasick soldiers to long for landfall also induced the German command to suspend the daily surface ship patrols of the Channel. In addition, Allied bombers destroyed the enemy's radar stations at Cape Barfleur and elsewhere on the invasion coast. The Allies also jammed enemy radars. No one in the armada compromised radio security. Finally, Allied forces staged feints and other ruses to divert enemy attention from Normandy (see map page 130). As a result, the Allies achieved complete strategic and tactical surprise. The Germans learned of the Allied presence only when their few remaining coastal radars picked up surface contacts around 03:00 on the morning of June 6.

The American Landings
Thanks to thorough planning, intensive training, skillful execution, and just plain good luck, the great majority of Allied ships and craft arrived off Normandy on time and at their appointed stations.

The selection of June 6, when the sun rose at 06:00 and high tide occurred between 09:45 and 12:45, meant the time of landing

(H-Hour) on the invasion beaches would be as follows: *Utah* and *Omaha*, 06:30; *Gold* 07:25; *Juno* 07:35-07:45; *Sword* 07:25.

Beginning around 02:00, British and US minesweepers began their dangerous work in the transport areas, the fire support areas, and the approach lanes to *Utah* Beach. Right behind them came the ships of the bombardment group, which anchored in their assigned areas, 11,000 yards (9,900m) offshore for battleships and cruisers and 5,000 yards (4,500m) offshore for destroyers.

At 04:05, under the gaze of Adm. Moon in US transport *Bayfield*, troops began to scramble down cargo-net ladders into craft that rose and fell in the strong swell. Even though the *Utah* landing force would have to navigate 11 miles (17km) of ocean to reach the shore, Pointe de Barfleur and Pointe du Hoc extended out into the Channel on either side of the beach approaches, moderating the sea state. Consequently, Moon's landing craft were able to stay in formation as they headed for the shore. In addition, patrol craft (PC) and control landing and control landing craft equipped with radars and radios were on hand to guide the force to the beach. Landing craft with mounted artillery pieces and multiple five-inch rocket tubes accompanied the assault landing craft to provide them with direct fire support.

Benefiting from the element of surprise, at 05:30, naval forces landed a detachment of Army troops on the St. Marcouf Islands located only four miles (6km) offshore in the middle of the landing zone. The soldiers quickly took control of the position, which soon served as an anti-aircraft artillery site. Meanwhile, a German battery had opened up on US destroyers *Fitch* and *Corry*. To silence the German guns, Rear Adm. Morton Deyo, commander of the bombardment force at *Utah*, ordered his units to open fire. The thunderous salvoes disoriented the Germans, whose response was desultory and ineffective. US battleship *Nevada*, a veteran of

Pearl Harbor, and US cruisers *Quincy* and *Tuscaloosa* lofted hundreds of shells at the German coastal gun redoubts near the center of the invasion beach. Later in the day they fired their shells far inland, knocking out German tanks, artillery, and troops that menaced the US 101st Airborne Division. British monitor *Erebus* and cruisers *Hawkins* and *Black Prince* worked over the enemy defenses on the flanks. Ironically, the latter cruiser operated off the port of St. Vaast-la-Hougue, where English King Edward III and his son, the "Black Prince," landed in 1346 at the head of an invasion army. British light cruiser *Enterprise*, Dutch gunboat *Soemba*, and eight destroyers poured their fire directly into enemy defenses, especially in front of St. Martin-de-Varreville. The naval bombardment at *Utah* was especially accurate and within a short period of time the Allies had silenced German counter-battery fire and reduced other defensive positions to rubble.

Not for the first or last time in modern warfare, however, enemy mines exacted a toll of men and ships. German mines that Allied minesweepers failed to detect embedded in an offshore sandbank exploded and sank destroyer *Corry*. During the first ten days of the operation, these lethal enemy weapons sank in the *Utah* area another destroyer, a destroyer escort, two minesweepers, a patrol craft, and five landing craft. Mines also damaged another 25 vessels.

As the first waves of the landing force approached the objective, LCTs prepared to release into the water 32 DD amphibious tanks. These armored vehicles, intended to provide the infantry with direct fire support were equipped with special canvas skirts, or "bloomers," designed to keep them afloat on the approach to the shore. Lt. (j.g.) John B. Richer, USNR, the commanding officer of control vessel *PC-1176*, realized that the water was much too rough for the planned launch 5,000 yards (4,500m) offshore. He directed the commanders of the LCTs to carry the tanks into the relatively calm waters just off the beach. As a result of Richer's clear appraisal of the situation and bold action, not one of the precious amphibious tanks fell prey to the treacherous seas, as happened elsewhere on D-Day.

Meanwhile, other naval forces rapidly cleared lanes through enemy beach obstacles, which were not extensive and which the Germans had not mined. Then, at 05:42, one of the key patrol craft hit a mine and sank. Because of the loss of this and other guide vessels, strong cross-beach currents, and battle smoke over the *Utah* area, the first waves of assault vessels veered off toward the southeast. Thus, when the combat infantrymen of the US 4th Division debouched from their landing craft at exactly 06:30, they were a little over one mile (1.6km) from the beach they had planned to storm. Fortunately for the attacking American soldiers, the beach they actually landed on was much less heavily defended than their original objective.

Right: Operation *Neptune* beach landing maps for the Western Task Force, American sector, showing top, *Utah* and bottom, *Omaha* Beaches. The maps show positions and types of beach obstacles. Both maps are dated April 6, 1944. *D-Day Museum, Portsmouth*

The first-wave troops at *Utah*, supported ably by the DD tanks, quickly established positions ashore.

The men of 11 Navy underwater demolition teams (UDT) landed with the second wave and began clearing beach obstacles. By the end of the day, they had destroyed or removed steel and concrete structures from 1,600 yards (1,440m) of *Utah* Beach. Despite

minor setbacks, the assault at *Utah* of 27 assault waves went especially well and by 18:00 Adm. Moon's task force had landed over 21,000 troops, 1,700 vehicles, and 1,700 tons of supplies.

Omaha, the target of the US 1st Infantry Division and the second beach to be stormed by the assault formations of Adm. Kirk's Western Task Force, proved to be the Allies'

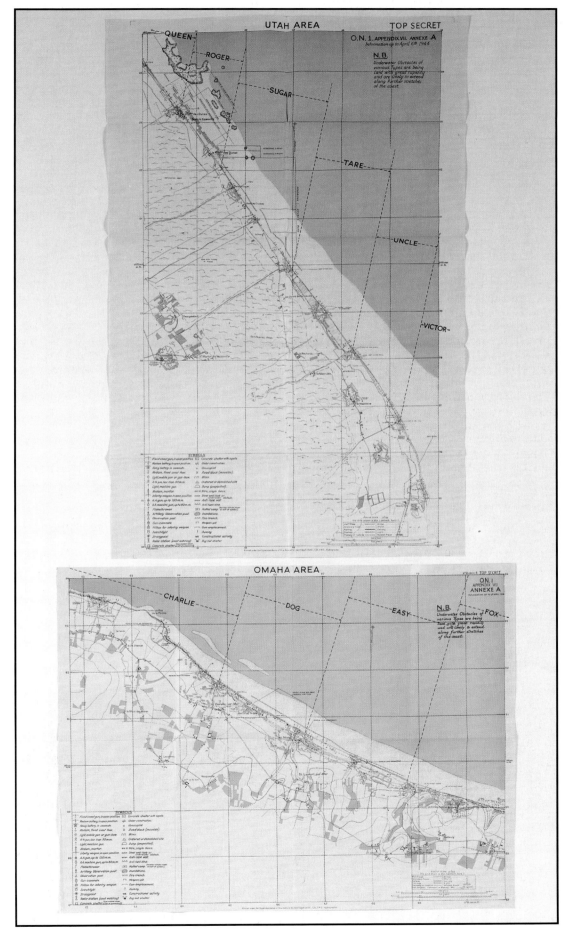

greatest D-Day challenge. The pre-invasion air bombardment of beach defenses was not especially effective at *Omaha*. Moreover, Kirk decided that his bombardment group would open up on the German coastal guns in his sector only 40 minutes before H-Hour, which contrasted with the two hours the British had allotted for their preparatory bombardments. As a result, there was not sufficient time to neutralize all the big German weapons trained on the landing area. Compounding the difficulties, Allied intelligence of the enemy's defenses at *Omaha* was inadequate. As an illustration, the 14-inch guns of US battleship *Texas* fired 250 rounds into the German coastal gun site on top of Pointe du Hoc before US Army Rangers discovered it empty of the enemy's big guns. *Arkansas*, the other American battleship off *Omaha*, French cruisers *Georges Leygues* and *Montcalm*, and British cruiser *Glasgow* leveled their guns against enemy defenses in the vicinity of Port-en-Bessin and St. Laurent but with limited success.

Furthermore, as at *Utah*, the landing ships at *Omaha* lowered their smaller craft into the water some 11 miles (17km) off the beach, in contrast to the British, who established their lowering points four miles (6km) closer in. Adm. Kirk was concerned that if he moved his transports any closer, they would fall prey to the German long-range coastal guns. As a result of this decision, however, it took the American landing craft almost three hours to close with the shore. And, in the waters offshore, not protected by the geography as at *Utah*, many landing craft fell out of formation. Landing waves became intermixed. In

contrast to *Utah*, the LCTs on the left flank at *Omaha* launched their DD tanks into the sea about 5,000 yards (4,500m) offshore. The result was catastrophic. Twenty-seven tanks, most with their crews, foundered and sank in the heavy seas. Only five reached the relative safety of the beach. On the right flank, however, Lt. D. L. Rockwell, USNR, correctly assessed the danger and decided not to disembark his 32 tanks until the transporting LCTs touched sand.

The rough waters off *Omaha* took a heavy toll of Allied assault craft, including DUKWs laden with critical artillery pieces and boats specially designed to destroy offshore obstacles and clear lanes through to the beach. Seizing the initiative, several American commanders used their vessels to smash through the barriers and open passages to the beach. Some vessels got through, but others were damaged or sunk in such attempts. Many more were forced to mill around outside the defensive belts searching for a cleared lane to the beach.

Working mightily to create openings in the obstacle belts were 16 joint teams of Navy UDTs and Army combat engineers. Although German fire wiped out two of the teams, almost to a man, their comrades managed to detonate explosive charges and blow eight channels through the defensive works. The rising tide eventually forced the demolition men to suspend their efforts.

Witnessing the distress of the Army units on the beach, Capt. Harry Sanders, Commander Destroyer Squadron 18, ordered his ships to close with the shore to support the troops. Risking grounding and counter-

battery fire, eight "tin cans" moved to within 800 yards (720m) of land and poured hundreds of rounds into German pill boxes, mortar positions, troop units caught in the open, and emplacements blocking the key exits from the beaches. US destroyer *Emmons* even knocked down part of the Colleville church tower from which enemy spotters were adjusting fire on to the beach.

By 11:00 the crisis at *Omaha* had passed. Heroic army officers, sergeants, and individual soldiers rallied the knots of men around them and stormed through the beach exits and over the bluffs which dominated the beach. Soon tanks, artillery, troops, and supplies began to pour ashore. The bravery and determination of American soldiers was key to the victory at *Omaha*, but the contribution of the small boat commanders, demolition men, and battleship, cruiser, and destroyer sailors was equally vital. At the end of that momentous day, Maj. Gen. Leonard T. Gerow, commanding general of V Corps then pushing inland from *Omaha*, sent a message to Adm. Kirk's flagship, the cruiser *Augusta* in which he simply said, "Thank God for the United States Navy."

The British Landings
The drama at *Gold*, *Juno*, and *Sword* beaches began around 05:00, when the British five-man midget submarines *X-20* and *X-23* surfaced, after remaining submerged for three days, and flashed green lights seaward to mark the parameters of Adm. Vian's Eastern Task Force landing sites. Soon afterward, as the naval force approached its objective, German Adm. Krancke, Commander Naval

THE LANDING BEACHES AND THEIR SECTORS
The division of the invasion coast into areas and sectors was laid down in *Neptune* Orders

ON1 Appendix VIII Annexe B. Contrary to popular belief, the famous code names *Utah*, *Omaha*, *Gold*, *Juno*, *Sword*, though now refered to as "beaches" were actually names

given to landing *areas*. To aid navigation and identification, these areas were subdivided into sectors — *Tare*, *Uncle*, *Victor*, *William* in the case of *Utah*. The assault beaches

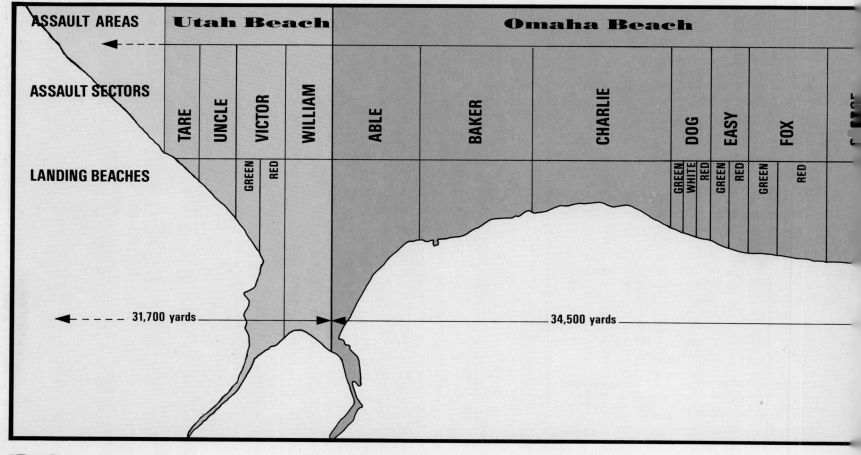

Group West, dispatched against it from Le Havre three torpedo boats: *T-28, Jaguar,* and *Möwe.* The vessels loosed a spread of torpedoes at the Allied fleet, sinking the Norwegian destroyer *Svenner,* and escaped through a smoke screen.

The approach to *Gold* beach was to be no easy matter. There, the Germans had emplaced 2,500 obstacles, consisting of 900 tons of steel and concrete, on a coastal front of three miles (5km). It proved virtually impossible to clear lanes through these barriers until the tide went out. For much of the morning, Germans holed up in the village strongpoints directed a withering fire on to the beach, which added to the troubles of the assault units. Many landing craft, especially those transporting No. 47 Royal Marine Commando, were damaged or destroyed. As a result of this difficulty and strong German ground opposition, it took two days and 200 casualties before the commandos could seize their D-Day objective, Port-en-Bessin, which the Allies had hoped to develop as a logistics hub.

Critical assistance to Commodore Douglas-Pennant's *Gold* assault forces came from the bombardment group, composed of British cruisers *Ajax, Argonaut, Emerald,* and *Orion,* Dutch gunboat *Flores,* and 13 destroyers. In fairly short order the Allied formation eliminated opposition from enemy coastal gun emplacements in the vicinity of Arromanches. The *Gold* ships put a number of 6-inch rounds right through the embrasures of the Longues position, destroying both guns there. By nightfall on June 6, Task Force G had successfully landed all three brigades of the British 50th Infantry Division.

At *Juno* beach to the east, naval forces experienced some difficulty getting the units of the 3rd Canadian Infantry Division to shore. Allied leaders had scheduled the landing on the right flank of *Juno* 20 minutes later than on the left flank. Staff planners figured that the landing craft would need higher water to traverse what aerial photographs suggested were underwater rocks, but which actually turned out to be floating seaweed. Another ten minutes was lost to difficulties during the passage of Task Force J from England. When the units approached the beach, they discovered that the water was too high for demolition personnel to clear lanes through the beach obstacles. Consequently, landing craft had to disembark their troops among the obstacles or smash through them. Vessels transporting No. 48 Royal Marine Commando had an especially tough time breaching the obstacles and a number of the wooden-hulled vessels were sunk or badly damaged.

Meanwhile, cruisers, destroyers, and rocket ships off *Juno* pumped hundreds of rounds into German gun positions, redoubts, communication trenches, and other defenses.

Like his decisive American colleagues on the other beaches, the British commander of the landing craft carrying the first-wave DD tanks at *Juno* ordered his landing craft commanders to deposit the armored vehicles safely on the beach.

By that evening, Task Force J had successfully landed the Canadians and preparations were being made to deploy ashore the follow-on formation, the British 7th Armoured Division and the British 51st (Highland) Division.

Like the eastern flank DDs at *Omaha,* the DDs at *Sword* had a tough time navigating the rolling seas. Forty DD amphibian tanks and a number of mine clearance tanks were launched 5,000 yards (4,500m) offshore, and eight of them promptly went down. Following the DDs came the infantry landing craft, whose crews skilfully traversed the extensive German beach obstacles. Leading the assault at *Sword,* the eastern-most landing beach, were two LCIs loaded with 176 French marines of No. 4 Commando. The first troops of the British 3rd Infantry Division hit the beach just after H-Hour. An entire brigade was established ashore only 18 minutes later than scheduled. However, German opposition steadily mounted on the beach and succeeding landing craft found the going rougher. German guns and mortars zeroed-in on landing craft, and mined beach obstacles sank or damaged many others. Some vessels got stuck in the sand as the tide ebbed.

Assisting the landing craft flotilla and the troops ashore were two British battleships, *Warspite,* a veteran of the Battle of Jutland in World War I, and *Ramillies,* together with British monitor *Roberts.* These ships neutralized the heavily casemated German guns enfilading the landing site from the east. In addition, five cruisers knocked out enemy guns positioned directly behind the beach. Guns encased in concrete were especially difficult to disable, but the *Sword* bombardment force scored a direct hit on one of two

themselves were then identified in each sector by using the codenames *White, Green, Red* (in what appears to have been quite an informal order). Thus on *Omaha,* a certain infantry unit on D-Day would be targeted to *Dog Green.* (See Chapter 5 for details of the landing sectors and beaches.)

The distances given for each landing area are those given in *Neptune* Orders. Thus, officially, the entire assault area stretched along the Normandy coast for 108,600 yards, or 61.7 miles (98.9km).

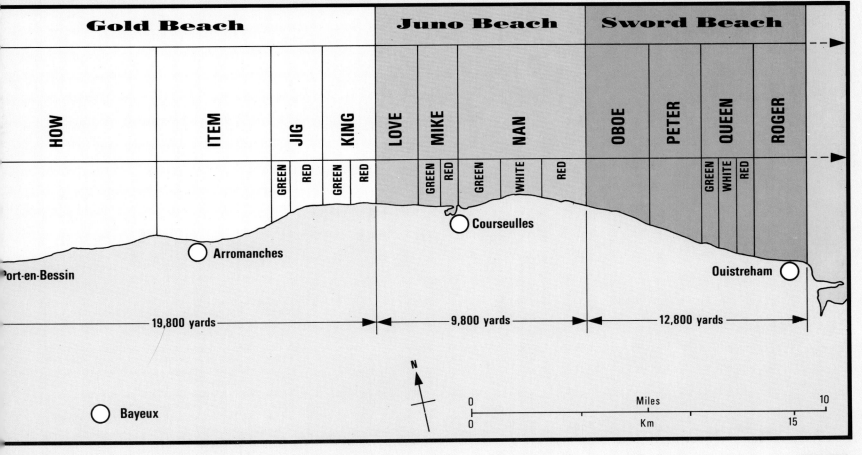

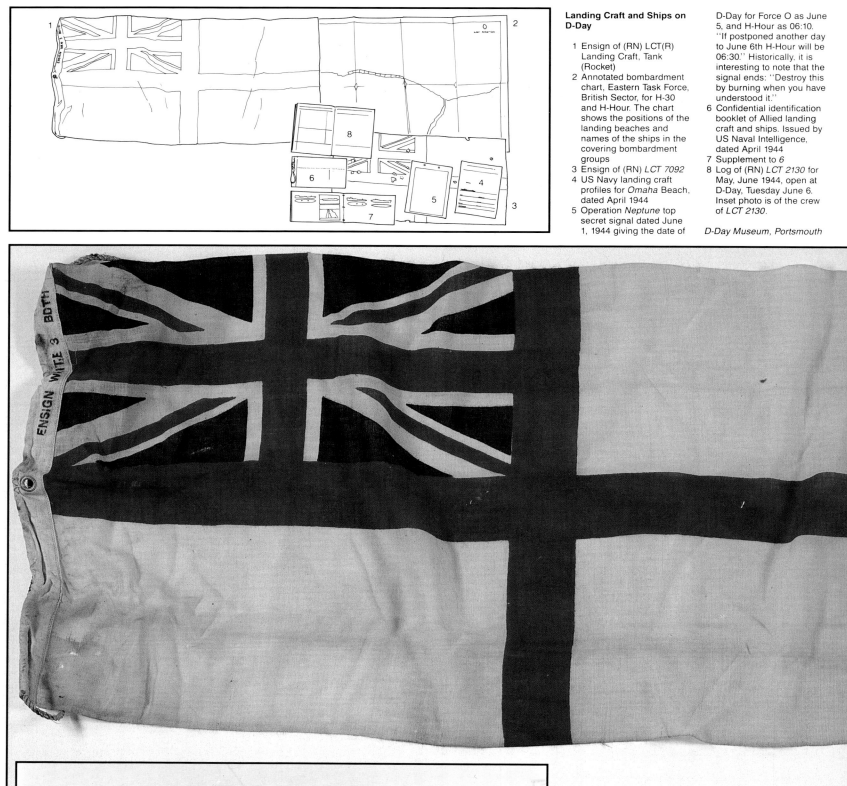

Landing Craft and Ships on D-Day

1 Ensign of (RN) LCT(R) Landing Craft, Tank (Rocket)
2 Annotated bombardment chart, Eastern Task Force, British Sector, for H-30 and H-Hour. The chart shows the positions of the landing beaches and names of the ships in the covering bombardment groups
3 Ensign of (RN) *LCT 7092*
4 US Navy landing craft profiles for *Omaha* Beach, dated April 1944
5 Operation *Neptune* top secret signal dated June 1, 1944 giving the date of D-Day for Force O as June 5, and H-Hour as 06:10. "If postponed another day to June 6th H-Hour will be 06:30." Historically, it is interesting to note that the signal ends: "Destroy this by burning when you have understood it."
6 Confidential identification booklet of Allied landing craft and ships. Issued by US Naval Intelligence, dated April 1944
7 Supplement to *6*
8 Log of (RN) *LCT 2130* for May, June 1944, open at D-Day, Tuesday June 6. Inset photo is of the crew of *LCT 2130*.

D-Day Museum, Portsmouth

On D-Day, *LCT 2130* sailed with the Western Task Force to the American sector. Its log (*8*) reports that on June 2 at 00:45 she loaded up at Dartmouth with: "5 track rec' cars & 5 x 57mm guns; 4 jeeps & 3 trailers; 1 2½ ton truck." A Lt. Elias was in charge of the load. She then sailed escorted, to Brixham (on the Devon coast) where she waited.

After joining the fleet and making the Channel crossing, she arrived off *Utah* at 06:30, but it was not until 11:20 that she beached at (Victor) Green. All vehicles and troops landed safely.

At 11:30: "Off beach, up [ramp] door. Shells dropping all round, one close to our Port bow, causing slight damage . . . no fire." At 14:00: "Proceed and join "S" Force traveling close to coast, every battery shelled us, just missing ship stern. Alter course immediately." At 23:00: "Dropped anchor just off Ouistreham. Which was burning fiercely."

such protected weapons in the Houlgate battery. Because of this naval gunfire support and hard fighting by the infantry brigade ashore, Rear Adm. Talbot's Task Force S was able to land the division's other two brigades in the afternoon. Marring the day's otherwise exemplary performance, anti-aircraft gunners afloat and ashore mistook Allied aircraft overhead as German and shot down several fighters and transport planes.

In addition to troops, on D-Day the Eastern Task Force put on the beach 900 tanks and other armored vehicles, 240 field guns, 280 anti-tank guns, 80 light anti-aircraft guns, 4,500 vehicles, and 4,300 tons of ammunition and supplies.

When he surveyed the scene from his flagship *Scylla*, off *Juno* that evening, Adm. Vian could be pleased that all had gone reasonably well.

A little less than 17 hours after the first American infantryman debouched from an assault vessel onto *Utah* beach, the combined navies of the Allied Expeditionary Force had landed close to 133,000 soldiers in Normandy.

The German Navy Responds

With the beachhead won, the Allies now had to hold it in the face of German counter-attacks not only on land but at sea and in the air. But the transport ships and craft that

carried the Allied combat divisions and logistical support forces from England to France during the weeks after D-Day were protected by an almost impervious shield of naval and air forces. Try as they might, German surface units, aircraft, and submarines did little to impede the invasion.

On D-Day the German naval command ordered submarine flotillas in Brittany, Norway, and the mid-Atlantic to move against the Allied landing force. A formidable contingent of 16 German U-boats sortied from Brest and La Pallice bound for attack positions south and west of the Isle of Wight. Another 19 submarines formed a defense line off Brittany to contest any Allied move

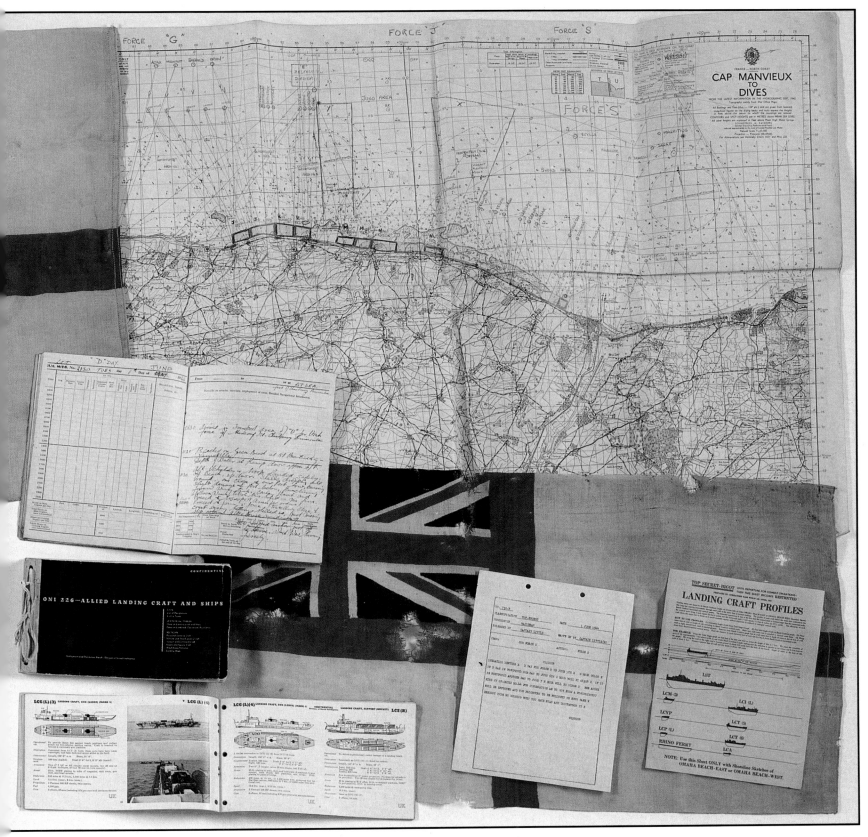

against that strategic peninsula. Even as this occurred, Allied air and sea patrol units were on the hunt for U-boats. Within hours, British aircraft sank *U-955*, damaged five other boats, and forced the remainder to run submerged, limiting their combat effectiveness. British Sunderland, Liberator, and Mosquito aircraft sent another five enemy vessels to the bottom during the next three days. These losses forced the German naval command to recall to Brittany all but the most capable units, those six equipped with the sophisticated "schnorkel" breathing system. Another five schnorkel boats were dispatched from Norway on June 9. Canadian and British aerial attackers soon sent two of these boats to the bottom. On June 24 and 25, the RAF's Coastal Command and the Royal Navy's surface forces combined to sink no fewer than three German submarines on the western approaches to the invasion convoy routes.

The German U-boat fleet scored only a few successes during June. On the 15th, *U-767* and *U-764* each torpedoed a British frigate in the Channel and *U-621* sank a US LST at the western edge of Adm. Kirk's landing area off Normandy. Then, on the 29th off the southern English coast, *U-984* torpedoed and sank three Liberty ships bound for France. These victories were a small return for the many brave submariners and boats sacrificed by the German high command in its fruitless attempt to halt the invasion.

German surface units fared little better than the U-boats. British fighters caught three German destroyers bound for Cherbourg off Brittany on June 6 and strafed them so savagely that the enemy force had to put in at Brest. Joined by another destroyer, on June 8 the formation sortied for another attempt to reach Normandy. This time the aircraft that spotted them called in a flotilla of eight British, Canadian, and Polish destroyers guarding the western approaches to the Channel. The battle was joined at 01:25 on June 9 when the Allied force opened fire at 5,000 yards (4,500m), evaded torpedoes, and closed with the enemy. The bold Allied dash disrupted the enemy formation and sent the German destroyers fleeing in two directions. The Canadian destroyers *Haida* and *Huron* gave chase to the German destroyers *Z-24* and *T-24* and heavily damaged *Z-24* before both of the hunted ships reached the safety of Brest. Meanwhile, the British and Polish units chased down and sank *ZH-1*. Finally, the Allied force converged on *Z-32*, set her afire, and forced her to beach. While this latter action was taking place, US destroyers and MTBs encountered a number of German E-boats off Cape Barfleur and drove them away from the invasion forces.

Below: Operation *Neptune* beach landing maps for the Eastern Task Force, British sector, showing from the top, *Gold*, *Juno* and *Sword* Beaches. The maps show the positions and types beach obstacles and are all dated April 6, 1944. *D-Day Museum, Portsmouth*

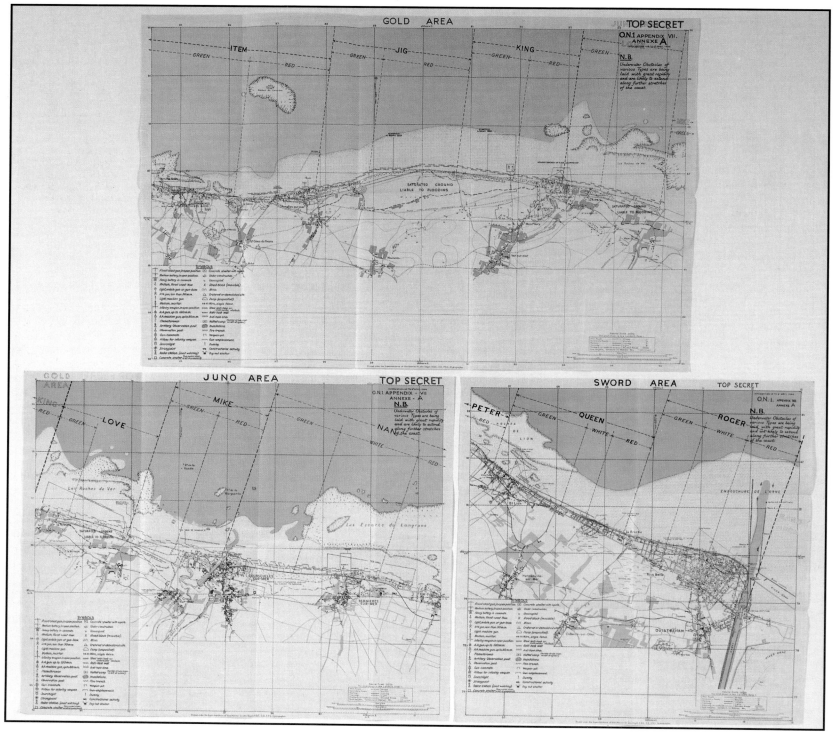

On June 13, British Beaufighter aircraft pounced on a group of E-boats and R-boats off Le Touquet, sinking four of the enemy units. The following night, 325 British Lancaster bombers devastated the German flotilla at Le Havre, destroying 11 E-boats in their concrete shelters and sinking two torpedo boats and 40 other craft in the harbor. Adm. Krancke characterized the Le Havre raid as "catastrophic" to his force. One day later, RAF Bomber Command visited similar destruction on the German light naval units at Boulogne, eliminating the surface threat to the Normandy beachhead for some time. German surface units were only able to sink two LSTs and nine smaller vessels.

The once-vaunted German Luftwaffe did little to impede the Allied invasion. During the entire month of June, German planes managed only to sink US destroyer *Meredith*, British destroyer *Boadicea*, frigate *Lawford*, and a few small craft.

Greater damage was done to the Allies by German mines laid before and after the invasion. The Americans suffered the most losses to mines early in June but toward the end of the month, British naval forces, operating closer to the enemy's air and surface minelayer bases in France proper, took a number of heavy hits. German mines sank nine warships and other vessels and damaged seven more, including Adm. Vian's flagship *Scylla*, which had to be towed back to England for repairs.

As Gen. Eisenhower and Adm. Ramsay already knew when they arrived off the invasion beaches in British minelayer *Apollo* soon after the landing, the great Normandy enterprise would fail if the troops ashore were not reinforced, armed, and supplied on a massive scale. Until "Lightning Joe" Collins' US VII Corps seized Cherbourg on

June 26, the Allies had to rely totally on the few small ports in the invasion area and over-the-beach supplies.

The heavy seas made offloading of cargo ships difficult and hazardous during the first few days after D-Day. Over 100 LSTs and other vessels were forced to idle offshore until Adm. Vian and Adm. Kirk took bold action. They directed the LST skippers to beach their ships, even though they realized that the vessels would be caught high and dry with the ebbing tides. Despite its unorthodoxy, this approach worked. The naval leaders also reinforced the ship-to-beach logistic effort by diverting LCTs and similar craft from cross-channel transport duties. In addition, Adm. Vian quickly made use of the harbor facilities of Port-en-Bessin and Courseulles, which had not been damaged badly in the first day's fighting. And, in short order, hard-working engineering parties had emplaced the *Gooseberry* boat shelters and *Mulberry* artificial ports.

Then, in the early morning hours of June 19, a threat arose that was much greater than anything the Germans could pose. The wind from the northeast rose to gale-force strength, whipping up the sea and compelling Allied naval commanders to halt logistic traffic to and from England. They also stopped unloading and transport operations in the invasion areas. For the next three days, the wind and sea of perhaps the worst June storm in the Channel in 40 years pounded the Allied Expeditionary Force. The American *Mulberry* at St. Laurent was damaged beyond repair. Hundreds of landing craft, small boats, and other light vessels were sunk or smashed on the shore and 800 craft were grounded. The force of the storm dragged ships' anchors across the bottom and caused cables to part. Sections of partially completed

Above: British Naval Uniforms and Equipment. From the left: Royal Navy captain's service uniform, cap and shoes. RN captain's shoulder boards. Rating's hat with HMS *Belfast* on cap tally. Center: service wool, bridge (duffle) coat with inflatable life belt, bridge binoculars, speaking trumpet and bosun's whistle. Rating's hat with white cover. Merchant marine officer's shoulder boards and cap badge. Right: Sailor's dress, "square rig." *Memorial Museum, Bayeux*

breakwaters broke loose and battered hapless vessels in their path.

Allied forces were bruised but not beaten by the fierce Channel gale. Small boat captains and crews often braved the weather to deliver ammunition and other vital supplies ashore. When this was not possible, the naval units made use of the *Gooseberry* boat shelters, which proved a godsend, to ride out the worst of the weather. Seamen of many nations kept their ships afloat, protected precious cargoes from damage, and prepared to resume operations. So, when the wind finally died down and the sun shone through the clouds on the evening of June 22, the combined naval force regrouped and resumed the buildup of the Allied armies.

When Adms. Kirk and Vian turned over their commands and returned to England in late June and early July it marked the end of Operation *Neptune*, the largest and most complex amphibious landing in military history. Cooperation among the Allied naval, air, and ground forces in the monumental effort was extraordinary. In the words of the British official history of the Normandy invasion, "where *Neptune* will long, and perhaps for ever, remain unique is as a feat of inter-service organization. Never before had so many soldiers, sailors and airmen been assembled and trained to achieve a joint purpose."

D-Day

5

Roger Cirillo • Stephen Badsey

The American First Army Plan

On February 1, 1944, the *Neptune* Initial Joint Plan revised COSSAC's original *Overlord* plan by adding a landing beach on the eastern face of the Cotentin Peninsula, thus putting Cherbourg, a key invasion objective, in closer reach. Lt. Gen. Bradley's First Army was ordered to assault and develop two beachheads astride the Carentan estuary between Vierville-sur-Mer and Colleville-sur-Mer. In the west, on First Army's right flank, the VII Corps would assault *Utah* Beach at the base of the Cotentin Peninsula. After cutting across the peninsula's neck, it would take Cherbourg whose port was the logistical lifeline that would make a substantial Allied buildup possible. East of the estuary on the Calvados coast, V Corps would attack *Omaha* beach between Carentan and Bayeux, and move south to cover British Second Army's advance.

The Cotentin would not be an easy place to start an invasion. The new landing area designated *Utah* Beach was small, with its dunes rising onto ground flooded by the Germans. If the exits were blocked, the invaders would be trapped.

The flooded areas covered most of the terrain inland to less than two miles (3km) from the shore; the ground rose steadily to an elevation of about 45 yards (50m). This high ground dominating the landing areas was part of the bocage country, territory covered with a complex latticework of man-made hedged fields. The open fields and frequent orchards could be acres large, but the hedgerows posed tactical problems. These hedges were often reinforced by extensive dirt embankments and interspersed with trees. Narrow dirt tracks dominated by hedges whose over-arching greenery could

reach a dozen feet (3.6m), canalized military movement, and made any paths fire lanes for anti-tank or automatic weapons. The hedges themselves were impenetrable to vehicles and often so for soldiers.

Intelligence showed a strong defensive crust with reserves located near critical points. Rommel intended to destroy the invasion at the water's edge. Allied intelligence identified two divisions in the peninsula belonging to General der Artillerie Erich Marcks's LXXXIV Corps. The 709th Coastal Division's two regiments held the 50 miles (80 km) of eastern beaches facing the Calvados coast. The 243rd Infantry Division held Cherbourg and the peninsula's western coast.

Below: To prevent the landing of Allied airborne forces, likely sites were strewn with "Rommelsspargel," but many sites did not feature the wire and mines of shells that would have made Normandy distinctly unhealthy.

The American Air Assault

The February airborne plan tasked the 101st Airborne Division to seize the western exits to *Utah* Beach, help expedite VII Corps' moves to cut the peninsula, and then swing northwards to Cherbourg. When additional aircraft gave the Americans a second drop division, the 82nd Airborne planned its drop west of the Douve River, to seize St. Sauveur-le-Vicomte and control the roads from the coast.

Hitler's intuition saw a threat to Cherbourg. Rommel did too, personally traversing the peninsula energizing local commanders to improve defenses in every potential Allied landing area. Rommel saw the Cotentin as a prime airborne objective. His response soon dotted numerous fields. "Rommelsspargel," "Rommel's Asparagus," were poles roughly a foot (.3m) in diameter and six feet (1.8m) high placed vertically in fields to disrupt

parachute drop zones or to block glider landing zones. Rommel wanted 1,000 per square kilometer (about 3,000 per square mile) with wire linking the stakes, which would be topped by mines or artillery shells rigged to detonate when the wires were hit.

Hitler sent the 91st Airlanding Division to occupy the Cotentin's center. As Seventh Army's reserve, it backstopped the beach defenses as a counterattack force. Additionally, the 6th Parachute Regiment and a Panzer battalion were added south of Carentan, both threatening the planned American landings.

At May's end, with the 91st's presence confirmed and thousands of Rommelsspargel appearing on air photos of the 82nd's drop zones, the airborne plan appeared to be compromised. Gen. Bradley felt the airborne was essential for the *Utah* landing and Montgomery agreed. Air commander Sir Trafford Leigh-Mallory predicted catastrophic losses recommending cancelling the drops behind *Utah*. Eisenhower disagreed. The American air drops would go ahead.

The 82nd's drop zones moved east astride the Merderet River, with Ste. Mère-Eglise the east end of the objective area. The 101st's drop was compressed, easing its D-Day mission to assist the VII Corps.

The 101st would get the invasion off the beaches. The division would capture the four exits and causeways leading from the beach, and the lock and bridges controlling the water obstacles and traverses throughout the invasion area. Its three parachute infantry regiments (PIRs), one airborne field artillery battalion, and one airborne engineer company planned to begin their drops between 01:15 and 01:30 on D-Day. Small fields and Rommelsspargel limited the use of gliders in darkness; but two glider lifts would come in at 04:00 and 21:00.

The 82nd's drops would begin a few minutes later, with two PIRs west of the Merderet and one northwest of its objective at Ste. Mère-Eglise. Its gliders were scheduled for three group landings, one after the 101st's 04:00 lift, one following the 21:00 lift, and one in twilight at 23:00.

All American aircraft approached from the west, dropping the pathfinder troops about 00:15 hours and the main body one hour later. The drops were scattered. Pilots evading anti-aircraft fire flew erratic courses or dived below prescribed drop altitudes. Many mis-identified drop zones. Some pathfinders were mis-dropped and, with only minutes to light their drop zones, opted to bring in the arriving lifts where they were. The 101st estimated that about 1,500 of its 6,600 paratroopers fell outside the division's battle area.

Left: Helmet, jump jacket, belt and equipment worn by Gen. James M. Gavin. Gavin was assistant commander of the 82nd Airborne on D-Day and was promoted to command the division in August 1944. *Helmet: Airborne Museum, Ste. Mère-Eglise; jacket and equipment: West Point Museum, West Point*

Above: Men of the 82nd Airborne Division's 508th Parachute Infantry Regiment make last-minute checks before boarding their Douglas C-47 transports for the flight from Saltby in Lincolnshire to their drop zone to the west of the Merderet River in the Cotentin Peninsula.

By 01:30, the German Seventh Army had received reports of airborne drops stretching from Caen to the Cherbourg Peninsula. But, with most of its troops sticking to their defenses and hesitant to root out the invaders, no coherent pattern appeared. As dawn approached, the German commander estimated that the paratroop plan was "to tie off the Cotentin Peninsula at its narrowest point."

In the north, the 502nd PIR and a supporting artillery battalion planned to land on Drop Zone (DZ) "A" just west of the high ground between its objectives, exits 3 and 4 at St. Martin-de-Varreville. Every plane load missed the DZ, scattering troopers to the north and south or onto Drop Zone "C." One battalion was so scattered that it was not heard from on D-Day. The 502nd's 3rd Battalion, landed near the 82nd's objective, Ste. Mère-Eglise, and had to reform and fight its way towards its objective. Finding the northern causeway's exits undefended, a small group under Lt. Col. Robert G. Cole ambushed fleeing Germans late in the morning and by 13:00 had established contact with the 4th Division's 8th Infantry moving in from the landing areas.

Meanwhile, the 2nd Battalion which was also scattered gathered enough men to move towards the German battery positions behind exit 4 and to establish road blocks throughout the area. Exit 4 was clear but skirmishes were frequent throughout the day with elements of A Company attacking the small village of Foucarville.

Exits 1 and 2 in the south were assigned to the two battalions of the 506th PIR and one from the 501st landing in DZ "C" in the division's center. Two battalions of the 501st Regiment and the remaining battalion of the 506th would land north of Carentan and east of the Douve River and marshes in DZ "D" to capture the la Barquette lock and the nearby bridges, while destroying the rail bridge northwest of Carentan to seal the southern part of *Utah's* landing area.

The southern exit forces were luckier than those in the north. More than half of the 506th dropped east of its DZ but gathered forces and began moving on exit 1 with orders to ignore the second objective.

Simultaneously, 101st commander Maj. Gen. Maxwell D. Taylor, lacking reports from any of his units, also ordered a battalion from the division reserve to move towards exit 1 and accompanied the force himself. The division reserve commanded by Lt. Col. Julian J. Ewell captured Pouppeville by noon, establishing a road block while awaiting the landing force, which soon arrived making the first airborne and seaborne linkup. The battalion originally sent to capture the exit fought several engagements en route and arrived after Ewell's battalion's success. With all four beach exits under control, Taylor focused his attention on capturing the southern bridgehead.

DZ "D"'s force was likewise scattered. The lock fell without a fight, but the scramble to

capture and destroy the bridges reflected the haphazard attempts of mixed forces, assembled from individuals separated by misplaced drops, the darkness, and the bocage.

The only real opposition met in the German 709th Division's sector was towards the Douve River at St. Côme-du-Mont and at Carentan then held by one of the division's battalions and the 6th Parachute Regiment. By nightfall on D-Day, 101st's southern

Above: Glider pilots were among the first men of the US Army to land on France. They took part in operations in German rear areas and were then evacuated. This group of pilots has just embarked in an LCVP for the short trip from the beach to a ship lying offshore.

line consisted of groups from three companies, not the planned full regimental defense of three battalions.

The 101st glider Landing Zone (LZ) "E" was southwest of DZ "C." Rommel's asparagus and the hedgerows restricted the 52 gliders taking in troops from the 327th Glider Infantry, some anti-tank guns, and supplies in their pre-dawn landing. The first glider crashed, killing Assistant Division Commander, Brig. Gen. Donald F. Pratt, D-Day's senior Allied casualty. About 30 troopers were killed, injured or missing in mishaps when most of the gliders missed their LZs. A second lift of 32 gliders landed at 21:00 but due to Leigh-Mallory's protests, and a lack of glider pilots, most of the 101st's glider troops arrived by sea on *Utah* Beach.

By day's end, the 101st Airborne had suffered at least 1,200 casualties and could account for slightly more than a third of its total strength, but its missions of clearing the beach exits and protecting the invasion were accomplished.

The 82nd Airborne's three drop zones placed the division on the edge of the German 91st Division's concentration area in a distorted triangular configuration astride the Merderet River west and northwest of Ste. Mère-Eglise. Even more badly scattered than the 101st, Maj. Gen. Matthew B. Ridgway's division lost the use of two of its regiments in its D-Day missions. The division successfully captured Ste. Mère-Eglise due to a fortuitously good drop of the 505th PIR. Taken in a hasty attack in darkness using grenades

Below: An American soldier of the 101st Airborne Division lies dead in the wreckage of his glider, which also holds the "Jeep" it was carrying; somewhere to the north of Carentan on June 7, 1944. All too many gliderborne troops suffered a similar fate.

THE AMERICAN AIRBORNE ASSAULT

Landing on the far western flank of the invasion area, the American airborne assault would be made by two full divisions, the 101st and the 82nd; 13,000 paratroopers in total. The objectives of their pre-dawn landings were: secure the four exits from *Utah* Beach prior to the seaborne attack; this was vital, as these four causeways were the only routes over the flooded land which covered the western end of the *Utah* area. To the southwest, capture and secure two bridges and one lock over the Douve River and to destroy the main rail and road bridge over that river. These objectives were given to units of the 101st Airborne, which were to land at Drop Zones "A," "C," "D." To the west of the 101st's landing area, the 82nd Airborne was to secure the west bank of the River Merederet and hold a bridgehead; destroy two bridges on the Douve, and capture the town of Ste. Mère-Eglise. The 82nd's Drop Zones were "N" and "T" and "O." The paratroopers would be reinforced by glider drops during the day. For clarity this map omits the glider Landing Zones "E" and "W," around les Forges.

The first transports bearing the airborne troops took off from airfields in southern England at 22:15 June, 5. Gen. Eisenhower was present at one of the fields to see off men of the 101st.

The landings of neither 101st nor 82nd were to go according to plan. Dropping at night and often without navigational aids, both divisions were widely scattered and suffered casualties on landing; despite the fact that drop zones and units became confused, objectives were found, captured and held.

By 13:00 on D-Day, the four exits from *Utah* had been secured by units of the 101st. At the northern exits (3 and 4), parachutists had linked up with men of the 4th Infantry Division coming inland from the beaches. The bridgehead over the Douve had been secured but the road and rail bridges targeted for destruction were still in enemy hands.

The 82nd Division's attack on Ste. Mère-Eglise was made by about 360 men of the 505th Parachute Infantry. Using speed, surprise and the cover of darkness, the town was infiltrated by 04:30. Communications to Cherbourg were cut and pockets of German resistance were dealt with. By 09:30 the first town in France to be liberated was under American control though by 12:00 a serious German counterattack had developed from the south.

Elsewhere in the 82nd's area, the situation remained very confused. Many units had been dropped into flooded marshland along the Merederet, where many had drowned. On the east bank of the river, bridgeheads had been fought for at la Fière and Chef-du-Pont, but scattered groups of men dropped west of the river would remain isolated until D + 4; their objectives on the Douve unreachable. By the end of D-Day the 82nd had not made any contact with forces from the beaches.

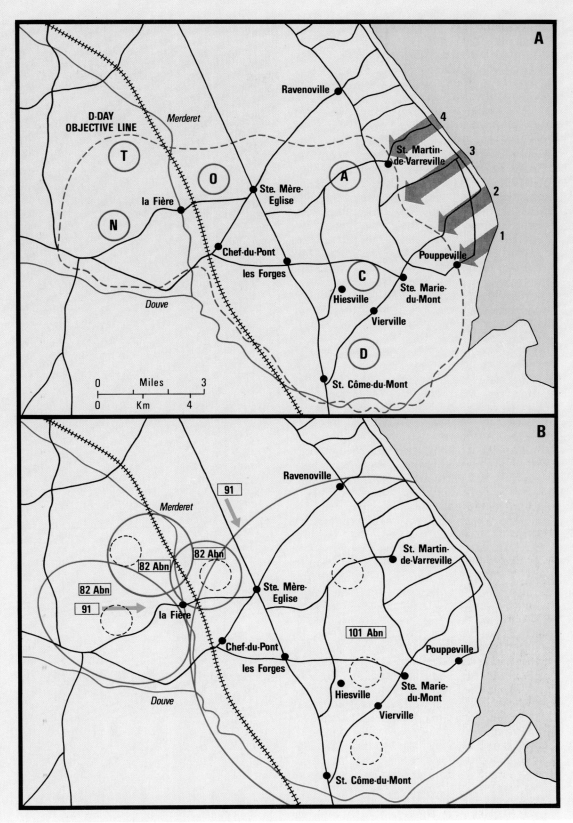

and knives but little gunfire, Ste. Mère was the first town liberated by the Allies. The enemy reacted immediately. Soon German forces appeared from different directions all to be held up and driven off.

The 507th and 508th Regiments whose missions were to hold the west banks of the Merederet, found no lighted DZs. Their pathfinders found German positions in the fields and marked no landing areas. The resulting confusion and the individual decisions of scores of transport pilots put troopers all over the division sector, dropping many into flooded fields and swamps. Surprised by the flooded areas and laden with equipment, many drowned in waist-deep water. Much of the division's equipment was lost in the

swamps, and with few troops to hold a wide perimeter, the division was forced into a small bridgehead between the two roads running west of Ste. Mère-Eglise and the Merederet with two small pockets at the opposite end of the swamp. The airborne was holding its own, but no contact was made with either the 101st division to the east or the invading forces moving inland from the sea.

The 82nd's 04:00 lift used 52 gliders carrying guns from an airborne anti-aircraft battalion plus forward parties for signals, artillery, and the division headquarters landing on DZ "O." Additional elements followed, with 76 gliders landing on LZ "W" after 21:00 and a further 100 at 23:00. Nearly 300 pilots and troopers were casualties due to flak

or crashes. The 82nd suffered about 1,200 D-Day casualties, and by nightfall reported that it had less than 40 percent of its infantry under division control.

While the 82nd formed the outer perimeter of VII Corps' landing, Gen. Dollman commanding the German Seventh Army ordered concentric attacks from the 91st and the 709th Divisions west of the Merederet and the 6th Parachute Regiment south in Carentan. Totally uncoordinated, none of these attacks gained ground. By nightfall, one German division commander lay dead from an ambush, while the other commanders and the corps headquarters generally felt the same "fog of war" that descended over the entire airborne battlefield.

Utah Beach
H-Hour 06:30

Utah is located in the Dunes of Varreville. The designated assault zones *"Tare Green"* and *"Uncle Red"* were about 1,000 and 1,300 yards (900-1,170m) wide respectively. Located astride exit 3 and stretching north toward exit 4, Maj. Gen. J. Lawton Collins's VII Corps assault would use the 4th Infantry Division's 8th Infantry Regiment, landing with two battalions abreast. Reinforced by the DD tanks of the 70th Tank Battalion, the attack would begin with four rifle companies in the first wave with two tank companies floating ashore under their own power.

But the 4th Division's soldiers were not the first in the corps to land. Both airborne divisions were attached to the corps on landing, and from the main body, the dismounted troopers of the 4th and 24th Cavalry Squadrons landed at H−2 hours, 04:30, on the heavily mined islands of St. Marcouf, whose shores were thought to hide guns which would imperil the transport area.

German radars missed the invasion's buildup, but coastal guns began firing about 20 minutes before the fleet's preparation bombardment, starting at 05:50. Within minutes, 276 B-26 Marauder aircraft dropped more than 4,400 bombs on seven designated target areas. Most missed, with at least one third of the bombs falling into the sea between the high and low water marks. A fire support group including rocket-equipped vessels drenched the beach just prior to landing while the landing craft began their final run-in.

The 8th Infantry's first troops touched down at 06:30, missing the planned assault areas. Both primary control vessels for the red and green beaches struck mines and sank and with a single control vessel left, the amphibious tanks led the assault in after leaving their carrying craft about 3,000 yards (2,700m) from the beach instead of the 5,000 yards (4,500m) as planned.

The first wave had 20 landing craft each carrying 30-man assault platoons and was followed immediately by a second wave of 32 craft, which included combat engineers and naval demolition teams to begin obstacle clearing. At H+15 minutes a third wave was scheduled to arrive with dozer tanks and then followed by a fourth, landing two engineer battalions.

Though formed according to plan, the landing force soon faced an unforeseen situation. With strong currents and perhaps confused by smoke and haze, the boat groups veered south making landfall astride exit 2, on *Victor* Beach about 2,000 yards (1,800m) south of their planned beachheads.

First ashore was the 2nd Battalion, 8th Infantry, followed within minutes by the 1st Battalion. Of the 32 dual-drive tanks, some 28 made the beach 15 minutes after the first wave. Simultaneously, Lt. Col. Cole's paratroopers arrived at exit 3, awaiting the planned landing there.

Right: American soldiers clamber down nets from their LCI to an LCA for the last lap of their journey to France. The number "9" on their helmets may indicate the 9th Infantry Division, a follow-up formation for Maj. Gen. J. Lawton Collins's US VII Corps.

Above: US Navy memorabilia of the landings. This material was used by Lt. (jg) Joseph McFalls, commanding officer of *LCT 474*, which operated off *Utah* and *Omaha* Beaches. The *Neptune* orders and their delivery bag were carried by McFalls in early May 1944 when he acted as courier for LCT Groups 10, 11, 12 and picked up the orders from Plymouth. During the landings McFalls was holding the code book (top right) in his hand when a near miss shredded the book and blew him off the bridge into the LCT. The Purple Heart was awarded to him for wounds received.
Joseph McFalls Collection, Newtown Sq. PA

UTAH BEACH
Designated assault sectors:
Tare Green, Uncle Red
Assault Division:
US 4th Infantry: US VII Corps

The leading elements of Task Force U — its minesweepers — arrived off the Normandy coast at approximately 02:00. By 02:30 the *Bayfield*, Adm. Moon's flagship was on station and the order was given to unload the landing craft. It was still four hours to H-Hour, but the landing craft would have to travel 11 miles (17km) to reach the beach. There was an 18-knot westerly wind causing waves four feet (1.2m) high. In the dark and at that distance, the coast wasn't even visible.

The long-suffering assault troops finally began to scramble down into their landing craft at 04:05. The initial landing at H-Hour would comprise four waves of landing craft carrying infantry, engineers and demolition teams. They would be supported by the DD tanks.

At about 05:30 ships began to be shelled by German shore batteries: in reply the Task Force opened up its bombardment.

On time — at 06:30 — the first wave of troops hit the beach. But it was the wrong one. The strong current and poor visibility created by the bombardment caused the landing craft to beach 2,000 yards (1,800m) south of the allotted sector. They had arrived on the less defended *Victor* Beach. Arriving with the first wave, Assistant Division Commander Brig. Gen. Roosevelt quickly realized what had happened and ordered the division to advance. By H+3 hours (approximately 09:30) exits 1, 2, and 3 had been secured and by 12:00 contact had been made with units of the 101st Airborne around the village of Pouppeville near exit 1.

By the end of June 6, the 4th Division had pushed inland about four miles. Contact had been made with elements of the 101st, though the airborne units on the Douve were still out of reach. To the west, the 4th's 12th Regiment were only a mile (1.6km) away from the 82nd Airborne's perimeter, though firm contact would not be established until the morning of D+1. The Germans were still in a position to launch serious counterattacks and the lodgment area was far from secure.

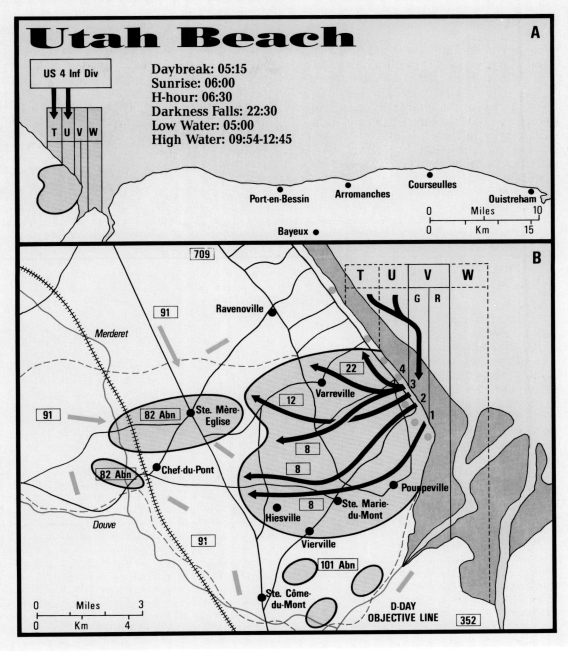

Utah Beach

A

US 4 Inf Div

T U V W

Daybreak: 05:15
Sunrise: 06:00
H-hour: 06:30
Darkness Falls: 22:30
Low Water: 05:00
High Water: 09:54-12:45

Port-en-Bessin • Arromanches • Courseulles • Ouistreham

Bayeux •

0 — Miles — 10
0 — Km — 15

B

709

91

T U V W
G R

Merderet

Ravenoville

91

22

12 Varreville

4
3
2
1

82 Abn • Ste. Mère-Eglise

91

8

82 Abn • Chef-du-Pont

8

Pouppeville

Douve

8 • Ste. Marie-du-Mont

Hiesville

91

Vierville

101 Abn

0 — Miles — 3
0 — Km — 4

Ste. Côme-du-Mont

D-DAY OBJECTIVE LINE 352

The 4th Division's Assistant Division Commander, Brig. Gen. Theodore Roosevelt, Jr., landing with a first wave assault company, immediately recognized that the initial waves were put ashore on the wrong beach. Amid occasional mortar bursts and without waiting for his forces to finish disembarking, Roosevelt moved ahead reconnoitering the dunes and locating the critical causeway leading inland.

Roosevelt decided that the rest of the division's units would follow the 8th Infantry at exit 2. His orders were concise, "We're going to start the war from right here."

The mislanding was a boon; unknown to the planners, the exit 2 area was both less obstructed and less heavily defended than the planned landing site.

The division's plan called for the 8th Infantry to move east to link up with the 101st and then to move southeastward onto the high ground north of Carentan.

Successively at H+85 minutes and at H+4 hours, the 22nd and 12th Regiments would land, the 22nd to move northwest clearing the beaches and the high ground overlooking it to the northwest. The 12th would move directly inland wheeling onto the 22nd's left flank. Both regiments would, in effect, relieve the 101st Airborne from the responsibility

Left: The transport *Empire Lance* loads LCAs with US troops on her way to the beachhead in June, 1944. The ship was one of the 13 US Maritime Commission C1-S-AY1 transports built by the Consolidated Steel Corporation and transferred to the United Kingdom under Lend-Lease.

American Airborne Uniforms and Accoutrements

1 M1942 paratroop jump jacket. Note insignia of 82nd Airborne Division
2 M2 pocket knife and cricket
3 Oil cloth arm brassard
4 Mk 2 grenade
5 Training gas mask in case
6 M1942 jump pants
7 M3 fighting knife, with M8 scabbard
8 Leather jump boots
9 M1C helmet. Note chin cup and first aid packet
10 M1942 officer's jump jacket. Note insignia
11 Formation ID brassard
12 Binoculars, 6x30 with M17 carrying case
13 Hand torch TL-122-C
14 OD wool sweater
15 Leather airborne gloves
16 M1C helmet, camouflaged
17 Carbine jump bag for *18*
18 M1A1 .30 caliber carbine with folding wire stock for airborne forces
19 Assault gas mask and case
20 Griswold bag
21 M1 Garand rifle .30 caliber
22 M1C helmet and M1944 goggles for glider troops
23 Accoutrements, see caption
24 M1936 canvas field bag with poncho
25 Wrist compass
26 M1941 OD field jacket with wool field trousers
27 Gas brassard
28 Pistol belt, see caption
29 M1938 canvas leggings
30 Service boots

Tony Stamatelos; Russ Pritchard: 17, 18, 20, 21

Note, on jacket *26*, the sleeve insignia of the 101st Airborne. It was not until April 1943 that plans to form airborne divisions were accepted. An airborne division was small, only 8,400 men compared to 15,000 in a regular infantry division. The cricket (*2*) was developed specifically for D-Day. Originals are rare and the device is a reproduction. The glider trooper's helmet (*22*), carries the insignia of the 327th Glider Infantry Regt. The Griswold bag (*20*) was padded and attached to the parachute harness. It held a disassembled M1 rifle. The accoutrements (*23*) include: M1926 cartridge belt with M1936 combat suspenders, M1919 entrenching tool with cover and improved M1910 canteen and cover. The pistol belt (*28*) is the M1936, and carries a leather holster and M1911A1 pistol and M1938 wire cutters and case.

for the invasion's northern flank. They would also be in position to advance on Cherbourg.

Roosevelt's decision sent the 8th Infantry inland to immediately reduce the complex of beach fortifications and move towards their original inland objectives. Single companies assaulted the forts blocking the beach exits while other troops cleared individual houses in the area. Exits 1 through 3 were cleared within three hours, but troops moving inland were forced to wade through areas flooded to waist level to reach exit 4 and to move on objectives to the north. By noon, the 4th Division with its supporting 70th Tank Battalion, pressed inland and linked with the 101st at Pouppeville.

By nightfall, the 8th Infantry alone had achieved its D-Day objectives. The 12th and 22nd Regiments failed to make their deep swing to the northwest, while a pocket of Germans controlled a two-mile (3km) finger on the ridge north of les Forges, at the edge of the 101st and 82nd divisional boundaries. But all four exits were clear, the 4th and 101st were linked, and though neither yet realized it, the 82nd and 4th Divisions were a mile (1.6km) apart, a mile unoccupied by Germans. The 4th Division's casualties totaled fewer than 20 dead and 200 wounded. The *Utah* gamble of an extended beachhead and a two division airborne drop inland now verged on success.

Omaha Beach
H-Hour: 06:30

Omaha was the westernmost assault beach under the original COSSAC plan. Located between Port-en-Bessin and the River Vire, its sectors stretched over 7,000 yards (6,300m), and was the largest of *Overlord*'s assault areas. Maj. Gen. Leonard T. Gerow's US V Corps planned to land two regimental combat teams abreast, one from each of the corps' assault divisions.

Assault Force "O" included the 1st Infantry Division (Maj. Gen. Clarence R. Huebner) headquarters, its own 16th and 18th Infantry Regiments, and the 115th and 116th Infantry Regiments drawn from the 29th Infantry Division. Attached were artillery, tanks, the Special Engineer Brigade, and the Provisional Ranger Force of two battalions (the 5th and 2nd). Together, there were over 34,000 men and 3,300 vehicles.

The beach was backed by high bluffs, which merge into high cliffs at each end of the landing area. The area behind the sand exposed by the withdrawing sea was heavy shale with seawalls in the western area. Five draws provided small exit corridors off the beach and onto the high ground behind, three with dirt tracks, one with a paved road, and one merely a steep draw leading to a rough road. These were seen by both sides as key to a possible landing. At the end of three of these were villages whose stone buildings made natural defense strongpoints.

The *Omaha* sector had 12 strongpoints, and beginning in April the Germans began fortifying the area with three bands of obstacles. Starting with huge gate-like obstacles some 250 yards (225m) from shore, a second band consisted of posts or logs driven seaward and mined about 225 yards (200m) from the water's edge, and the final belt consisting of mined, triple-pronged

hedgehogs, each 5½ feet high (1.5m) and some 130 yards (117m) from shore. The tidal sands were free of mines, but the trek inland and the approaches to the draws were heavily booby-trapped.

The German 352nd Division took over this area in May, and was a complete surprise to V Corps who still expected to find a reinforced battalion in the sector and not the two regiments that they encountered holding the bluffs and the ground behind.

Huebner planned to land two battalions from the attached 116th Infantry on the right, and two battalions from his own division's 16th Regiment on the left. Their D-Day objective was the ridge line parallel to the main coastal road ranging from two to three miles (3-5km) inland.

Additionally, the 116th was responsible for seizing Pointe du Hoc's coastal battery with two attached Ranger battalions. This battery located to the west, about four miles (6km) from *Omaha*'s right flank, and about seven (11km) from *Utah*'s left, was a significant component of the German coastal defense. Its six French-made 155mm guns, two thought to be casemated, could reach 25,000 yards (22km) and hit both corps transports and landing craft.

Three companies from the 2nd Rangers would scale the 85-100 foot (25-30m) cliffs and assault the guns, while another company landing with the 116th moved on the position from inland.

Omaha's violence contrasted with *Utah*'s relatively bloodless success. At H–50, two companies of DD tanks launched 6,000 yards (5,400m) from the beach. Heavy seas sank 27 tanks, drowning many crewmen; three of the five making the beach were actually put ashore by a craft whose ramp malfunctioned. Heavy seas also swamped ten landing craft making the 11-mile (17km) run to the beach. DUKWs ferrying artillery to the beach also foundered, losing most of the guns of two battalions and a separate cannon company. Additional guns were lost when landing craft struck mines.

Below: The scene eastward along *Omaha* Beach was photographed from an emplacement for an enfilading 88mm gun, and reveals the difficult task facing the US 1st Infantry Division during its D-Day landing.

OMAHA BEACH
Designated assault sectors:
Dog Green, Dog White, Dog Red, Easy Green, Easy Red, Fox Green
Assault Divisions:
US 1st Infantry, US 29th Infantry: US V Corps. Plus two battalions 2nd and 5th of the Provisional Ranger Force

On D-Day, minesweepers of Task Force O were at work off the beach by 00:55. The bombardment ships arrived at 02:20. At 03:00 the transports had arrived on station, 11 miles (17km) offshore. The unloading of the assault troops began. The first landing craft headed for the beach at 04:30, 45 minutes before first light. The sea was rough enough to cause a great deal of seasickness amongst the assault troops, as well as cause flooding to many of the smaller landing craft.

Each one of the designated beaches was to be assaulted by six LCAs or LCVPs (Landing Craft, Vehicle Personnel). Some 2 miles (3km) offshore they reached the line of departure marked by control craft. It was at this point that things began to go wrong. The strong easterly tide combining with that morning's westerly wind began to drive both the control and landing craft off course eastwards. At the same time the sea conditions were also having a devastating effect on the DD tanks.

Launching at H–50 minutes some 5,000 yards (4.5km) offshore, the tanks were scheduled to land at H–5 minutes. Those DDs designated to the western beaches (*Dog Green, Dog White, Dog Red* and *Easy Green*) in support of the 116th Infantry Regiment were launched as planned and promptly sank in the heavy swell. Landing craft on approach were forced to pass by the surviving tank crews as they floundered helplessly in the water. Of 32 tanks only 5 made it to the beach. In the eastern sectors (*Easy Red* and *Fox Green*) all 32 tanks in support of the 16th Infantry Regiment were delivered directly onto the beach, as the commanders of their LCTs decided not to risk the open sea.

Under these sea conditions and with the coastline obscured by the smoke and dust caused by the naval bombardment, navigation into the designated beach sectors broke down completely. All but two companies of the assaulting troops were emplaced on the wrong beaches, and in one case Company I of the 16th drifted all the way to *Gold* area.

This breakdown of the landing plan was to have a catastrophic effect on the assault. Individual companies had been given specific tasks in specific areas, and the success of the attack and the advance inland depended on these missions being completed swiftly and in concert. If companies became lost or leaderless, then the attack would stall.

The situation on landing rapidly deteriorated. At about 1,000 yards (1,600m), the landing craft began to be subjected to intense enemy fire. Most craft grounded at least a hundred yards (90m) offshore; heavily laden troops leapt into water sometimes 6 feet (1.8m) deep: many drowned, weighed down by their equipment. If the troops did manage to get ashore, then there was still over 200 yards (180m) of open beach to cross before they reached the cover of the sea wall. German fire throughout was accurate and intense, both from the bluffs overlooking the beach and from enfilading positions.

The 5th Ranger Battalion under the command of Lt. Col. Max Schneider had been given the mission of landing on *Dog Green* and supporting the 2nd Rangers in the attack on Pointe du Hoc to the west. The battalion instead landed on *Dog White* (at 07:40), and while unable to undertake its original mission, it was in the right place to lend its weight to the advance off the beach.

Inspired by the leadership of Maj. Gen. Cota, who had landed at 07:30, the attack up

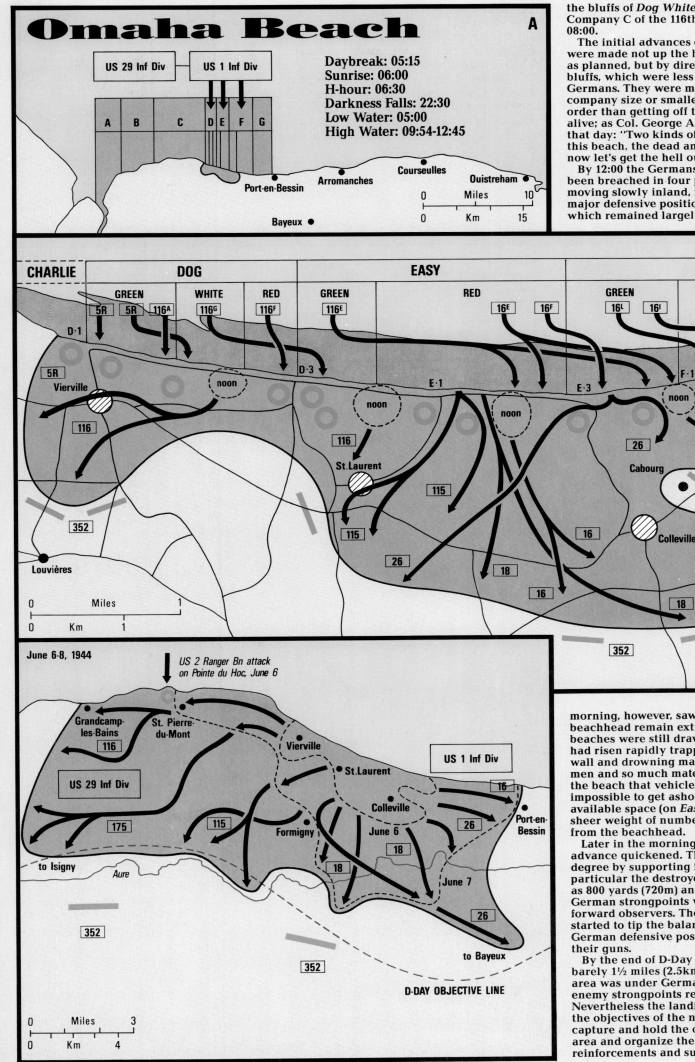

Omaha Beach

A

US 29 Inf Div   US 1 Inf Div

A B C D E F G

Daybreak: 05:15
Sunrise: 06:00
H-hour: 06:30
Darkness Falls: 22:30
Low Water: 05:00
High Water: 09:54-12:45

Port-en-Bessin   Arromanches   Courseulles   Ouistreham

Bayeux

0 —— Miles —— 10
0 —— Km —— 15

B

CHARLIE   DOG   EASY   FOX

GREEN   WHITE   RED   GREEN   RED   GREEN   RED

5R 5R 116A   116G   116F   116E   16E 16F   16L 16I

D-1

5R

Vierville

noon   D-3   noon   E-1   noon   E-3   F-1   noon

116

352   116   St.Laurent   115   26   le Grand Hameau

Louvières   115   115   16   Cabourg   16

26   18   Colleville

16   18

352

0 —— Miles —— 1
0 —— Km —— 1

June 6-8, 1944

US 2 Ranger Bn attack
on Pointe du Hoc, June 6

Grandcamp-
les-Bains   St. Pierre-
du-Mont   Vierville   US 1 Inf Div

116   St.Laurent   16

US 29 Inf Div   Colleville   26   Port-en-
Bessin

175   115   Formigny   June 6

to Isigny   Aure   18   June 7

18   26

352   June 7

352   to Bayeux

D-DAY OBJECTIVE LINE

0 —— Miles —— 3
0 —— Km —— 4

---

the bluffs of *Dog White* was begun by Company C of the 116th Infantry at about 08:00.

The initial advances off *Omaha* on D-Day were made not up the heavily defended draws as planned, but by direct assault over the bluffs, which were less heavily manned by the Germans. They were made by mixed units of company size or smaller, often with no other order than getting off the beach and staying alive; as Col. George A. Taylor of the 16th said that day: "Two kinds of people are staying on this beach, the dead and those about to die — now let's get the hell out of here."

By 12:00 the Germans' first line defenses had been breached in four places and troops were moving slowly inland, flanking the Germans' major defensive positions above the draws, which remained largely intact. The early

morning, however, saw the situation on the beachhead remain extremely hazardous. The beaches were still drawing fire, and the tide had risen rapidly trapping men against the sea wall and drowning many wounded. So many men and so much materiel was crammed onto the beach that vehicles and artillery found it impossible to get ashore. When they did find available space (on *Easy Green* and *Easy Red*), sheer weight of numbers clogged up the exits from the beachhead.

Later in the morning, the tempo of the advance quickened. This was aided to a great degree by supporting fire from the Navy; in particular the destroyers, which got in as close as 800 yards (720m) and fired directly at German strongpoints without the help of forward observers. The arrival of tanks also started to tip the balance, as one by one German defensive positions began to fall to their guns.

By the end of D-Day the advance had gone barely 1½ miles (2.5km) inland; the beachhead area was under German artillery fire and enemy strongpoints remained intact. Nevertheless the landing had been made, and the objectives of the next two days would be to capture and hold the original D-Day lodgment area and organize the beach for the arrival of reinforcements and supplies.

American Assault Troops' Uniforms and Accoutrements

1 M1941 wool cap, worn under M1 helmet
2 M1 helmet with the insignia of the 29th Infantry Division
3 M1944 goggles
4 M1941 field jacket
5 M1943 high neck sweater
6 M1911A1 pistol .45 caliber, in waterproof cover
7 Accoutrements, see caption
8 OD wool field trousers
9 M1938 canvas leggings
10 Service shoes
11 M1928 field pack with M1910 entrenching tool
12 Assault gas mask and case
13 Assault vest, developed for the Normandy landings

14 M26 inflatable life preserver issued to invasion troops
15 M1 helmet with medical ID
16 OD wool shirt with shoulder patch of the 4th Infantry Division
17 Red Cross brassard
18 Private purchase fighting knife and sheath
19 M1938 dispatch case
20 First aid pouch
21 M1 Garand .30 caliber
22 M1 helmet with netting and burlap (sacking) camouflage
23 M1943 camouflage jacket of herring bone twill
24 Trousers for 23
25 Accoutrements, see caption
26 Ammunition bandolier

Tony Stamatelos: 1-6, 8-20, 22-26; Russ Pritchard: 7, 21

The American assault forces that landed on the Normandy beaches were arguably the best armed and equipped invasion force to date. The accoutrements (*7*), include: M1936 pistol belt with leather holster, improved M1910 canteen with cover, Mk II fragmentation grenade and M1942 first aid pouch. The M1943 camouflage uniform (*23* and *24*) was issued to some US troops in Normandy, but was quickly withdrawn when it was found to be too similar to the camouflage uniforms worn by the Waffen-SS. The accoutrements (*25*) include: M1936 suspenders, M1923 cartridge belt, modified M1910 canteen with cover and M1910 entrenching tool with cover. The bandolier (*26*) can be seen with an eight-round clip of .30 caliber M1 rifle ammunition. Ball, armor-piercing and tracer was also available. Each bandolier held six eight-round clips.

Starting without hope of tank or artillery support, the infantry suffered more severely. Lateral currents dragged units hundreds of yards from their objectives, landing them on a strange beach out of sight of rehearsed objectives and in front of heavy enemy opposition. Though the Germans claimed that the preparatory bombardment exploded entire inshore minefields, beach defenses were neither destroyed nor suppressed. The defense rapidly recovered and brought its weapons to bear.

Heavy machine gun and mortar fire greeted inbound boats whose equipment-burdened soldiers were often dumped in waist-to-neck deep water, causing many to discard equipment or drown. The scrambled landing bunched units in two areas, two companies in front of the D-3 draw (les Moulins) and four companies astride the E-3 draw near Colleville. Right flank companies landed on the wrong beaches; one company's boats were pulled so far from their objective that they circled offshore for 90 minutes.

The Ranger company and company of the 116th at the right beach exit lost more than half of their men to mortar fire and small arms before making the seawall. The 29th's landing force decided to bring its DD tanks all the way into the beach rather than floating them in, but artillery fire rapidly destroyed eight of the 16 tanks before their tracks hit dry

sand. Further to the east, two full tank companies made the beach in their landing craft to find their assigned infantry teams either missing in the tangled landings or withering away under heavy fire.

Subsequent waves piled onto a confused mass of men pinned to the beach. With leaders downed by fire, others rose to take their places. With the German defense pinning the invaders to the seawall or behind obstacles, the naval demolitions and Special Brigade troops were unable to clear obstacles, soon adding 40 percent of their number to the rising casualty list. With a tide rising four feet (1.2m) and shrinking the dry beach 80 yards (72m) each hour, obstacles were soon covered with water compounding the danger to shorebound boats. Wounded too weak to crawl faster than the advancing water drowned.

After nearly an hour and a half of what appeared to be impending disaster, the flow of battle started to change. Several destroyers risked grounding and fired on visible enemy activity from close inshore. The surviving tanks moved forward giving supporting fire as groups of men attempted to crack the defense by climbing the bluffs and attacking the defense line that blocked the exits.

Above: Willys-Overland Model MB "Jeep." This vehicle was the personal transport of Gen. C.H. Gerhardt, commander of the 29th Infantry Divison. It landed with him on *Omaha* on June 7 and carried him throughout the war in Europe. *Maryland National Guard Historical Society, Baltimore, Md*

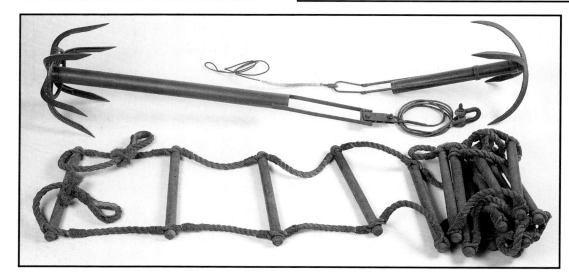

Above: Invasion currency signed by officers of the 5th Ranger Battalion on HMS *Leopold* prior to landings on *Omaha*. The signatures are of: Lt. Pepper, Co. B; Lt. Shaddock (artillery observer); Capt. Whittington, Co. B; Capt. Heffelfinger, batt. exec.; Lt. D. Anderson (killed on D-Day); Capt. Byren, batt. intelligence; Lt. Zepelski; Lt. Col. Max Schneider, CO and second in command of Ranger operations. *D-Day Museum, Portsmouth*

Below: This US Coast Guard-crewed LCVP burst into flames after German machine gun fire had exploded a hand grenade as it approached the French coast on D-Day, but reached the shore and disembarked its troops before the fire was successfully extinguished.

Above: Ranger scaling equipment. These four-prong and six-prong grapnel hooks were used by the 2nd Ranger Battalion in their assault on the Pointe du Hoc. The objects were recovered from the area after the battle. *Musée du Débarquement, Arromanches*

The 2nd Ranger Battalion's three companies (D, E and F) landed at Pointe du Hoc at 07:10 40 minutes late — victims of currents and rough seas. While the Rangers scaled the cliffs with one company to the west and two companies to the east of the promontory, the destroyers USS *Satterlee* and HMS *Talybont* provided effective suppressive fire from close inshore. Once atop the cliffs, small groups rushed the casemates finding them empty with the actual battery hidden farther inland, unmanned and unguarded. After destroying the guns, the Rangers endured heavy counterattacks and were besieged for two days while V Corps expanded its beachhead.

While the Rangers were overrunning the Pointe, V Corps and Gen. Bradley were receiving observer reports from a liaison boat circling offshore. Through the smoke, enemy fire was seen to be hitting troops who

were pinned on the beach. Bradley later was said to have considered pulling troops off and relanding them at *Utah*, which was probably an impossibility.

But what couldn't be seen were the four

Above: Men of a US Army Ranger battalion are seen in their landing craft before leaving an English port for France. Note the M1 rifles, "bazooka" anti-tank rocket launcher, and pack of "Lucky Strike" cigarettes. The main Ranger landing on D-Day took Pointe du Hoc.

Below: The moment of truth approaches for these soldiers of the US Army as their US Coast Guard-crewed LCA nears the French coast on D-Day. the location is probably *Omaha* Beach, which would make these men an element of the US 1st Infantry Division.

thin penetrations made in the defense, two in each regiment's sector. A score of nameless leaders emerged to form small groups to move forward and reduce defenses.

After they individually landed some time after H + 1, Gen. Cota and Col. Canham of the 29th Division, and Col. Taylor of the 16th Infantry, each started tying together independent group actions, galvanizing the pinned-down troops who were already beginning to fight back.

Waterlogged radios and the nature of the terrain made coordinating attacks impossible, but the picture developed identically in each of the footholds gained. The independent fire of the destroyers had inflicted significant losses on the defenders whose thinning ranks focused more heavily on blocking the key exits. Once assaulting troops cleared the fireswept beaches, they found that stretches of the dominating bluffs were undefended. Gaining these heights, the assault groups began moving inland to become entangled in hedgerows.

Even with troops moving inland, the situation was tenuous. The beach area remained under fire, and follow-on waves were restricted to narrow columns by uncleared obstacles. By mid-morning, large landing craft ignored obstacles, ramming their way to the beach while destroyers moved closer to continue firing on targets. By midday, the battle devolved into three independent battles for the villages of Vierville, St. Laurent, and Colleville, the villages controlling the east-west road and the keys to capturing the ridgeline, which determined if the landing force could survive serious counterattacks.

Nightfall

By D-Day evening, First Army held firm beachheads. On *Utah*, the 4th Division and a reinforcing regiment were ashore and linked with the 101st Airborne. Although the planned northern edge of the bridgehead still had to be taken and the 82nd Airborne was

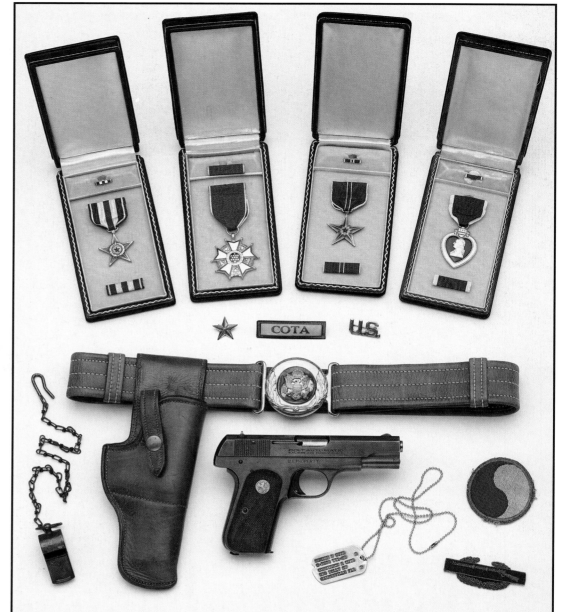

Above: Memorabilia of Gen. Norman S. Cota. Gen. Cota was Assistant Division Commander of the 29th Infantry Division and went ashore on D-Day at *Omaha* at 07:30, with that division's 116th Infantry.

Decorations, left to right: Silver Star, Legion of Merit, Bronze Star and Purple Heart with service ribbons and lapel rosettes in original presentation cases. Collar insignia: Silver Star, name tag and "US" device. Brass command whistle, Colt M.380 pocket automatic with general officer's waist belt and holster. Cota's "dog tags." Division shoulder patch and silver bullion Combat Infantryman's badge.

Eisenhower Library and Museum

Below: Suppression of the German positions left intact by the air bombardment before D-Day was entrusted to the Allied navies. Seen here are two cruisers, HMS *Glasgow* (foreground) with 12 6in guns and USS *Quincy* with nine 8in guns.

Above: American infantry start the lengthy trek to the shore from the beached position of their LCA. The prone men ahead of them are either dead or seeking what cover they can from the storm of machinegun fire from undamaged German strongpoints.

Below: A US Army chaplain's stole and service Bible. The stole is a poignant reminder of those terrible events on *Omaha*. It was found on that beach on June 7 by Stoker James Cook, a crewman of Royal Navy *LST 367*. *D-Day Museum, Portsmouth*

Below: Assault troops of the 16th Regimental Combat Team's 3rd Battalion shelter under "A" Cliff near Colleville. The division was faced by the cliffs and the German 352nd Infantry Division and could not reach the Isigny-Bayeux road that was its first objective.

Above: Under a pall of smoke, men of the US 1st Infantry Division move ashore on *Omaha* Beach. Under the command of Maj. Gen. Huebner, on D-Day, the division landed its 115th and 116th, and 16th and 18th Regimental Combat Teams.

yet to be contacted, VII Corps was in a good position to move inland, receive reinforcements, and begin its fight for the peninsula and Cherbourg. The predicted airborne disaster failed to materialize.

V Corps on *Omaha* recovered from what appeared to be impending disaster during the first hours and held the major exits, the three villages, and a broken line that was a mile and a half (2.5km) at its deepest point. The right flank units and the Rangers at Pointe du Hoc held isolated pockets. Reinforcements, particularly in artillery and armor, were needed before any move inland could be attempted. V Corps estimated its losses at about 2,400 in killed, wounded and missing.

The British Second Army Plan

British Second Army's landing area, with Caen as its main objective, stretched for nearly 25 miles (40km) from the seaside village of Port-en-Bessin (a little beyond Bayeux and next to the American landing beach at *Omaha*) eastwards along the coast to the flooded estuary of the River Dives at Cabourg. Between the offshore shoals, three sandy beaches, each about two miles (3km) long, offered suitable landing points, separated by between five and ten miles (8-16km) from each other. The British invasion would start with 6th Airborne Division dropping northeast of Caen before dawn, followed by amphibious landings by XXX Corps, led by 50th (Northumbrian) Division at *Gold* Beach with Bayeux as its objective, and by I Corps with 3rd Canadian Division

Below: Canadian troops of the North Nova Scotia Highlanders board an LCI(L) of the 2nd Canadian (262nd Royal Navy) Flotilla during a training exercise in May 1944. The Canadian assault area was *Juno* Beach between the British *Gold* and *Sword* Beaches.

Above: Men of the Highland Light Infantry of Canada stream up the two bow ramps of *LCI(L) 276* during a May 1944 exercise. With a full-load displacement of 384 tons, the American-built LCI(L) had a complement of 24 and could carry 388 troops at a maximum of 14 knots.

at *Juno* Beach, and 3rd Division (usually known as 3rd British Division to distinguish it from the Canadians) at *Sword* Beach directly north of Caen. 6th Airborne Division would come under I Corps once contact was made.

The landing beaches themselves were gently shelving sand, fronted by little holiday villages which the Germans had turned into strongpoints. Other gun positions, obstacles and minefields of the Atlantic Wall stretched from the water's edge to between 400 and 800 yards (360-720m) inland. Away from the beaches, the ground rose up into farm country of rolling ridges which reached down to the sea as cliffs at the western edge of *Gold*, separating it from *Omaha* by about ten miles. The River Orne, flowing with the Canal de Caen through the city of Caen and into the sea at Ouistreham just east of *Sword*, was the only major water obstacle on the British sector, except for the flooding of the Dives to the east.

The value of Caen and Bayeux to the British was obvious. Any town or city made a good defensive position, costly and time-consuming to capture. If the Germans could hold the old medieval town of Bayeux (once William the Conqueror's capital as Duke of Normandy) they could prevent a firm link-up between the British and the Americans from *Omaha* Beach, and deny them the use of the roads leading into the heart of Normandy. Even more important, the British planned to build their *Mulberry* harbor at Arromanches, just west of *Gold*, and to use Bayeux as their main administration and supply centre. The

Left: Tetrarch light airborne tank. A regiment of these landed in Hamilcar gliders on the evening of D-Day, in support of 6th Airborne Division operations on the Orne River; their first objective was the village of Troarn. *Bovington Tank Museum*

THE BRITISH AIRBORNE ASSAULT

The British 6th Airborne Division was to land on the eastern flank of the invasion area. The division's objectives were: capture and hold the bridges over the Caen Canal and Orne River, southeast of Ouistreham; destroy the bridges over the flooded River Dives; attack and destroy the gun battery at Merville; secure the flank of the invasion area on the ridge running from Troarn through to Bréville and the sea. The division planned to land in nine major drops throughout D-Day.

Drop I, to Drop Zones (DZ) "X" and "Y," by glider at 00:16+; the "coup de main" operation to take the river and canal bridges. Drop II, to DZs "N," "K," "V" by parachute, at 00:20; parachute pathfinders with radar beacons. Drop III, to DZ "N," "K," "V" at 00:50, by parachute; forward units of 5th Parachute Brigade. Drop IV, to DZ "N," by glider at 03:30; Divisional HQ with division commander plus anti-tank guns. Drop V by glider; support equipment for the Merville battery assault. Drop VI, by glider on the Merville battery with support equipment for the assault. Drop VII, to DZs "N," "K," "V," by parachute, support equipment and reinforcements. Drop VIII, to DZ "K," by glider, support equipment. Drop IX, to DZs "N" and "W," by 256 gliders, by 20:52; the 6th Airlanding Brigade and divisional troops.

The landings were to take place in three phases. The majority of these drops took place as planned, except for the landings of support equipment for the Merville battery attack; Drop V disappeared; Drop VI landed in a field amongst Rommel's Asparagus which destroyed the gliders, the equipment and killed most of the crews.

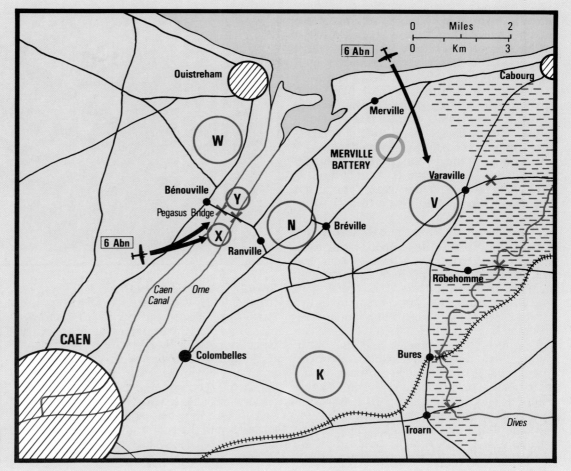

same argument applied with even greater force to Caen, a city of 50,000 inhabitants with its own aerodrome at Carpiquet, and the most important Allied objective on D-Day. If they could hold Caen, the Germans could use the city as a defensive block to hold up the whole 21st Army Group advance.

For this reason, Montgomery placed great stress on his British and Canadian forces getting rapidly inland. For D-Day the first three divisions to land were reorganized into four assault brigades each, by the addition of extra armor, engineers and specialist troops, including two brigades of commandos. If everything went well, Montgomery hoped for British Second Army to capture the whole of its landing area from the Germans on D-Day, including Caen and Bayeux and the road linking them, to join up with the Americans, and to get armored forces well inland as far as Villers-Bocage and even Falaise. Against that, the worst fate which could befall the landings was to be destroyed on the beaches without ever getting inland at all.

The British Air Assault

The plan called for 6th Airborne Division to drop between the rivers Orne and Dives, so as to cover the flank of the landings at *Sword* Beach. Unlike his American counterparts, the flamboyant Maj. Gen. Richard ("Windy") Gale of 6th Airborne Division planned to use his men like airborne commandos, in small parties to take specific objectives. "What you

get by stealth and guts," he told them, "you must hold with skill and determination." In order to secure their objectives before the first amphibious landings, the airborne forces would land by night, relying on darkness to hide their numbers and confuse the Germans. Night landings carried a high risk of failure, and Gale depended on the training of his men to carry his plan through.

On June 6, at a few minutes after midnight, high over the Normandy coast, the British liberation of France began as the first of Gale's men, 181 assault troops in six gliders under Maj. John Howard of 2nd Oxfordshire

and Buckinghamshire Light Infantry (the "Ox and Bucks"), cast off their tow ropes and began the silent glide down to land. Their target was the bridges at Bénouville over the Canal de Caen and the Orne, the only bridges between Caen and the sea, guarded by about fifty German troops and wired for demolition. Gale wanted these bridges intact, as the link between his division and the commandos landing at *Sword*.

At 00:16, Howard's lead glider skidded to a halt only yards from the Canal de Caen Bridge, probably the first Allied troops to land in Normandy on D-Day, followed seconds

Right: Maj. Gen. Richard Gale gives last words of advice and encouragement to men of his British 6th Airborne Division before they emplane for their part in *Overlord*, namely the seizure of objectives on the extreme eastern flank of the Allied lodgment.

later by two other gliders. Bombing of the area by the RAF had already started, and the bridge's defenders hardly noticed the dark shapes of the gliders until Howard's men burst from them, guns blazing. In 10 minutes it was all over, and for the loss of two men dead and five wounded the British had captured the bridge intact. Although it was wired for demolition, the Germans had not yet placed the explosives. At the same time two more of Howard's gliders, coming down by the Orne Bridge, discovered that its defenders had fled. The sixth glider missed the target altogether, landing beside a bridge over the Dives.

While the glider troops dug themselves in around the bridges, the main airborne drop had already begun, and within an hour the first paratroopers of 5th Parachute Brigade arrived. Throughout the night there were sharp firefights as Germans drove up out of the dark, only to find the bridges blocked. By morning the defenders had fought off more than one attack by tanks, and the battle swung back and forth as more airborne troops joined in. Finally, at just after noon, the men on the bridges heard the distinctive sound of bagpipes, heralding the arrival of reinforcements from 1st Special Service (Commando) Brigade under Lord Lovat, coming from *Sword* Beach. In honour of the "Pegasus" divisional insignia of British airborne troops, the Canal de Caen Bridge was later renamed Pegasus Bridge.

Gale's other main target for the night was a well-defended German gun battery position at Merville, across the Orne estuary from

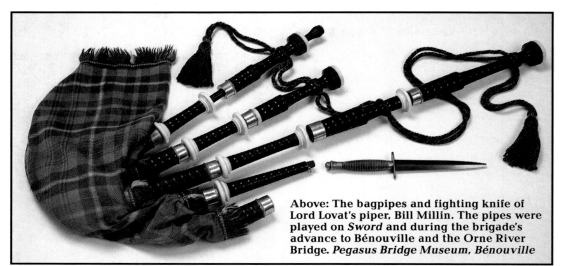

Above: The bagpipes and fighting knife of Lord Lovat's piper, Bill Millin. The pipes were played on *Sword* and during the brigade's advance to Bénouville and the Orne River Bridge. *Pegasus Bridge Museum, Bénouville*

Sword. The silencing of this battery was entrusted to Lt. Col. Terence Otway of 9th Parachute Regiment, who devised an elaborate plan involving the bombing of the German battery by the RAF, support from Canadian paratroops with special equipment, the storming of the battery by his own battalion accompanied by a simultaneous glider landing, and a final bombardment from British warships just as dawn broke. In the confusion of the night this plan broke down completely. The RAF bombers missed the battery, nearly killing Otway's advance party instead. Only just over 150 men reached the rendezvous in time for the attack, and little of the special equipment arrived. Clearing their way through a minefield protecting the battery, the paratroops launched their

Above: Personal memorabilia of Lt. Den Brotheridge, Ox and Bucks Light Infantry. The lieutenant flew in the lead glider with Maj. Howard and men of A-Able platoon. He was mortally wounded leading his men in the Pegasus Bridge assault. The spirits flask was carried by him in the attack. The map case is contemporary, as is the map of the "coup de main" assault area. *Pegasus Bridge Museum, Bénouville*

Below: Maj. John Howard, commander of the "coup de main" assault on the Orne River bridges. He led the first Allied troops to land on D-Day. Both bridges — over the Caen Canal and Orne River — were captured intact within 15 minutes of the landing.

Below: Memorabilia of Maj. Howard. His helmet, with sniper's bullet hole received June 7; compass; silk escape map of France; escape and evasion kit issued to airborne personnel; and divisional and regimental insignias. *Pegasus Bridge Museum, Bénouville*

The Glider Assault on Pegasus Bridge

Right: A reconnaissance photo of the assault area around the Caen Canal (Pegasus) Bridge. Taken after the attack, the photo also shows the landing positions of the three gliders which carried the assault party. Howard's total force to capture and hold this, and the Orne River Bridge 400 yards (360m) away, comprised six platoons of 2nd Battalion Ox and Bucks, plus 30 sappers from 249 Company Royal Engineers. In total 181 men (plus pilots) in six Horsa gliders. The first of these took off at 22:56 on June 5, the last at 23:01. They crossed the French coast at 00:07, seconds into D-Day. Below and below right: The precision with which the gliders hit their target was remarkable. Tows were cast at 6,000 feet (1,800m) the first glider landed 47 yards (42m) from the bridge, without landing aids.

Once the bridges were taken, Howard's troops had to hold them until relieved, first by men of the 5th Parachute Brigade (at about 01:00) and later in the day by Lovat's 1st Special Service Brigade. Contrary to legend, Piper Millin did not play over Pegasus Bridge — German machinegun fire and mortaring were too great; he did, however, play the commandos over the Orne River Bridge. Bottom: Café Gondrée and Pegasus Bridge as they looked in the early 1990s. There were plans to move the bridge to the nearby Pegasus Bridge Museum in Bénouville and replace it with a new one.

British Airborne Uniforms and Equipment

1 Distinctive maroon 'red' beret and cap badge of The Parachute Regiment
2 Pattern 1940 serge battle dress blouse
3 Binoculars
4 Accoutrements, see caption
5 No. 2 Mk I Webley revolver .38 caliber, with lanyard
6 Battle dress trousers
7 Pattern 1937 canvas web gaiters
8 'Ammunition' boots. Note not jump boots
9 Airborne pattern steel helmet with netting. Note chin strap
10 Officer's Denison smock
11 Ammunition bandolier, .303 caliber
12 Toggle rope carried by assault troops
13 Sten Mk III submachine gun, 9mm, with clip below
14 Grenades, see caption
15 Fairbairn-Sykes fighting knife with sheath
16 Folding map case
17 Late pattern airborne helmet with camouflage net and scrim attached
18 Denison smock for other ranks, introduced 1941
19 Accoutrements, see caption
20 Maroon beret with cap badge insignia of the Glider Pilot Regiment
21 Glider pilot's Type C flying helmet
22 Oxygen mask for 21
23 Parachute smock
24 British X-Type parachute

Memorial Museum, Bayeux

The toggle rope *12* was specially designed for assault troops. Each rope had a toggle at one end and a loop at the other. Each man carried a section which could be linked with others to create a sizeable scaling rope.

The distinctive cap badge of The Parachute Regiment seen on beret *1*, was first introduced in 1943. The insignia on battle dress blouse (*2*) includes the shoulder insignia of The Parachute Regiment, the parachutist's qualification wings, and the distinctive "Pegasus" badge of the Airborne Division. The accoutrements (*4*) include a Pattern 1937 web waist belt, web ammunition pouch, web holster, plus No. 4 bayonet and scabbard with frog. The grenades (*14*) are, left: offensive plastic concussion grenade No. 69; and right: Mills No. 36 fragmentation grenade. The accoutrements (*19*) include Pattern 1937 webbing, ammunition pouches and water bottle. The parachute smock (*23*) was worn over the Denison smock and battle dress and under the parachute harness. It was used during drops and taken off on landing.

attack at 04:30. Just as they did so, two of the expected gliders flew over the battery, missed it entirely, and crashed nearby. To this accompaniment, Otway's men stormed the battery casemates, driving the Germans back and taking 30 prisoners, but in the smoke and darkness underground failed to realize that they had only damaged, and not disabled, the four 100mm guns. With dawn coming up and nearly half his men killed, wounded or missing, Otway pulled his force back from the battery, having achieved his objective of silencing it for D-Day.

Throughout the night, the paratroops and gliders continued to land, roughly half of them where the plan intended and the rest

scattered between the Dives and the sea. Small parties of men, largely from 3rd Parachute Brigade, succeeded in destroying the five bridges over the Dives next to their landing area, so sealing off the landing from serious German interference. Others became lost and were taken prisoner, or fought with equally lost German patrols. Soon after dawn, Gale, who had established his headquarters near Pegasus Bridge, could feel confident that his division had achieved its objectives, and with daylight the main glider force of 6th Airlanding Brigade could start its landings. Any Germans trying to reach *Sword* Beach across Pegasus Bridge would find their way securely blocked.

Gold Beach
H-Hour: 07:25

Dawn over Normandy came almost exactly at 06:00, three hours after the start of the main RAF bomber attack on the Atlantic Wall positions in the landing area. As the light improved, the gathering flotilla of warships offshore joined in the bombardment. Expecting hard resistance from the village strongpoints facing them on the beaches, the British delayed the start of their landings until almost an hour after the Americans, choosing assembly areas only seven miles (11km) offshore for a shorter final assault by their landing craft. The first troops of 50th Division were expected to land at 07:25, a few minutes behind the DD tanks, and press inland to Bayeux, followed by commandos who would swing westward overland to Port-en-Bessin, linking up with the Americans.

The bad weather on D-Day seriously affected this plan. German gun emplacements on the cliffs near Arromanches were not properly destroyed by bombing or naval gunfire, the tide was running high, and a fierce current and force five wind meant that the DD tanks were almost certain to sink. Rather than launching at sea, their crews brought them into the beach still in their landing craft, 5 minutes behind the first infantry. *Gold* was wide enough to land two brigade groups side by side, 231st Brigade at the little villages of le Hamel and 69th Brigade at la Rivière. At le Hamel, 1st Hampshire Regiment hit the beach unsupported by armor, as the tanks which got ashore either bogged down or were crippled by German fire, to find that the wire was not cut. Wading chest deep through the water, the men were briefly pinned down, but with help from one surviving flail tank and an AVRE were eventually able to press

Below: One of the many specialised tank types that proved invaluable in the Normandy landing was the Churchill AVRE (Armoured Vehicle Royal Engineers) of the type seen in the foreground. These came in variants such as Fascine with a gap-filling bundle of chestnut pales, Bobbin with a large roll of road-improving matting, and Petard.

Above: Centaur Mk IV tank, with 95mm gun-howitzer, of V Troop, 5th Independent Battery, Royal Marine Armoured Support Regiment. This tank was knocked-out shortly after landing. It was renovated in 1975.
Pegasus Bridge Museum, Bénouville

Below: Universal (otherwise known as Bren Gun) Carriers of the British 50th Infantry Division come ashore from a flotilla of LCTs beached on the shallowly sloping shoreline of *Gold* Beach. The division's primary objective was the ancient city of Bayeux.

GOLD BEACH
Designated assault sectors:
Jig Green, Jig Red, King Green, King Red
Assault Division:
British 50th (Northumbrian) Infantry Division:
British XXX Corps

Task Force G arrived off *Gold* area, ten miles (16km) east of *Omaha*, at 05:30. Reefs off the coast at this point made it necessary to delay H-Hour until 07:25, by which time the flood tide would have been running for over an hour. The delay allowed the preliminary bombardment — starting at 05:45 — to last over an hour and a half. With the sea running high, it was decided to land the DD tanks directly from beached LCTs. This, however, brought them in ahead of the demolition parties and supporting infantry, and all the tanks but one were shortly destroyed or put out of action.

The infantry assault waves came in on time, but the number of beach obstacles and the fast-rising tide created problems for the landing craft, many of which were damaged. Most of the coastal German defenses were lightly manned, but enfilading strongpoints at la Rivière and Asnelles (near Arromanches) had to by bypassed and reduced later.

No. 47 Royal Marine Commando landed at 09:30; its mission was to take Port-en-Bessin and link up with the Americans from *Omaha*. Unfortunately a bad landing delayed the capture of the town until D + 1, and as of the end of D-Day there was no sign of the Americans.

By nightfall the *Gold* lodgment area covered nearly five square miles (13km²), the division's reserves were ashore and patrols were near the outskirts of Bayeux.

The following written landing instructions were handed to units heading for *Gold*:

LANDING INSTRUCTIONS — SECRET
1. You are about to take part in the invasion of Europe. The operation will be known by the codeword 'OVERLORD'. Do not disclose this codeword nor any of those which follow, to anybody and do not use them in conversation among yourselves.
2. You will be landed on one of 3 beaches. The code names of these are ITEM, JIG, KING. Wherever you land, carry out the following instructions. (A) Go at once to the Beach Transit Area, which will be marked. Go straight there do NOT hang about looking for your friends or your own section. If you are on foot go to the Personnel Park, if you are with a vehicle go to the Vehicle Park and carry out the first stages of dewaterproofing. DO NOT wait for orders — get on with it SPEED in clearing the ships and beaches is essential. WASTE NO TIME.
Courtesy of the D-Day Museum, Portsmouth

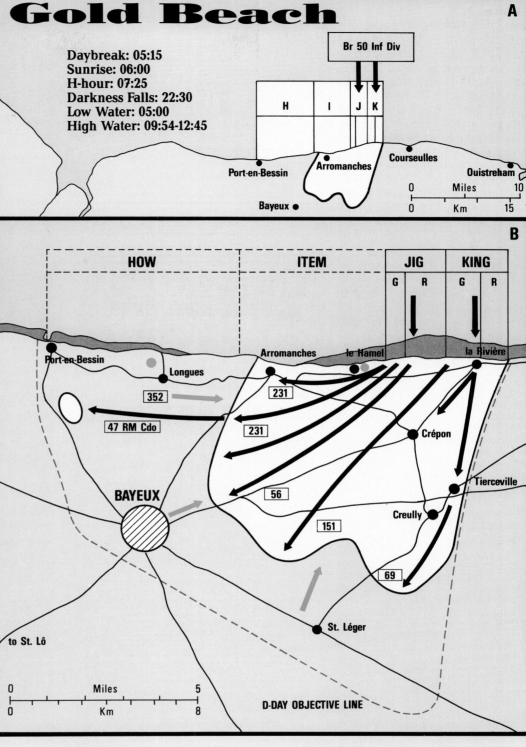

Gold Beach

Daybreak: 05:15
Sunrise: 06:00
H-hour: 07:25
Darkness Falls: 22:30
Low Water: 05:00
High Water: 09:54-12:45

Br 50 Inf Div

H I J K

Port-en-Bessin   Arromanches   Courseulles   Ouistreham

Bayeux

0 Miles 10
0 Km 15

A

B

HOW   ITEM   JIG   KING
G R   G R

Port-en-Bessin   Longues   Arromanches   le Hamel   la Rivière

352   231   231   47 RM Cdo

Crépon

56   Tierceville

Creully

BAYEUX

151

69

to St. Lô   St. Léger

0 Miles 5
0 Km 8

D-DAY OBJECTIVE LINE

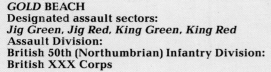

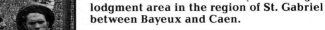

Left: Passing men of another unit resting on the roadside, infantrymen of Maj. Gen. D.A.H. Graham's British 50th Division move inland from the beachhead, thereby extending the lodgment area in the region of St. Gabriel between Bayeux and Caen.

forward. The Hampshires were surprised to find that many of the "German" defenders in their pillboxes were unwilling Asiatic conscripts from the southern Soviet republics, put into the front lines by the Germans.

To the east, the Victoria Cross was won by CSM Stanley Hollis of 6th Green Howards. As Hollis's company advanced off the beach at Mont Fleury it passed two German pillboxes which the company commander ordered to be checked. In the words of Hollis's citation, "When they were 20 yards [18m] from the pillbox, a machine gun opened fire from the slit and CSM Hollis instantly rushed

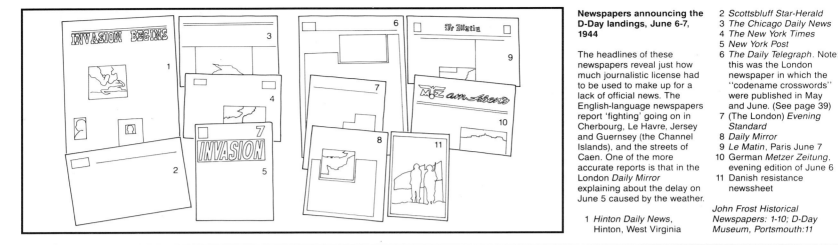

Newspapers announcing the D-Day landings, June 6-7, 1944

The headlines of these newspapers reveal just how much journalistic license had to be used to make up for a lack of official news. The English-language newspapers report 'fighting' going on in Cherbourg, Le Havre, Jersey and Guernsey (the Channel Islands), and the streets of Caen. One of the more accurate reports is that in the London *Daily Mirror* explaining about the delay on June 5 caused by the weather.

1 *Hinton Daily News*, Hinton, West Virginia

2 *Scottsbluff Star-Herald*
3 *The Chicago Daily News*
4 *The New York Times*
5 *New York Post*
6 *The Daily Telegraph*. Note: this was the London newspaper in which the "codename crosswords" were published in May and June. (See page 39)
7 (The London) *Evening Standard*
8 *Daily Mirror*
9 *Le Matin*, Paris June 7
10 German *Metzer Zeitung*, evening edition of June 6
11 Danish resistance newssheet

John Frost Historical Newspapers: 1-10; D-Day Museum, Portsmouth:11

straight at the pillbox, recharged his magazine, threw a grenade in through the door and fired his Sten gun into it, killing two Germans and making the remainder prisoner. He then cleared several Germans from a neighbouring trench." As the company advanced past Crépon later in the day it was fired upon by a field gun and machine guns. Taking cover with his men in a nearby house, Hollis used a PIAT to destroy the gun and pulled back, only to find that two of his men had remained in the house. "In full view of the enemy who were continually firing at him he went forward alone using a Bren gun to distract their attention from the other men," so allowing them to escape. Hollis's

Victoria Cross was the only one won in Normandy on June 6.

While the battle to drive the last of the Germans out of their emplacements continued, the beach was laboriously cleared of mines and obstacles, with much assistance from a Hobart's Funnies. By midday the division was ashore, and ready to move off the beach complete with its remaining brigades, 151st and 56th, while the next division (the famous "Desert Rats" of 7th Armoured Division) prepared to land. Meanwhile, despite losing many of their assault craft on the approach, No. 47 Royal Marine Commando had moved off the beach along a clifftop route to Port-en-Bessin to link up with the Americans,

but had not quite reached the village by nightfall.

Clearing its way through the Atlantic Wall, 50th Division did not quite achieve the objectives set for D-Day, pushing to within a mile (1.6km) of Bayeux while linking up with the Canadians from *Juno* and almost reaching the Caen-Bayeux road. By nightfall the division had three brigades in line and ready to advance next day, while 231st Brigade secured Arromanches for the arrival of *Mulberry*. The division's big anxiety, and part of the reason for the slow advance towards Bayeux, was that its western flank was hanging in the air. There was no sign of the Americans from *Omaha*.

The European newspapers (*9-11*), reveal other points of view in reporting D-Day. The official press in occupied countries, represented by the French paper *Le Matin* (*9*) leads with headlines which can only be described as collaborationist: "France again becomes a battlefield . . . The enemy admits to having lost 25,000 men during the first day . . . By evening the invader has been forced to evacuate several of his bridgeheads." In contrast is the *Free Dane* "Invasion Issue" (*11*): "Joy and expectation all over Denmark. It had happened — the big one, the wonderful . . . So there was joy in our hearts from the early hours of June 6th — and we just could not hide our joy, despite informers and other vermin." The *Metzer Zeitung* is more low key: it says the invasion was long expected. The Atlantic Wall remains unbreakable, despite heavy aerial bombardment.

Juno Beach
H-Hour (delayed): 07:45, 07:55

Like *Gold, Juno* beach was wide enough to land two brigades side by side, Canadian 7th Brigade at Courseulles and 8th Brigade at Bernières. The Canadian landing was deliberately delayed in the plan, to give the rising tide time to cover underwater shoals near the landing area, revealed by air reconnaissance (it was later discovered that many of these "rocks" were floating seaweed). The tide, the rough weather and the high wind delayed the approach of the landing craft still further, and both brigades touched down ten minutes later than planned, the troops at Courseulles at 07:45, and those at Bernières at 07:55, the last of the first wave to land. As at *Gold,* the sea was far too rough to risk launching the DD tanks ahead of the infantry. Most came in by landing craft, but a few were launched from close to the shore, and reached the beach ahead of the infantry at Courseulles as planned. But the rising tide covered more of the beach obstacles, and the current pushed landing craft out of position. "The heavy seas meant that people who should have been in front were behind," remembered one sapper, "and we ourselves were twenty minutes late." The Regina Rifles had to endure 20 minutes on their

Below: British Commando, Special Service and Combined Operations insignia. From top left, 41, 46, 47 and 48 Royal Marine Commandos which made up 4th Special Service Brigade. No. 47 landed on *Sword,* the rest on *Juno.* Insignia of 3, 4, 6 (Army) and 45 (Royal Marine) Commandos, which made up Lovat's 1st Special Service Brigade which landed on *Sword.* Other insignia include the Special Service dagger, and the eagle-anchor-machinegun of Combined Operations. Insignia of other units include Beach Ordnance, Beach Signals and Royal Navy Beach Commando, eight of which were landed on D-Day.
Royal Marines Museum, Portsmouth

Above: An LCA loaded with men of the Royal Winnipeg Rifles approaches *Juno* beach, where the Canadian assault was launched by the Canadian 7th and 8th Brigades. The 9th Brigade arrived in the second wave between the two assault units, and forged toward Caen.

Below: Royal Marines of No. 48 Commando disembark from an LCI (Small) at St. Aubin, near the junction of *Juno* and *Sword* Beaches. Numbering 100 in all, these wooden-hulled craft each had a full-load displacement of 110 tons and carried 102 troops.

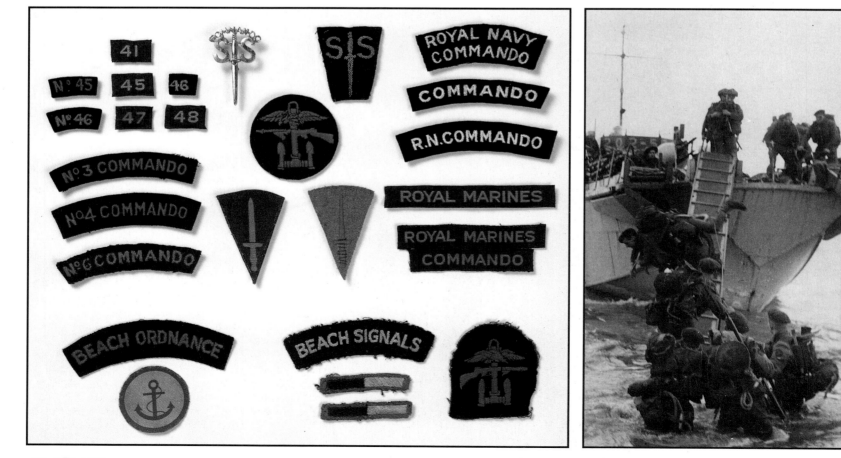

JUNO BEACH
Designated assault sectors:
Mike Green, Mike Red, Nan Green, Nan White, Nan Red
Assault Division:
Canadian 3rd Infantry Division; British I Corps

Task Force J, bearing the Canadians, arrived offshore without incident. Unlike the task forces in the American sector, which disembarked their troops 11 miles (17km) from the beaches, the task forces in the British sector chose a lowering point for the landing craft only seven or eight miles (11 or 12km) offshore. Although the sea conditions were the same as in the American sector, the shorter distance made the journey to the beaches a little easier.

The later H-Hour, however, caused its own problems with the incoming tide. Beach obstacles were already partially submerged when the assault began. The result of this was that demolition teams could not get to work, and so landing craft were forced either to avoid them as best they could or drive forward and hope for the best. Heavy losses resulted; nearly 30 percent of all landing craft employed on *Juno* were either destroyed or damaged.

As on the other beaches that morning, the enfilading fire of the German defenses took the assaulting forces by surprise. Despite thorough reconnaissance it was not realised until D-Day that German gun positions did not point out to sea but instead faced along the line of the coast, with heavy protection on the seaward side.

By mid-morning and after a bitter infantry fight, the town of Bernières was in Canadian hands and the divisional commander Gen. Keller had set up his HQ (see page 108). Meanwhile No. 48 Royal Marine Commando had disembarked and was fighting its way east towards *Sword*.

Progress inland was good. With the prompt arrival of some of its armored units, the division achieved part of its D-Day objective line by getting tanks onto the Caen-Bayeux road. A link-up with the 50th Division from *Gold* was achieved a few miles south of la Rivière. This was in the western part of the landing area.

To the southeast and east, towards Caen and Ouistreham progress was more difficult. Units of the Canadian 9th Brigade began to find resistance stiffening as they neared the area around Carpiquet. The commandos could not make contact with the British 3rd Division from *Sword*, and a gap of two miles (3km) divided the two landing areas. The only major German counterattack on the day was to occur in this area, when the 21st Panzer Division attempted to reach the coast.

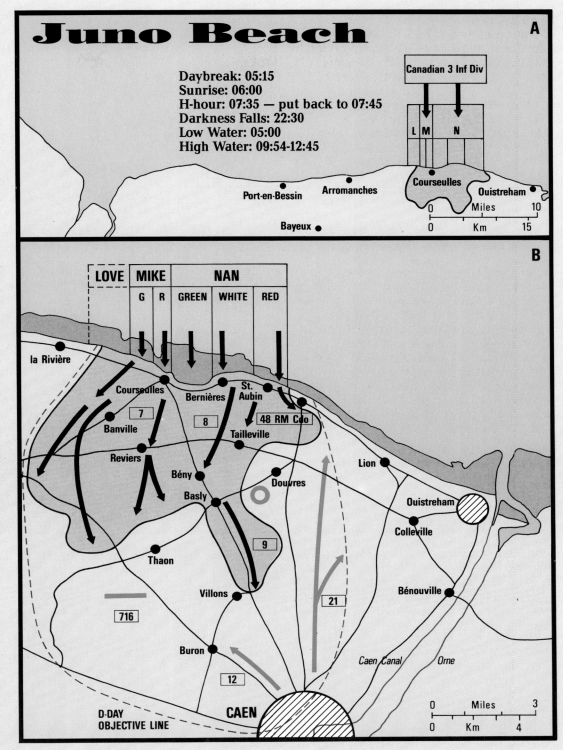

Juno Beach

Daybreak: 05:15
Sunrise: 06:00
H-hour: 07:35 — put back to 07:45
Darkness Falls: 22:30
Low Water: 05:00
High Water: 09:54-12:45

Canadian 3 Inf Div

Port-en-Bessin   Arromanches   Courseulles   Ouistreham
Bayeux

B

LOVE   MIKE   NAN
G   R   GREEN   WHITE   RED

la Rivière
Courseulles   Bernières   St. Aubin
7   Banville   8   48 RM Cdo
Reviers   Tailleville
Bény   Lion
Basly   Douvres   Ouistreham
Colleville
9
Thaon
Bénouville
Villons   21
716
Buron   Caen Canal   Orne
12
D-DAY OBJECTIVE LINE   **CAEN**

Left: Canadian sailors of HMCS *Prince Henry* rescue a British infantryman after his landing craft had been sunk. Allied naval losses offshore were small, but in the beach area the British alone lost 258 landing craft due to mines and other obstacles.

landing beach before the first armor arrived. It was nearly 08:15 before the last troops of the two brigades finally struggled ashore. Just 30 minutes later, No. 48 Royal Marine Commando of 4th Special Service (Commando) Brigade came ashore and moved off eastwards along the coast to link up with the forces from *Sword*.

3rd Canadian Division's objective for D-Day was the Caen-Bayeux road and Carpiquet aerodrome, forming a link between the two British lodgments. As on the other beaches, on *Juno* the Canadians found that the extra firepower from the DD tanks or the Funnies often made all the difference

between overcoming a German strongpoint or being held up. Between the beach obstacles and German fire, mainly from mortars, onto the beach the landing craft had a difficult passage. One Canadian naval officer recalled that he was just disembarking the troops from his landing craft when "a wave lifted it onto an obstruction. The explosion that followed ripped the bottom out of the craft." Despite severe injuries to a boat officer, all the troops got ashore safely.

Bypassing positions that they could not take quickly, the Canadians moved inland. The French Canadian Régiment de la Chaudière of 8th Brigade recorded that "the French were very welcoming and greeted us heartily in the midst of the ruins of their houses." Some Canadians of Polish origin also found that their "German" prisoners were Poles, surprised to hear a familiar language. By mid-afternoon, the 3rd Canadian Division was ashore and its third brigade, 9th Brigade,

Above: Men of the North Nova Scotia Highlanders and Highland Light Infantry of Canada land near Bernières on D-Day. That these men are not in the assault wave is indicated by the leisure in which they are moving, and by impedimenta such as bicycles.

Below: Maj. Gen. R.F.L. Keller (in beret) was commander of the Canadian 3rd Division, and is pictured here with some of the officers of his headquarters group, including Brig. R.A. Wyman (right), at Bernières on _Juno_ Beach, where the Canadian 8th Brigade landed.

Above: Royal Marines of No. 48 Commando make their way inland from St. Aubin-sur-Mer. The brigade landed between *Juno* and *Sword* Beaches, and during the afternoon of June 6 faced a counterattack by the 21st Panzer Division.

Below: The first German prisoners captured by the Canadians on D-Day are guarded on the beachhead by military police and soldiers with fixed bayonets. Ships evacuated Allied wounded also ferried such prisoners of war to incarceration in Britain.

started its advance through the remaining German defenses. To the west, the division made good progress and its leading armor reached almost to the Caen-Bayeux road. But closer to Caen the German resistance intensified. Neither the Canadians, nor the commandos who were held up at Langrune, could break through to close the gap between themselves and the men coming off *Sword* Beach. By evening the Canadian line conformed roughly to that of 50th Division to the

Above: British commandos pass through the small town of la Délivrande on their way towards Caen. This city was to have been captured on D-Day, but the British and Canadians were checked by the steady defense of the German 716th Infantry Division.

west, a few miles short of its objectives, but still in a strong position. But to the east a gap of two miles (3.2km) still separated them from the troops from *Sword*, and the airborne forces beyond.

Sword Beach
H-Hour: 07:25

The landing of 3rd Division at *Sword* and the capture of Caen was the most important event in Montgomery's plan for D-Day. Between the offshore shoals and the estuary at Ouistreham, the beach itself at the little hamlet of la Brèche d'Hermanville was wide enough only for one brigade at a time to come ashore, the first — 8th Brigade — at 07:25 to coincide with the landing at *Gold*. While the four brigades of 3rd Division fought their way inland towards Caen, Lovat's commandos would cross the bridges at Bénouville and reinforce 6th Airborne Division, which continued to receive glider reinforcements throughout the day. Problems of landing and stiff German resistance at *Sword* meant that Lovat arrived a few minutes late, but in good time to help secure the bridges against further German counterattacks.

Above: Typical of the men who faced a long and deep wade to the shore are these infantrymen of the 1st Battalion, Royal Norfolk Regiment, which was part of the 185th Infantry Brigade, the second of the British 3rd Infantry Division's three brigades to land.

Below: Lord Lovat's personal piper, Bill Millin, lands from *LCI(S) 519* on *Queen Red* beach near la Brèche d'Hermanville as part of the 1st Special Service Brigade's operation. Lord Lovat is the single figure on the right of the column wading to the shore.

Above: This photograph, taken at 08:00 from the starboard side of *LCT 854*, reveals the beach obstacles and other hazards faced on *Sword* Beach by the British assault forces, which comprised mainly British 3rd Infantry Division with support from 27th Armoured Brigade. The main assault was flanked on its left and right by Army and Royal Marine Commandos, which were to smash inland to the areas seized by the British 6th Airborne Division and occupy the area east of Caen.

The terrain at la Brèche is explained by its name, which means 'the breach'; a dip in the ground leading from the beach inland to the village of Hermanville. This proved irresistible to Maj. "Banger" King of the 2nd East Yorkshire Regiment, who went in with the first wave reciting "Once more unto the breach!" from Shakespeare's *Henry V*, while nearby a rescue launch played "Roll Out the Barrel" over its loudhailer. The first landings went well, with the first troops of 8th Brigade touching down one minute late, and nearly all the DD tanks and specialist armor, including the leading elements of 27th Armoured Brigade, reaching the beach safely. The strongpoints at la Brèche itself were subdued by 10:00, and while the last of the German guns and machineguns were silenced, and the barbed wire entanglements cleared away, Lovat's commandos (some of them on folding bicycles) pushed inland towards the waiting airborne troops. No. 4 Commando, including Commandant Kieffer's force, moved eastward to secure Ouistreham. Kieffer's men successfully assaulted the sea-front at Ouistreham, known as Riva-Bella, including a German strongpoint at the old casino. "All my fellow commandos," one of Kieffer's men mused, "idealists or madmen, saints or rogues, sailors or daredevils, united by a love of danger, are going back to where we started — France." It was a small but important gesture: Gen. de Gaulle's Fighting French had returned.

The bad weather showed little sign of abating, and as the morning wore on the rising tide reduced the narrow beach to a strip of sand only 10 yards (9m) from the seafront to the water's edge. Engineers and frogmen trying to clear obstacles in the surf found themselves swept out to sea. Although infantry continued to land without much trouble, most of 3rd Division's armor and vehicles

SWORD BEACH
Designated assault sectors:
Queen Green, Queen White, Queen Red
Assault Division:
British 3rd Infantry Division: British I Corps, plus Commandos of 1st Special Service Brigade.

Landing with Lord Lovat's Commandos of 1st Special Service Brigade was war correspondent Doon Campbell of the news agency Reuters. He was one of the first seaborne correspondent's ashore (other correspondents had landed with the airborne forces). He describes the landing in his own words:

"At six minutes past nine of that dull, grey morning of D-Day, June 6, 1944, I landed in Hitler's Europe. It was a wet landing. The ramp thrown down from the landing craft was steep and slippery and I fell chest deep into the sea lapping the mined beaches. Their faces smeared with camouflage grease the commandos charged ahead, eager to join battle . . . My pack, sodden, waterlogged, strapped tight round my shoulders, seemed made for easy drowning . . . Ahead lay the beach, sandy cemetery with unburied new dead and the half dead, missing arms and legs, their blood clotting the sand, scattered about. Behind through fountains of water raised by exploding shells from coastal batteries, little ships were nudging in to the shallows and behind them a vast armada of battleships, cruisers, destroyers and close support vessels put down a paralysing bombardment . . . This was war in its totality — theatrical and terrifying. The greatest combined operation in history was underway. And this time I was not just ringside but on stage; in a devastated corner of France."

Campbell moved off the beach, crossed a road and under heavy fire took cover with the wounded in a ditch 200 yards (180m) farther inland:
"We fought to stay alive in that shallow furrow. We clawed at the soggy soil for depth that at least made us feel more safe from a withering fire of mortars and shells. The moaning minnies [Nebelwerfers] and 88s, most of them falling short or whistling overhead, never let up. Earth spurted in with every near miss and more water seeped through our clothes."
The correspondent then tried to type his first dispatch:
"I got a sheet of paper in and started pecking at the keyboard. But it was hopeless. Every time I tried to type, a mortar exploded a few yards away or hit the lip of the ditch and a shower of dirt clogged the keys. Worried stiff about getting copy back to *Reuters* that the invasion was underway, I tore a page from a school exercise book and scribbled a few lines . . .

'A few minutes ago, just after 9am, I landed in Hitler's Europe. I came ashore with the commandos who are thrusting inland impatient to get to grips with the enemy. On a huge scale the invasion is now well underway. Everywhere thousands of men and hundreds of aircraft and ships — the Channel is chocablock with ships: ships with guns blasting in ear-splitting bombardments, ships bulging with reinforcements edging into the shallows, ships smoking, even a few sinking. Every minute more men and guns, tanks, vehicles and supplies are landing. The dead and the half-dead, blood staining the sand, lie about. First prisoners have been taken — I counted 60 lined up in front of me: young men who look staggered at the weight of Allied shipping. Our planes dominate the skies. For the moment with the wounded I'm staying behind in a ditch where we claw at the soft earth for more cover from German shells and mortars. Moaning minnies sometimes fall too close for comfort'."
Extracts courtesy of Doon Campbell

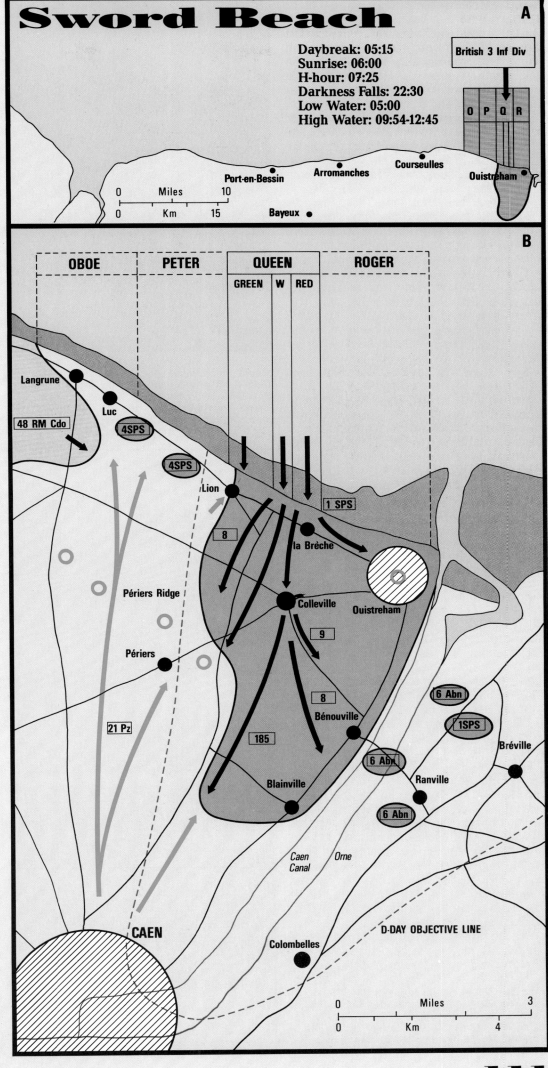

Sword Beach

Daybreak: 05:15
Sunrise: 06:00
H-hour: 07:25
Darkness Falls: 22:30
Low Water: 05:00
High Water: 09:54-12:45

British 3 Inf Div

O P Q R

0 Miles 10
0 Km 15

Port-en-Bessin   Arromanches   Courseulles   Ouistreham
Bayeux

OBOE   PETER   QUEEN   ROGER
GREEN W RED

Langrune
48 RM Cdo
Luc
4SPS
4SPS
Lion
1 SPS
8
la Brèche
Ouistreham
Périers Ridge
Colleville
9
Périers
8
Bénouville
6 Abn
1SPS
185
Bréville
6 Abn
Ranville
Blainville
6 Abn
21 Pz
Caen Canal   Orne
CAEN
D-DAY OBJECTIVE LINE
Colombelles

0 Miles 3
0 Km 4

were packed close together on the beach or waiting offshore to land, and the beach remained under fire. There was, remembered one tank officer, "a terrible jam on the beach where no organisation appeared to be operating and no marked exits were to be seen." With only one road off the beach, vehicles had to land at exactly the right spot.

Advancing only a short distance inland, many of the available tanks of 27th Armoured Brigade were drawn in to help the infantry fight their way past two German strongpoints, codenamed *Morris* and *Hillman* by the British, just beyond Hermanville and Colleville. A further brigade, 185th Brigade, was able to move off the beach soon after 11:00 as the spearhead of 3rd Division's drive on Caen, but only by leaving most of its tanks and heavy weapons behind, to catch up as best they could. By late afternoon the leading troops of 185th Brigade had reached the villages of Beuville and Bieville, only two miles (3km) short of Caen itself. The division's last brigade, 9th Brigade, was still assembling, having disentangled itself from the beaches.

For a moment it seemed that Caen was within the British grasp. But by mid-afternoon the leading units of 185th Brigade started to report German tanks or assault guns emerging northwards from Caen, and German infantry on the Périers ridge north of the city. These were the leading troops of 21st Panzer Division, which the British had expected to find much further south. Without much armor support of their own, the infantry halted to engage the tanks, giving up any further advance.

It was the crisis of D-Day for British Second Army. Having checked the advance, the Germans were ready to launch their big attack to throw the British back into the sea. The two-mile (3km) gap between 3rd Division and 3rd Canadian Division was still not closed, and at 19:00 21st Panzer Division launched a charge of 50 tanks into it, trying to split the British landing in two. But 3rd Division were waiting for the PzKpfw IVs with artillery, fighter-bombers, and another surprise, the "Firefly" Sherman, fitted with a 17-pounder anti-tank gun instead of the smaller 75mm gun of normal Shermans. In exercises back in England, the commander of 27th Armoured Brigade's Staffordshire Yeomanry had analyzed the ground and the German plan. "They will form up their squadrons, give out their orders, then drive straight for their objective," he had predicted. "What they do not know is that I have three troops of Fireflies which I will station on the Hermanville ridge and leave as a backstop." Thirteen German tanks were knocked out for the loss of one British M-10 tank destroyer. It was an important lesson — the British might be slow in the advance, but they were almost unbreakable in defense.

Whether any of the German tanks actually reached the coast at Lion-sur-Mer along with their infantry is debatable. But just as the

Right: The DD-Sherman tanks of the 27th Armoured Brigade were intended to provide the main punch for mobile operations as the British 3rd Infantry Divison advanced inland, but were slowed by the need to support the hard-pressed infantry near the beach.

Above: A crowded scene on the beach near Lion-sur-Mer after the landing of the 4th Special Service Brigade. This is "A" Troop of No. 41 Royal Marine Commando, and the standing figure is Lt. Paddy Stevens. No. 41 was the brigade's left-hand element.

Below: The counterpart of No. 41 Royal Marine Commando at the eastern end of *Sword* Beach was an army unit, No. 4 Commando of the 1st Special Service Brigade. Here men of the commando move inland from Ouistreham toward the areas seized by airborne forces.

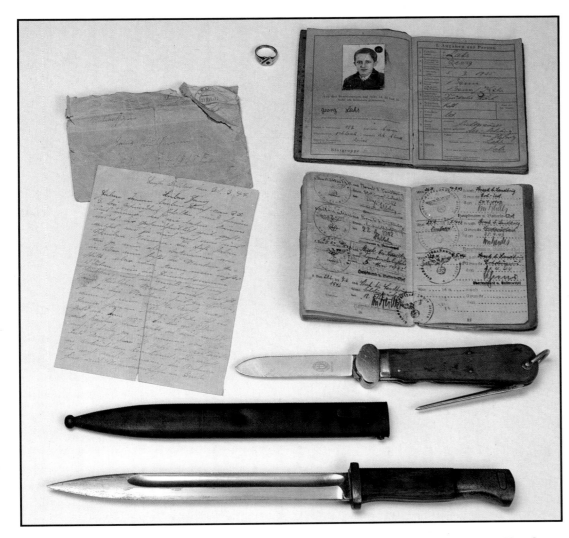

Left: German items picked up on the assault beaches. Top book — a "Wehrpass," issued to 25/5/172/4 Georg Lahs, a gunner from Bonn. Lower book — a "Soldbuch," issued to gunner A/158/II/243 Kanonier Wilhelm Gloystein from Oldenburg: it records details of leave, travel and issue of kit. The latest entry is April 21, 1944. To the left is a soldier's ring found by a member of 47 (RM) Commando at Port-en-Bessin. The family letter was found on *Omaha* and is dated May 31. Below are a gravity knife and rifle bayonet. *Personal letter: D-Day Museum, Portsmouth; remainder: Royal Marines Museum, Portsmouth*

who pulled back towards Caen. The German threat to *Sword*, like the British threat to Caen, had been ended for the day.

Nightfall

At the end of D-Day, the British and Canadians were off all three of their beaches, through the Atlantic Wall, and inland on a front of about twenty miles (32km). The average penetration inland was about six miles (9km), barely half what had been planned. The position was not yet continuous or completely secure, but it was defensible, and the chances of the Germans pushing the invasion back into the sea as Rommel had hoped were virtually gone. In these terms, D-Day had been a major success for British Second Army. The landings had also been much lighter in casualties than had been feared in planning. As far as can be told, of 6,250 men of 6th Airborne Division who had landed, 650 were casualties by the end of the day, while nearly 25,000 men had landed at *Gold*, 21,500 at *Juno* and 29,000 at *Sword*, for the loss of 3,000 casualties evenly spread between the three beaches. Of the German forces opposing them, 716th Static Division had been virtually destroyed and 21st Panzer Division had taken serious losses.

To the east of the Orne, 6th Airborne Division was still intermingled with German troops, including arrivals from 21st Panzer Division. Not only the village of Cabourg, but the coastline almost up to the Orne estuary remained in German hands. The British would not actually reach their extreme eastern D-Day objectives until August. The link-up between 6th Airborne Division and 3rd Division still depended entirely on Pegasus Bridge, but that was strongly held. 3rd Division had failed to take Caen, far less get past it to Falaise, while the gap west of *Sword* remained open. 3rd Canadian Division had failed to reach the Caen-Bayeux road in any strength, but was securely linked up with 50th Division, which in turn had just failed to reach Bayeux. The western flank of the entire lodgment was threatened by the absence of the Americans from *Omaha*. All these were relative problems: what mattered was that the landing had succeeded.

The retreating Germans would abandon Bayeux without fighting next day, the only town in Normandy to be captured without serious fighting. But their hold on Caen meant that the British were restricted to a lodgment area only a few miles deep, from which a breakout either eastwards or southwards would be extremely hard to achieve. The fight for Caen would dictate the shape and nature of the remaining battle for Normandy, distorting Montgomery's "master plan" as it did so.

attack faltered, at 21:00 in the gathering dusk, there came one of those chance events by which battles are sometimes decided. Still trying to press forward, the German tank crews were astonished to see in the sky above them a force of over 250 British gliders, which swept over their heads like giant bats and came to land just behind them, close to Pegasus Bridge. This was the final fly-in of the day by 6th Airlanding Brigade, and by sheer coincidence it had arrived just in time to completely demoralize the German survivors,

Below: Universal Carriers of the 2nd Battalion, King's Scottish Light Infantry, an element of the 3rd Infantry Division's 185th Brigade, sweep through Lion-sur-Mer and in process pass a Churchill AVRE of the 253rd Field Company, Royal Engineers.

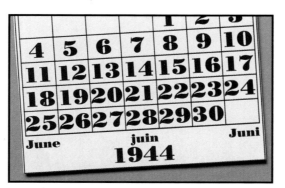

The Buildup

6

Charles Kirkpatrick

Logistics governed all planning for *Overlord* and dominated the selection of landing beaches, initial objectives, and the size and composition of the assault force. Once the Allies were ashore, the first combat task was capturing enough space to permit the installation of depots and a supply system adequate to maintain a constantly growing expeditionary force in France. The beachhead had to be enlarged to give it greater depth, and therefore greater security, to provide the ground to conduct the logistical buildup, and only then to provide the room for maneuver essential to a breakout.

Field Marshal Erwin Rommel, who understood the Allied style of fighting as well as any German officer, privately held out little hope for the eventual outcome of the fighting in Normandy. If, he believed, the Germans allowed the "overwhelming industrial capacity of the United States" to make itself felt on the continent of Europe, then the war was certainly lost. "Tactical skill," he warned, "could only postpone the collapse . . ." The only hope of success was to defeat the landings or to crush the beachhead immediately, a fact that Gen. Montgomery well understood when he correctly predicted that Rommel would use all forces available, from divisions down to individual rifle companies, to make constant assaults against the Allied perimeter.

The lines were clearly drawn. It was crucial for the Germans to repel the invaders as quickly as possible, and at any cost. The Allies had to create a large enough beachhead to permit the rapid buildup of forces that the *Overlord* plan called for, to outpace the countervailing German buildup, and to secure what Eisenhower called the "elbow room" to maneuver for a breakout into the

interior of France. Thus the supreme commander turned his attention from the initial problem of getting the assault forces ashore and focused instead on keeping them ashore and, Gallipoli and the more recent experience at Anzio clearly in his mind, preventing a stalemate from developing.

Three interlocking factors influenced Eisenhower's task. The first was that the logistical plan to support operations on the continent of Europe had to be properly developed and carried out. The second was that the nature of the terrain on which the soldiers had to fight considerably complicated the tactical problem. The third was the ability of the British, Canadian, and American soldiers to develop the beachhead in accordance with the *Overlord* plan.

The Logistical Plan

To support combat operations, *Overlord* planners had arranged the pre-stowage of eight days of supplies in various landing craft, small freighters, and modified Liberty ships. Following a 13-day transition period, the

WE ARE AT WAR! Please Do Not Take Photographs On This Beach All Films Will Be Confiscated

majority of resupply would begin to arrive in Normandy via the larger Liberty ships. By D + 41, planners intended the majority of the logistical requirements to be met by using deep-draft cargo ships berthing at ports the combat forces would by then have captured, supplemented by smaller vessels delivering materiel from England.

To accommodate those ships, planners intended using Cherbourg, Lorient and Brest, minor ports in Brittany and at the mouth of the Seine, and artificial *Mulberry* harbors to be laid off American and British invasion beaches. The *Mulberries* were initially the most important, because the Germans were expected to fight hard for the ports and demolish them if forced to withdraw. *Mulberry* A, for example, planned for *Omaha* beach, was to be emplaced by D + 4 and to handle seven Liberty ships, five large coastal freighters, and seven medium coastal freighters at one time. The open beaches, counting the tonnage of beached landing craft and lightered cargo in addition to the *Mulberry* ports, were expected to handle almost 15,000 long tons (1 long ton = 2,240lb, 1,016kg) of cargo each per day by D + 10, rising to almost 46,000 long tons per day by D + 90.

Such large trans-shipments of war materiel demanded careful beach organization, a task assigned to several special engineer brigades. Planners had learned through the painful experience of previous amphibious operations that specially trained troops had to be on hand to clear minefields and obstacles from the beaches and beach exits, manage the landing operations of succeeding waves of troops and the delivery of supplies, and to create and operate depots within the beachhead. Traffic control, both afloat and ashore, loomed as an important challenge, as did the requirement to maintain local security after the assault troops moved inland. To accomplish all these tasks, the engineer special brigades were organized not only with engineering units to emplace, maintain, and operate the artificial harbors and pierheads, but also with transportation, port and amphibian truck companies, quartermaster service and railhead companies, and ordnance, chemical, medical, military police and signal units.

While the beaches would be the principal and initially most important focus of the lines of communications, major combat operations could be contemplated only if the Allies had the use of regular ports. The planners expected to bring a few of the smaller ports into operation quickly, Cherbourg and other of the smaller ports by D+30, and the major ports of Lorient and Brest a month after that. Looking at the situation realistically, no one expected that ports would be ready to use immediately; some reconstruction to repair war damage or intentional demolition would be necessary. For that purpose, engineer and transportation troops were detailed to bring the ports into usable condition by D+90, when deep water facilities were to take the burden of all supply operations.

The scale of the logistical requirements was imposing. In the simplest terms, an infantry division in combat required roughly 700 tons of supplies per day. Projections for early September called for 37 divisions to be ashore, consuming 26,000 tons of supplies each day. That cumulative total of 780,000 tons per month defined a hand-to-mouth existence for the armies. Before they could seriously consider extended offensive combat, reserves, particularly of ammunition and fuel had to be built up, and provision had to be made to replace combat losses in tanks and other major pieces of equipment. Logistics, as Gen. Bradley said, was "the dullest subject in the world," but obviously the "lifeblood of the Allied armies in France."

Acknowledging the many practical difficulties, Prime Minister Churchill told Eisenhower that "if by the coming winter you have established yourself with your 36 Allied divisions firmly on the Continent, and have the Cherbourg and Brittany Peninsulas in your grasp, I will proclaim this operation to the world as one of the most successful of the war." Eisenhower, more confident, predicted that the Allies would stand on the borders of Germany by the coming winter. Everything depended, however, on the speed and success of the buildup in Normandy. In June and July, the race was on to see whether the defenders or the attackers could reinforce the battle front faster.

As events unfolded, developments on the battlefield quickly reduced the carefully phrased logistical plans to chaos. Neither the British nor the Americans captured ports on schedule, and German demolition work, especially in Cherbourg, was much more

Above: The "workhorse" of amphibious operations, the DUKW was a 2½ ton amphibious truck first introduced in 1942. This vehicle has the markings of 101 Co. (Amphibian) RASC, part of British 3rd Division. *D-Day Museum, Portsmouth*

Below: Although designed for the assault landing of tanks, the LST was a remarkably versatile type, and ships of this type shuttled back and forward between Normandy and England with vehicles, reinforcements and supplies for the fighting men.

complete than anyone thought probable. That port did not become operational until July 16, and then handled only 2,000 tons of supplies per day. It remained the most important port until well into August, by which time it could handle around 12,000 tons a day. Other ports, such as Le Havre and Rouen, unloaded substantially less. The ports of Lorient and Brest never became available, and the tenacity with which the German garrisons defended them right to the end of the war gave Gen. Bradley occasion to wonder how much more stubbornly the German soldier would fight when defending his own

land. Thus the logistical plan, dependent on good ports, began to unravel and improvisation became increasingly important.

It was therefore fortunate that the special engineer brigades worked with great efficiency and developed the landing beaches into something resembling major ports. Again, the examples of the American beaches are typical. By the end of the second week after the assault (Sunday, June 18), the engineers had cleared the beaches of almost all wrecked landing craft and were well on their way to clearing the minefields behind the sea walls. They pushed additional roads inland to

support the increasing number of trucks that were being landed. Trucks, both regular and amphibious, were the key factor that allowed the beach depots of supplies to be built up and moved forward. Toward the end of June, the beaches were handling nearly 100 percent of their planned tonnages each day, in addition to the continued landings of combat troops and evacuation of casualties.

The complicating factor was a storm that arose in the English Channel on June 19 and lasted through June 22. Although not a particularly powerful gale by Channel standards, it was enough to wreck *Mulberry* A

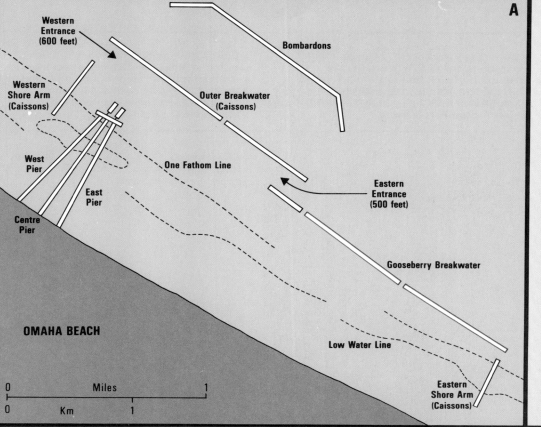

THE LAYOUT OF *MULBERRY* A

This was the organization of *Mulberry* A as envisioned in the pre-invasion plans. The harbor was situated off *Omaha* Beach opposite the village of St. Laurent. Like *Mulberry* B its elements were towed to France and assembled under the auspices of Operation *Neptune*, and was commanded by Rear-Adm. W.G. Tennant RN; though the harbor was built and operated in the American sector by the US Navy and the US Army.

By D+10 (June 16), some of the piers, caissons and a *Gooseberry* breakwater were in position, and the harbor unloaded its first LST on June 17. Unfortunately before it was fully assembled the harbor's working life was dramatically cut short. On June 19, a storm blew up which completely wrecked the harbor. Winds blowing from the northeast at up to force 7 forced seas through the breakwaters which did catastrophic damage to the fabric of the harbor and the ships inside. When the storm abated on June 22, caissons and piers were smashed, blockships were wrenched out of position, and ships, landing craft and barges were piled up on the shore. Damage to the harbor was so great that the decision was made not to repair it. Instead men and materiel were delivered directly over the beach, and attempts were made to utilize what unloading capacity was to be had from the smaller Normandy harbors such as Port-en-Bessin and Courseulles. On June 27, with the major port of Cherbourg in Allied hands, the decision was taken to abandon *Mulberry* A altogether. Any elements of the harbor still usable were transfered to *Mulberry* B.

THE LAYOUT OF *MULBERRY* B

This was how the assembled elements of *Mulberry* B were to look according to *Neptune* planners. The harbor was situated in the British *Gold* Beach area off the town of Arromanches, three miles (4.8km) to the west of assault areas *Jig* and *King*. It was constructed and operated by the Royal Navy and British Army. Assembly of the harbor proceeded at a slower rate than that of *Mulberry* A. This, and the fact that it was situated in more sheltered water than the American harbor, prevented it from receiving as much damage when the storm struck on the 19th. Work on its completion, however, was seriously delayed by severity of the storm. Unloading did not begin again until June 29, and the final pier did not come into operation until July 29. Despite this late start, over 250,000 men were landed through the harbor together with 40,000 vehicles, and up to 11,000 tons of stores a day. This success led to an extension of the harbor's working life and a strengthening of its sea defenses in August.

The *Mulberry* stayed in operation until November 19, 1944 when it was officially closed and its piers and roadways disassembled. The *Phoenix* caissons remained in place, however, and over half a century later many could still be seen off the coast at Arromanches — a remarkable achievement for a prefabricated harbor originally designed to last only 90 days.

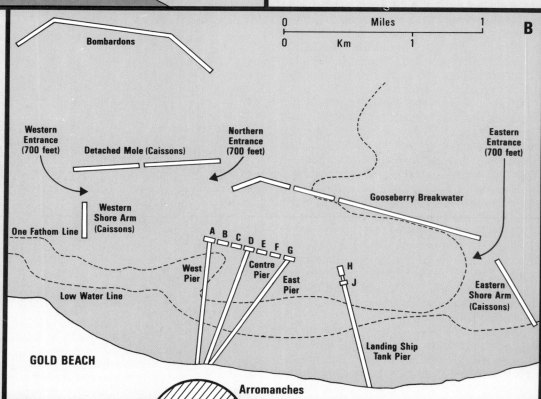

and beach as many as 800 ships, wrecking around 300. The immediate result was that, while roughly 80 percent of the soldiers landed according to schedule, the cumulative volume of supply at D + 15 only reached 61 percent of that which was planned. To compensate, the Allies resorted to an extremely inefficient way of delivering critical supplies, but the only one available under the circumstances. For three days, the air forces used their C-47 transports to deliver 500 tons of artillery ammunition each day to Bradley's troops, and particularly to his VII Corps, then poised for the final assault on Cherbourg.

Right: One of the major elements in the Allied success in *Overlord* was *Pluto* (Pipe Line Under The Ocean). After the pipe had been unrolled from ''bobbins'' towed across the Channel and allowed to sink to the bottom, fuel was pumped to France from England.

Left: Another key element in the Allied success was the pair of *Mulberry* floating harbors assembled from prefabricated sections. This is part of *Mulberry* B at Arromanches which was severely damaged in the violent storm of June 19-22.

Elsewhere on the American front, Bradley drastically reduced ammunition expenditure, a step that virtually halted forward momentum in V Corps. The problem was so severe that a number of coastal freighters loaded with ammunition were beached and had holes cut in their sides to allow unloading. In the long run, the loss of *Mulberry* A and disappointments with activating captured French ports affected Allied operations all the way to the Siegfried Line. In the short term, tactical problems that kept the forces close to the beaches tended to ameliorate shortcomings of the logistics system.

Below: The storm of June 19-22 also played havoc with Allied shipping, as this photograph of wrecks off *Omaha* testifies. The vessel in the background is *LSK 7*, a conversion outfitted with kitchens and food supplies for the creation of hot meals on a large-scale.

The Normandy Battlefield

Probably no military operation had ever been planned more thoroughly, or with more thought given to the possible contingencies that might arise, than the landings on the Normandy beaches. The great oversight, as almost every senior commander has subsequently confessed in his memoirs, was that no-one gave adequate thought to the problem of continuing operations once the beaches were secure, and particularly to the difficulties of fighting in the Norman terrain.

The Allies chose the battlefield chiefly on the basis of beach requirements; the choice entailed inevitable compromises, and planners perforce had to accept as given the terrain that lay behind the beaches. The Caen-Falaise plain, which opened before British Second Army, was open, rolling farm and pasture land that was both dry and firm. It was ideal for armored operations. The drawback was that, equally aware of that fact, the Germans did their best to deny it to the Allies. To fend off attacks by the armored divisions the British landed on the first day, the Germans drew toward Caen all the soldiers that could be spared elsewhere in Brittany, divisions from the south of France, and units from the Netherlands. Caen was the essential connecting link between German forces in Normandy and the Fifteenth Army in the Pas de Calais. To maintain connection between the two armies, Caen had to be held. If that connection were sundered, the German Seventh and Fifteenth Armies could operate together only if they made a long withdrawal from the coast to reestablish contact. Thus the German command concentrated the strongest divisions, and the bulk of their available armor, 7½ divisions by the end of June, at Caen and prepared for a hard fight to hold that critical city. In contrast to the 150 heavy tanks (Tigers and King Tigers) and 250 medium tanks confronting the British, the Germans sent the equivalent of only a half division of tanks — 50 medium tanks and 26 Panthers — to defend against American operations in the V and VII Corps sectors.

Below: After a hard struggle, Tilly-sur-Seulles was finally captured on June 19. The town was badly damaged by shellfire, and the British found, in addition to many wrecked German tanks and other vehicles, mined streets that had to be cleared with extreme caution.

Above: British infantrymen rush forward along a country lane near le Tourneur. The nature of the countryside, with roads sunk deep between banks surmounted by thick hedgerows, presented the attackers with many problems and made momentum difficult.

Below: Conversely, the bocage country was ideally suited to the Germans' defensive needs, and virtually any hedgerow could be turned into a strongpoint for weapons such as this 75-mm anti-tank gun, which could be concealed to deliver short-range fire.

Left: The bocage continued deep into the Normandy countryside, and here a group of British infantrymen shelter from German mortar fire on August 4 as armored elements of the British Second Army probe toward Ondefontaine in the region south of Caumont.

They could well afford to do so, for when the Americans moved off the beaches, they advanced on to ground that was ideal for a defending force weak in mobility and armor. Passing from the Caen-Falaise plain on the Allied left flank the character of the ground rapidly changed the further one moved to the west. Between the Orne and Vire rivers was a broad mass of broken terrain, the small hills, valleys, and low ridges gradually rising in elevation to the south. Further to the west, at the base of the Cotentin Peninsula, the land was low-lying and very marshy, frequently crossed by slow-moving streams and drainage ditches. Compounding the problem, the Germans had flooded broad stretches of that low country. Approaches to the interior were accordingly limited, with vehicular traffic constricted to a few easily-defended causeways and embanked roads that crossed the flooded areas.

The use to which French farmers had traditionally put the land increased American difficulties. The entire area into which the First Army was attacking was known as the bocage, a general term given to the Norman hedgerow country. Hedgerows were fences, usually half earthen and half hedge, that subdivided the land into individual fields. Those parapets around each plot of land varied from one to four or more feet (.3-1.2m) in thickness and might be anything from 3-12 feet (.9-3.6m) high. On top of the parapets grew characteristically a compacted mass of thorn, brambles, trees, and vines that could increase the height of the barrier to 15 feet (4.5m) or more. The irregularly and unpredictably shaped fields, rarely more than 200 yards (180m) wide and 400 yards (360m)

Below: One of the methods developed by the Americans of breaking through the bocage hedges was to weld one or two large metal spikes on to the front of tanks. These would punch holes into the hedgerow into which would be placed explosive charges.

Above: The Germans proved themselves to be remarkably adept at close-quarter operations in the close country of Normandy. This as an MG42 machine gun position cunningly worked into the natural cover provided by one of the area's myriad hedgerows.

Below: An M4 Sherman medium tank, probably of the 747th Tank Battalion, smashes through a typical hedgerow with the aid of its special nose-mounted steel attachment. The invention of this simple device transformed Allied capabilities in the bocage.

British, American and German Mortars, Ammunition and Equipment

1 Tube of British 3-inch mortar
2 Mortar bipod with elevating and traversing screw
3 Mortar base plate
4 Leather tube cover
5 Leather mortar sight case
6 Projectiles for 3-inch mortar. Note the fuze cap has been removed on the right-hand projectile
7 Metal box for 3-inch mortar ammunition
8 Metal box for mortar projectile fuzes
9 US 60mm M2 mortar on M2 bipod and baseplate

10 Sight, collimator M4
11 One 60mm HE round with fiber storage tube
12 German 8cm Granatenwerfer 34 (81mm mortar)
13 Wicker carrying case for three 8cm mortar rounds
14 Two 8cm mortar rounds in metal three-round carrying box
15 Wooden carrying box for 8cm mortar rounds
16 German mortar sight and protective metal box
17 German 70cm coincidence range finder (Entfernungsmesser)
18 Metal cleaning rod for Granatenwerfer 34

Memorial Museum, Bayeux

long, abutted each other and were linked by trails that were often sunken lanes that ran among them and gave access to openings through the hedges to allow farm traffic to enter the fields.

Such terrain gave the defenders enormous tactical advantages. Each field was, in effect, a small earthen fort, and a connected series of them constituted a fieldwork that could easily be organized for defense in depth. It was a simple matter to position anti-tank guns to cover the approaches to the fields, as American armor quickly found out to its cost. Driving tanks over the hedgerows was no better solution, however, for the tank then exposed its relatively unprotected belly as its front climbed the parapet. Dense vegetation obscured observation and fields of fire and made artillery difficult to employ with any effectiveness. The effects of artillery were also diminished by the many and very effective earthen blast walls that gave protection from individual shell bursts.

To fight in the hedgerows was to make a series of deliberate attacks on a well-prepared defensive position that, once taken, was merely the prelude to yet another well-prepared defensive position. American infantrymen learned with dismay that the bocage, to which they usually referred simply as "this goddam country," was almost 50 miles (80km) in depth.

Because the hedgerow country severely restricted maneuver, it took away the chief advantage of American tactical organization — mobility. Combat in such terrain assumed many of the aspects of a bar-room brawl. The only advantage was that, when American tanks encountered German tanks, the conditions were more nearly even, for the short combat distances of 150 to 400 yards (135-360m) neutralized the great German advantage of being able to kill at ranges out to 2,000 yards (1,800m) and put the more maneuverable Sherman within a range at which even its weaker 75mm gun could be effective. Finally, Americans found a solution to the mobility problem. Curtis G. Cullin, Jr.,

Inset photograph: a British 4.5-in mortar being fired in a Normandy orchard; about D + 8. The mortar became one of the most important and effective infantry support weapons in Normandy, where the dense cover of the bocage gave these light, portable quick-firing weapons an edge, both in attack and defense. The Germans, with a lack of conventional field artillery, relied on them a great deal. A German infantry division, for example, would have up to 60 8cm mortars and 20 120mm mortars. By the end of July, some estimates had German mortars causing up to 70 percent of British infantry casualties.

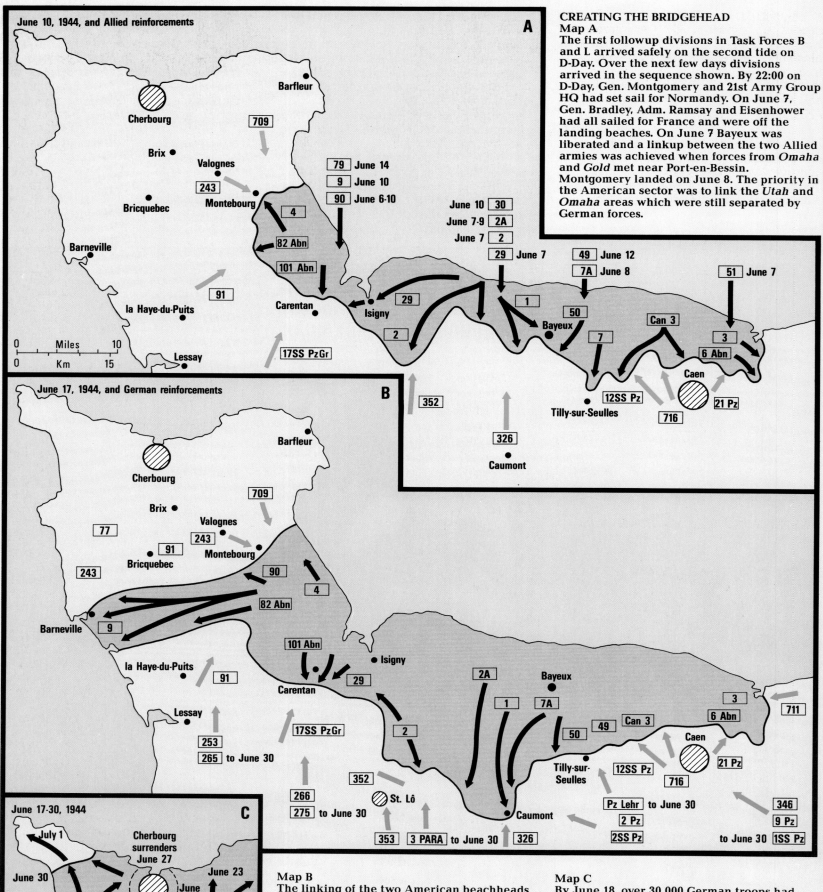

A

June 10, 1944, and Allied reinforcements

Barfleur

Cherbourg

709

Brix •

Valognes

79 June 14

243

9 June 10

Bricquebec •

Montebourg

90 June 6-10

4

June 10 30

Barneville

82 Abn

June 7-9 2A

101 Abn

June 7 2

29 June 7

49 June 12

91

7A June 8

51 June 7

la Haye-du-Puits •

Carentan

29

1

50

Can 3

3

Miles 10

Isigny

2

Bayeux

7

6 Abn

Km 15

Lessay •

17SS PzGr

12SS Pz

Caen

Tilly-sur-Seulles

716

21 Pz

B

June 17, 1944, and German reinforcements

352

326

Barfleur

Caumont

Cherbourg

709

Brix •

77

Valognes

243

91

243

Bricquebec •

Montebourg

90

4

82 Abn

Barneville

9

101 Abn

la Haye-du-Puits •

Isigny

29

2A

Bayeux

91

Carentan

1

7A

3

Lessay •

29

6 Abn

711

253

17SS PzGr

2

50

49

Can 3

265 to June 30

352

Tilly-sur-
Seulles

12SS Pz

Caen

21 Pz

266

St. Lô

716

346

275 to June 30

Pz Lehr to June 30

9 Pz

353

3 PARA to June 30

326

Caumont

2 Pz

2SS Pz

to June 30 1SS Pz

C

June 17-30, 1944

July 1

Cherbourg
surrenders
June 27

June 30

June 23

June 22

4

June 30

9

Brix •

Valognes

79

Bricquebec •

June 17

Barneville

CREATING THE BRIDGEHEAD
Map A
The first followup divisions in Task Forces B and L arrived safely on the second tide on D-Day. Over the next few days divisions arrived in the sequence shown. By 22:00 on D-Day, Gen. Montgomery and 21st Army Group HQ had set sail for Normandy. On June 7, Gen. Bradley, Adm. Ramsay and Eisenhower had all sailed for France and were off the landing beaches. On June 7 Bayeux was liberated and a linkup between the two Allied armies was achieved when forces from *Omaha* and *Gold* met near Port-en-Bessin. Montgomery landed on June 8. The priority in the American sector was to link the *Utah* and *Omaha* areas which were still separated by German forces.

Map B
The linking of the two American beachheads was not achieved until June 12 when the 101st Airborne took Carentan, supported by the 29th Infantry's attack on Isigny. By June 15 the US VII Corps had begun to attack west and north to cut off the Cotentin Peninsula and the port of Cherbourg. Crossing the Douve River, the advance was led by the 9th Infantry Division.

Progress was swift, and the peninsula was cut on June 18. To the east around Caen, the first British offensive to take the city, Operation *Perch*, began on June 10, but met strong resistance from Panzer Lehr and the 12th SS Panzer "Hitler Jugend."

Map C
By June 18, over 30,000 German troops had been trapped in the Cotentin Peninsula. They began an ordered withdrawal towards Cherbourg. Facing them were the American 9th, 90th, 79th and 4th Divisions. The southern part of the offensive line was secured by the 82nd Airborne. On June 22 at 14:00, after air bombardment, the final attack on the Cherbourg area began. By the 23rd, the German defensive line had been breached, mainly by the 9th Division's drive from the west. On the 24th, American troops attacked the city itself. The Germans retreated into fortified areas; the last of which surrendered on July 1.

a sergeant in the 102nd Cavalry Reconnaissance Squadron, welded steel scrap to the front of a tank to form a pair of scythe-like blades. Using them, the tank rammed itself into the hedgerow and then drove through the wall by main force, carrying a bit of earth and vegetation with it as camouflage and entering the field with its guns firing. Maj. Gen. Walter M. Robertson, commanding 2nd Infantry Division, showed the improvisation to Gen. Bradley, who ordered as many tanks converted as possible. Using such expedients, but also suffering many casualties, the American attack slowly gained momentum.

In the planning for *Overlord*, some staff officers believed that the bocage would give the Allies ability to hold on to their beachhead against heavy German counterattacks while the British advanced with their armor through Caen, outflanking the difficult country. Eisenhower, Bradley, and Montgomery, deeply concerned with the problems of putting a powerful enough force ashore at Normandy, gave the bocage little thought. But it turned out that the pre-invasion concerns of some senior British officers about the defensive utility of the Norman countryside were well founded. Field Marshal Sir Alan Brooke, Chief of the Imperial General Staff, and

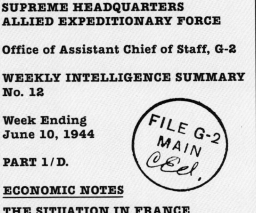

SUPREME HEADQUARTERS ALLIED EXPEDITIONARY FORCE

Office of Assistant Chief of Staff, G-2

WEEKLY INTELLIGENCE SUMMARY No. 12

Week Ending June 10, 1944

PART 1/D.

FILE G-2 MAIN O.Bel.

ECONOMIC NOTES

THE SITUATION IN FRANCE

It is too early to assess any economic measures taken by the enemy and the French authorities as a result of the Allied landing, or to know whether their plans for rounding up the male population have been successfully put into effect.

The Germans have taken strict emergency measures in "certain departments" — presumably in the zone of operations — aiming at the total immobilization of the French population. These include a curfew, a ban on the use of vehicles and cycles, the closing of restaurants and places of entertainment, and a ban on the sale of alcohol. No evacuation may take place except on the order of the military authorities. In the zone of actual operations the civilian population are also forbidden to be out of doors during the day.

The Germans announce that these measures will not apply to PARIS if the population remains calm.

Courtesy of the Dwight D. Eisenhower Library

Lt. Gen. Frederick E. Morgan, as COSSAC one of the chief British *Overlord* planners, had both warned of serious difficulties to be anticipated in the hedgerows.

Unfortunately for Eisenhower, the Allied attack appeared headed for stalemate not just in the bocage, but also in the more favorable terrain around Caen. By the end of July, around D + 50, his troops stood on ground they were supposed to have captured by D + 5. These difficulties had not been apparent on June 6-7. After the euphoria of the successful landings, the hard fighting and slow progress behind the beaches came as a shock that could not be explained entirely by the stiffness of the German resistance and the difficulty of the terrain.

The Military Situation
As night fell on June 6, Eisenhower had reason to feel cautious satisfaction with the progress that had been made. British, Canadian, and American assault troops were established all along the 61-mile (97km) stretch of coast, and the additional men and supplies brought by succeeding waves of landing craft made the lodgment ever more secure. From the west, where US VII Corps had easily overcome German resistance and stood six miles (9.6km) inland, to the east, at the mouth of the River Orne, where the British I and XXX Corps also stood well inland in the approaches to Caen, the beachhead was firmly held. Even in the middle, where the most heavily fought actions occurred, US V Corps had finally cracked the German defenses and moved to the bluffs above bloody *Omaha* Beach.

Beyond the obvious need to supply the combat forces, the immediate object of the combat power that the logistical buildup could generate was twofold. First, Eisenhower wanted to base a large number of fighter-bombers in Normandy to provide quick, responsive, overwhelming tactical air support for the armies. Second, he wanted to develop operations into areas in which the Allies' great tank strength could be used to advantage. For both of those needs, the land to the south and southwest of Caen was

Above: British officers and other ranks tour the medieval streets in the center of Bayeux after the town's liberation. Bayeux became the main supply and medical center for the British Second Army. Its capture allowed the consolidation of a single lodgment area.

essential, and captured the attention of armor commanders, logisticians, and airmen. The rolling, open ground there was ideal tank country that offered a direct route to the Seine and Paris. Moreover, the open fields offered adequate space to build the 27 airfields needed to support the 62 squadrons tabbed for early deployment to the continent. Then too, Caen had a small but important port facility that was necessary to sustaining an adequate rate of supply to the armies ashore.

Therefore the plan called for the British Second Army to capture the wide plains situated south of Caen; for the American V Corps to move inland abreast of the British; and for the American VII Corps to cut off the Cotentin Peninsula and seize the port of Cherbourg as quickly as possible, thereby easing the resupply problems. Intelligence estimates predicted the heaviest fighting around Caen, adjacent to large German forces positioned in the vicinity of the Pas de Calais. Eisenhower expected the Germans to maneuver those divisions to contain the Allied landings. Operating with speed and surprise, however, Caen and Cherbourg might be captured quickly, satisfying conditions for wider operations on the continent.

The divisions ashore on D-Day were the point of a powerful Allied wedge poised in England to exploit the landings, and the Allies enjoyed a considerable advantage over the German defenders. The most important fact was that the core of the German Army was deployed against the Soviets, and that the German high command had, for a long time, systematically looted divisions posted to occupy France for their best and youngest manpower and most modern equipment. Fighter squadrons of the Luftwaffe deployed in France had been recalled to the desperate air defense battles over the Reich, replacing units consumed in the steady Allied bomber offensive, or those redeployed to the Eastern

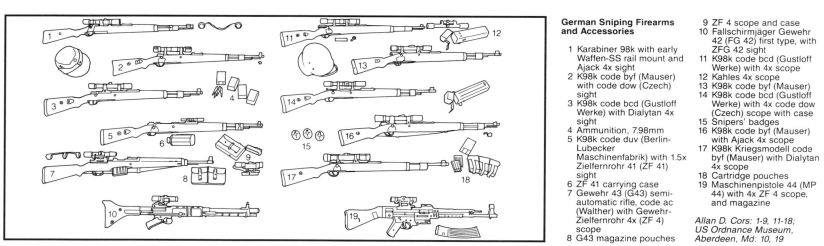

German Sniping Firearms and Accessories

1 Karabiner 98k with early Waffen-SS rail mount and Ajack 4x sight
2 K98k code byf (Mauser) with code dow (Czech) sight
3 K98k code bcd (Gustloff Werke) with Dialytan 4x sight
4 Ammunition, 7.98mm
5 K98k code duv (Berlin-Lubecker Maschinenfabrik) with 1.5x Zielfernrohr 41 (ZF 41) sight
6 ZF 41 carrying case
7 Gewehr 43 (G43) semi-automatic rifle, code ac (Walther) with Gewehr-Zielfernrohr 4x (ZF 4) scope
8 G43 magazine pouches
9 ZF 4 scope and case
10 Fallschirmjäger Gewehr 42 (FG 42) first type, with ZFG 42 sight
11 K98k code bcd (Gustloff Werke) with 4x scope
12 Kahles 4x scope
13 K98k code byf (Mauser)
14 K98k code bcd (Gustloff Werke) with 4x code dow (Czech) scope with case
15 Snipers' badges
16 K98k code byf (Mauser) with Ajack 4x scope
17 K98k Kriegsmodell code byf (Mauser) with Dialytan 4x scope
18 Cartridge pouches
19 Maschinenpistole 44 (MP 44) with 4x ZF 4 scope, and magazine

Allan D. Cors: 1-9, 11-18; US Ordnance Museum, Aberdeen, Md: 10, 19

The Karabiner 98k (1) has a solid walnut stock, and muzzle cover in place. It has a short rail variant mount for the sight. The K98k (11) has a long side rail mount for its scope, code duv, and long safety. Note the sheet metal rail cover and windage wrench. The sniper's badges (Scharfschutzenabzeichen) (15) were instituted on August 20, 1944. They are from left to right, the 3rd, 2nd and 1st Class badges, indicating 20, 40 and 60 confirmed kills. They were awarded to all services. These badges were worn on the right forearm of the tunic. The K98k Kriegsmodell (17) has its scope on a high turret mount with short milled safety. The Maschinenpistole 44 (MP 44) is shown with its 35 round magazine unclipped. Though renowned for being the world's first assault rifle, this weapon was totally unsuitable for sniping operations.

Front. The number of German divisions in the west, apparently greater than that which the Allies could muster, was deceptive because those divisions were generally not at full strength, were manned in some cases by Russians or other volunteer formations, and were equipped with a hodge-podge of obsolete, obsolescent, and foreign weaponry. The task, to cite only one example, of supplying ammunition to more than 30 different types of artillery was very nearly insurmountable.

Along the coast, the German divisions defending the beaches in the Seventh Army sector occupied frontages of approximately 50 miles (80km) each, making the defensive "crust" fairly thin indeed. The first-rate divisions, including the armored divisions on which Rommel and von Rundstedt counted to smash an invasion attempt, were concentrated largely in Fifteenth Army or in the high command reserve, well back from the coast. The "Transportation Plan," the systematic Allied bombing campaign that had largely destroyed the French rail network and cut both rail and roadway bridges into Normandy, effectively isolated the German defenders both from speedy reinforcement and from adequate resupply. From the beginning of the battle, it was clear that the Germans would have to make do with what was on hand on June 6. Allied air supremacy

made German maneuver behind the battlefield virtually impossible in daylight and destroyed many valuable tanks, assault guns, and artillery pieces committed to the counterattack, as well as delaying German concentration of forces. German war diaries reported that British and American fighter-bombers "strangled" every attempt at tactical maneuver. Largely because of the Allied use of air power, Eisenhower was already winning the race to reinforce the beachhead.

Allied assault troops also benefited from the concentrated firepower of an enormous battle fleet, the guns of which could range far inland to overcome the smallest resistance to the advance of Bradley's and Montgomery's troops. German accounts of the battle speak of the paralyzing effect of overwhelming bombardments that shattered the offensive spirit of the infantry and halted almost every attempted counterattack, notably that of the 12th SS Panzer Division against the British on June 7. Naval artillery and air power together achieved the crucial effect of preventing the Germans from using their armored and mechanized units in large-scale and coordinated attacks on the perimeter of the beachhead. Small-scale attacks, even where they achieved a measure of success, could always be dealt with. Compounding the German dilemma was the accident that the invasion came when many commanders were away from their headquarters at a war game, and that confusion ruled in the critical first hours of the battle.

Such circumstances augured well for success, and Eisenhower had no doubts that fairly quickly his troops would secure the several essential and minimum objectives for the Normandy landings to succeed. Beyond that, he entertained hopes that Allied military operations could attain what he called "reasonable expectations" of success beyond the scope of the plan. Finally, there lay the "realm of hope," of which he was optimistically thinking when he described future operations to Mr. Churchill. At first, the supreme commander's thinking was entirely too optimistic, and it appeared that even the minimum objectives set for *Overlord*'s opening days would not be met.

This first became apparent on *Omaha* Beach, where Maj. Gen. Leonard T. Gerow's US V Corps met stiffer resistance than expected, where the majority of the DD tanks were lost, and where soldiers struggled through the high surf encumbered by individual equipment loads that exceeded 60 lb (27kg) for a rifleman. Despite having assigned a regiment of the experienced 1st Infantry Division to the *Omaha* assault, Gen. Bradley found that soldiers were stunned by the withering defensive fire and halted at the tide line. Finally, heroic leaders led the drive to the bluffs above the beach, but for some hours Bradley worried that he would have to evacuate his troops from *Omaha*. American VII Corps, far more successful on June 6 and driven by the dynamic Maj. Gen. J. Lawton Collins, made more impressive gains. In the event, that corps took Cherbourg on D + 20, rather than on D + 8 as planned, and the Germans managed a systematic destruction of the port that kept it out of action for a considerable time.

Eisenhower's greatest disappointment however, was at Caen, which Montgomery had intended to capture on June 6 as a prelude to pushing his tanks as far inland as Falaise. The Germans had repulsed what could only be described as a feeble attempt to take Caen on June 6, and likewise halted all movement toward the town on the next day. Throughout the remainder of the month of June, the Germans continued to hold the British and Canadian forces at bay, and when the Allies finally captured portions of Caen by July 10, the choice airfield sites were still out of reach. In the end, the British did not break out of Caen until after the American breakthrough at St. Lô on July 19, and the Allies never realized the potential advantage of an early armored attack in the direction of the Seine, outflanking the ideal defensive terrain of the bocage.

The conspicuous lack of progress all along the landing front, particularly in view of the truly enormous advantages the Allies enjoyed over the Germans, can be attributed only partially to difficulties imposed by terrain, weather, and unexpected delays in developing the logistical base. It was unfortunately also true that the Allied armies were neither as aggressive nor as capable as they might have been.

Since the opening of the North African campaign, senior British officers had privately derided the fighting quality of American soldiers and the generalship of their commanders. Over the intervening 18 months, Americans who had indeed shown all of the characteristics of untried troops had become more battle-ready and at least the combat equals of any soldier in the alliance. Still, even American commanders acknowledged a lack

Below: Insignia of American units. Top: 12th Army Group. Second row, from left: 1st; 3rd Army; ETO Advance Base. Third row: V; VII; XII; XV; XIX; XX Corps. Third row: 1st; 2nd; 4th; 5th; 8th; 9th; 28th Divisions. Fourth row: 29th; 30th; 35th; 79th; 80th; 83rd; 90th Divisions. Fifth row: 2nd; 3rd; 4th; 5th; 6th Armored Divisions; Tank Destroyer Forces. Sixth row: 82nd Airborne Division; XVII Airborne Corps; 101st Airborne Division; Army, Navy, Engineer amphibious units. Seventh row: Troop Carrier Command; Glider Command cap and shoulder insignia; Ranger Battalions; 2nd Ranger Battalion.

of aggression in the infantry and a pervasive tendency to allow the artillery to fight the war as much as possible. According to some analyses, the American practice of expending materiel, rather than men arose from an institutional appreciation of the political consequences of a high casualty rate, an awareness that some believed stemmed all the way back to the Battle of Antietam, in the American Civil War.

The tactical consequence was the kind of caution that could easily produce inertia on the battlefield. When, as Gen. William Simpson, the commander of US Seventh Army, put it, commanders would "never send in infantryman in to do a job that an artillery shell can do for him," the inevitable consequence was a loss of time and momentum. Historian Russell Weigley concluded that American practice in Europe reversed the traditional formula of fire and maneuver, wherein firepower held the enemy in position while the infantry maneuvered to attack. Instead, American infantry maneuvered to locate the enemy and then used artillery fire to destroy him. While respecting the material superiority of their enemy and the general excellence of American artillery and air power, German commanders considered that Americans were timid soldiers who often missed opportunities through a want of initiative. They were not, as one German officer phrased it, "tactically at all clever." American tactics, according to Gen. Max Simon, commander of the XIII SS Corps, were "based on the idea of breaking down a wall by taking out one brick at a time."

The costs of such tactics were high, and not all American divisions, or American combat commanders, were up to it. High casualties typified hedgerow combat. The survivors became battlewise and wary, but the demands of battle gave the veterans little time or opportunity to pass on their hard-won knowledge to the constant stream of

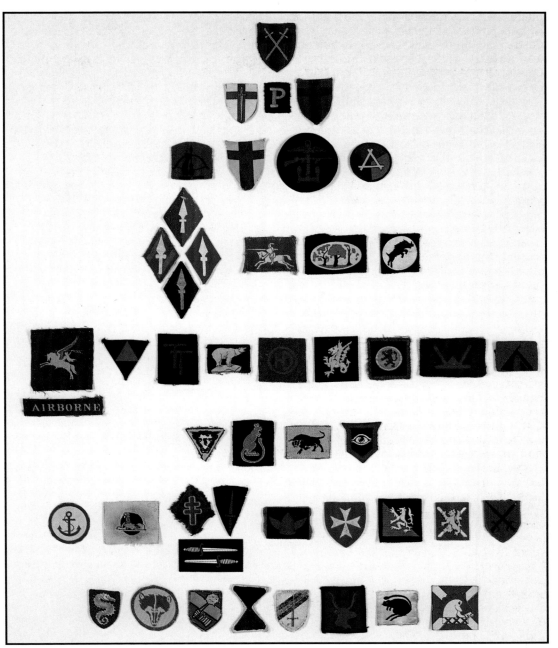

replacements. Hedgerow combat was costly. The 4th Infantry Division, as one example, suffered 6,000 casualties, or roughly half of the division's strength. The usual experience of an American infantry regiment in 1944 and 1945 was that it would replace its entire strength about every 90 days. Thus even veteran divisions might be somewhat shaky. Other divisions, particularly including the 79th and 90th Infantry, did not fare as well and continually disappointed Bradley and Eisenhower. Reliefs from division command were far more common in the US First Army than in the rest of 21st Army Group.

British and Canadian ground operations were similarly timid, despite the fact that Montgomery, like Bradley, decided to use veteran divisions in the assault and immediate attacks to deepen the beachhead. The 7th Armoured Division, the famous

Left: Insignia of Canadian and Allied units. Top: Shoulder flash. Second row, from left: Canadian HQ; First Army. Third row: Shoulder flash. Diamond insignia, from left, clockwise: 1st Army Artillery; II Corps; II Corps Artillery; 2nd Armoured Brigade. Fifth row: 2nd; 3rd; 4th Canadian Infantry Divisions. Sixth row: 1st Polish Armoured Division; 1st Belgian 'Piron' Brigade; Royal Netherlands Brigade; Czechoslovak Brigade.

Above: British and Allied unit insignia. Top: 21st Army Group HQ. Second row: Second Army; "Phantom" Army; 21st Army Group. Third row: Anti-Aircraft Command; Communications; Combined Ops; Airfield Construction. Fourth row: I Corps (x4); VIII; XII; XXX Corps. Fifth-sixth rows: 6th Airborne; 3rd (inverted); 50th; 49th; 51st; 43rd; 15th; 53rd; 59th; 79th Armoured; 7th Armoured; 11th Armoured; Guards Armoured Divisions. Seventh row: Combined Ops; 56th Inf. Brig.; 1st Special Service Brigade (x3); 234th; 231st; 44th; 46th; 115th Ind. Inf. Brigs. Eighth row: 27th; 8th; 34th; 37th; 6th Guards; 22nd; 4th; 30th Independent Armoured Brigs.

"Desert Rats" from North Africa and Italy, and the proud 51st (Highland) Division both turned in disappointing performances, appearing tired and overly cautious. It was the judgement of Lt. Gen. Brian Horrocks, the XXX Corps commander, and Maj. Gen. G. L. Verney, who took command of the 7th Armoured in Normandy, that the men were tired, unprepared for fighting in the restrictive terrain of France, and had been in battle long enough to have had dash replaced by caution. The same, they believed, was true of the veteran 51st Division, proud of its past victories but no longer, as Montgomery reported to Brooke, battle worthy. Other divisions performed similarly.

Command philosophy had something to do with it, for it was accepted in 21st Army Group that the need to keep down casualties was a pivotal consideration. Although it now appears that there were some 100,000 uncommitted infantrymen in the United Kingdom — possible evidence that Churchill still harbored doubts about the ultimate success of *Overlord* — in practical terms the British contingent of 21st Army Group was as large and as powerful on June 6, 1944, as it would ever be. There were no more reserves to be committed, and Montgomery lived in a world of ever-declining resources. While more American units were available, the British began *Overlord* at maximum strength. The concern to limit casualties inevitably had an effect on the aggression with which the divisions fought and their willingness to take chances and exploit opportunities. Instead, careful battle preparation, already a Montgomery trademark, was the hallmark of 21st Army Group operations.

Like the Americans, the British and Canadians preferred to let the artillery do the fighting wherever possible. The men did not lack courage, but did lack boldness. In general terms, as historian Carlo D'Este has concluded, Commonwealth infantrymen took a piece of terrain that invited counterattack, then used their machine guns in what was essentially a tactic of attrition little changed from the days of World War I. Because there were doctrinal problems in tank-infantry co-operation that stemmed from a British understanding of armor as an independent, exploiting force, tank units also

Above: A Canadian soldier is silhouetted near Fleury-sur-Orne during some of the night fighting for Caen. The warfare in this sector was extremely bitter as the German defense was strengthened to hold what was sensibly the best exit from the Allied lodgment.

Below: The bodies of two American infantrymen rest where they were thrown by the explosion of the mine, or possibly the mortar bomb, which killed them. The dead were swiftly recovered and buried by the specialized graves registration units.

suffered heavily in the Normandy fighting. German criticisms of the fighting quality of British and Canadian infantry were much like their criticisms of American infantry, assessing fighting morale as not very high, finding little willingness to engage in close combat, and observing an excessive dependence on artillery support, without which they would not advance.

Throughout the Normandy fighting, it was the Germans who impressed. Given their enormous disadvantages in manpower, fire support, lack of mobility, lack of logistical sustainment, and above all lack of air power, and considering the countervailing Allied superiority in every one of those categories, the German ability to contain the beachhead for so long was a very impressive achievement. Hitler's order that his troops stand and fight in Normandy derailed the *Overlord* plan. It also, however, resulted in the destruction of the fighting power of the German Army in the west. Despite, and in fact as a consequence of, the difficulties they faced and the slow advance they managed, the British and American forces methodically ravaged German divisions. By the end of the battle in Normandy, not only were the coastal defense divisions destroyed, but also many of the first-class armored and mechanized divisions. Three months after the landings, the Germans could muster no more than 120 of the 1,300 tanks and assault guns they had committed to battle in Normandy, and the average Panzer division could count fewer than ten tanks. Perhaps just as damaging, the Germans lost more than 15,000 vehicles of

Below: A German soldier typical of those who fought in Normandy. This young man, a member of the 12th SS Panzer Division "Hitler Jugend", is an MG42 machine gunner wearing camouflaged battledress and carrying an ammunition belt round his neck.

Above: The British placed considerable emphasis on heavy and well-directed artillery fire to keep casualties down. This gunner is helping to unload shells for his battery's 5.5-in guns, which could deliver their projectiles to a range of 16,200 yards (14.5km).

other types, further crippling their tactical mobility. It was the destruction of the Panzer divisions in the hedgerows that made it possible for the Allies, once they broke out of the beachhead, not only to catch up with the *Overlord* plan, but to exceed it, racing all the way to the German frontier by September.

It was, however, the overwhelming materiel superiority, coupled with overwhelming air superiority and artillery firepower, rather than tactical and operational acumen, that allowed the Americans and the British to prevail. That fact amply justified the *Overlord* planners' preoccupation with logistics and with the development of the continental logistical base. The Allies' often-criticized battlefield caution helped to minimize casualties, and is the more understandable in view of their clear decision to use American industrial might, not men, in what Churchill called "merely the proper application of overwhelming force." The palm for tactical adroitness in Normandy must be awarded to the Germans, but it is worth noting that tactical skill and small-unit initiative and aggression were not so much virtues as essential, in view of German military shortcomings in almost every other way.

Despite any actual or perceived problems at the tactical level, the difficult ground battles of June and July were important Allied victories that it would be wrong to discount. Hard fighting in front of Caen, on the Cotentin Peninsula, and in the morass of the bocage made reality of Eisenhower's boast to Churchill about standing on the German frontier by winter.

The Air Battle

7

Alfred Price

During the spring of 1944, as part of the general preparations for the invasion, Spitfires, Mosquitoes, Mustangs, and Lightnings of Allied reconnaissance units flew many hundreds of sorties over France and Belgium. Their cameras took tens of thousands of photographs which revealed details of the German coastal defensive system running from Holland to the Spanish frontier. Most of the photographs were taken from medium and high altitude, and showed the targets vertically, from above. Additionally, low-flying aircraft fitted with sideways-looking or forwards-looking oblique cameras took close-ups of important objectives. Aircraft flew high-speed runs over the beaches at low altitude, taking photographs for the coxswains of landing craft and platoon commanders to show the appearance of their objectives as seen from the seaward approaches. It was vitally important that the aerial activity should not betray the invasion area, so for each sortie flown over western Normandy three were flown over the Pas de Calais.

Also at this time, fighter-bombers set about the important task of knocking out radar stations along the French and Belgian coasts. During the ten-week period prior to the invasion, Typhoons, Spitfires, and Mosquitoes of the RAF 2nd Tactical Air Force flew nearly 2,000 sorties against radar sites. These targets were well defended, and on occasions the attackers suffered serious losses. But by June 5 the fighter-bombers would have put out of action all but 16 of the original 92 sites and left no radar fully operational overlooking the invasion area.

During this phase, medium bombers of the 2nd Tactical Air Force and the US 9th Air Force carried out systematic attacks on transportation targets. Following a careful analysis of the railway system in northern France, Prof. Solly Zuckerman devised a clever plan of attacks that would isolate Normandy while giving the impression that the invasion would take place somewhere in the Pas de Calais area (the "Transportation Plan"). A total of 72 specific objectives were singled out for attack: 39 in western Germany and 33 in France and Belgium. The targets included railway junctions, marshaling yards and rolling stock repair shops. Fighters and fighter-bombers flew over the rail network shooting up the rolling stock with the aim of clogging the repair system with damaged units. By the beginning of June, of 2,000 steam locomotives that had been available in

Below: The Allied forces were well served by their intelligence departments, which could draw on the efforts of many sources including photo-reconnaissance aircraft such as this Supermarine Spitfire PR.Mk XI, which could fly with any of three camera installations.

northern France and Belgium, 1,500 had been immobilized as a result of direct air attack or lack of maintenance.

The US 9th Air Force also delivered concentrated attacks on bridges and airfields. By June 5, of the 24 bridges over the Seine between Paris and the sea, 18 had been destroyed and three were closed for repair. Also, during the final six weeks prior to the invasion, 36 Luftwaffe airfields in France, Holland and Belgium were attacked.

Eve of D-Day

By the eve of D-Day the Allied air forces possessed a clear qualitative and quantitative superiority over the Luftwaffe in the west. Between them the US Army Air Force and the RAF could send into action some 2,800 heavy bombers, 1,500 medium and light bombers and 3,700 fighters and fighter-bombers. Luftflotte 3 (Air Fleet 3), which controlled all Luftwaffe units based in France, Holland and Belgium and was responsible for countering the invasion, possessed only about 140 medium bombers, 90 anti-shipping aircraft, 200 fighters and fighter-bombers and 56 night fighters. Once the invasion began it was planned to reinforce Luftflotte 3 with a further 400 single-engined fighters from home defense units in Luftflotte Reich. Even with this transfusion of strength the Luftwaffe units in the west would still be heavily outnumbered. In the pre-invasion address delivered to his forces Gen. Eisenhower felt able to make a jaunty prediction on the outcome of the battle in the air: "Don't worry about the planes overhead. They will be ours..."

On the afternoon of June 5 all aircraft earmarked to take part in supporting the invasion were hastily painted with distinctive

LION — SUR — MER

black and white stripes on their wings and fuselages, to assist in identification. As darkness fell and the invasion fleets set sail, from more than a hundred airfields throughout the length and breadth of Britain there came the thunder of aero engines as planes roared into the air to fulfil their allotted tasks.

Six squadrons of RAF Mosquito night fighters maintained standing patrols over the English Channel and France to safeguard the huge armada of ships, and the streams of bombers, transport aircraft and gliders heading for Normandy. The night fighter operation was completely successful — not a single enemy aircraft was able to interfere with the enterprise. The only combat over the Channel that night was by a Mosquito of No. 409 (Canadian) Squadron, which engaged a Junkers 188 on reconnaissance off the south coast of England and claimed it ''probably destroyed.''

Twenty anti-submarine aircraft of RAF Coastal Command equipped to carry out night attacks — Sunderland flying boats, Wellingtons, Liberators, and Halifaxes — headed for their designated patrol lines off the coast of Cornwall. The appropriately named *Cork* patrols would be flown round the clock throughout the weeks ahead and were intended to saturate a 20,000 square mile (50,000km²) area of sea between Brittany and the Irish Coast. Any U-boat attempting to reach the invasion area from its base on the French Atlantic coast would have to run the gauntlet of air patrols cruising most of the way on the surface, for the distance was too far to cover submerged. And while it was on the surface, a U-boat was liable to suffer repeated attacks from the air.

As the U-boat hunters moved into position, aircraft from RAF Bomber Command — 551 Lancasters, 412 Halifaxes, and 49 Mosquitoes — headed out to bomb ten coastal batteries situated at strategic points along the Normandy coast. Most of the objectives were covered in cloud, so Pathfinder Mosquitoes fitted with the highly accurate *Oboe* radar attack system dropped pyrotechnic markers to point out the targets for the rest of the force.

Shortly before midnight, heavily laden transport planes staggered into the air and headed south. Three divisions of troops and their equipment were being committed in the largest airborne assault operation ever attempted. Making for the Drop Zones

Right: On D-Day the Allied air forces put in a massive effort. This photograph reveals a German radar installation shrouded by the smoke of exploding rocket projectiles fired by Hawker Typhoon Mk IB fighter-bombers, each capable of carrying eight such weapons.

Above: Issued in March 1944, this composite was intended as an aid to coastal recognition rather than for navigation as such, and was derived from photographs taken by an aircraft flying ''on the deck'' about 1,000 to 1,500 yards (900-1,350m) off the shore.

Below: A member of the specialist ground crew loads an F.52 vertical camera into the bay behind the cockpit of a Supermarine Spitfire PR.Mk XI of No. 541 Squadron, an RAF photo-reconnaissance unit operating from Benson in central Oxfordshire.

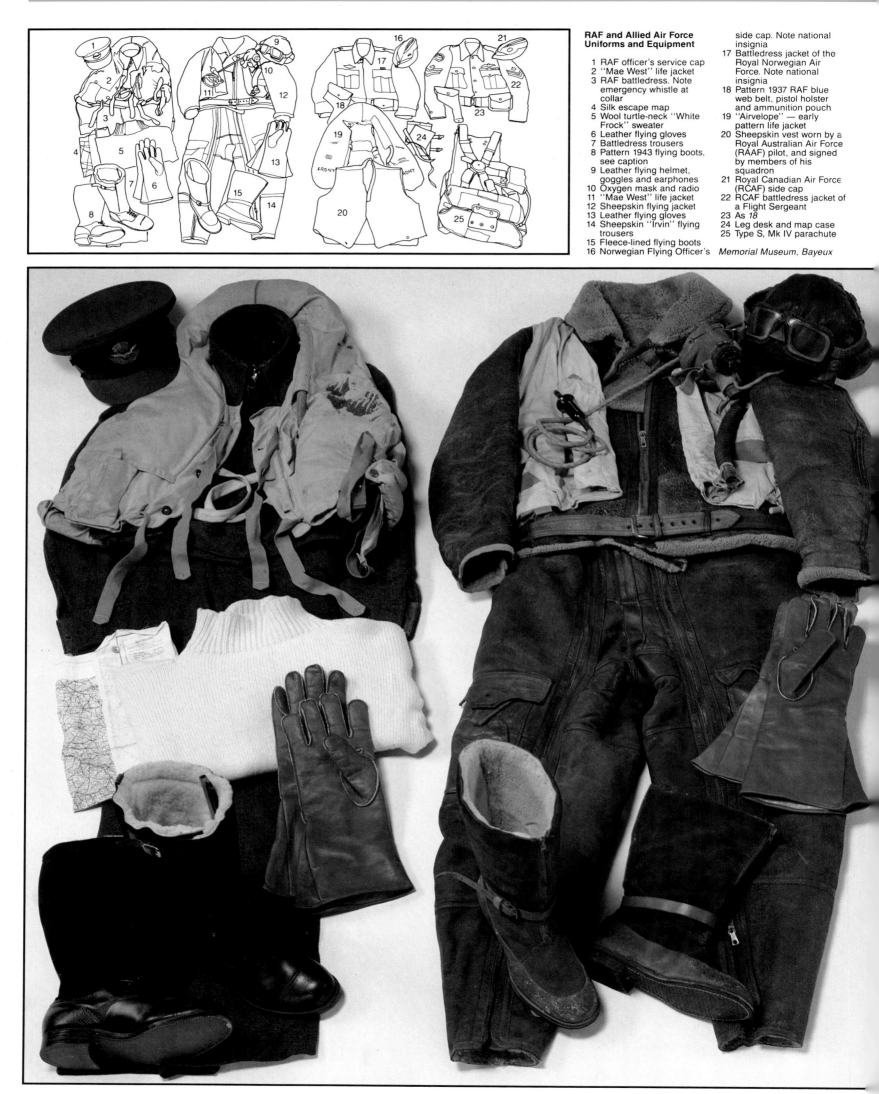

RAF and Allied Air Force Uniforms and Equipment

1 RAF officer's service cap
2 "Mae West" life jacket
3 RAF battledress. Note emergency whistle at collar
4 Silk escape map
5 Wool turtle-neck "White Frock" sweater
6 Leather flying gloves
7 Battledress trousers
8 Pattern 1943 flying boots, see caption
9 Leather flying helmet, goggles and earphones
10 Oxygen mask and radio
11 "Mae West" life jacket
12 Sheepskin flying jacket
13 Leather flying gloves
14 Sheepskin "Irvin" flying trousers
15 Fleece-lined flying boots
16 Norwegian Flying Officer's

side cap. Note national insignia
17 Battledress jacket of the Royal Norwegian Air Force. Note national insignia
18 Pattern 1937 RAF blue web belt, pistol holster and ammunition pouch
19 "Airvelope" — early pattern life jacket
20 Sheepskin vest worn by a Royal Australian Air Force (RAAF) pilot, and signed by members of his squadron
21 Royal Canadian Air Force (RCAF) side cap
22 RCAF battledress jacket of a Flight Sergeant
23 As 18
24 Leg desk and map case
25 Type S, Mk IV parachute

Memorial Museum, Bayeux

All of the Allies who flew with the RAF, particularly those from occupied countries, tried to retain some vestige of their national uniform, usually the cap and rank insignia. The RAF pilot (items *1-8*), flew in Normandy from forward airfield B3. The Pattern 1943 flight boots (*8*) were specially designed to help the escape of downed aircrew. In occupied territory the tops of the boots could be cut off thus creating a pair of civilian shoes. The knife incorporated to make the alteration can be seen in the right-hand boot. The Norwegian pilot (items *16-18*), flew in Normandy from airfield B16 in August 1944. The non-issue RAAF sheepskin vest (*20*) was signed by personnel of No. 453 Squadron at forward airfield B11 in July 1944. Despite their disparate origins Allied airmen performed admirably under the most trying conditions.

covering the west flank of the landings were 821 USAAF troop-carriers — C-47s and C-53s (the latter a modification of the former, equipped for glider towing), together with 104 Horsa and Waco gliders. These carried the two US airborne divisions to their Drop Zones. Meanwhile, heading for Drop Zones covering the east flank of the landings were 266 Halifaxes, Stirlings, Dakotas, and Albemarles, and 98 Horsa and Hamilcar gliders, carrying the British airborne division. During the small hours of the morning the aircraft put down their troops and equipment with varying degrees of accuracy. Twenty-one US and seven British transport aircraft were lost in the operation.

In one of many unusual operations flown as part of *Overlord* shortly before dawn, a pair of Douglas Boston bombers of No. 342 (French) Squadron flew low over the sea along the western flank of the invasion fleet to lay a smokescreen to shield the columns of ships from visually aimed fire coming from German coastal batteries along the Cotentin Peninsula. At ten-minute intervals, relays of bombers arrived to renew the curtain of smoke which significantly reduced the accuracy of the enemy's long range artillery. Bostons of No. 88 Squadron RAF carried out a similar operation along the eastern flank of the invasion force. Two aircraft were lost in the course of these operations.

At 04:30 the first day fighter units arrived to relieve the Mosquito night fighters patroling the invasion area. Six Groups of P-38 Lightnings of the US 8th and 9th Air Forces flew on a rota designed to maintain two full squadrons on continuous patrol over the concentrations of ships throughout the period between dawn and dusk. The Lightning, with its unique and unmistakable twin-boom layout, was particularly suitable for the task, for it was the type least likely to be misidentified by naval gunners liable to engage any aircraft within range unless they were sure it was friendly.

To provide defense in depth, squadron-sized formations of Spitfires, Thunderbolts, and Mustangs ranged far and wide over Normandy to block the path of enemy planes making for the landing areas.

As the landing craft approached the beaches, battleships and cruisers lying off shore loosed off broadsides at the enemy shore batteries, assisted by spotter planes. One of the latter, a Seafire of No. 866 Squadron piloted by Lt. Dick Law RN, corrected the fire from the battleship HMS *Warspite* as she engaged a coastal defense battery of six 155 mm guns near Trouville. "The battleship was a magnificent sight as she lay at anchor, loosing off four-gun salvoes with her main 15-in guns," he recalled. "During one of the early salvoes I was a little over-enthusiastic in positioning myself to observe the fall of the shells, with the result that some 35 seconds after *Warspite* fired my Seafire suddenly shivered and I actually saw one of the giant shells, weighing almost a ton, go sizzling close past me on its way to the target. During subsequent salvoes I made good and sure that I was well to the side of the line of fire! From time to time the German batteries returned *Warspite's* fire; when that happened we were treated to the spectacle of a giant-sized tennis match. During one of these exchanges a salvo straddled *Warspite*, but she received only slight damage."

While Law was directing the battleship's fire, 1,077 B-17 Flying Fortresses and B-24 Liberators of the US 8th Air Force laid carpets of bombs along the shore lines where Allied troops were about to land. One of the heavy bombers was shot down by flak.

Among the US 9th Air Force units providing direct support for the initial landings was the 366th Fighter Group with some 45 fighter-bombers — P-47 Thunderbolts — each carrying two 1,000lb (400kg) bombs. The Group commander, Lt. Col. Norman Holt, later wrote: "The sky was quite gray but brightening rapidly as the definite line of the French coast moved toward us. Preparing to dive-bomb our primary targets, shore gun batteries, terse commands came from the squadron leader, 'Relic Squadron, echelon right, flights in trail.' Inching slowly over into formation, we stole a quick look down at the beach as often as we could, at the same time we looked around for any enemy aircraft which could be very troublesome during the crucial forming of the beachhead. Below us, for a three or four mile [4-6km] stretch, we could pick up innumerable water craft of all sizes, shapes and types. There seemed to be thousands of them! Battleships standing off-shore were firing broadsides

Above: National insignia and squadron badges of Commonwealth units serving with the RAF. By June 1944 the RAF had a total of 487 serving squadrons, 100 of which were manned by personnel from countries of the Commonwealth. Of these, Canada provided 42 squadrons, South Africa 27, Australia 16, and New Zealand 6. There were also 9 squadrons from India and a large number of personnel serving with the RAF from other Commonwealth countries such as Rhodesia. *Memorial Museum, Bayeux*

Below: National insignia and squadron badges of Allied air force personnel. Together with the personnel from the Commonwealth, the RAF also had under its 'wing' the men and women of the Allied air forces. By June 1944 they mustered 31 squadrons based in Britain ready to take part in the invasion. These included 4 Czechoslovak, 4 Norwegian, 7 French, 2 Belgian and 2 Dutch. Another 26 Allied squadrons including 3 Greek and 1 Yugoslav served overseas. *Memorial Museum, Bayeux*

over the other craft. Their firepower was helping pin down and hamper return fire from the enemy. At the shore line, landing craft were spewing out men and equipment at an astonishing rate. We could see them scattering like kids from school." After the Thunderbolts had delivered their bombs they flew inland to strafe targets of opportunity.

Allied medium bombers were also active against enemy positions, attacking from altitudes much lower than usual to ensure accurate bombing. For example, 54 A-20 Havocs of the 416th Bomb Group, 9th Air Force, descended to 1,700 feet (510m) to deliver a devastating attack on the Argentan crossroads. The target was undefended and all of the aircraft returned safely.

Eighteen squadrons of RAF Typhoon fighter-bombers supported the landings in the British sector. As the first troops went ashore, three squadrons dive-bombed strongpoints immediately in front of them. Throughout the day relays of squadrons flew "cab rank" patrols, orbiting over the beachhead waiting for their forward air controllers to call on them to attack enemy positions that were holding up the advance. If there was no suitable target near the beachhead, the Typhoons were sent south to attack targets of opportunity in the areas around Bayeux and Caen.

The Luftwaffe Reply

The initial Allied landings came as a complete surprise to the Luftwaffe. No German reconnaissance aircraft reported the approach of the armada, and initially there was no reaction from the defenses. Even when Luftflotte 3 had firm evidence that the landings had

Above: By far the largest number of Allied air force squadrons from continental Europe were supplied by the Poles. A total of 12 Polish squadrons were serving in Britain in June 1944 in Fighter, Bomber and Coastal Commands, as well as a small number of personnel serving in RAF squadrons. As well as operations over France before and during the invasion, the Poles scored notable successes against the V-1s aimed at London, claiming 190 destroyed up to March 1945. *Sikorski Institute*

begun, the powerful defensive umbrella prevented it from mounting effective air attacks. During one attempt to reach the shipping, Mustangs of the 355th Fighter Group intercepted a gaggle of Junkers Ju 88 bombers and shot down nine of them and forced the remainder to jettison their bombs and run for home.

A few German fighters did succeed in reaching the landing area that morning, however. In a well-known incident a pair of Focke-Wulf Fw 190s piloted by Oberst Josef Priller, commander of Jagdgeschwader 26,

and his wing man Unteroffizier Heinz Wodarczyk delivered a strafing attack on *Sword* Beach. Elsewhere, a dozen Messerschmitt Bf 109s bounced Typhoons of No. 183 Squadron as the latter were engaged in strafing a column of German Army vehicles, and shot down three before the remainder were able to fight them off. The total Luftwaffe effort during the day amounted to about a hundred sorties, mainly by fighters,

Above: Seen on its English base, this Consolidated B-24 Liberator bomber was one of the many 8th Air Force assets that were used for the tactical bombing effort before D-Day, when road, rail, river and canal communications to northern France were hit.

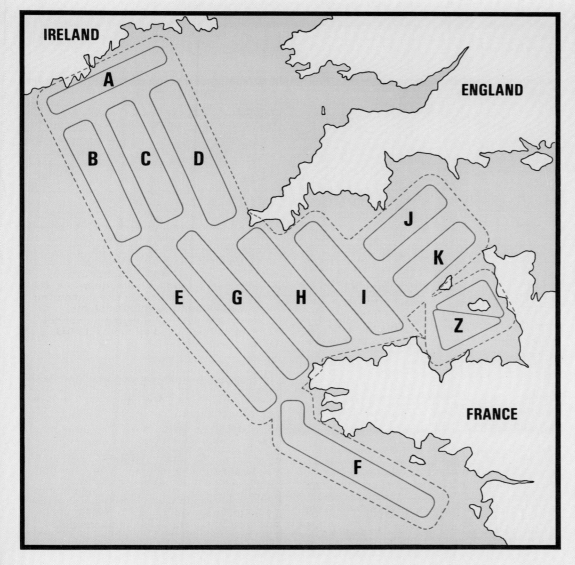

THE ANTI-SUBMARINE *CORK* PATROLS OF RAF COASTAL COMMAND IN THE WESTERN APPROACHES

From the eve of D-Day and for weeks afterwards, anti-submarine aircraft of No. 19 Group, RAF Coastal Command flew round the clock to keep German U-boats away from the invasion fleet.

The patrol aircraft, including Sunderland flying boats, Wellingtons, Halifaxes, and Liberators were supplied with information from *Ultra* about U-boat movements, and were supported in their task by a sizeable naval force which included destroyers, frigates, and flotillas of torpedo, and gun boats.

Anti-submarine patrols took place on both the northern and western flanks of the invasion fleet, but it was in the Western Approaches, closest to the U-boat pens in Brittany and in the Bay of Biscay, where the effort was greatest.

The map shows the enormity of the task. The patrol areas covered every square mile of sea from the Brittany coast to Ireland. The solid line shows the patrol areas of the aircraft, while the dotted line shows the range of their on-board radar. The radar, known as the ASV III, could spot a surfaced submarine at a distance of up to 12 miles (19km). The tight patrol pattern and the range of the radar ensured that patrol areas effectively overlapped.

The total area patrolled was so big that U-boats moving into the invasion area from the west, especially those without the "schnorkel" breathing system, would have to surface somewhere within it to recharge their batteries, thus opening them up to attack from either air or surface forces.

The success of this massive, but largely unheralded operation, was extraordinary. On D-Day, 16 U-boats were ordered into the Channel from the west. By June 10, six had been sunk, five damaged, and the threat of U-boat operations in the Western Approaches effectively eliminated.

fighter-bombers and fighter-reconnaissance aircraft.

The IIIrd Gruppe of Schlachtgeschwader 4, a ground attack unit with some 50 Focke-Wulf Fw 190Fs, was one of the Luftwaffe units sent in during the initial stages of battle. On the morning of D-Day the Gruppe received orders to move from its bases in the south and east of France to forward operating airfields at Laval and Tours. During such combat deployments a mechanic was carried in the rear fuselage of each Focke-Wulf, to assist in the rapid turn-around of the aircraft when it arrived at the new base. Unfortunately for those on board, as the German fighter-bombers were in transit, several of them were intercepted by Mustangs and Thunderbolts. Five of the German planes were shot down and, lacking parachutes, the mechanics had no means of escape. Their pilots refused to bail out and leave them, and of the ten men on board the planes, eight were killed.

Left: Chaff was used by the Royal Air Force with codename *Window*, and the dispersal of bundles of this metal foil, filled the German radar screens with thousands of echoes in which it was very difficult to pick out the real aircraft, if any.

Above: The aircraft of the US 9th Air Force also played a prominent part in the approach to D-Day. This is a Douglas A-20G Havoc with fixed armament, a dorsal turret and provision for up to 4,000 lb (1,800kg) of bombs carried internally and externally.

ALLIED DECEPTION OPERATIONS, JUNE 5/6
To mask the real invasion area, a whole series of deception operations were brought into play on the night before D-Day. Organized under the *Fortitude South* plan, the object of these elaborate and devious schemes was to fool the Germans into thinking that an invasion force was heading towards the Pas de Calais area, while masking the movement and arrival of the real invasion force in Normandy.

Beginning at dusk on June 5, aided by naval craft, bombers over the Channel began Operations *Glimmer* and *Taxable*, the creation on German radar of "phantom" invasion fleets by the systematic dropping of *Window* (see inset B). At the same time night-fighters flew *ABC* patrols over the Somme area to create the impression of a major pre-invasion air attack. Meanwhile over the real invasion fleet, aircraft flew radar jamming missions in the *Mandrel* operation. A similar operation, *Big Drum* was flown off Cherbourg.

As the hour for invasion drew closer, and to confuse the German land forces, Operation *Titanic* dropped *Rupert*, the dummy parachutists, onto the unsuspecting defenders. (See page 39.)

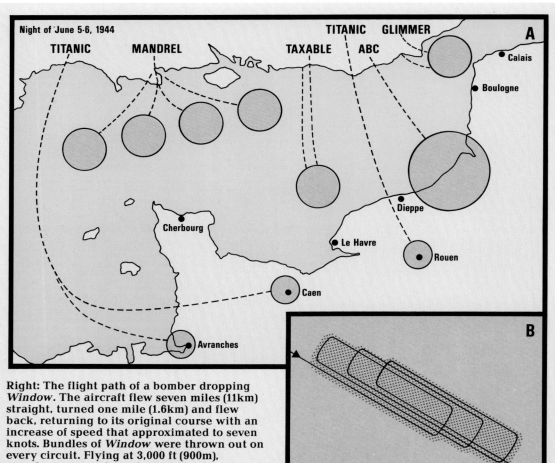

Right: The flight path of a bomber dropping *Window*. The aircraft flew seven miles (11km) straight, turned one mile (1.6km) and flew back, returning to its original course with an increase of speed that approximated to seven knots. Bundles of *Window* were thrown out on every circuit. Flying at 3,000 ft (900m), squadrons created a radar shadow 14 miles (22km) long.

Above, left: Luftwaffe ground combat camouflage smock with M1940 helmet and M1943 Luftwaffe field cap. Right: Luftwaffe service cap, lightweight summer flying jacket and trousers. *Military History Shop; Andrew Xaras and Pritchard Collections*

Flying from the new bases late on the afternoon of D-Day, the Gruppe mounted three attacks against *Sword* Beach with a total of 13 aircraft. Allied fighters prevented one raiding force from reaching its target, the other two got through to the beachhead but the volume of anti-aircraft fire forced them to make fleeting attacks which caused little damage.

That night there were violent skirmishes

Left: With its twin engines, the Lockheed P-38 Lightning was well suited to long-range missions involving overwater flight, and its fixed armament could be supplemented by the heavy underwing loads that made it a fearsome ground-attack fighter.

at the western end of the English Channel, as U-boats from the bases along the Biscay coast tried to force their way past the *Cork* patrols. The patrol planes obtained contacts on 22 U-boats and converted seven of these into attacks. Two U-boats were sunk and four were damaged to such an extent that they were forced to turn back.

At dawn the surviving U-boats submerged, for a daylight passage was far too dangerous to attempt. After darkness fell on the evening of June 7, the U-boats surfaced and doggedly continued their move eastwards trying to recharge their depleted batteries. The patrol planes were again in action and one of them, a Liberator of No. 224 Squadron RAF commanded by Flying Officer Kenneth Moore, achieved the unique feat of sinking

two boats — *U-373* and *U-629* — within a space of 15 minutes.

In the days following the initial landings Allied bombers and fighter-bombers continued their round the clock attack on the road and rail networks leading into Normandy. On the night of June 8/9, 24 Lancasters of No. 617 Squadron RAF carried out a precision attack on the Samur rail tunnel using

12,000 lb (5440 kg) "Tallboy" deep penetration bombs. The exploding bombs collapsed the tunnel and the line was blocked for a considerable period.

Also that night, Luftflotte 3 sent about 130 bombers to attack the concentrations of Allied shipping off the coast. During their approach flights the attackers suffered losses not only from the Allied night fighters, but also from German flak batteries long accustomed to regarding all aircraft as hostile. Those bombers that reached the beachhead area encountered so violent a reception that in many cases they were forced to break off their attacks prematurely. The only Allied losses were the headquarters ship *Bulolo* and the destroyer *Lawford*, both of which were sunk by radio-controlled glider bombs.

THE STRAFING OF *SWORD* BEACH ON D-DAY
On D-Day, numerous German aircraft attempted to fight their way through to the landing area, but only a few managed to. Two Focke-Wulf 190s that succeeded were flown by Oberst Josef "Pips" Priller, the commander of Jagdgeschwader 26 (shown in the inset in his plane "Jutta") and his wing man Unteroffizier Heinz Wodarczyk. The pair reached *Sword* and carried out a brief strafing attack on British troops.

The Story of One Fighter Gruppe

Under the long-prepared Luftwaffe plan, when the Allied landings began, home defense fighter Gruppen were to move from Luftflotte Reich to France to stiffen the defenses there. We shall follow the fortunes of one such unit, IInd Gruppe of Jagdgeschwader 1, which flew its 25 Focke-Wulf Fw 190s from Rheine in western Germany to Le Mans on the afternoon of D-Day. On June 7 the Gruppe mounted three full-strength fighter sweeps over roads along which German reinforcements were moving and, remarkably, encountered no Allied aircraft. On the next day, June 8, the unit was ordered to load bombs on its Fw 190s for an attack on shipping off the coast. The pilots had no previous experience of fighter-bomber operations, and although they reached the invasion area and dropped their bombs, from

Above: A German ammunition truck explodes under the fire of a Republic P-47 Thunderbolt, a massive and sturdy fighter of which the fixed armament of eight 0.5-in machine guns could be complemented by rockets or bombs in the important ground-attack role.

Allied records we know that no ship was hit. The German pilots described the flak they encountered as "terrific" yet, again, all of the aircraft returned though some had minor

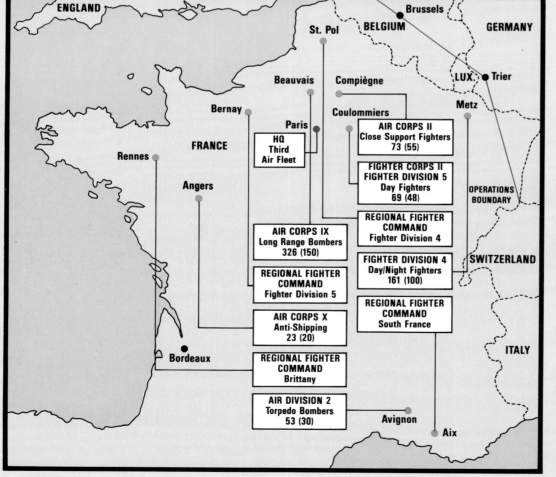

THE LUFTWAFFE IN FRANCE, MAY 1944
When the Allied invasion came, the Luftwaffe in France was organized into Luftflotte (Air Fleet) 3. Under the command of Field Marshal Hugo Sperrle (see photograph page 55.) The Luftflotte had been in the west since 1940 when it had participated in the fall of France and the Battle of Britain. Now four years later, it faced the combined might of the Allied air forces in the west.

The map shows the locations of the Luftflotte's various unit headquarters around France. The figures given are some of the units' total aircraft on-strength, and those actually serviceable (the figures in parentheses). Note that these are locations of headquarters, and would not necessarily be where all a unit's aircraft would be based.

The subsidiary units of Luftflotte 3 included Fighter Corps II, made up of Fighter Divisions 4 and 5; II Air Corps, fighters; IX Air Corps, bombers; X Air Corps, anti-shipping. This corps also included Air Division 2 which flew torpedo bombers. On paper, Luftflotte 3 had in service a total of about 890 aircraft of all types including reconnaissance, transport and anti-shipping. Of this figure, it is estimated that only 497 were serviceable in late May. Estimates for the number of Allied aircraft available to actually counter the invasion are as low as 319.

The Allied air assault after June 6 quickly overwhelmed Luftflotte 3. Despite a transfer of aircraft from Luftflotte Reich in Germany, and the use of a variety of new weapons (see pages 146-147) the Luftwaffe in France was powerless to stop the advance of *Overlord*, and the destruction of German land forces from the air. Field Marshal Sperrle was relieved of his command in August 1944 and transferred to the reserve.

Right: A selection of Luftwaffe qualification badges. Top row, from left: ex-flyer's commemorative badge in case; Luftwaffe ground combat badge; parachutist's (Fallschirmjager) badge, in original case; anti-aircraft artillery (flak) award with its original cardboard box. Bottom row from left: pilot's badge with case; observer's badge with original case; air gunner/flight engineer's badge with envelope; wireless operator/air gunner's badge with case.
Fistrovich Collection

damage. A similar operation on the following day was also unsuccessful, but still the unit's run of luck held and there were no losses.

On the night of June 10/11 a force of more than a hundred RAF Lancasters and Halifaxes bombed Le Mans airfield. Craters pock-marked the landing ground, but prudently the Gruppe had dispersed its aircraft into the surrounding fields and none was damaged. Lacking mechanical earth moving equipment, however, it took six days of hard work to fill in enough craters by hand to provide a flat strip for take-offs. As soon as the Focke-Wulfs were able to get airborne they moved to Essay, and from there they flew fighting patrols over the battle area for the next four days. Then the unit transferred to a field landing ground near Alençon, where its charmed existence came to an abrupt end. Soon after the German fighters landed, a force of Mustangs swept over the airfield at low altitude and, in a series of coordinated strafing runs, destroyed 15 of the Fw 190s and effectively put the Gruppe out of the battle.

As a result of the continual harassment of Luftwaffe units in France from the Allied air forces, the German ground troops received minimal air support.

Above: Allied air superiority was so complete that effective camouflage was an essential ingredient of aircraft survival between missions. These are Focke-Wulf Fw 190 fighters of Jagdgeschwader 26, commanded by Oberst Josef "Pips" Priller, who scored 101 victories.

Below: Short of fuel and skilled pilots, the German air force was also forced to operate large numbers of old warplanes such as this Messerschmitt BF 109 fighter, shot down near Tilly-sur-Seulles during an abortive attack on June 13.

Below: Caught by the camera gun of a Republic P-47 Thunderbolt fighter flown by Lt. Col. L.T. Houck of the US 9th Army Air Force, a column of German trucks catches fire as each vehicle in succession is hit and its load of fuel or ammunition explodes.

Headquarters Attack

Allied fighter-bombers and bombers flew large numbers of sorties against German troop positions, and headquarters were priority targets for attack when these could be found. On June 10, RAF aircraft bombed three sites thought to be the locations of major headquarters. Only one of the attacks, that against Château-la-Caine south of Caen, was successful but it brought handsome dividends, for the building housed the headquarters of Panzer Group West. Forty Typhoons of Nos. 181, 182, 245 and 247 Squadrons fired rockets into the château then 71 North American Mitchells of Nos. 98, 180, 266 and 320 Squadrons carried out a horizontal attack on the area from 12,000 feet (3,600m) dropping large numbers of 500 lb (200kg) bombs. The headquarters was wrecked and the Chief of Staff, Gen. von Dawans, and many of his staff officers were killed.

By now construction was well advanced on the first landing grounds in the beachhead, and from June 13 Allied fighter and fighter-bomber squadrons used these to refuel between missions. A couple of days later, units took up residence on the new bases.

Off the coast of Normandy the Luftwaffe anti-shipping units continued to suffer heavy losses in their attempts trying to attack the assembled vessels. In the ten days following the invasion, IIIrd Gruppe of Kampfgeschwader 100, a Dornier Do 217 unit equipped with glider bombs, lost ten aircraft and eight crews. During that period only two destroyers and three smaller vessels were lost to direct air attack. Shortly afterwards the Luftwaffe abandoned direct attacks, and sent its bombers to sow mines in the shallow waters off the coast. The newly developed pressure mine was difficult to sweep, but ships were safe provided they kept their speed to a minimum while passing through the shallows. The mines caused considerable inconvenience, but few ships were lost.

HAWKER TYPHOON
RAF Typhoons of No. 245 Squadron, flying from a base near Creully, deliver a rocket strike on 21st Panzer Division HQ near Falaise on August 10. Squadron Leader Jack Collins has just fired his eight 60lb (27kg) rockets and is pulling sharply away to avoid enemy tracer rounds. The inset photo is part of a gun camera sequence from a Typhoon of No. 247 Squadron during a rocket attack on Panzer Group West HQ near la Caine, June 10, 21:05.

German "Secret Weapon"

In mid-June the Luftwaffe sent one of its new "secret weapons" to France: the *Mistel*, a Junkers Ju 88 bomber with the crew compartment replaced by a 6,200 lb (2800 kg) high explosive warhead and with a Messerschmitt Bf 109 fighter mounted rigidly on top. The Bf 109 pilot was to fly the combination to the target area, align it on the target and lock in the autopilot on the Ju 88. Then he fired explosive bolts to release the fighter, leaving the explosive-laden bomber to continue on and smash into target. The first *Mistel* unit, Kampfgruppe 101, deployed to St. Dizier near Reims and went into action on the night of June 24/25. Hauptmann Horst Rudat, the commander, led four of the ungainly aircraft into the invasion area and the pilots aimed their explosive Ju 88s at ships off the coast. Hits were claimed but the only Allied report of damage that links with this attack was from the headquarters ship HMS *Nith*, which suffered extensive splinter damage when an explosive Ju 88 exploded on the sea nearby.

During that and subsequent *Mistel* operations against shipping off the coast about ten explosive Ju 88s were launched. At least one hit was claimed on a "battleship" but this is not confirmed in Allied records. An explanation that fits the known facts is that the victim was the old French battleship *Courbet*, which had been abandoned and sunk in shallow water to form part of the breakwater for the *Mulberry* artificial harbor.

Heavy Bombers Support the Land Battle

Operation *Goodwood*, the powerful thrust past the east of Caen by British and Canadian divisions on July 18, called for the use of large numbers of medium and heavy bombers to blast a path through enemy defenses. In the heaviest and most concentrated air attack yet made in support of a ground action, nearly 2,000 bombers were to lay carpets of bombs across designated target areas ahead of the advancing troops. RAF Bomber Command opened the attack at dawn, when Pathfinder Mosquitoes marked the five target areas which were then bombed by 1,013 Lancasters and Halifaxes. Later that morning, 571 B-24 Liberators of the US 8th Air Force attacked five more target areas. Then 318 medium bombers of the US 9th Air Force — A-20 Havocs, B-25 Mitchells and B-26 Marauders — attacked a further five target areas. During these attacks seven heavy bombers were lost, all of them to flak.

The bombs fell across positions manned by the 21st Panzer Division and the 16th Luftwaffe Field Division and caused considerable losses and disruption to their defenses. One company of 21st Panzer, laagered in farm buildings around the village of Guillerville, was hit particularly hard. It had 15 of its tanks put out of action and the area was cratered to such an extent that its surviving vehicles were unable to move. During the hours immediately following the bombing the attacking troops advanced rapidly, but then the defenders recovered and were able to halt their progress.

On July 25/26 in a similar series of attacks in a prelude to Operation *Cobra*, large forces of Flying Fortresses and Liberators of the US

Above: In the ingenious *Mistel* (mistletoe) weapon, the pilot in the Messerschmitt Bf 109 upper component flew this composite machine to the terminal stage of the attack, when he separated and left the Junkers Ju 88 bomber to impact the target with its huge warhead.

Below: Another German technical success was the Henschel Hs 293 rocket-boosted glider bomb, which was a line of sight, radio-controlled weapon intended for the anti-ship role and carried in pairs by converted Dornier Do 217R bombers.

8th Air Force put down a carpet of bombs along the Périers-St. Lô highway and some 1,200 yards (1,000m) in front of troops of the US First Army who were preparing to attack. On this occasion the targets were too close to US forward positions for safety, however, and several sticks of bombs fell across US Army positions causing more than 600 casualties and leaving some units in a dazed condition. As a result the subsequent land attack achieved little. The lesson was clear: when heavy bombers were used to support the land battle, a separation of at least 3,000 yards (2,700m) from the nearest Allied positions was necessary if such losses were to be avoided.

Jets Join the Battle

At the end of July the Luftwaffe moved another of its "secret weapons" to France: the revolutionary new Messerschmitt Me 262 jet aircraft. Hitler had insisted that these planes be modified to carry bombs and used to disrupt the Allied seaborne invasion. Due to various problems with the novel engines, the aircraft was not ready in time to combat the initial landings but if the Allies landed in the Pas de Calais area, as the Führer still believed they might, the "Blitzbombers" would be in position to strike, each carrying two 550 lb (250 kg) bombs. The first jet fighter-bomber unit, part of Kampfgeschwader 51 and equipped with nine Me 262s, began operations from Châteaudun near Paris early in August.

In the event the jet planes achieved little. To minimize the risk of losses their pilots had strict orders not to descend below 13,000 ft (4,000m) while over enemy territory, and from that altitude accurate bombing was impossible against small battlefield targets such as bridges or vehicles.

Throughout the Battle of Normandy, Allied field commanders received frequent and comprehensive photographic coverage of the enemy positions in front of their forces. Their German counterparts, in contrast, often knew nothing of Allied movements until the attacking units came within sight or sound of their forward positions. Luftwaffe reconnaissance aircraft attempted to fly low

Above: A fighter that could have achieved a serious erosion of Allied air superiority, had it been available in large numbers for operation by experienced pilots, was the jet-powered Messerschmitt Me 262, seen here in the form of an Me 262A-2a fighter-bomber.

Below: Another type that could have played a major role was the Arado Ar 234C Blitz, a potent reconnaissance bomber powered by four turbojet engines and possessing excellent performance. Only 19 of the type were built, however, and its impact was limited.

to attack the bridges at night. During these operations one bridge suffered minor damage but it continued in use, and six of the bombers were shot down.

In a move aimed at overcoming the lack of effective aerial reconnaissance over Normandy the Luftwaffe committed another of its "secret weapons": the Arado Ar 234 jet reconnaissance plane. Two of these aircraft, both prototypes, were dispatched to Juvincourt near Paris, and on the morning of August 2 Lt. Erich Sommer took off for the world's first jet reconnaissance mission. Flying at 34,000 ft (10,000m) at 460 mph (270 k/mh), the German pilot made three long photographic runs over Normandy. The skies were clear, but if any Allied fighter attempted to intercept the Arado the latter's pilot never noticed it. In a flight lasting less than 90 minutes Erich Sommer achieved more than the entire Luftwaffe reconnaissance force in the west had done during the previous eight weeks; he photographed almost the entire Allied lodgment area, from one end to the other. When the films were

altitude photographic sorties by day, and high altitude photographic missions at night using flares. The powerful Allied fighter defenses covering the beachhead and its approaches took a heavy toll of these planes, and those that survived usually did so by breaking off their missions prematurely.

This lack of effective aerial reconnaissance had serious consequences for the defenders. At the end of July American troops broke out of the western side of the lodgment area and, undetected by the German high command, advanced in force down the western side of the Cherbourg Peninsula. On the 31st the advancing units seized the bridges over the Rivers Sée and Sélune at the southern end of the peninsula intact. Exploiting his unexpected opportunity, Gen. Patton poured his troops across the bridges and into the undefended countryside beyond.

For the Germans, the road between the two bridges now became a "fighter-bombers' paradise": mile upon mile of vehicles jammed nose-to-tail and moving slowly along the one narrow road. But by day the German fighter-bombers were quite unable to penetrate the thicket of defensive patrols. In a desperate attempt to stop the advance, Dornier Do 217s carrying glider bombs were sent

Below: The elegant but frightening pattern of tracer rounds, which were only a tithe of the total fired, provides evidence of the awesome AA firepower at the Allies' disposal for tasks such as protection of convoys to Cherbourg. Even so, this German raid sank one ship.

**American Air Force
Uniforms and Equipment**

1. Pilot's summer flying cap, Type B-1
2. Demand oxygen mask, Type A-14
3. Life jacket, Type B-4 "Mae West"
4. Summer flying suit, Type A-4
5. Winter flying suit, Type A-9
6. Leather G1 shoes
7. Leather flying helmet, Type A-11, with earphones Type ANB-H-1 and flying goggles, Type B-8
8. Headset, Type ANB-H-1, made by Western Electric
9. Officers' issue "crusher" service cap
10. Leather Type A-2 flying jacket, emergency whistle at throat
11. Sun glasses
12. Flying jacket F-2, note senior pilot's badge
13. Throat microphone, Type 30-V
14. Pilot's winter cap, Type B-2
15. B-3 Shearling jacket
16. A-3 Shearling trousers
17. Non-regulation Shearling gloves
18. Winter flying shoes, Type A-6A
19. Aircrew body armor, Type 1
20. Aircrew armored helmet, Type M3
21. Type M4 armored helmet
22. Type M4A2 armored helmet
23. Aircrew steel 'flak' helmet, Type M5

Stamatelos Collection: 1-13, 21-23; West Point Museum Collection: 14-20

As American flyers conducted longer high altitude raids, the need for special flying suits to keep out the cold increased. Even the heavy Shearling suits were insufficient and various types of electrically heated suits were used. At altitude the cold was so intense that gloves had to be worn at all times to stop hands freezing to the aircraft.

Anti-aircraft fire was another concern of crews. It was often so heavy that at the end of a mission shrapnel could be swept out of an aircraft with a broom. To help keep casualties down, various types of body armor and helmets were devised for aircrew. The body armor (*19*), was first devised in the US in 1942. It is made of manganese steel plates. Though heavy and uncomfortable, they proved popular, and by 1944 over 13,000 were in service with the aircrew of the 8th Air Force.

developed it took a twelve-man team of interpreters more than two days to produce an initial assessment of what the photographs revealed; that is hardly surprising, for by then the Allies had landed more than 1½ million men and 300,000 vehicles. Detailed examination of the prints took several weeks. From then on high-flying Arados flew regular photographic missions over the Allied rear areas. Yet the time had almost passed when such intelligence might play a decisive part in the land battle. By now the US armored units were streaming out from the Cotentin Peninsula, and their spearheads were thrusting east, west and south into the hinterland and meeting little opposition.

On August 7 the German Army launched Operation *Lüttich*, a powerful counter attack by five Panzer divisions and elements of a fourth with the intention of driving west to cut off the American advance. That morning a cloak of mist prevented air operations, allowing the German troops to make good progress. By noon the skies had cleared, however, and for the first time since D-Day Allied fighter-bombers went into action against columns of enemy vehicles moving in the open by day. Nineteen squadrons of rocket-firing Typhoons maintained a shuttle service of attacks against the tank columns. Meanwhile, Spitfires, Mustangs, Thunderbolts, and Lightnings strafed the soft-skinned

vehicles and mounted barrier patrols to prevent German fighters from interfering. By the end of the day the German advance had been halted for the loss of more than a hundred tanks. Despite determined attempts to renew the assault, the scale of Allied air power thwarted troop movements during the daylight hours and this, combined with a stiffening of resistance on the ground, forced the abandonment of *Lüttich*.

Now in an exposed salient and unable to advance, the German Army began to pull back its forces. And again there were lucrative targets for the marauding Allied fighter-bombers. During an armed reconnaissance mission along a road near Carrouges on August 13, for example, a Thunderbolt pilot of the 366th Fighter Group caught sight of a couple of trucks parked under trees. As he pulled round to line himself up for a strafing attack he suddenly noticed what looked like trees growing in the middle of the road.

Above: The large tonnages delivered onto German tactical targets required that the 8th Army Air Force expand its already huge bomb dumps. Handled here with care but confidence, these bombs lack their stabilizing fins and all-important fuzes.

Above: Armorers reload the outer wing troughs with the 0.5-in ammunition for the eight machine guns of this Republic P-47 Thunderbolt. Ammunition capacity was 425 rounds per gun, reduced to 267 rounds per gun when bombs were carried.

Below: A group of GIs, standing in front of a Piper L-4 Grasshopper observation aircraft, watch the first P-38 Lightning land on a newly created airstrip in Normandy on June 10. Such forward-based aircraft could provide very quick reaction when needed.

Below left: With its armament of four 20mm cannon and eight rockets or two 1,000lb (450kg) bombs, the Hawker Typhoon Mk IB was a superb anti-tank weapon flown by such units as No.185 Squadron, one of whose aircraft is being rearmed at Thorney Island on June 15.

Below: These Republic P-47 Thunderbolt heavy fighters are operating from a forward airstrip in the Normandy lodgment, where they could be rearmed, refuelled and undergo minor repairs, though anything more extensive required a return to England.

Above: The A-2 jacket of 1st Lt. Melvin J. Strunk, navigator of B-17G "L'il Eight Ball." Lt. Strunk flew with the 447th Bomb Group, 8th Air Force. The artwork on the back of the jacket was painted by an American NCO in England. Top: A photograph of "L'il Eight Ball" in England. In front of the aircraft is her crew chief Master Sgt. Michael Kashak.
Jacket courtesy of Melvin J. Strunk

Examination revealed about 30 heavily camouflaged tanker trucks in the area and at least six tanks taking on fuel. The pilot summoned the rest of the Group by radio and the fighter-bombers carried out repeated bombing and strafing runs. When the aircraft departed, having expended their munitions, they left behind a line of blazing vehicles more than a mile (1.6km) long. Elsewhere that day, Thunderbolts of the 36th Fighter Group located a column of several hundred vehicles on the move near Argentan and destroyed a large number of them.

Meanwhile, the American armored thrust plunged deep into France. As other units headed towards Paris and other important cities, the US XV Corps swung north for Argentan. At the same time Canadian and Polish troops advanced on the Falaise area, threatening to envelop the 16 German divisions pulling back from positions to the west of those towns. By August 16 the net was drawing tight and the network of narrow roads leading out of the pocket filled with vehicles of all types moving eastwards. Allied fighter-bombers attacked with bombs, rockets and cannon destroying hundreds of vehicles and creating numerous road blocks, that prevented movement altogether in some areas. The German troops abandoned their vehicles and heavy equipment, and fought their way out of the pocket on foot.

Operation *Dragoon*

On August 15 Allied troops launched Operation *Dragoon*, an assault landing on the French Mediterranean coast. The Luftwaffe had about 65 Junkers Ju 88 torpedo bombers and 25 Dornier Do 217s carrying glider bombs based within reach of the landing area, but there were no fighters in the area until a single Gruppe of Messerschmitt Bf 109s was rushed there from Italy. The ships were well protected by land-based and carrier-based fighters, and the German attempts to strike at them had little success. Only one ship, an LST, was sunk by direct air attack, while air-dropped mines accounted for a few small craft. Within a few days of the landings Luftwaffe air activity over southern France ceased altogether.

By mid-August the Luftwaffe units in France were on the brink of collapse. Luftflotte 3 was down to its last 75 single-engined fighters and their number was dwindling rapidly. To cover the withdrawal of ground forces a further four Gruppen of fighters were transfered from Germany. One of the units to arrive at this time was IInd Gruppe of Jagdgeschwader 6, an Fw 190 unit that had been recently formed with pilots from disbanded twin-engined bomber-destroyer units. The Gruppe flew to Herpy near Reims on August 23, and one of its pilots, Feldwebel Fritz Buchholz, recalled: "Our airstrip at Herpy was nothing more than a piece of flat cow pasture surrounded by trees in which our aircraft could be hidden; nearby was our tented accommodation. The Allied fighter-bombers seemed to be everywhere and our survival depended on the strictest attention to camouflage. As part of this we even had a herd of cows which moved on to the airfield when no flying was in progress; as well as giving the place a rustic look, these performed the valuable task of obliterating the tracks made on the grass by the aircraft. Such attention to detail paid off and there were no attacks on Herpy while I was there."

The Gruppe flew its first major operation on August 25, when it mounted an offensive patrol with some 40 aircraft over the St. Quentin area. The Focke-Wulfs surprised a dozen Lightnings of the 367th Fighter Group, 9th Air Force in the act of strafing the airfield at Clastres, and shot down six of them. The American pilots' distress calls summoned the other two squadrons of the Group to the area, and when these joined the fight they quickly turned the tables. Numerically the two forces were almost equal, but the German pilots lacked experience in dogfighting and suffered accordingly. In the resulting mêlée the Gruppe lost 16 aircraft destroyed and several more damaged, and accounted for only one more Lightning. Fritz Buchholz survived the encounter but on the next day he was bounced by a Mustang, shot down and wounded.

The withdrawal of the Luftwaffe from France quickly disintegrated into a rout. The fighter Gruppen sent from Germany to cover the move all suffered heavy losses, and they made no noticeable difference to the predicament of the German army units which had to face repeated attacks from the air as they headed east. With the exception of its one small reconnaissance unit, the Luftwaffe played no effective role in this phase of the land battle. One German soldier who took part in the Battle of Normandy and the subsequent retreat later commented with some bitterness: "If the aircraft above us were camouflaged, we knew they were British. If they were silver, we knew they were American. And if they weren't there at all, we knew they were German!" His pungent remark sums up, more effectively than any statistical list of aircraft involved or damage inflicted, the degree of air supremacy achieved by the Allied air forces during the Battle of France.

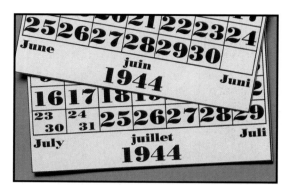

The Normandy Battleground

8

Nigel de Lee

By June 10, the Allied forces had established and secured a lodgment in Normandy. Four corps were ashore, with their forward elements well inland of the assault beaches, connected by a continuous perimeter. They enjoyed the benefits of safe logistic and administration areas, and mutual support.

The US VII Corps was pressing northwards against Montebourg, westwards to force the line of the River Merderet, and south to invest Carentan. To the southeast of the US VII Corps, the US V Corps, having bounced across the marshy flood plain of the River Aure, was pushing south towards the River Elle. East of their area the British XXX Corps was struggling through the bocage south of Bayeux. British I Corps was deployed astride the River Orne, held to the north of Caen, with the troops east of the river crowded into a shallow bridgehead overlooked by enemy positions. Reinforcements and supplies poured in across the beaches; the minor ports were being cleared, and the two *Mulberry* harbors, one off *Omaha* beach and one near *Gold*, were being assembled.

Rommel's plan to contain the landing forces on the beaches with his fortified positions, and destroy them between the tidelines, had failed. Because of Hitler's belief that the Allied assault on Normandy was a feint, he was reluctant to release the mobile reserve forces that von Rundstedt and Geyr von Schweppenburg wanted to launch in a counterstroke. Those German units that were ordered to Normandy were hindered and delayed by the effects of Operation *Pointblank*, the offensive patrols of the 2nd Tactical Air Force, and disruption caused by the French Resistance. The German forces were unable to mount a major counteroffensive; all they could do was to defend and make

local counterattacks. In the American sector, these were directed towards clearing the area around Carentan, in an attempt to force the US VII and V Corps apart. But the fall of Carentan to a pincer attack by both US corps on June 12 frustrated these German efforts. In the British sector, the most dangerous counterattacks were made by 21st Panzer Division, which continuously probed the defences of the bridgehead east of the Orne.

As the Allied buildup continued, the senior commanders considered their plans. Montgomery had expected that once the hard crust of coastal defenses had been penetrated, the Germans would conduct a fighting withdrawal, using counterattacks, ambushes and blocking actions to reduce and delay the Allied armies, until they reached strong positions on the Seine. He had planned to make the whole Allied beachhead absolutely secure, and build up an overwhelming superiority of men and materiel.

Once certain of this superiority, he would launch breakout operations on both flanks simultaneously. The Anglo-Canadian armies in the east would pivot on Caen, swing to their left, and drive for the Seine. In the west, the American forces were to break out on an axis selected by Gen. Bradley. Once through the enemy lines, they were to send one army southwestwards to liberate Brittany. Another army was to move to the southeast, and advance parallel to the Anglo-Canadian troops, to the Seine. Once on the Seine, the Allies would have to prepare for a succession of opposed crossing operations.

But it was apparent by June 10 that the Germans would not conform to Montgomery's expectations, and that his plans would have to be changed. Contrary to the conventional military doctrines, the Germans did not conduct a withdrawal after the beach defenses had been overrun. Hitler insisted that his soldiers must defend every inch of ground, and die in position rather than yield. This meant that the Allied armies did not advance as rapidly as intended. In the British sector, operations were particularly inhibited by the failure to take Caen as planned on D-Day. Caen was of critical importance as the most important center of communications in the British area. The Germans proved to be tenacious and very skillful in making the best possible use of the ground they were defending. They were assisted by the weather.

Left: M1915 Adrian helmets, revolvers and brassard used by the FFI/Resistance. The revolvers are, left: a Smith and Wesson M1917, and right: a French M1892. The Cross of Lorraine brassard and the right-hand helmet were used by the commanding officer of the Resistance in Caen, Leonard Gille.
Memorial Museum of Bayeux

Spells of heavy rain deprived the Allies of the benefits of their superiority in air power and in artillery.

Allied plans and actions were modified in accordance with the enemy behavior and adverse circumstances. The British Second Army mounted a series of offensive operations which aimed to take Caen and advance south of the city. An attack eastwards was barred by the inundated valley of the Dives, where the German engineers had worked to extend the flooded area. An attack south to the west of Bayeux would be impeded by a series of steep ridges, and dense bocage country. The British offensives, *Perch*, *Epsom*, *Charnwood*, and *Goodwood*, did not achieve a breakout. But they did maintain pressure on the German Army, so that it was never able to assemble a reserve big enough to make a successful counterattack. The British offensives also drew in German reinforcements. Highly mobile Panzer units were employed in static containment operations, digging in to hold ground. When not involved in making major offensives, the soldiers of the British Second Army kept up the pressure by constant local attacks and aggressive patrolling. These offensive activities were not decisive, but did have a great effect on the Germans. The Panzer reserves were held in waiting in front of the Second Army's sector, because it was closest to Paris and to Germany, and therefore, according to conventional military thinking, the most likely place for the Allies to attempt their decisive attack. This meant that the German Army was never able to seize the initiative, and suffered from a very limited maneuver.

Like Montgomery and Dempsey, Bradley gave top priority to securing his base in Normandy. He felt confident that given a secure beachhead he could build up a local superiority that would guarantee victory, and was in no mood to risk a setback by optimistic and premature offensives. By mid-June he decided that his first aim must be to clear the Cotentin Peninsula and take Cherbourg. If the Cotentin remained in enemy hands, it would be a permanent menace to the rear of the US First Army. Furthermore, the German division in the Channel Islands and other formations located in Brittany might be sent into Cherbourg to reinforce the threat. On the other hand, once captured and cleared, Cherbourg would be a major asset to the Allied logistic infrastructure. Again, the fall of such

Above: Gen. Montgomery gives his first press conference to Allied War Correspondents at his tactical HQ at Creully, Normandy, June 12. The Reuters correspondent Doon Campbell, whose D-Day dispatch is quoted on page 111, is sitting to the right of Monty.

a strongly fortified and garrisoned port would be bound to damage the morale of the German Army.

Once the Cotentin and Cherbourg were clear, Bradley could choose a suitable place for a breakout to the south. He was intent upon breaking through the German defenders, and conducting a war of maneuver deep in their rear. Pushing back the enemy was bound to be a slow process, and costly in casualties. Bradley wanted a swift, decisive operation to minimize casualties. But it was not easy to pick a good axis for the breakout attack. In the far west of the American sector there were desolate moorlands strewn with rocks, bad going for armor and affording little cover for infantry. Inland of the moors were extensive marshlands, extended by German hydraulic engineers, crossed by long straight causeways, too deep for wading and too shallow and reedy for boats to cross. Beyond the marshes lay the bocage country, hills and deep, narrow streams, the hills one-third woodland and orchard, the rest a patchwork of tiny fields surrounded by hedgerows. In the extreme east of the American sector lay the great Forêt de Cerisy, dense woodland traversed by a few roads and rides which would canalize any large-scale movement.

The key ground to the south of the US First Army was the town of St. Lô, which had been scheduled for capture by June 12. St. Lô was at the center of the major road network in west Normandy, and commanded crossings of the Vire, the most important river in the American sector. The town had been flattened by incessant bombing between June 6 and 12, but remained in German hands. As Bradley was deciding to take Cherbourg before moving south, the German command concluded that St. Lô was more important than the Cotentin. Accordingly, the German plan was to hold St. Lô, not only to retain a

center of communication, but also to test the morale and resolution of the American Army and if possible to break its spirit.

Bradley knew that the capture of St. Lô would cost his army bitter fighting and heavy casualties and was reluctant to attack the town directly. But the logic of geography was inexorable. Having attempted to push his troops across the marshes to the west of the Vire, and probed the moorlands beyond, Bradley was eventually driven to the conclusion that there could be no breakout until St. Lô was taken. Thus, just as in the British sector the vital operations were centered on Caen, in the US sector the most important and vicious battle was fought for St. Lô. Once St. Lô fell, on July 18, the way was clear for operation *Cobra* — the decisive breakout attack.

Operation *Perch*

The first major British offensive began on June 10. The plan for Operation *Perch* was to make a wide outflanking maneuver to the west of Caen, crossing the River Odon to seize high ground near Evrécy. The XXX Corps was to employ the 50th Division to break defensive positions held by Panzer Lehr in the area of Tilly sur Seulles, Juvigny, Hottot and la Senaudière. Once the way was clear, 7th Armoured Division was to drive through to Evrécy, taking Villers-Bocage on the way. Montgomery arranged for Allied tactical aircraft to provide reconnaissance. The initial attack by 50th Division was also supported by the fire of two cruisers and a battleship.

Despite the lavish support, the attack by 50th Division made little progress. This was due in part to the inherent difficulty of movement through the bocage. But it was also because of the sheer quality of the enemy, the élite Panzer Lehr Division, which was effectively supported by the 12th SS Panzer

Left: Shoulder and breast patches of US War Correspondents and photographers. Though non-combatants, these individuals risked their lives in the war zones. Every army had similar personnel covering the conflict.
Stamatelos Collection

British Army Uniforms and Equipment

1. Royal Armoured Corps pattern steel helmet
2. Beret with the insignia of the Royal Tank Regt.
3. Armored crew denim overalls
4. Binoculars and P.37 compass pouch
5. First aid kit for armored fighting vehicles
6. Royal Tank Regt. designating pennant
7. P.37 web gaiters dyed black for armored personnel
8. Mk III steel helmet
9. P.37 webbing equipment
10. Battle dress blouse and trouser of a corporal, York and Lancaster Regt. 146th Brigade, 49th (West Riding) Division
11. P.37 web gaiter
12. Mk I steel helmet
13. Battle dress blouse of Maj. Royal Engineers with corduroy (whipcord) jodhpurs
14. Web map case, P.37 web waist belt and compass pouch
15. Web satchel for field signals
16. Tin of chocolates
17. Tin of cigarettes
18. Officer's service dress cap with the insignia of the Royal Engineers
19. Pre-1942 pattern officer's service dress jacket and trousers, bearing insignia of the Royal Engineers, XXX Corps
20. Sam Browne belt
21. Service boots

Memorial Museum, Bayeux

Division (Hitler Youth) from the east. On June 10 the Germans launched their own pre-emptive attacks on the forward positions of 50th Division. On the left side of 50th Division, the 8th Durham Light Infantry (DLI), newly in possession of the village of St. Pierre, next to Tilly, were vigorously attacked. From across the River Seulles they were subjected to heavy artillery and mortar bombardment by Panzer Lehr. From the east the 12th SS sent tanks to shell the village, and infantry to infiltrate through the orchards and gardens. These infiltration teams established machine gun posts to pour concentrated fire onto the Durhams. The 24th Lancers were deployed on Point 103, north of St. Pierre, to support the Durhams. But neither they nor the Sherwood Rangers who relieved them for the night of June 10/11 could move forward because the slope south of the hill was covered by the fire of Panzer Lehr's heavy tanks and self-propelled guns, dug in on higher ground west of the Seulles.

The Germans made four strong attacks on St. Pierre and Point 103 on June 11. The most violent occurred in the evening, described by an officer of the 24th Lancers:

''. . . a number of Tigers penetrated our positions, up to Brigade HQ. Six of our tanks were knocked out in as many seconds. We withdrew to the west of the hill. Hidden in the trees we sighted our guns onto the advancing monster Tigers and Panthers. The Shermans shook with the recoil of their guns. Most of our armour-piercing shells were bouncing harmlessly off the enemy . . . the few remaining tanks were called up, those that mounted the new enormous 17 pounder . . . An ear-splitting crack, a vivid flash — and whoosh — the leading Tiger stopped, smoked, and then burst into flames. The others began to withdraw. Meanwhile the German infantry were working their way up the left flank of the hill. I could hear the bullets pattering on the outside of my tank. The infantry could hardly lift their heads. The firing became intense . . . we held. Slowly darkness fell. The enemy withdrew.''

THE BATTLE FOR CAEN

Map A
Operation *Epsom*

This was the second major British offensive, the first, Operation *Perch*, had ended on June 15 (see page 151). Caen had been found to be too tough to take directly, and so *Epsom*, like *Perch*, was meant to outflank the city from the west. The operation was given to VIII Corps, together with elements of I and XXX Corps. The attack was divided into two phases. Phase I — the capture of high ground around Hill 112; Phase II — an advance eastwards across the Orne. *Epsom* began on June 26. The Hitler Youth soldiers of the 12th SS Panzer had built up their defenses in and around Cheux and progress through these fortified villages was slow. A bridge over the Odon River was captured, but the bridgehead and the road southeast, known as "Scotch Corridor" could not be held securely enough to maintain a presence of the 29th Armoured Brigade on Hill 112, which was coming under heavy German counterattack. On June 29, with seven Panzer divisions now deployed against the bridgehead, Hill 112 was evacuated and Phase II of *Epsom* cancelled.

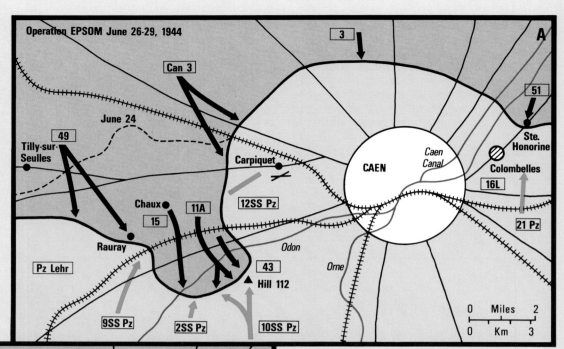

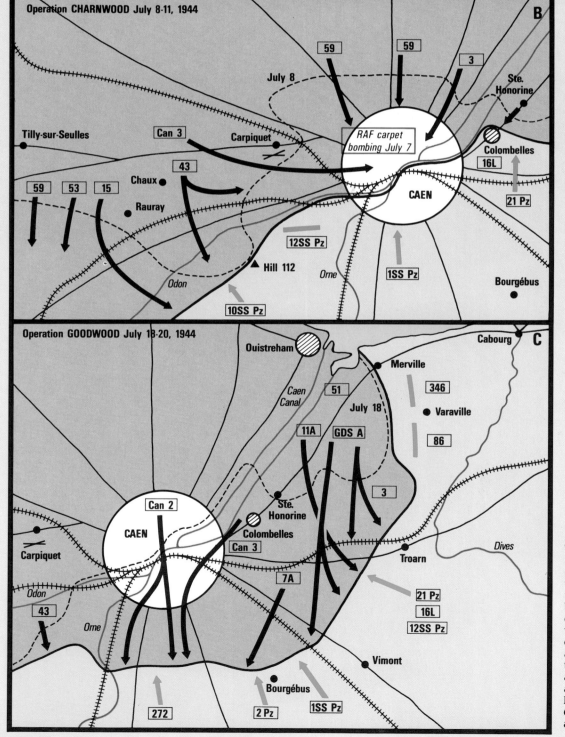

Map B
Operation *Charnwood*

Having failed twice to outflank Caen's defenses, Montgomery took the decision to storm them from three sides. On the left flank of the city, in July 4, the Canadians launched an attack to take the aerodrome and village of Carpiquet, held by tanks and Panzer Grenadiers of the 12th SS Panzer Division. The Canadians took four days to take these positions in the face of a fanatical defense by the heavily outnumbered Hitler Youth troops.

In support of the opening attack of *Charnwood*, on July 7 the northern areas of Caen were subjected to a massive carpet bombing. Over 2,000 tons of bombs were dropped on the city, devastating a huge area and killing 3,000 civilian inhabitants. The following day, Canadian and British troops found that their progress into Caen was hindered not only by the Germans, but also by the sheer scale of the destruction. By the end of the 8th, the center of the city had been reached by a brigade of the Canadian 3rd Division, but by then the German defenders had already pulled back across the Orne River destroying the remaining bridges as they did so.

Map C
Operation *Goodwood*

Any hope of reaching the open country to the south of Caen through the area of Hill 112, or through the center of Caen itself, had gone. The only avenue of advance left to the British Second Army was on the left flank west of the Orne. The plan was to use three armored divisions of VIII Corps in an all-out charge. Some 700 tanks would take part, largely unsupported by infantry or artillery, but having the benefit of tactical air cover and a massive preliminary air bombardment.

On July 18 2,000 bombers dropped 7,000 tons of fragmentation bombs on German postions. As the bombardment lifted, the tanks rolled south, their initial objectives being the Caen-Troarn railway and beyond that the vital ridge around Bourguébus. At first progress was good, through German units stunned by the weight of the air bombardment, but as the tanks approached Bourguébus they began to be destroyed in large numbers by the highly-organized system of German anti-tank weapons. The sheer number of tanks and the efficiency of their destruction soon threw the advance into chaos. By the end of the 18th, 220 tanks of VIII Corps had been destroyed for an advance of only six miles (9km). On the 19th, attacks continued towards Bourguébus, but late in the day the weather broke and *Goodwood* ground to a halt amongst rain, mud and burning tanks.

Next morning the HQ Squadron of 24th Lancers discovered a whole company of Panzer Grenadiers, lavishly equipped with close-range anti-tank weapons, who had infiltrated into their midst during the night.

On June 12 the enemy attacks abated. The 8th DLI were withdrawn from St. Pierre, having been reduced to half their effective strength.

Further west, 231st Brigade attempted to push south towards Hottot and Longraye, but were held up in the hedgerows. The German defenders had prepared successive defensive positions, and supported them with mobile counterattack groups of armor and infantry. They employed mines and antitank weapons to separate tanks from infantry, and snipers to kill leaders at all levels. The British attackers found it difficult to counter these tactics, and to coordinate their artillery and air support in the close country.

On June 12, the XXX Corps commander, Gen. Bucknall, decided that he must change the plan. Whilst the 50th Division continued to attack to hold Panzer Lehr, the 7th Armoured Division would move further west. Here they would advance through positions held by the German 352nd Division, which had been heavily engaged for six days and was showing signs of demoralization. During the afternoon of June 12, the 22nd Armoured Brigade, followed up by 131st Motorized Infantry Brigade, moved round the western flank of Panzer Lehr, skirting the inter-army boundary beyond which the US V Corps was advancing on Caumont. Enemy resistance was light, and early on the morning of June 13, the 7th Division's leading elements passed through Villers-Bocage unopposed. At Point 103, on the road to Caen, A Squadron of the County of London Yeomanry (CLY) and A Company of the 1st Rifle Brigade halted. As the sentries were being deployed, the column was attacked by a detachment of German tanks led by SS-Hauptsturmführer Michael Wittmann, who had driven west from Baron-sur-Odon in search of action. Wittmann's approach had been masked by the bulge of the ridge, and the noise of his tanks' engines muffled by the trees and drowned by the sounds of CLY's own vehicles, so he achieved complete surprise. The first round from the 88mm gun on his Tiger destroyed the leading vehicle in the British column, so immobilizing the tanks and halftracks stretching behind it into Villers-Bocage. As his accompanying four Mark IV Panzers engaged the head of the column, Wittmann motored along it, putting a shell into each vehicle as he passed. Wittmann drove through the town, then returned to attack the confused British troops in it again. On his third pass through the town centre, a Sherman Firefly waiting in ambush, using the shopwindow opposite the square as a mirror, knocked out the Tiger with a hit on the engine. Wittmann and his crew fled on foot, pistols in hand, and got clean away.

Meanwhile, German tanks and infantry from the 2nd Panzer Division began to arrive in small detachments, and attempted to break into Villers-Bocage from the south. By late afternoon the Germans were making well-coordinated attacks with infantry and artillery, and the 22nd Armoured Brigade

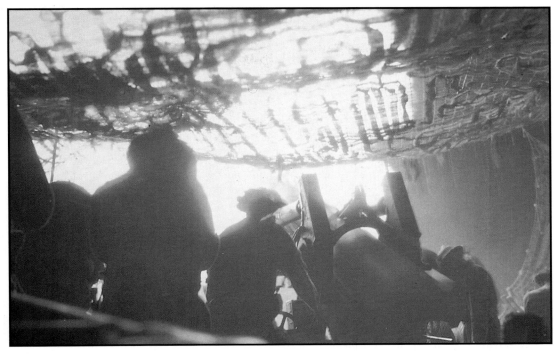

moved back westwards to occupy a position just east of Amaye-sur-Seulles. Here the brigade set up a box position. This position withstood a series of German attacks: noisy attacks made by armor and infantry with substantial support from mortars and artillery, and silent infiltration by infantry. Meanwhile, the 7th Armoured Division HQ ordered the 131st Brigade to keep open the line of communication to 22nd Armoured Brigade, and hoped that 50th Division could advance to reach the box. However, the corps commander decided that 7th Armoured Division was vulnerable to isolation, and ordered it to withdraw. During the night of June 14/15, with massive support from the corps artillery, 7th Armoured Division withdrew to positions in conformity with the 50th Division's front line. The 2nd Panzer Division attempted a pursuit, but was severely checked by the 7th Division's rearguard. The operation had not reached its objectives, indeed 50th Division did not secure Hottot until June 19, and Villers-Bocage was not taken until early August. However, German plans to insert 2nd Panzer Division along the inter-army boundary had been frustrated.

Operation *Epsom*

The next major British offensive, *Epsom*, was carried out by VIII Corps, which was forming up in Normandy. The assembly of the corps, and the offensive, were delayed by the storm of June 19-22. The attack began on June 26. The plan for *Epsom* had two phases. For Phase I the objectives were Hills 112 and 113 near Evrécy, as in Operation *Perch*. Once this high ground had been taken it was to be the base for Phase II, an advance eastwards across the Orne, to seize key ground south of Caen, so threatening that city with encirclement. The axis of advance for Phase I was east of Tilly-sur-Seulles, and ran across the front held by 3rd Canadian Division, part of I Corps. To the immediate west of the VIII Corps' avenue of attack was the Rauray Spur, a ridge of high ground which dominated ground to the east and south, and covered the road running from Villers-Bocage to Caen. The 49th Division, part of XXX Corps, was ordered to take

Above: The British 5.5-in gun was an excellent piece of field artillery firing by day or night, and the pounding given to the Germans by gun crews such as this were instrumental in destroying the cohesion of some units and demoralizing many others.

this feature on June 25. On the other flank, 3rd Canadian Division was to continue its attempts to take the aerodrome at Carpiquet. Before the ground troops moved forward, German positions south of the start line were to be attacked by a mass of strategic bombers. Tactical aircraft based in the theater were to cover the flanks of the VIII Corps sector, and interdict enemy forces moving into the area. Phase I was to commence with a massive artillery barrage fired by 552 field, 112 medium, 48 heavy and 24 heavy anti-aircraft guns drawn from all three corps and Army Troops. The Navy would provide additional support from three cruisers and a monitor. The 15th Scottish Division was to lead the attack for Phase I, with two brigades forward, following a creeping barrage, supported by Churchill tanks of the 31st Tank Brigade. Once the 15th Division had cleared the bottleneck at the village of Cheux, provided all was going well the 11th Armoured Division was to advance through 15th Division on two axes, seize bridges over the Odon, and go on to take Hills 112 and 113. The 43rd Division would consolidate the captured ground whilst 15th Division moved up to support the armored division. If the 15th Division was held up, then 11th Armoured would be held back until an opportunity for exploitation was perceived. The 4th Armoured Brigade was attached to the corps for use as a mobile reserve.

In the event, the enemy and the weather combined to disrupt the plan for *Epsom*. The Germans were acutely aware of the importance of the Rauray Spur, and determined to hold it. The attack by the 49th Division on June 25, made with two brigades forward and an armored brigade in support, was repulsed. The village of Rauray was eventually taken late on June 27, but the Germans continued to contest control of the village and Spur with repeated counterattacks. This

Waffen-SS Uniforms and Equipment

1 2nd type camouflage helmet cover
2 2nd model field cap
3 2nd type camouflage smock in plane tree pattern. Note reversible Fall (autumn) colors at neck
4 Camouflage clothing rank insignia, see caption
5 M-42 steel helmet with ''SS'' decal
6 Officer's visor cap. Note silver cords
7 Officer's M-42 field cap
8 Officer's first pattern M-42 field cap
9 Field gray tunic and trousers of assault gun unit, of 2nd SS Panzer
10 SS officer's field belt
11 Binoculars, 7x50, slide rule, plotting board and compass
12 2nd Model field cap
13 Officers' early pattern service cap
14 Helmet and cover of 1st pattern camouflage with sniper's rope face veil
15 1st type camouflage smock in palm tree pattern. Note reversible Fall (autumn) colors
16 Leather marching boots
17 German ID tag
18 Collar insignia of SS-Obersturmbannführer Lt. Col.
19 SS shoulder straps
20 M1940 forage cap
21 Jacket of SS-Sturmmann (private)
22 Belt and buckle
23 Trousers for 21

Memorial Museum, Bayeux

Camouflage smock *3*, was found near Caen, and was probably used by personnel of the 9th "Hohenstaufen" or 10th "Frundsberg" SS Panzer Division. The camouflage clothing insignia (*4*), was introduced in 1943. Top row, left to right: SS-Unterscharführer, SS-Scharführer, SS-Oberscharführer, SS-Hauptscharführer, SS-Sturmscharführer, (corporal, sergeant, color-sergeant, sergeant-major, warrant officer). SS-Untersturmführer, SS-Obersturmführer, SS-Hauptsturmführer, (2nd Lt, 1st Lt, Capt). SS-Sturmbannführer, SS-Obersturmbannführer, SS-Standartenführer, (Maj., Lt. Col, Col). Camouflage smock (*15*), was collected in Caen and was used by a member of the 1st SS Panzer Division. The SS-Sturmmann's jacket (*21*) was worn by a member of the 17th Panzer Grenadier Division "Götz von Berlichingen."

meant that throughout *Epsom*, the right flank of the VIII Corps, axis of advance was insecure, and the road from Villers-Bocage via Noyers-Bocage was open for Panzer counterattacks. On the morning of June 26 the weather in England was too bad for the strategic bombers to fly, so they could not bomb ahead of the start line as planned.

The weather in Normandy was wet, but this did not prevent the artillery from preparing the way for the infantry; 240 field guns and 80 medium guns fired a creeping barrage from the start line just south of Bretteville-l'Orgueilleuse and Brouay, whilst the other guns did counterbattery shoots or put concentrations on the flanks and targets in depth.

This effort employed the largest concentration of guns used so far on the Allied front. Behind the barrage the infantry advanced, the 46th Brigade, with two battalions leading, heading for Cheux, and the 44th Brigade in similar formation moving on St. Manvieu. They were closely accompanied by Churchill tanks. The ground ahead was held by the Engineer Battalion of 12th SS Panzer.

Initially, the Scots advanced briskly. The Hitler Youth soldiers deployed in the cornfields had been stunned and driven deep into their rifle pits by the bombardment; when they raised their heads they were assailed by furious Scotsmen yelling and hurling grenades. But around le Mesnil-Patry an

German Armored Unit Uniforms and Insignia

1 Officer's field cap
2 NCO Panzer jacket
3 Panzer marksmanship lanyard
4 Panzer trousers
5 General officer's collar tab
6 Lieutenant general's shoulder tab
7 Throat microphone
8 Vehicle intercom headphones
9 Officer's cap
10 Major's shoulder strap
11 Pair of lieutenant's shoulder straps
12 NCO's shoulder straps
13 Helmet with cover
14 Self-propelled gun crew NCO jacket
15 Army waist belt and holster for P.38
16 M1943 helmet
17 Trousers for 14
18 General officer's vehicle pennant
19 Waffen-SS Panzer field service cap
20 Waffen-SS Pea Pattern camouflage Panzer uniform
21 Pistol belt and Radom P.35p holster
22 Web gaiters for 23
23 Short combat boots
24 Four SS shoulder straps, see caption
25 SS divisional cuff titles, see caption
26 Luftwaffe officer's service cap
27 1st Lt. Panzer jacket and trousers
28 Luftwaffe enlisted man's waist belt
29 Luftwaffe web gaiters

Memorial Museum, Bayeux

On cap *1*, note the Panzer service color, pink, on the reverse chevron. The color also appears on items *9-12*. On jacket *2* appears the "Afrika Korps" cuff title, an entitlement of the 21st Panzer Division. Insignia of jacket *14* carries the artillery service color, red. The vehicle pennant and cover (*18*), was found at the Panzer Group West HQ at Château-la-Caine. The SS shoulder straps (*24*) are those of (from left to right) major, lieutenant, captain, corporal; the latter carries the embroidered monogram of the 1st SS Panzer Division. The SS divisional cuff titles (*25*) are, from top: 17th SS Panzer Grenadiers; 10th SS Panzer; 1st SS Panzer; 2nd SS Panzer; 12th SS Panzer; 9th SS Panzer; and 1st SS Regiment which was part of 2nd SS Panzer. Item (*27*) is that of Panzer Division "Hermann Goering" a Luftwaffe unit which was fighting in Poland in July '44.

anti-tank minefield stopped the Churchills accompanying the 46th Brigade, leaving the infantry to press on alone. The going was heavy due to the rain, and south of the River Mue, the infantry fell behind their creeping barrage. The Hitler Youth sappers had thoroughly prepared Cheux and St. Manvieu for defense; the villages had been loopholed, mined and garnished with booby-traps. By the time the British assaults began, the German defenders had recovered from the effects of the barrage. The 44th Brigade took St. Manvieu by noon, but were then mortared and shelled continuously, except during two counterattacks made from the east by 12th SS Panzer and 21st Panzer in the afternoon.

The 46th Brigade had to clear Cheux by close-quarter fighting house to house, in which the 2nd Glasgow Highlanders lost 12 officers and 200 soldiers. It proved impossible to drive the Germans out of le Haut-du-Bosq, a straggling settlement southwest of Cheux, running up the rising ground towards Rauray. The Germans on the Rauray Spur and in le Haut-du-Bosq supported each other very effectively. The official history of the VIII Corps remarked of the situation on the afternoon of June 26 "The wooded areas from the southern slopes of le Haut-du-Bosq to the west and southwest were unsubdued and filled with small parties of infantry, supported by tanks, often dug in, and anti-tank guns

Götz von Berlichingen

Frundsberg

Adolf Hitler

Das Reich

Hitlerjugend

Hohenstaufen

Deutschland

which, through their effective concealment and rapid changes of position, gave much trouble."

In the early afternoon the Northamptonshire Yeomanry, reconnoitering for 11th Armoured Division, struggled through the ruins of Cheux. Just south of the village they were attacked by infantry with sticky bombs. On reaching the Ruisseau de Sabley they were fired on by anti-tank guns directly to the south. The 29th Armoured Brigade moved southwards through Cheux with difficulty, but did not attempt to rush the Odon bridges.

On the evening of June 26, the 227th Brigade, the third brigade of the 15th Division, moved forward, but was stopped on the Ruisseau de Sabley. During the night the 43rd Division relieved the 44th and 46th Brigades, which prepared to resume the attack next day. On the morning of June 27 all attempts to move down the western axis to take the bridges at Gavrus were stopped. Indeed, in the morning a German armored force fought its way up the road covered by the Rauray Spur and got into Cheux for an hour. But on the eastern flank the British made progress. German attempts to concentrate forces for counterattacks attracted attacks by RAF 83 Group Typhoons, which broke them up. The 227th Brigade forced its way, in column of battalions, down the road through Colleville and Tourville to seize the bridge at Tourmauville. The battalions of the brigade dug-in and held the road. This was uncomfortable, and dangerous, for the enemy held higher ground south of the Odon in its steep wooded valley. The road, now known as "Scotch Corridor," was fired upon by nebelwerfers, mortars, artillery and anti-tank guns. The soldiers could do nothing but simply had to sit in their foxholes and endure the bombardment. Despite the shelling, 29th Armoured Brigade raced down the road, across the Tourmauville bridge, and on to Hill 112.

Below: A field conference of the commanders of SS Tank Battalion 101 takes place in front of a Tiger Ausf E. The tank ace Michael Wittmann commanded the battalion's 2 Kompanie. The variety of uniforms worn by Panzer troops in combat is very evident.

Above: Troops of an SS division, possibly the 12th SS Panzer, counterattack through a field of crops around Caen, during the bitter struggle for that city. The variety of types of camouflage used is noticeable in the uniforms of these young SS soldiers.

Later in the day the 159th Brigade, the motorized infantry of 11th Armoured Division, moved up to form a defensive perimeter around the bridge. This relieved the 2nd Argyll and Sutherland Highlanders, who went off on an adventure of their own. In the late afternoon patrols sent westwards along the banks of the Odon discovered that the bridges at Gavrus were undefended; the Germans had created a strong position on the road to the north. The whole battalion moved to secure the bridges. This was a difficult move; according to Maj. McElwee, a veteran of the action, it was "a nightmare trek through the thick woods lining both banks of the Odon. All-round defence in such country was impossible. The going was vile, and at one place the whole march was held up for over an hour while the anti-tank guns were man-handled over a sticky patch. Any well-planned ambush might have proved fatal." Once at Gavrus the Argylls deployed, and waited for the road north to be opened, but it never was. Instead the battalion was isolated by persistent attacks. Attempts by the 15th Division to force the road through the German positions at le Valtru failed. Indeed, this was the area of the strongest and most frequent German counterattacks. Eventu-

ally the battalion withdrew on the night of July 1-2, having been cut off for four days.

Meanwhile, 11th Armoured Division had made the most of the eastern axis. On June 28, the 29th Armoured Brigade, reinforced by 44th Royal Tank Regiment, had cleared and secured the crown of Hill 112. Next day the Germans were driven from their positions on the south slopes of the hill. The 29th Armoured Brigade enjoyed excellent views across the valley of the Orne to the rolling downlands south of Caen.

However, Gen. O'Connor, the commander of VIII Corps, was concerned. The enemy continued active resistance on the western side of his axis. The wooded Odon valley was vulnerable to infiltration by infantry. Scotch Corridor, the only line of communication to Hill 112, was subject to enemy observation and under heavy fire. There was intelligence that the II SS Panzer Corps was moving into the area to deliver a counterstroke. Accordingly, on June 28, O'Connor ordered that there was to be no further advance until the area between Cheux and the Odon had been thoroughly mopped up. On June 29 the Germans showed their strength by preparing five counterattacks. A column of three battalions mixed with armor attacked up the road from Noyers-Bocage and broke into Cheux; an infantry assault pushed eastwards into Grainville; there was a push on Gavrus which forced the Argylls out of the village; 29th Armoured Brigade was forced back up the south slope of Hill 112 and a force of 40 tanks moved westward from Caen. These attacks were all greatly disrupted by British artillery and tactical air power. The Panzers motoring out from Caen were caught in the open near Carpiquet by Typhoons and dispersed. The other attacks were crushed by massive artillery bombardments. The Germans made no serious attacks on June 30, but on July 1 attempted to push along four axes, from east and west, simultaneously. Once again, the artillery broke up these attacks before they could make an effective impact. The sheer volume of high explosive demoralized the

German soldiers; the commander of 2nd Panzer Division, von Luttwitz, remarked: "The incredibly heavy artillery and mortar fire of the enemy is something new both for the seasoned veterans of the Eastern Front and new arrivals."

But the German counterattacks on June 29 had been effective, for they persuaded O'Connor that he could not proceed to Phase II of *Epsom*, and should withdraw 29th Armoured Brigade from Hill 112. The 29th Armoured Brigade felt disappointed, but, as Gen. Roberts, the divisional commander, observed, they were ". . . out on a limb". The brigade evacuated Hill 112 on the night of June 29. The VIII Corps was reinforced by 53rd Division and 32nd Guards Brigade, and consolidated its gains. *Epsom* had gained about six miles (9.6km) and inflicted serious damage on the enemy, especially during the repeated and unsuccessful counterattacks made by the Panzer formations. Apart from 12th SS Panzer, these included Panzer Lehr, 2nd Panzer, 21st Panzer, 1st SS Panzer, 9th SS Panzer and 10th SS Panzer. All the divisions could have been employed more effectively in the offensive role had they not been drawn to contain the Odon bridgehead. In fact, *Epsom* had forced Rommel to commit his entire strategic reserve in Normandy, and convinced him that the German Seventh Army should make a fighting withdrawal to the Seine. But Hitler absolutely forbade any withdrawal; he argued that in the face of Allied superiority in airpower and artillery the only sensible policy was to dig in deep and defend every inch of ground.

Operations *Charnwood* and *Goodwood*

Having failed to take Caen on D-Day, and made two fruitless attempts to compromise the garrison of the city by flanking maneuvers, Montgomery decided that the British Second Army must storm it. He had considered an offensive operation from east of the Odon, but ruled it out because the bridgehead was small, congested with troops, and overlooked by the enemy from three sides. However, there was no doubt the Germans would exact a very high price for Caen.

On July 4, the Canadian 3rd Division attacked and took the village of Carpiquet, but were repulsed from the airfield by 12th SS Panzer. The main attack on Caen, Operation *Charnwood*, was made on July 8. The I Corps deployed the 3rd Canadian Division to the west, British 59th Division in the center and the British 3rd Division on the east. In order to overawe the enemy and hearten the attacking troops, Bomber Command devastated the city in a massive raid on the evening of July 7. But the Germans had located most of their defensive positions so close to the British front line that the bombs missed them. In fact, the physical effects of the bombing made the task of clearing Caen much more difficult for I Corps. However, they fought through the German defenses and cleared the city up to the Orne. The Germans, however, retained the industrial quarters east of the river.

Ten days later, Second Army launched Operation *Goodwood*, the last great British attack before the breakout in the west. By mid-July Montgomery was under political

Above: Men of the 1st Battalion of the Welsh Guards (32nd Guards Brigade of the Guards Armoured Division), prepare to move forward from a concealed position near Cagny on July 19. This area was about the farthest south penetrated by the British during *Goodwood*.

pressure to do something decisive, or at least spectacular, to appease the press and public opinion. The success of the landings on June 6 had created a euphoria and expectation of easy victory which had been disappointed. Montgomery's critics at SHAEF, in particular Air Marshal Tedder, claimed that the Allied breakout had been delayed because Montgomery was too cautious. This pressure made Montgomery apprehensive. He was also aware that in the American sector Bradley was having difficulty; his plan to advance down the west side of the Cotentin to Coutances had stalled, and progress towards St. Lô was slow and costly. The Germans had reinforced Seventh Army with infantry, and were planning to create a mobile armored reserve with which to make a major counter-

Right: Photographed in the western suburbs of Caen in the first few days after D-Day, motorized units and Panthers of the 12th SS Panzer Division advance to meet the Canadians who are coming from the *Juno* area towards Carpiquet aerodrome.

Below: A Hitler Youth flag, bearing an organization number top left. This flag was taken from a building by a French liaison officer with the US First Army on the advance from *Utah* to Cherbourg.
Memorial Museum, Bayeux

Waffen-SS and German Army Uniforms and Equipment

1 Waffen-SS Panzer M1943 (M-43) field cap, first pattern
2 Italian Navy black leather uniform worn by armored personnel of 12th SS Panzer Division "Hitler Jugend"
3 Waffen-SS belt and buckle
4 P.35 Radom holster
5 Short laced boots
6 Waffen-SS M-43 cap of Army splinter pattern camouflage material
7 Waffen-SS M-40 new style field cap
8 Waffen-SS jacket and trousers of armored personnel in Italian camouflage material, known as "Normandy Pattern" used by personnel of the 12th SS Panzer Division "Hitler Jugend"
9 Army issue 'pullover' shirt: rayon and cotton blend
10 Short laced leather combat boots
11 Lt. Col. of Artillery (Army) field jacket and riding breeches (Reithose)
12 Army officer's two piece aluminum buckle and web belt
13 P.38 holster
14 M-42 camouflaged steel helmet
15 Army officer's M1933 field cap
16 Officer's leather greatcoat (Ledermantel)
17 Officer's leather boots, private purchase

Memorial Museum, Bayeux

move in the US sector. But it was difficult to decide where to attack; *Perch* and *Epsom* had tested the possible avenues west of Caen; the city itself was still choked with rubble and partly held by the enemy. Only the Orne bridgehead remained, and this was the area through which *Goodwood* was launched, despite its inherent disadvantages. Chief amongst these was the constricted and crowded nature of the bridgehead; this meant that only one armored brigade of the main attacking force could be assembled there before the offensive began; it also meant that there was no room to deploy extra field artillery behind the start line, so the fire support provided by 25-pounder field guns could

cover only the first few miles of the advance from positions west of the Orne. These considerations did not deter Dempsey, commander of the Second Army, who believed that the German army in Normandy had been so worn down by attrition that it was no longer capable of effective resistance. According to his intelligence, the enemy facing I Corps east of the Orne consisted of the 346th Infantry Division, 16th Luftwaffe Field Division and 21st Panzer, all seriously depleted and exhausted, deployed in a defensive position four miles (6km) deep. In fact, Rommel had realised that the open rolling country between the Orne and the Bois de Bavent ridge to the east was good going for

tanks, and had taken measures to defend it. The German defenses were actually eight miles (12km) deep, and very well designed.

The forward posts were held by the 16th Luftwaffe Field Division and 346th Infantry Division; behind them, on the slopes of the Bourguébus Ridge was a network of stone-built villages, each held by antitank guns protected by infantry, and with overlapping arcs of fire, under the 21st Panzer Division; along the crest of the Ridge were 78 88mm guns of the II Flak Corps; on the reverse slope of the Ridge three counterattack groups were in waiting, each of some 40 tanks and a battalion of Panzer Grenadiers. The general artillery reserve of guns, mortars and nebelwerfers

was concealed in the woods of Garcelles-Secqueville, also on the reverse slope. On the eastern flank, around Emiéville, a detachment of Tigers lurked amongst the copses and manor houses, with excellent views across the open fields towards Caen. In Colombelles, the Germans had observation posts on the chimneys of the steelworks which gave a panorama of the whole area. The 1st and 12th SS Panzer Divisions were ready to reinforce this area if necessary.

The Second Army plan drawn by Dempsey envisaged a massive air raid by 2,000 aircraft to destroy all enemy positions ahead of the start line, then a rolling barrage to work over the first four miles (6km) of the advance. The main attack, from between Ste. Honorine-la-Chardonnerette and Escoville, was to be made by VIII Corps. For *Goodwood*, VIII Corps consisted of 11th Armoured Division, Guards Armoured Division, and 7th Armoured Division, advancing in echelon in that order. The 29th Armoured Brigade was to follow the barrage, leaving the Division's motorized infantry, 159th Brigade, to clear the villages of Demouville and Cuverville on the eastern outskirts of Caen, then race forward southwards over the Bourguébus Ridge, as far as possible towards Falaise. Guards Armoured and 7th Armoured were to follow as swiftly as possible, the armor leaving the infantry brigades behind if they could not keep up once beyond range of the 25 pounders; Typhoons were there to provide any close support required. But Dempsey believed the Germans were demoralized and on the verge of collapse, and that it might be possible to push light forces into Falaise, so cutting the line of retirement of all German forces west of the Orne. Whilst the VIII Corps was racing southwards, the II Canadian Corps was to slog through and clear the industrial suburbs of Caen, on the western flank. On the eastern side of the VIII Corps axis, 3rd Division was to advance along the Bois de Bavent Ridge, taking the villages at the foot, clearing the woods on the crown, and seize Troarn.

Montgomery considered Dempsey's plan far too optimistic, he had a much greater respect for the German defenders. He altered the plan to set VIII Corps objectives just beyond the Bourguébus Ridge; his aims were to tie down, draw, and reduce the German armor, and to expand and make safe the Orne bridgehead. Gen. Roberts, commanding the 11th Armoured Division, had doubts about the plan; he thought it was unsound to push his tanks forward without their infantry. His comments were discounted by O'Connor and Dempsey, who believed that the weight of the aerial bombardment and sheer number of tanks would overwhelm the enemy.

July 18 was a fine day, and the heavy bombers of Bomber Command arrived over the battlefield at 05:45 to attack the villages along the flanks of VIII Corps' sector. They were followed by medium bombers which carpeted the main axis with fragmentation bombs; the intention was to destroy enemy personnel and equipment without cratering the ground. The artillery fired counter-battery missions against German flak during these air raids. At 07:45 the main barrage commenced, as a third wave of aircraft attacked Troarn and Bourguébus.

German Flak Weapons

Below: Four-barreled 2cm Flak 38 on a quadruple mount. The Flak 38 was clip fed, firing 180 rounds per minute with a range of 3,500 ft (210-240m) and a 360° field of fire. With high explosive (HE) and armor-piercing rounds, it could be used against ground targets, having a horizontal range of 5,000 yards (4.5km).

Its weight of 1.68 tons allowed it to be either static mounted or carried aboard mobile trailer or vehicle to defend convoys against air attack.
Memorial Museum, Bayeux

Left, clockwise, A: a Spitfire strafing attack on German positions; B: a German flak battery engages a high-flying target; C: a single Flak 38 on a Czech LT-38 chassis; D, E: camouflaged Flak 38 manned by Fallschirmjäger; F: the 88mm AA gun.

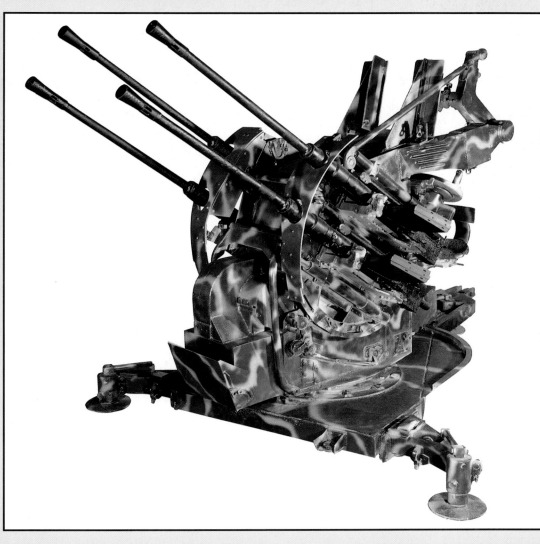

The heavy bombing on the flanks was effective. Half of the Tigers in the heavy tank unit at Emiéville were knocked out, and the commander, Lt. von Rosen, recalled that under the stress of the bombardment two of his men committed suicide and one went mad. Later in the morning, soldiers of the 3rd Division moving up the eastern flank found, "villages that were battered beyond description. Those Germans left conscious were far too dazed to offer any resistance." But by the time the 3rd Division's leading elements reached the outskirts of Troarn and the Caen-Troarn railway, the Germans had recovered, and mounted a stout defense. Despite strenuous efforts, the 3rd Division could not take Troarn or the hamlets around Emiéville.

In the center, the 29th Armoured Brigade advanced through the positions of the 51st Highland Division. They were delayed and disordered by having to pass through a defensive minefield laid by the 51st, but kept moving forward. Until they crossed the Caen-Troarn railway they were opposed only by snipers hiding in the corn. The 159th Motorised Infantry followed, then swung west to clear and secure Demouville and Cuverville. The 29th Armoured Brigade pushed on alone. The armored brigade of Guards Armoured Division was held up by a traffic jam on the approaches to the bridges over the Orne and Orne Canal; the Guards were on time, the leading elements of 7th Armoured Division were ahead of schedule.

The 29th Armoured Brigade was alone, with only its integral battalion of half-track infantry the 29th Armoured Brigade was alone, when it reached the Caen-Vimont railway. The 3rd Royal Tank Regiment were on the right, 2nd Fife and Forfar Yeomanry on the left, with the 23rd Hussars in reserve. As the leading regiments ascended the gentle concave slope of the Bourguébus Ridge they came under concentrated crossfire from anti-tank weapons in the villages, backed up by 88s from the crest of the Ridge.

The tanks of the 29th Armoured Brigade continued to fight, and tried to find ways forward. But they lacked the means to attack the villages, because they were short of infantry and were beyond the range of the field artillery. Their own self-propelled guns were insufficient to suppress the antitank batteries. Above, a "cab rank" of Typhoons flew, but were unable to give close support as planned. This was because the brigade had only one Forward Air Controller with them, at Brigade Tactical HQ, and, according to Gen. Roberts's memoirs, "Only minutes after the armored brigade's Tac HQ had arrived at their 'embankment' position and the RAF had first got contact with the 'cab rank,' a shell scored a direct hit on the armoured car, the RAF officer was badly wounded and the armoured car was a write-off." When the self-propelled guns attempted to mark enemy targets with pink smoke, the enemy replied in kind. The pilots could not tell friend from foe in the confused mêlée on the Bourguébus Ridge.

Meanwhile, the Guards Armoured Division advanced into battle for the first time. The tanks were delayed by the 51st Division's minefield, and found the Germans recovered from the successive shocks of the bombing and the artillery barrage. Gen. Adair,

Above: A patrol of the Canadian 3rd Infantry Division picks its way past the church of St. Etienne in shell-torn Caen on July 10. Inset: The battle for Caen was prefaced by an extremely heavy artillery bombardment, and a pall of smoke soon enveloped the city.

commanding the division, recalled in his memoirs, ". . . my tank had two near-misses from a bazooka team lying in a cornfield." Ahead of the general, the 2nd Grenadier Guards led the division, but found that, "Every advantage lay with the defenders; the ground haze was thickened by the dust churned up by the armour, and thick hedges and belts of tall trees limited the vision of the tank commanders as they peered through their fieldglasses, trying to pick out the enemy guns in the corn and root fields. Three tanks of the leading squadron were hit when they were still over a mile (1.6km) from Cagny, and as it was impossible to escape the fire by maneuvering to left or right the squadron was brought to a standstill." The Grenadiers were engaged from the front, by anti-tank guns in le Prieuré Farm, and from their left by the Tigers around Emiéville. As the armor of the division shifted westwards to support the 29th Armoured Brigade, Gen. Roberts gave warning that the village of Cagny was highly dangerous and strongly held. He was in error, for Cagny was occupied by only four 88s, one tank and a section of infantry, but the 88s had opened fire suddenly on the Reserve Squadron of the 23rd Hussars and done great damage, and this had impressed the general. The Guards duly took warning, and made formal attacks, with infantry support, on le Prieuré and Cagny.

The fighting on the Bourguébus Ridge continued. On two occasions troops of Shermans managed to reach the crest, using the smoke of burning tanks to cover their movement; but each time they were pushed back by an enemy counterattack group. Late in the morning, the commander of 22nd Armoured Brigade (of 7th Armoured Division) arrived on a recce, and according to Roberts, said: "There are too many bloody tanks here already, I'm not going to bring my tanks down yet." In his view, O'Connor's scheme to rush the enemy defenses with a mass of armor had simply provided the German anti-tank gunners with a big juicy target. When the 2nd Irish Guards arrived northwest of Cagny they observed, ". . . a confused mass of tanks shooting in all directions . . . the little rises in the ground and occasional hedges, combined with the standing corn, gave excellent cover from which the Tigers and Panthers could shoot up the steady stream of Shermans as they came across open country."

The Guards cleared Cagny and its outposts in the afternoon, and tried to press on southeastwards along the railway to Vimont. But they made little progress, because the Germans had posted tanks and anti-tank guns protected by infantry in the hedgerows on the rising ground from Emiéville to Frénouville. The approaches to this belt of dense cover were open, and in places the ground was soft. As the Guards closed with the enemy, according to the history of the Irish Guards, the attack lost cohesion, ". . . dissolved into isolated games of hide and seek among the

Above: Canadian Universal Carrier T-16. This was a fully tracked reconnaissance and combat vehicle used extensively by Commonwealth forces. Some 34,000 of the T-16 were produced by Ford Canada alone. *Memorial Museum, Bayeux*

corn stacks and hedges . . ." As the day wore on, "In the failing light the tanks were on top of each other before they fired." After nightfall the exhausted tank regiments fell back and went into laager. Infantry came up to consolidate the captured ground, and to mop up pockets of resistance in the rear. Some went forward to explore the enemy positions, and came to close quarters.

By the end of the fighting on July 18, VIII Corps had lost about 220 of the 700 tanks committed to the attack. The Germans had lost some 120 of the 240 tanks they had put into the battle. The corps had gained approximately six miles (9km) of ground. On the western flank the Canadians had fought a bitter battle to annihilate the German defenders of Colombelles and Vaucelles; Caen was now completely in Allied hands.

On July 19, the Guards Armoured, 11th and 7th Armoured Divisions mounted a series of attacks on the villages along the Bourguébus Ridge, using coordinated groups of tanks, infantry, engineers and artillery. These set-piece attacks succeeded in taking villages from the Panzer Grenadiers of the 1st SS Panzer Division. But the Germans were already rolling back to form a new system of defense in depth on the next suitable ridge to the south. Late on 19th the weather broke and rain stopped play; tanks were bogged in the mire, the infantry were stuck, artillery suffered from reduced visibility. So the battle of *Goodwood* ended.

The American Sector

Until the end of June, whilst the British Second Army was concentrating its attention on Caen, the US First Army was occupied in securing the link between the *Utah* and *Omaha* beachheads, clearing the Cotentin, and capturing Cherbourg. In order to connect the two beachheads it was essential to capture and secure Carentan. This was difficult, because the approaches to the town were cut by numerous water obstacles, which were crossed by causeways and bridges. The Germans had demolished bridges and zeroed their artillery and mortars on the causeways. Between the causeways were marshes, within which islands of higher ground were covered with bocage.

The use of armor was extremely hazardous, as German 88s in the town could reach out over the marshes 2,000 yds (1,800m) along the causeways. The town had to be taken by infantry using close-combat techniques, clearing defensive positions with grenade and bayonet. The Germans delayed the progress of the infantry of the 101st Airborne and 29th Divisions by counterattacks.

Whilst the town was being closely invested, the soldiers of the US VIII and VI Corps also maneuvered to seal off the outer approaches. On June 10 the 327th Glider Infantry advancing across the Lower Douve from the west met the 29th Division's recce troops moving up from the east at Auville-sur-le-Vey.

On June 11 Gen. McAuliffe took command of Task Force F, the 501st and 506th Parachute Infantry, and 327th Glider Infantry. In accordance with his plan, Carentan was heavily bombarded during the night of June 11. Early on the 12th, Task Force F made a double pincer attack on Carentan; two battalions of the 327th advanced into the town from the northeast; battalions of the 506th moved to the southwest to forestall attempts at relief or counterattack. The outer arms of the double-pincer helped to secure Carentan, but did not meet in sufficient time to prevent the retirement of the survivors of the garrison. The Germans reacted violently. On June 12 and 13 they launched counterattacks from the southwest. The second of these was made by the 6th Parachute Regiment and elements of 17th SS Panzer Grenadier Division, and was thrown back by a counterstroke by Combat Command 'A' of the 2nd Armored Division. The US forces consolidated, and pushed outwards from Carentan; the VII and

Left: A German 88mm gun in action. Developed primarily as an anti-aircraft weapon, this legendary piece of ordnance was also able to function as a deadly anti-tank weapon as a result of its high muzzle velocity and the flat trajectory imparted to the shell.

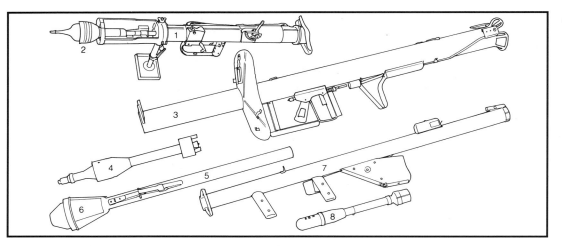

Anti-Tank Weapons

1 Projector, Infantry Anti-Tank (PIAT). A British weapon which was operated by means of a spring-loaded spigot detonating a charge in the projectile (2)
2 PIAT 2.5lb (1kg) projectile; high explosive, hollow charge
3 German 8.8 cm Panzerbuchse 53 (Panzerschreck — ''Tank Terror'') an electronically fired smoothbore weapon with gunner's protective shield in place
4 Panzerbuchse 53 round; shaped charge, about 7.25lb (3kg)
5 German Panzerfaust 100m, a one round, recoilless weapon which

fired a shaped charge (6). The launcher was reloadable or disposable
6 Warhead or bomb for the Panzerfaust. The weapon's simple firing instructions can be seen on the charge head
7 US M1A1 Rocket Launcher, 2.36 inch ''Bazooka.'' A smoothbore weapon which fired a hollow charge rocket projectile. Introduced in 1942 this was the weapon from which the Germans developed the Panzerbuchse
8 Bazooka training round. The live HE round was painted OD and had a pointed shell

US Ordnance Museum, Aberdeen PG, Md

V Corps were firmly in contact. Subsequently, V Corps expanded southwards, obstructed by the extensive marshes south and east of Carentan, and held back by shortages of ammunition. VII Corps was to advance westwards and northwards, to cut off the Cotentin from the south, and to take Cherbourg. Bradley gave priority of supply to formations in the Cotentin. Despite this, the VII Corps, and also — later — the VIII Corps, had much difficulty and delay in the Cotentin. This was primarily because of the inherent difficulties of operating in the peculiar terrain. The German forces in the Cotentin were heavily outnumbered and exhausted, but knew how to use the ground to maximum advantage. They

could probably have made the American advance more slow and costly had they not been subjected to detailed and irrational interference by Hitler.

On June 10 VII Corps was held by the Germans on good defensive ground to north and west. The US Army Historical Division, description of the ground to the north remarks, ''The ground rises gently giving the defender commanding heights liberally crisscrossed with hedgerows. Fortifications supported the German defense in depth. A backstop line was anchored to the coast at Quinéville, it stretched inland along a high ridge to Montebourg, and then bent southwest. It was part of VII Corps' D-Day

objective, but five infantry regiments took a full week, from June 8-14, to reach and secure it.''

The 4th Division had to take this line by close-quarter fighting, hedgerow by hedgerow, with artillery and air support. On the coast, infantry had to rely on cooperation with sappers to take the fortifications. Some of the batteries in the area of Quinéville were still shelling *Utah* beach, hindering reinforcement. But by June 14, the 4th Division was through, breaking the Germans' main defensive line in the north.

VII Corps also had difficulty moving west, across the Rivers Merderet and Douve. On June 8 the 325th Infantry had attempted an

assault along the causeway at la Fière. The movement was preceded by heavy artillery preparation, and supported by direct fire from tanks. Even so, the attack was too difficult. The Historical Division recorded: "The men had been told that they were to cover the exposed, 500-yard (450m) causeway in one sprint. But the long run in the face of small arms and mortar fire proved to be too much for most only a handful made the initial dash others, who hesitated, were hit the first casualties induced more hesitation and the causeway became congested with the dead, the wounded and the reluctant."

Next day, Bradley directed VII Corps to cut off the Cotentin. On June 10 attempts to force the Merderet at la Fière and Chef-du-Pont had limited success, because of the inherent difficulties of such assaults. However, the American pressure was relentless, and gradually the Germans were forced back from the west bank of the floodplain. But progress was still very slow; a regimental attack could take all day to push a few hundred yards. Every yard was paid for in blood; the 357th Regiment was losing an average of 150 men a day. The attacking troops had to learn to reapply the basic principles of tactics in combat, if they lived long enough to appreciate the lessons of experience.

On June 15 Gen. Collins, Commander of VII Corps, sent the 82nd Airborne and 9th Infantry Divisions into the drive west of the Merderet. At the same time, the Germans had decided to swing back on to an east-west line in order to reduce their commitments. This meant that the 82nd and 9th met only blocking parties and rearguards. The 82nd seized St. Sauveur-le-Vicomte and bridged the Douve on June 16. At once Collins saw and grasped his opportunity. He ordered the 82nd

Below: Seen in an aerial photograph taken on June 21, Cherbourg was the only major harbor available to the Allies by a comparatively simple westward expansion of their lodgment, and its capture was vital to exploitation of the Allied position in northern France.

Above: Cherbourg's defense was entrusted to Lt. Gen. Karl-Wilhelm von Schlieben (center) with Adm. Nennecke as his naval subordinate and Maj. Gen. Robert Sattler as his deputy commander. Despite its strength, the defense folded after five days of bitter fighting.

and 9th to form four regimental columns and charge down main roads westwards to the coast, and not to worry about flank guards. The speed of this movement took the Germans by surprise; the regiments in columns of battalions reached the coast during the night of June 17/18. On the northern side of the axis, the 60th Infantry Regiment (9th Division) set up blocking positions, and intercepted columns of the German 77th Division which had been ordered to evacuate the Cotentin.

The Germans attempted no substantial counterattack: their forces were too weak. On June 15, the German LXXXIV Corps had formed two Kampfgruppen ("battlegroups") in the Cotentin: "Hellmich," of elements of the 77th and 91st Divisions, which had been ordered to move south but was not trapped in the peninsula; and "Von Schlieben," of the remnants of the 709th and 243rd Divisions, intended to defend Cherbourg. Bradley and Collins realized that the German forces were too weak to hold a line all the way across the Cotentin. On June 16 they decided to advance north on a front of three divisions, from west to east the 9th, 79th and 4th, with the 4th Cavalry Group covering the gaps with light patrol forces. The important thing was to close in on the fortress of Cherbourg quickly, to minimize the Germans' chances of reinforcing and strengthening the defenses.

On June 19 the 4th Division used heavy artillery preparation, followed by an envelopment by armor and infantry to force the German garrison out of Montebourg, and clear the main highway to Cherbourg. Valognes was devastated by heavy air attacks, and was abandoned by the enemy. The advance north by the 4th Division was made in column of route. The 9th and 79th Divisions were impeded only by demolitions; on June 20, the Germans broke contact and moved to occupy the formidable defenses of Cherbourg. They would have done this days earlier had it not been for Hitler's insistence that every inch of ground must be defended. As it was, the line they attempted to hold before Cherbourg was too long for the 21,000 men available, being 30 miles (48km) from St. Vaast-la-Hougue to Vauville.

The Attack on Cherbourg

The main defenses of Cherbourg were on an arc of high ground extending four to six miles (6-9km) beyond the center of the port. A deep belt of fortifications covered all lines of approach and provided for mutual support. Anti-tank ditches and steel obstacles supplemented the streams which made natural obstacles to armor. Hedgerows were cut back to clear fields of fire. The actual works were protected by wire. In some areas they were concrete emplacements with machinegun turrets, mortar emplacements, antiaircraft guns and casemated artillery. In other areas they were well-made entrenchments. The

SUPREME HEADQUARTERS
ALLIED EXPEDITIONARY FORCE

Office of Assistant Chief of Staff, G-2

WEEKLY INTELLIGENCE SUMMARY
No. 17

Week Ending
July 15, 1944

PART 1/F.

MISCELLANEOUS

NOTES ON PRISONERS OF WAR

Physique and General Health

The physique of nearly all prisoners of war groups (i) [Germans] and (ii) [German Nationals] is distinctly poor, (particularly compared with Afrika Korps standards). They consist in the main of undeveloped youths and somewhat undersized men, many of whom were of indifferent health. There are many cases of men having been pulled out prematurely from convalescent homes and forced to join their units and several cases were encountered even among the SS of men who had minor wounds received in RUSSIA which had not healed. A Medical Orderly of the SS was found to be suffering from secondary syphilis.

. . . The main complaints of the German soldier are:
 (i) The lack of air support despite reiterated promises of assistance.
 (ii) The lack of artillery support.
 (iii) Shortage of rations in the front line.
 (iv) Behaviour of officers leaving NCOs to do their jobs and robbing the men of their comforts.
 (v) Lack of regular mail when in the line.
 (vi) In some cases lack of weapons.
 (vii) Dissatisfaction of specialist personnel such as engineers and reconnaissance at being used as infantry.
 (viii) Drafting to SS Infantry units of personnel who had never volunteered for this Corps and in certain cases were doing specialist work even with the Luftwaffe.

In conclusion it should be said that whilst fighting capabilities must be affected by physique, lack of training and mental outlook, there is no indication in the case of the Germans and German Nationals of the fighting spirit having been seriously impaired.

Courtesy of the Dwight D. Eisenhower Library

Above: From one of the concrete pillboxes that formed the German outer defense ring for the port, a US Army major surveys Cherbourg, where street fighting continued, and the large harbor whose facilities the Germans totally destroyed before their surrender.

VII Corps closed up to the outer works on June 20, and probed the positions in the night. All the patrols were sharply repelled. But Collins was encouraged by reports from prisoners of war who said that the garrision was a motley collection of detachments, exhausted and demoralized, and that the defenders were short of ammunition. Nevertheless, when Collins called on the German commander Gen. von Schlieben to capitulate on June 21, his message was ignored.

All the US divisions attacked the defenses on June 22, but the main assaults were made by 9th and 79th Divisions from the west and southwest. At 12:40, 10 squadrons of Mustangs and Typhoons attacked the defences with bombs and gunfire. They were followed at 13:00 by 562 fighter-bombers, who unfortunately hit friendly troops as well as the enemy, because smoke marking their targets had drifted south. At 14:00, 377 medium bombers attacked 11 major strongpoints. After these air attacks, which forced German infantry into underground shelters, the American infantry, sappers and armor moved up, protected by an artillery barrage. The assault forces proceeded to methodically reduce the German fortifications; intense machinegun and antitank gunfire directed at embrasures suppressed the defenders, and allowed the sappers to move forward. Once at the concrete works, the sappers used shaped charges and bazookas to blow in the steel doors, then hurled in phosphorus grenades and pole-charges until the Germans were finished.

Next day (June 23) the Germans attempted counterattacks, and some in by-passed strongpoints continued active resistance. But they were too weak to stop the progress of VII Corps. As the American forces, learning on the job, improved the coordination of their

tactical aircraft, artillery and infantry, the enemy was forced to yield ground. By the end of the 23rd, the 9th Division had seized the key ground of the Bois du Mont Roc southwest of the port. The advance was maintained from the east as well. On the 24th, the 3/12 Battalion from 4th Division attacked a position near Digosville as described in the Historical Division account: "Scouts came within 200 yards (180m) of the German emplacements before machineguns opened fire on them. The four tanks deployed, returned the fire and then overran the first gun positions. The tanks provided a base of fire with both 75mm guns and machineguns, and the platoons worked forward. Twelve P-47s dive-bombed and strafed the German positions, and, as soon as the last bombs fell, tanks and infantry closed in rapidly and destroyed the enemy in a short, sharp fight." On the same day, the German commander of Cherbourg, von Schlieben, complained to Seventh Army HQ that his forces were being crushed by the American artillery. The fire reached a crescendo on June 25, when the US Navy gave extra support from three battleships and four cruisers. With this support the VII Corps broke through into the town. The Germans systematically wrecked the port installations; strong fortifications like the Fort du Roule and the Arsenal were still resisting on June 26, but the Americans were in the town and German activity was uncoordinated. Gen. von Schlieben was discovered in a bunker at St. Sauveur, and surrendered. Some 10,000 German troops became prisoners of war. The Arsenal was persuaded to capitulate by a loudspeaker unit on June 27, and by the 29th the outlying forts of the harbor had been forced to submit.

The fall of Cherbourg had a depressing effect on the morale of the German Army in Normandy. A great port, very strongly fortified, had surrendered, against the express orders of the Führer. The Americans felt euphoria and relief. Bradley could now turn his full attention to organizing the breakout operation.

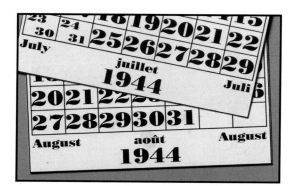

The Breakout

9

Nigel de Lee

In the US sector, while VII Corps advanced to Cherbourg, VIII Corps faced south and struggled towards the northern edge of the Carentan marshes. East of the marshes, the XIX and V Corps made a slow advance south. After the storm of June 19/22 these formations were severely rationed in their use of ammunition, and could not make progress. The Germans, principally the II Parachute Corps under the resourceful Gen. Meindl, made good use of the respite to survey the ground and prepare positions. Meindl's men complained bitterly that all their time was spent digging.

By June 21 Bradley was considering plans for a breakout. He regarded a penetration and mobile exploitation essential, because, as he wrote in his memoirs, "As long as the enemy confined us to the bocage. . .where we were forced to match him man for man, he could exact a prohibitive price for the few miserable yards we might gain." The essential thing was to find an area which gave sufficient room for the deployment of large-scale mobile forces. What Bradley wanted to do was find a weak place in the enemy line, concentrate sufficient force to break a hole in the line, then send mobile forces through it to exploit. These requirements entailed getting control of a line of departure south of the Carentan marshes, and finding a system of parallel roads sufficient to support the movement and supply of several divisions of mechanized troops. Bradley's analysis of the terrain led him to select the St. Lô-Coutances road as the ideal line of departure. From that straight highway, two adequate roads ran parallel along elevated ground to the southwest. A few miles south of the line of departure, beyond Marigny and St. Gilles, the whole country tilted so as to give the advantage to an army approaching from the north, and the bocage gave way to more open country.

Attacking the St. Lô-Coutances road

The immediate grand tactical question was how to secure control of the St. Lô-Coutances road. Bradley wanted to avoid a direct attack on St. Lô, because it was so strongly held. An advance across the Carentan marshes was uninviting; the use a skillful defender could make of such ground had been demonstrated in the Cotentin. Initially, the moorlands, hills and woods of Normandy's far west seemed most suitable as an avenue of attack. Accordingly, early in July, Bradley's plan was for V and XIX Corps to hold, whilst VII crossed the marshes and VIII advanced down the west

coast. However, the ground, weather, and enemy defeated this plan. Wet weather not only spread the marshes, but made all movement difficult. The VII Corps managed to cross the Vire and numerous other water obstacles and advance southwards, but much more slowly than anticipated. Attempts to boost the advance by pushing the 3rd Armored Division through the 30th Division (of XIX Corps) immediately west of the Vire led to congestion and confusion. The Germans responded to the advance west of the Vire by counterattacking on July 9, with the 17th SS Panzer Grenadier and 2nd SS Panzer Division. On the 11th, they mounted a major counterattack by the Panzer Lehr Division, newly arrived from south of Bayeux. These German attacks ran into exactly the same difficulties of movement, communication, and coordination as the American assaults had, and did not have the desired effect. But they did limit the VII Corps advance, so that by July 17 the forward elements were just by Pont-Hébert, still over 3 miles (6km) from the St. Lô-Coutances road.

Further west VIII Corps also ran into difficulty. The Mont Castre hills, thickly wooded and stoutly defended, could not be penetrated quickly. The advance was slow; by July 14 the corps had gained 12,000 yards (13km) in 12 days, and at a very high cost in life; in the fighting from July 3/10 the 90th Division had taken 5,000 casualties.

By July 10 Bradley had changed his mind, and decided he must grasp the nettle and

Left: A German paratrooper (Fallschirmjäger), dug in amongst the hedgerows of the bocage, keeps a watchful eye for Allied fighter-bombers. He is armed with the paratroopers' specially-designed semi-automatic rifle the FG 42, first type.

attack St. Lô. This was partly because VIII and VII Corps were not moving as fast as he had hoped, and also because there was political pressure on him to get on. But it was also due to the realization that he would need the road-net east of the Vire to sustain an advance southwest from his favored line of departure, and St. Lô was the center of that system.

The immediate question for the US First Army was, how to take St. Lô? The enemy in the area consisted of the II Parachute Corps. In the east stood the 3rd Parachute Division, consisting of two strong regiments of parachute infantry (Fallschirmjäger) — élite troops of great skill and determination. To the west of them were Kampfgruppen ("battle groups") of the 353rd, 352nd, and 266th Divisions. In support were the 12th Assault Gun Brigade, a nebelwerfer battalion, two batteries of 88s, plus 105mm and 150mm howitzers, and many heavy mortars. There were very few German soldiers in St. Lô itself, which lies in a depression; the defense of the town was based on the hills to the north and east. The II Parachute Corps could not man a continuous line of defense. Instead they occupied a number of intervisible mutually-supporting strongpoints covering all the approaches to the town. These strongpoints were not always on the higher ground, but were capable of denying such ground to the

enemy by use of fire. Such posts were effective and unobtrusive, and extremely difficult for aircraft or artillery spotters to locate. Facing these positions stood the American V and XIX Corps. The 2nd Division of V Corps was on the eastern flank, opposite Hill 192, mistakenly believed to be the highest point in the area. To the west of 2nd Division was the 29th Division.

Above: An American soldier scrambles away from a farmhouse on the Cotentin Peninsula. It seems possible that the building had been used by the Germans as an ammunition dump before their withdrawal to Cherbourg under pressure from the US VII Corps.

Gen. Gerhardt, commander of the 29th Division, believed that the key ground was Hill 122, which looms directly to the north of St. Lô, surmounted by the Church of St Georges de Montcoq. But Hill 122 was very strongly held and protected by a strong hedgerow position to the north at le Carillon, and a hilltop strongpoint at le Cauchais to the east. Therefore it would be advantageous to evade an assault on Hill 122, and to make an indirect approach by moving from east to west along the Martinville Ridge. According to Gerhardt, such a maneuver would threaten the line of retreat from Hill 122 and make it untenable. However, an attack on the Martinville Ridge could not succeed whilst Hill 122, to the east, remained in enemy hands. Gen. Corlett, commanding XIX Corps, agreed with Gerhardt's analysis. Accordingly, on July 11 the 2nd Division attacked Hill 192, and 29th Division advanced up onto the Martinville Ridge. Hill 192 had been attacked in regimental strength on July 16 and 19, but was still in enemy hands. The feature was a sugarloaf promontory about 150 feet (45m) higher than its surroundings. Lt-Col. Little recalled: "The Germans had built a tower in the trees on its summit, and from this tower on a clear day, one could see the shipping off *Omaha* beach, 20 odd miles [32km] to the north." The hill was held by two parachute battalions, who had done much to develop its defensive possibilities: according to the history of the 2nd Division: "The base of Hill 192 was zeroed-in by the Germans at every gap in the hedgerows. In dugouts tunneled under them a handful of men with machineguns could hold off a regiment simply by crossing each field with deadly close-range fire. They cut boxed-in apertures in the hedgerows at ground level through which

Left: A group of Fallschirmjäger manhandle a 3.7cm PAK anti-tank gun. Above left: A 3.7cm PAK 35/36 anti-tank gun armed with a 6.25-in shaped charge stick or rodded bomb. Also in view is the bomb's canister and crew's harness. *Memorial Museum, Bayeux*

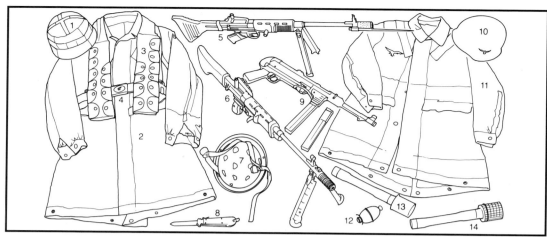

German Airborne Uniforms and Equipment

1 Luftwaffe paratrooper's helmet with splinter pattern camouflage cover. Note foliage loops
2 Second pattern Luftwaffe camouflage jump smock. Snap fasteners on the lower edge turn skirt of smock into "legs"
3 Paratrooper's 100-round bandolier for 7.92mm ammunition for 98k rifle. (See pages 44-45)
4 Luftwaffe waist belt and steel buckle. Note the leather braces hooked onto the belt
5 Paratrooper rifle M1942 7.92mm, first type
6 Paratrooper rifle FG 42, second type
7 Luftwaffe paratrooper

helmet, interior view. Note leather liner and chin strap
8 Luftwaffe flight utility knife (gravity blade knife) issued to flight crews and paratroopers
9 Machine pistol 1940 MP 40 with 32-round magazine
10 Luftwaffe paratrooper steel helmet with single Luftwaffe insignia decal
11 First pattern gray-green jump smock
12 M1939 hand grenade, with suspension ring
13 Stick grenade M1924
14 As 13 with fragmentation sleeve attached

Milwaukee Public Museum: 1-4; West Point Museum: 5-7, 9, 11; Pritchard Collection: 8, 10, 12-14

The German airborne troops, like those of other nations, were an elite force from inception. The distinctive paratrooper's helmet and jump smock, called a "bone bag," are readily identifiable. Such special equipment was introduced to the service in 1938. The FG 42 (Fallschirmjäger Gewehr 42) weapons series was specifically designed for airborne troops. The weapon was clip fed from the left hand side and included a folding bipod and spike bayonet. In all only 7,000 are thought to have been produced.

German paratroopers actually made very few combat jumps after the spectacular but costly victory on the island of Crete in May 1941, in which the German airborne suffered 25 percent casualties. Thereafter Fallschirmjäger fought as special ground troops although their uniform was retained.

their 88s and machineguns could sweep the fields, while remaining unobserved." The use of prepared hedgerows in an elastic system of defense in depth was reinforced by the construction of strongpoints in the four hamlets of Cloville, le Soulaire, St. Georges-d'Elle and la Croix-Rouge. The parachutists were very aggressive in defense, patrolling and raiding vigorously, especially at night. American reconnaissance patrols found it difficult to explore the German positions. The men of the 2nd Division felt dominated by the hill and the strong German defenses on it; one man remarked; "Every time I clean my teeth I feel some German is looking down my throat."

Hill 192

It was obvious that it would take a special effort to take Hill 192, and V Corps made the effort. The artillery support was exceptional. Besides the four battalions of 105mm howitzers from the division, corps provided two battalions of 155mm and two of self-propelled armored 105s and a company of chemical mortars. There was no limit on the expenditure of shells. The air force was to send four groups of P-47s, each 40 strong, to bomb and strafe the southern side of the hill once the attack had started. The artillery preparation began at 05:00 on July 11. For 50 minutes the medium guns fired on German batteries, command posts, reserve areas and

THE ATTACK ON THE ST. LÔ — COUTANCES ROAD, AND OPERATION *COBRA*
Map A

For nearly a month, the American First Army's advance south had stalled in vicious infantry fighting among the Carentan marshes and the bocage. Gen. Bradley knew that he needed to break a hole in the German line to give his army the space it needed to allow the tanks and motorized units space to engage. The St. Lô-Coutances road seemed to be the most promising area where the German front could best be attacked, but as St Lô itself was too heavily defended, it was decided to develop the attack from the west, beginning with the VIII Corps and bringing in the VII and XIX Corps in turn.

VIII Corps began the attack on July 3, but appalling weather conditions and stiff German opposition reduced the Corps' advance to just 6,000 yards (5,400m) in three days. VII Corps began its attack on July 4 along the Périers-Carentan road, but had made only 2,000 yards (1,800m) by July 7. The XIX Corps began its attack on July 7, its objectives being high ground west and east of St. Lô.

The XIXth crossed the Vire River on the first day, but strong counterattacks by German units including Panzer Lehr developed on July 10-11 and stopped the advance. In the light of

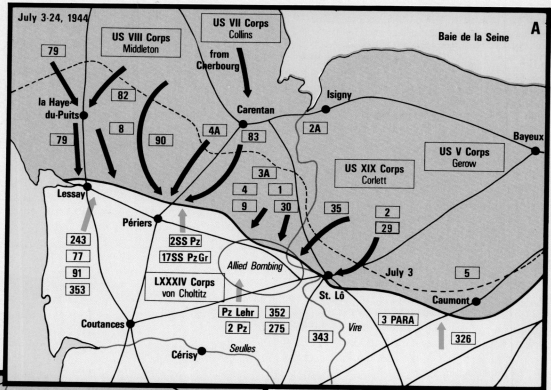

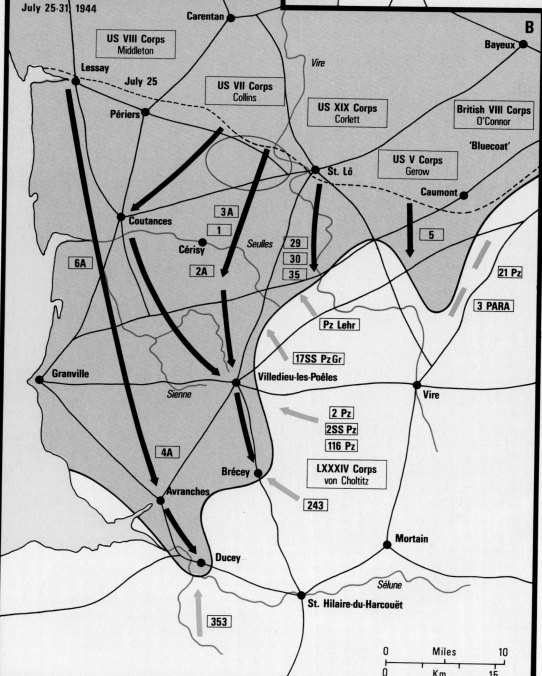

these developments it was decided to make an attack on St. Lô itself.

On July 11 the battle developed along the high ground to the north and northeast of the town (the Martinville Ridge and Hill 192). For five days the fighting went on, but the Americans made progress, and by the 17th this vital ground was in their hands. Realizing that their position was untenable, the Germans began a retreat from St. Lô on the same day.

Map B

Operation *Cobra*, the offensive to exploit the capture of St. Lô, began on July 25 on a 4.5-mile (8km) front with a massive, and at times inaccurate, air bombardment. In contrast to the small advances made early in the month, by the end of the first day, the 9th, 4th and 30th Divisions of VII Corps had advanced two miles (3.2km). The armored breakout that had been so long awaited began. On the 26th as planned, the 3rd and 2nd Armored Divisions passed through the infantry divisions and headed south and southwest. At the same time the 4th Armored, part of VIII Corps, attacked across the Périers-Lessay road towards Coutances. Realizing that it risked encirclement, the German LXXXIV Corps was ordered to retreat from the town. The 3rd Armored cut the Coutances-Granville road on July 29. Coutances was taken the following day by the 4th Armored, though the Germans had already gone.

At this point the German defensive line on the western side of the front began to crumble. By July 30, Gen. Patton had taken operational command of VIII Corps and ordered the 4th and 6th Armored to rush for Avranches supported by the 79th and 8th Infantry Divisions. On that day the 4th Armored took Avranches and pressed on to take the vital bridges at Pontaubault, west of Ducey. The roads to Brittany were now open for Patton's newly-established Third Army.

field kitchens, whilst the field guns bombarded all known mortar and machinegun posts
in the first three hedgerows. From 05:50
until 06:00 all the artillery, and all infantry
support weapons in the area, hit the first
hedgerow. The medium guns fired shells with
impact fuses, to collapse dugouts, the 105s
fired air bursts to catch personnel in the open.
Promptly at 06:00, the field guns commenced a rolling barrage, moving 100 yards (90m)
forward every four minutes. Behind the barrage advanced three battalions of infantry,
from the 38th and 23rd Regiments, closely
supported by four companies of tanks. Each
leading battalion could advance, halt, or
reverse the barrage. The medium guns dealt
with German artillery, as spotted by air observation posts. The barrage did not destroy the
German positions, but did suppress the
paratroopers, and screened the American infantry. The village strong points were
demolished by direct fire from the tanks and
self-propelled 105s. When the enemy retired
to tunnel systems, sappers threw in explosive
charges, and bulldozed five feet (1.5m) of
earth over the entrances. The attack was a
complete success, and the enemy proved
unable to mount effective counterattacks.
However, on arriving on top of the hill the
Americans discovered that Hill 101, to the
south, surmounted by St. Jean des Baisants,
was even higher.

To the west of the 2nd Division, the 116th
and 115th Infantry of the 29th Division were
due to attack the Martinville Ridge at 05:00
on July 11. But their attack was delayed by
enemy action against the 115th. The history
of the 115th in World War II remarks that
from 22:00 on July 10, German mortars and
artillery fired on the regiment and: "For the
men crouching in their foxholes this was the
heaviest artillery barrage experienced in
combat". At about midnight on June 10/11,
the fire concentrated on the 1st Battalion of
the 115th (1/115) then, "under cover of the
barrage a reinforced company of infantry infiltrated through the center and right. As the
artillery lifted, the Germans charged upon
the dazed men who were in their holes.
Flamethrowers and flares lit up the scene and

the Germans took advantage of the opportunity to smash through Company A . . . cut
the company into small isolated groups who
resisted with rifle butts, bayonets, hand
grenades, and anything else that could be
found." The Germans withdrew at dawn,
leaving 87 of their men behind; the 1/115 had
suffered 150 casualties. The attack on the
Martinville Ridge was delayed until late morning, and made very little progress.

To the east, the 116th Infantry had attacked adjacent to the 2nd Division area, at 06:00,
in column of battalions up the ridge and then
westwards along it, gaining some 3,000 yards
(2,700m). The 175th, the third infantry regiment of the 29th Division, moved up east of
the 116th, to exploit down the southern slope
of the Martinville Ridge, and establish firm
contact with the 2nd Division.

On July 12/13 the 29th Division attempted
to advance south and west. On the southern
slopes of the Martinville Ridge, the 175th was
stopped by fire from Hill 101 Ridge, directly
south. The 116th made some progress
westwards along the Martinville Ridge, but
was stopped on the 13th. The 115th closed up
to the foot of the western end of the ridge but
could not take or by-pass the enemy position
at le Cauchais.

Above: This hilltop provided a good vantage
point for observers investigating the route into
and through St. Lô, on whose western side the
US VII Corps was to spearhead the US First
Army's breakout from the Normandy
lodgment behind a "bomb carpet."

By July 12 Gen. Gerhardt had changed his
mind; he told Gen. Corlett that it was
necessary to take Hill 122, but that 29th Division, with no reserve available, could not
make the attack. On July 13 Gen. Corlett produced a new plan; Hill 122 was to be attacked by P-47s whilst the 115th advanced south
down the Isigny-St. Lô road, and the 116th and
175th moved west along the Martinville
Ridge. The disappointment of his advances
on July 13 led Gen. Corlett to revise his plans
yet again. The 35th Division was moved into
the area on the west of the 29th Division. On
July 15 the 134th Regiment would assault Hill
122, supported by tactical aircraft, artillery
and tanks. The 137th would slip past Hill 122
to the west, whilst the 320th occupied and
masked the enemy at le Carillon. At the same
time, the 115th would push down the road into St. Lô, supported by armor; the 116th and
175th would resume their attempts to move
westwards.

The 134th Infantry moved forward, supported by a rolling barrage on the morning
of July 15, and had reached Emélie by midday. In the afternoon the regiment was joined by 21 tanks and 3 tank destroyers and
sappers to form Task Force Sebree. At 20:00
a swarm of P-47s attacked Hill 122. The

Left: Command posts were established
wherever suitable cover could be found.
This one was located inside a family crypt in
St. Lô, and helped control the flood of US land
power pouring through the gap punched
through the German line.

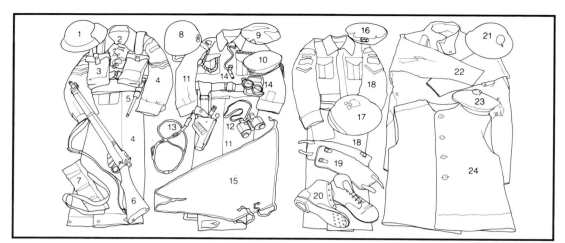

Canadian Uniforms and Equipment

1 Mk I helmet with netting and field dressing
2 Camouflage scarf
3 Pattern 1937 webbing
4 Battle dress blouse and trousers 'Cameron Highlanders of Ottawa'
5 No. 4 Mk II bayonet and scabbard
6 No. 4 rifle
7 Ammunition bandolier
8 Armored corps pattern helmet
9 Beret with insignia of Royal Canadian Tank Corps
10 Denim fatigue beret
11 Battle dress blouse and trousers, Maj. 4th Armored Division
12 Binoculars No. 2 Mk II
13 Enfield No. 2 Mk II

revolver in P.37 holster
14 Compass Mk III with belt pouch and officers' whistle
15 Nylon vehicle-aircraft recognition panel used by the 3rd Canadian Division during Operation *Tractable*
16 Service cap, French Canadian volunteers 'Le Régiment de la Chaudière'
17 Mk III helmet
18 Battle dress blouse and trousers — as *16*
19 P.37 web gaiters
20 Steel reinforced boots
21 Mk III helmet with insignia of the 'Black Watch of Canada'
22 Oil cloth raincoat
23 Balmoral bonnet of 'Black Watch of Canada'
24 Leather jerkin

Memorial Museum, Bayeux

artillery began to shoot at 20:15, and at 20:50 the Task Force advanced and overran the German positions. At once, the tanks dug in on the north slope of the hill; the sappers helped the infantry dig in on the forward slope, and protected the position with mines and wire. Meindl was acutely aware of the importance of this position, and organized two counterattacks on it on the 16th. The second of these temporarily displaced the 134th back to Emélie, but the regiment regrouped and charged back to secure the hill again.

To the east of the 35th Division, the 115th, supported by tanks, had set off for St. Lô at 05:15. But the ground off the road was soft, which impeded the armor. Further, as the history of the 115th says, ". . . Germans were still in position in woods to the right and a deep draw to the left". The regiment could not get forward and suffered heavy losses, C Company being reduced to fewer than 35 men. Up on the ridge, and beyond it, the 116th and 175th were also stopped after moving a few hundred yards. But the 116th had better luck in the evening of the 15th, when the attack resumed. The history of the 29th Division records: "It carried the 116th 1st and 2nd Battalions through the enemy's positions with unexpected swiftness. Division Headquarters was reluctant to let the attack progress too far in the dark, and, aware of strong enemy occupying the ridge, ordered the attack halted . . .". But this order never reached the 116th's 2nd Battalion, who moved on to take a position at the la Madeleine crossroads, on the outskirts of St.Lô. The Germans closed in behind it, and the battalion was cut off. However, Meindl was deeply anxious, because the Americans had taken Hill 122 and were infiltrating through his defensive positions. On July 16, besides the desperate attempts to recapture Hill 122, he launched two strong counterattacks eastwards along the Martinville Ridge. These attacks were beaten off. A force assembling south of la Madeleine to attack the isolated 2nd Battalion was, by chance, spotted by a group of P-47s which dispersed it.

Developments on July 17 convinced Meindl that he could no longer hold St. Lô. The 134th was firmly esconced on Hill 122, looking down directly into the market place of the town. The 116th and 115th managed to penetrate his defenses by using guile and fieldcraft rather than numbers and firepower. The 29th Division history describes how the 3rd Battalion 116th ". . . at 04:30, in a quick, silent move unheralded by artillery or small arms fire, slipped through the main German defense line . . . relying solely on the grenade and bayonet and the cover of an early morning fog," to join the 2nd Battalion at la Madeleine at 06:00. the 115th too, had realised that the enemy lacked the manpower to patrol the areas between their strong points. Late on the 17th, having made an attempt to storm the la Cauchais feature, the 115th sent its second battalion along a stream around the hill, to reach la Planche du Bois, west of the end of the Martinville Ridge, by the early hours of July 18. By then Gen. Meindl had already issued orders to his units to move south of St. Lô, but be prepared to return to the town if the opportunity arose. The German soldiers evacuated their positions at le Carillon, le Cauchais and Martinville. In the afternoon Gen. Norman Cota, Assistant Commander of the 29th Division, led Task Force C into the town. He was preceded by the 2nd Battalion 116th, carrying the body of their commander, Maj. Howie, on the leading jeep. The "Major of St. Lô" was placed on an improvized bier of rubble on the steps of the cathedral.

The XIX Corps rapidly consolidated the position at St. Lô, relying mainly on the artillery. The infantry were much depleted and very tired. According to the history of the 110 Field Artillery, Lt. Col. Johns, an infantry officer, said, "The infantry occupied St. Lô but . . . artillery held it. Three rifle companies, each down to 30 or 40 effectives, couldn't have done much in so large a town if the artillery had not kept the Germans out." The 29th Division had suffered particularly from exhaustion and loss; the rifle companies had suffered more than 200 percent casualties, and the division had been in continuous contact with the enemy since D-Day.

Operation *Cobra*

On the day St. Lô fell, Bradley's plan for *Cobra* was approved by Montgomery. The attack was scheduled for July 21, but was delayed until the 25th by bad weather. The weather was a key factor because the offensive was to commence with massive air attacks involving 2,246 aircraft. The first wave, 350 fighter-bombers, was to attack just south of the St. Lô-Périers road for 20 minutes. Then 1,500 heavy bombers, each loaded with 40 100lb (45kg) fragmentation bombs, were to saturate an area three and a half miles (5.5km) wide and one and a half miles (2.4km) deep, for one hour. Subsequently, the fighter-bombers were to return to give close support to the advancing ground troops. Then the medium bombers would attack the southern edge of the bombing box for 45 minutes. Bradley was particularly anxious that the bombers should fly laterally *along* the St. Lô-Périers road rather than *across* it, to minimise the risks of bombs falling on his attacking formations.

The ground attack was to be made by VII Corps, with the 4th, 9th and 30th Divisions advancing supported by 1,000 guns. Once the infantry had seized the roads leading south and cleared corridors along them, the 2nd and 3rd Armored Divisions and 1st Mechanized Infantry Division would pass through to exploit. Having passed through the enemy positions, 3rd Armored would swing west towards Brittany, the 2nd Armored would move southeast to Canisy and beyond, whilst the 1st Mechanized would make for Coutances.

Bradley was keen to attack as soon as possible, because the German Seventh Army was receiving reinforcements from Fifteenth Army and was planning to move two Panzer divisions across to the west. If the Germans were able to create a reserve opposite US First Army they could spoil his plans for maneuver. At the opposite end of the front, the Canadians attacked southeast of Caen to discourage any such development.

The weather seemed favorable very early on July 24, then it deteriorated. This was unfortunate, because one group of heavy bombers took off, and could not be recalled. Over Normandy, they approached the start line from the north, contrary to Bradley's wishes, and also bombed short. This inflicted casualties on the forward elements of VII Corps, and killed Gen. McNair, the most senior officer of the US Army. The incident also alerted the German commanders, who ordered a Kampfgruppe of 2nd SS Panzer Division to move across from the front opposite VIII Corps.

But the Germans had no time for a major redeployment, for on July 25 *Cobra* was unleashed. Once again, the heavy bombers flew in from the north and bombed the 9th and 30th Divisions, inflicting losses and delaying the advance. But the effects on the Germans south of the start line were devastating. The commander of Panzer Lehr, Gen. Bayerlein, had deployed his tanks in depth along the roads leading to St. Gilles and Marigny. After the war, Bayerlein remembered, "My flak batteries received direct hits which knocked out half the guns and silenced the rest. After an hour I had no communication with anybody. By noon nothing was visible but dust and smoke. My front lines looked like the face of the moon and at least 70 percent of my troops were dead, wounded, crazed or numbed. All my forward tanks were knocked out." Some of the German infantry, in deep bunkers, emerged in better condition and fought hard. The US 9th, 4th and 3rd Armored Divisions moved forward, and concentrated on clearing the key roads leading south. By the end of July 25 they had gained two miles (3km).

Gen. Collins studied reports of the action, and concluded that the enemy had no reserves in the area. So, on July 26 medium bombers attacked corridors along the main axis roads, and then the 2nd and 3rd Armored Divisions advanced down them towards St. Gilles and Marigny. German engineers mined and cratered the roads, but American tanks had been fitted with hedgecutters which enabled them to move through hedgerows, and by-pass these blocks. The few German armored vehicles left were still confined to the roads, and were easy targets for the roving bands of P-47s. The American tanks soon outran their artillery support, but each combat command now enjoyed the services of a Forward Air Controller, so coordination with the fighter-bombers was excellent. On the eastern side, 2nd Armored Division passed through St. Gilles unopposed, reached Canisy by dusk, and went on to seize high ground at le Mesnil-Herman, and secure the flank. On the western side, 3rd Armored Division supported by 1st Mechanized Infantry Division had to fight hard for Marigny, and faced the prospect of a counterattack from the west by 2nd SS Panzer and 17th SS Panzer Grenadier Divisions. But the enemy in the far west was under pressure from the north, as VIII Corps reinforced by 4th Armored Division attacked southwards.

On July 27 the 3rd Armored and 1st Mechanized Divisions swung westwards, threatening the eastern flank and rear of the

Left: German command arrangements were very flexible at their lower levels, local commanders (mounted as here in a radio-fitted Kübelwagen) having considerable discretion to co-ordinate operations under emergency conditions such as the US breakthrough.

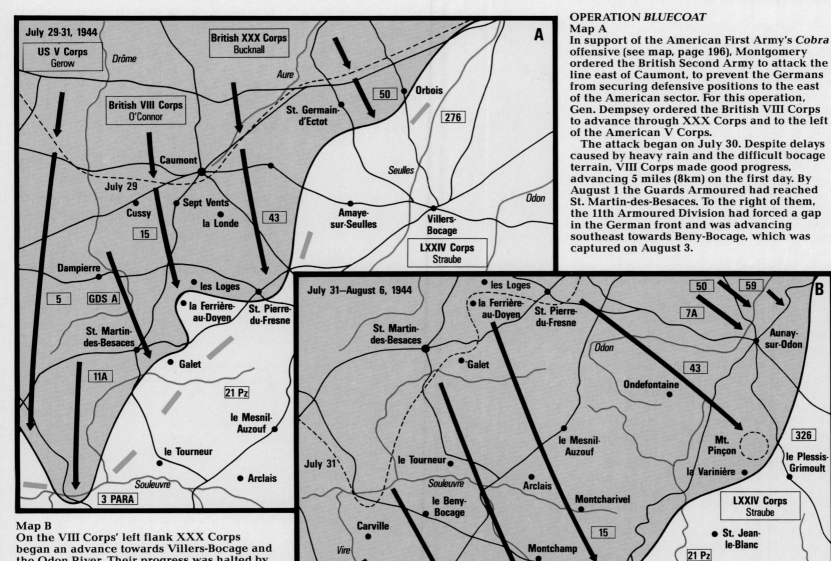

OPERATION *BLUECOAT*
Map A
In support of the American First Army's *Cobra* offensive (see map, page 196), Montgomery ordered the British Second Army to attack the line east of Caumont, to prevent the Germans from securing defensive positions to the east of the American sector. For this operation, Gen. Dempsey ordered the British VIII Corps to advance through XXX Corps and to the left of the American V Corps.

The attack began on July 30. Despite delays caused by heavy rain and the difficult bocage terrain, VIII Corps made good progress, advancing 5 miles (8km) on the first day. By August 1 the Guards Armoured had reached St. Martin-des-Besaces. To the right of them, the 11th Armoured Division had forced a gap in the German front and was advancing southeast towards Beny-Bocage, which was captured on August 3.

Map B
On the VIII Corps' left flank XXX Corps began an advance towards Villers-Bocage and the Odon River. Their progress was halted by the arrival of units of the II SS Panzer Corps. The situation eased only when Hitler ordered Panzer divisions west to take part in Operation *Lüttich*. By August 4 Villers-Bocage had been taken, though the lack of progress to date had led to Montgomery to sack the commanders of both XXX Corps and 7th Armoured Division. On August 5, the Odon was crossed and elements of the 7th Armoured Division were in Aunay-sur-Odon. Further south, Normandy's highest feature, Mont Pinçon was the object of a three-day siege as the 43rd Division battled to scale its heights.

Even compared with the losses suffered around Caen, Operation *Bluecoat* was particularly bloody for the British Second Army. Intelligent defense by crack German divisions took a heavy toll on both men and armor. By August 13, VIII Corps and XXX Corps had suffered nearly 9,500 casualties.

German LXXXIV Corps. The 2nd SS Panzer and 17th SS Panzer Grenadiers moved to block this advance, so opening the way for VIII Corps. Late on the 28th the 6th and 4th Armored Divisions met at Coutances. The German formations had dissolved into chaos; there was no front and no coordinated resistance.

Gen. Patton took over direction of VIII Corps, which raced south unopposed, seized the bottleneck at Avranches, and advanced into Brittany. The Luftwaffe made desperate efforts to destroy the bridge at Avranches, but failed. By August 4 Patton's forces had captured Vannes on the south coast of Brittany, and Rennes, the capital of the province. The day before, 30th Division had captured Mortain, and Bradley ordered

Patton to advance eastwards. By August 7 Patton's forward elements were at Le Mans, deep in the rear of the Seventh Army.

In the east, the Germans and British reacted to the success of *Cobra*. On July 27 von Kluge sent 2nd and 116th Panzer Divisions westwards; these formations were delayed by air strikes en route and arrived too late to contain the breakout. Immediately east of the Vire, the Germans attempted to hold fast, and resisted the US V and XIX Corps. Between July 26-30, V Corps advanced 3 miles (5km) in the teeth of bitter opposition. XIX Corps also pressed forward, but was unable to advance swiftly. Montgomery's reaction was to send his VIII Corps from the vicinity of Caen to attack through XXX Corps just east of Caumont, to compromise

the right flank and rear of any putative German defensive position on the east bank of the Vire. This offensive, *Bluecoat*, began on July 30, hindered by heavy rain, rough bocage terrain and extensive minefields. However, the 15th Division and 6th Guards Tank Brigade gained five miles (8km) on the first day. On July 31 11th Armoured Division, on the right flank, found a gap in the German line, passed through it, and went on to encounter and intercept elements of the II SS Panzer Corps moving westwards. On August 1 and 2 the VIII Corps swung southeast, whilst XXX Corps moved forward to assault Mont Pinçon, the highest hill in Normandy. These movements confronted the Germans with yet more demands on their inadequate reserves.

The Mortain Counterattack

By early August the German commanders in France realized that the game was up and were convinced that only a withdrawal to the Seine could save them from annihilation. The Allies were present in the theater in a great superiority of numbers and material, and could prevent German reserves and supplies from moving into the area. After *Cobra*, the Americans had ample room in which to use these advantages to decisive effect. Once again, Hitler disagreed. He perceived a great opportunity. On August 2 he ordered von Kluge to allow the Americans to pour into Brittany unchecked, then assemble every Panzer unit in Normandy to make a counterattack intended to retake Avranches and cut the lifelines to Patton's forces. In vain the German commanders argued that if they took all the Panzers away from the area south of Caen, they would lose Falaise. Hitler was adamant. Only the battered 12th SS Panzer Division remained facing the British and Canadians before Falaise. In an area east of Mortain the Germans assembled the Fifth Panzer Army, consisting of the 1st, 2nd and 9th SS Panzers, and the 2nd and 116th Panzer Divisions, which, in total, had only 250 tanks. The German forces not involved in the attack on Avranches must, as always, stand firm and not retreat, relying on willpower to resist the enemy when materiel means were insufficient. (See map, page 208.)

The preparations of Fifth Panzer Army were spotted by Allied aircraft, and Bradley reacted. He deployed five infantry divisions between Vire and Mortain, backed up by two armored combat commands and three more divisions around St. Hilaire. Driven by Hitler's insistence, protesting at the lack of time to prepare, and of materiel, the Fifth Panzer Army attacked on August 7. On the northern flanks 116th Panzer was checked by the US VII Corps pushing south from Vire and St. Sever. The 2nd Panzer Division advanced between Sourdeval and Mortain, gaining seven miles (11km) before it was stopped by encountering Combat Command B of the 3rd Armored Division. The 1st and 2nd SS Panzer Divisions to the south made less progress, because the 30th Division, deployed around Mortain, held on to hilltop positions which gave them good observation. The infantry of the SS Panzer divisions made repeated attempts to seize the hilltops, but the 30th Division would not be dislodged.

On 7th August the advance of Fifth Panzer Army had been covered by mist, but on the 8th the weather was clear. Allied tactical aircraft slaughtered the tanks and half-tracks of the Fifth Panzer Army as it struggled to move westwards. The VII Corps applied such pressure from the north that 116th Panzer was unable to advance at all. On the southern flank, Combat Commands of the 2nd and 3rd Armored Divisions moved northeast towards Ger and Domfront, to menace the rear of 1st and 2nd SS Panzer. By dusk on August 8 it was obvious to the German commanders in

Above: By the time American troops entered Argentan to the southeast of Caen, they had accomplished a major enveloping movement via St Lô, Avranches and Mayenne, and were placed to trap elements of two armies and one Panzer group against the British Second Army.

Below: Canadian troops advance across a field, against the backdrop of a burning ammunition truck, near Cintheaux during *Totalize* on August 8. The operation was designed to capture Falaise and so provide the northern half of the "Falaise pocket" trap.

Right: Universal Carriers of the Canadian 3rd Infantry Division tow 6-pounder anti-tank guns as they advance on Bretteville-le-Rabet on August 14. Though *Totalize* secured initial success, it was then slowed and halted by the resistance of several Waffen-SS divisions.

Above: A British artillery column moves along the Falaise road during Operation *Totalize*. On August 11 *Totalize* stalled halfway between Caen and Falaise. On August 14 after reinforcement and regrouping, the attack was renewed as Operation *Tractable*.

Below: Amid the burning remains of another Allied air attack, the crewman of this Panther tank of the 9th Panzer Division keeps a watchful eye on the skies. It is estimated that only 100 German tanks escaped the Falaise pocket and made it to the Seine.

SUPREME HEADQUARTERS ALLIED EXPEDITIONARY FORCE

Office of Assistant Chief of Staff, G-2

WEEKLY INTELLIGENCE SUMMARY No. 18

Week Ending July 22, 1944

PART 1/A.

MISCELLANEOUS

ENEMY CAPABILITIES

FILE G-2 MAIN CEd.

[The assassination attempt on Hitler] That a "military clique", as **HITLER** calls them, should have been plotting to liquidate him is encouraging; that they should have chosen this moment is exhilarating. Details of the attempted coup de main are lacking; but the very fact that the plotters reckoned that the time was ripe for a venture so complicated as the assassination of the **Führer** argues that they had good reason to hope for success not only in the first phase but also in the latter ones. Exactly who is implicated, apart from **ZEITZLER, BECK** and **STAUFFENBERG**, is still a matter that only **STOCKHOLM** is prepared to bet on. There seems, however, no reason to disbelieve **HITLER**'s assertion that it was an Army Putsch, cut to the 1918 pattern and designed to seize power in order to come to terms with the Allies. For, from a military point of view, the rebels must have argued, what other course is open? How else save something, at least, from the chaos? How else save the face of the German Army, and, more important still, enough of its blood to build another for the next war? And since now, more than ever before, the Party motto must be "Don't abdicate. Liquidate," recourse was had to the traditional bomb. It is only to be regretted that it wasn't a bigger and better bomb.

Courtesy of the Dwight D. Eisenhower Library

Normandy that the counteroffensive had failed, and that Fifth Panzer Army was in grave danger. But Hitler insisted on exerting control of his armies, and ordered a renewed attack on Avranches, oblivious of the danger.

Even as Fifth Panzer Army attacked westwards, the jaws of the pocket were developing. Part of Patton's Third Army was moving northwards on Eisenhower's orders, to advance in the direction of Alençon, the main supply depot of Seventh Army, Argentan and Falaise. By August 9 leading elements of the US XV Corps were only five miles (8km) from Falaise. In the north, the First Canadian Army, south of Caen, made an ingenious attack on the night of August 7. The plan for Operation *Totalize* was drawn by Gen. Simonds, commander of II Canadian Corps. He decided that the attack must be made without any artillery preparation, to gain surprize. The advance would be at night, in order to deprive the enemy of the advantage of the superior range of the 88s. For the first three miles (5km), all movement would be in vehicles, formed up in close columns four tanks wide. The infantry would travel in the hulls of self-propelled guns with the artillery pieces removed; anyone on foot was to be regarded as hostile. After three miles (5km), the infantry would dismount and attack the second line of enemy defenses.

The flanks of the main axis, which ran along the Caen-Falaise road, would be bombed by strategic aircraft of RAF Bomber

Uniforms and Equipment of the 1st Polish Armoured Division

1. Polish dress cap, or Rogatywka, of a Lt. Col.
2. Service dress, jacket and trousers of a Lt. Col. of the 10th Polish Dragoons
3. British Royal Armoured Corps steel helmet, with national insignia
4. British battledress, see caption
5. Black beret of armored units with Capt.'s insignia under eagle
6. British pattern 1937 web belt and holster
7. US Smith and Wesson military and police revolver
8. Brass cleaning rod for 7, carried on the side of holster 6
9. Tin of purification tablets
10. Cleaning compound for web gear
11. British Mk III goggles
12. Unit designation pennant, see caption
13. British jerkin
14. Battle dress blouse
15. Battle dress trousers with field dressing
16. Armored officer's beret, with Lt. Col.'s insignia
17. British issue goggles
18. Service jacket, see caption
19. Sam Browne belt
20. Armored officer's beret, with Lt.'s insignia
21. British Mk I helmet with Polish insignia
22. British gauntlets
23. Designation pennant
24. British Webley revolver

Sikorski Institute

The service dress uniform (2) carries the silver eagle device on the collar flashes, indicating a graduate of the Command and General Staff College. The device on the left sleeve is the "winged helmet" divisional insignia. The device on the right sleeve is an honorary badge from the county of Lanarkshire, Scotland. This also appears on 14.

The battle dress 4 bears the black epaulet indicative of armored units. The collar flashes indicate a motorized formation. The service ribbon is for the Cross of Honor. The insignia above this is the armored forces badge. The unit pennant 12 is that of the 2nd Squadron, 10th Polish Dragoons.

The jacket 18 is that of a Lt. of division engineers. Note the pre-war Flight Engineers badge over ribbon bar.

Command. Tracer fire, star-shells, searchlights and radio beams were to give directional guidance. The 2nd Canadian Division would attack west of the road, and the 51st Highland Division to the east. At dawn American heavy and medium bombers would attack enemy positions to assist a further advance by the 4th Canadian and 1st Polish Armoured Divisions. Facing the attack were the 272nd Division, the 89th Division, recently arrived from Norway, and, in reserve, the 12th SS Panzer Division. The advance began at 00:30 on August 8, and, inevitably, there was apprehension and con fusion, as described by Ian Hammerton, who was there commanding a troop of flail tanks:

"To say that we were apprehensive is an understatement. Tanks are almost blind at night . . . there were more dry mouths and butterfly stomachs than at any time previously including D-Day. We trundled forward, all eyes straining to see. As we reached the near edge of the German positions, our visibility was reduced to zero — so much smoke and dust that it was impossible to see even the pinpoint red rear lights of the tank in front. We proceeded by fits and starts, the radio filled with messages of bewilderment. I found there were no tanks in front of me. The next moment we plunged into a giant crater."

But despite the obvious difficulties, the tempo of the advance was maintained. The

THE FALAISE POCKET
Map A

By August 7, when the Canadians began Operation *Totalize* towards Falaise, the jaws of a vast pincer movement began to close on the German Seventh Army, Fifth Panzer Army, and Panzer Group Eberbach. On August 11 the US XV Corps, including Leclerc's 2nd French Armored Division was ordered north from Le Mans towards Argentan. It now became obvious that the only action that the Germans could take was to retreat as quickly as possible. On August 15 von Kluge ordered all German units to cross the Orne. But by then the whole German line was collapsing.

On August 17, the Canadian 2nd Infantry Division took Falaise, while the 1st Polish Armoured had (by mistake) advanced to les Champeaux, north of Mont Ormel on the Vimoutiers-Trun-Argentan road.

The Germans were now caught in a pocket 162 miles square (450 km²) which was contracting every hour under the massive weight of the Allied ground advance and ceaseless air attack.

On the same day Hitler sacked von Kluge as C in C West and replaced him with Field Marshal Walter Model. Model's first acts were to order all German units to retreat east of the Dives River. He also set in motion two counterattacks on the 18th: the first from the west by the II SS Panzer Corps towards Vimoutiers, the second from the east by the 2nd and 9th SS Panzer Divisions. The German retreat, however, was swiftly turning into a rout as the remains of over 20 divisions tried to escape.

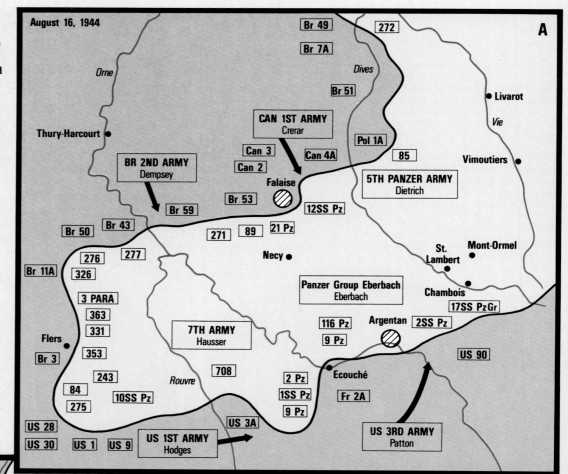

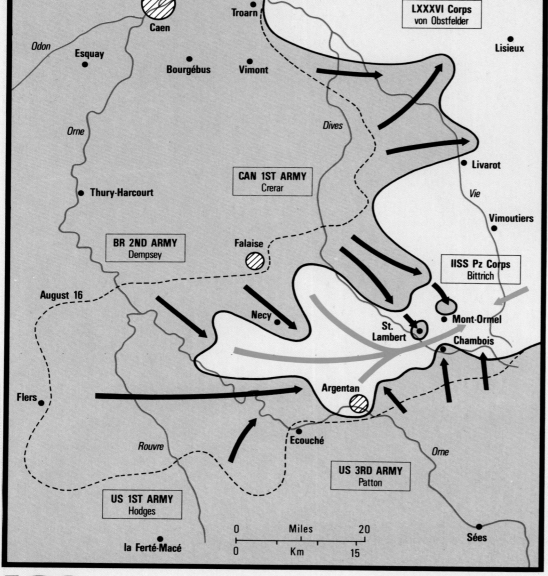

Map B

By August 18 the line of retreat for the Germans had collapsed into a narrow corridor between St. Lambert and Chambois, barely a thousand yards (1km) wide. Towards Chambois from the north, Maj. Gen. Stanislaw Maczeck, commander of the 1st Polish Armoured Division sent the 1st Polish Lancers and 10th Polish Dragoons; while advancing towards them from the south were units of the US 90th Division. Meanwhile, behind and to the west of the Poles, tanks and troops of the Argyll and Sutherland Highlanders of Canada — part of the 4th Canadian Armoured Division — were battling for St. Lambert.

The Poles entered Chambois at about 19:00, Saturday August 19, and encountered the 90th Division's 359th Infantry Regiment. The Falaise pocket was now officially "closed," but these Allied units now had to defend themselves against desperate German counterattacks.

To the east, other units of the 1st Polish Armoured had driven through les Champeaux and on the 19th had arrived on the heights of Mont Ormel, a ridge which dominated the surrounding lowlands. This position, soon to be known as the "Maczuga" or "Mace" to the Poles, would in Montgomery's later phrase become "the cork in the bottle."

The Polish units however, comprised only two armored regiments and three light infantry battalions — about 1,500 men supported by 80 tanks. It soon became clear to the Poles that the sheer weight of the German retreat had cut them off from support and supply, and though in an excellent position to wreak havoc on the Germans, they were in mortal danger themselves.

For three days the Poles fought off massed German attacks by infantry and tanks on their positions along the ridge, until their food was gone, ammunition was spent, and they had suffered nearly 30 percent casualties. The last German attacks occured on the morning of August 21. These once again were beaten off, and around midday contact was made to the north with tanks of the Canadian Grenadier Guards. The men on the "Maczuga" had been relieved.

German position was broken, the 272nd and 89th Divisions had collapsed. The 12th SS Panzer sent forward two Kampfgruppen which delayed the 4th Canadian and 1st Polish Divisions, whilst their comrades fell back to a new line on the River Laison, seven miles (11km) north of Falaise.

The Canadians forced the Laison on August 14. On this occasion they used smoke to blind the German anti-tank guns, and attacked in phalanxes of tanks and tracked infantry carriers. Strong tactical air support helped them close in to within 3 miles (5km) of Falaise.

To the west of the Canadian sector, the British Second Army was pushing south-eastwards through the tangled hills of the Suisse Normande. The pocket was forming. By August 16 when the Canadians captured Falaise, most of the Seventh Army was still west of the Orne. On the following day Hitler authorized a withdrawal to a new defensive line on the east bank of the Orne, but it was too late. On the same day the 4th Canadian and 1st Polish Divisions swung wide to the eastern flank and crossed the Dives. The US V Corps moved north through the XV and attacked towards Chambois and Trun on the Dives. The German Seventh Army and Fifth Panzer Army were trapped in a pocket 20 miles by 20 miles (32km x 32km), surrounded by higher ground: 100,000 soldiers, the remains of 20 divisions, were caught in an arena overlooked from all sides.

The Germans did not give up easily. To the south they used the Forêt de la Grande Gouffern to delay the advance north of the Americans. They attempted to break out of the pocket eastwards by forcing a way across the Dives and through the Auge Hills beyond. The II SS Panzer Corps made two attempts to break into the pocket from Vimoutiers, to establish a safe exit. But the 4th Canadian Division had seized the crossing over the Dives. The Poles had occupied high ground on Mont Ormel, and could not be driven off it, even when reduced to fighting armor with bayonets and bare hands because they were out of ammunition. South of the Poles, near Exmes, were the tanks of the Tactical Group

Above: Despite the reputation of the Germans' motorized and armored units, the majority of their army was still horse-drawn, a fact revealed in the Falaise gap where over 8,000 of these draught animals were killed by Allied air and ground fire.

Below: The fate of the Germans in the gap. It is estimated that 10,000 were killed and about 50,000 were made prisoner. Up to 50,000 are believed to have escaped. In material terms the Germans lost 344 armored vehicles, 2,447 motor vehicles, and 252 guns.

Below: The view from the Polish positions on the top of Mont Ormel. From here every German move could be targeted. Inset: the colors of two of the Polish regiments around Falaise. Left: 24th Lancers; right: 10th Dragoons. *Sikorski Institute*

de Langlade, part of the French 2nd Armored Division. They too enjoyed commanding views of the pocket, its exits and the retreating German forces.

Eventually only one ford and narrow track was still open to the Germans evacuating the area, and it was under concentrated artillery and air attack. By August 19 this route was so choked with wrecked vehicles, corpses and dead horses that it was impassable. Ever since that day it has been known as the "Couloir de Mort", the corridor of death. In the evening of the 19th the Poles, Americans and Canadians met in Chambois. For three more days the Germans inside and outside the pocket continued the fight, then they gave up. On August 22 the II SS Panzer Corps was ordered to join a general retirement towards the Seine. By that time the leading elements of US Third Army had already crossed that river in two places.

The Falaise pocket completed the ruin of the German Army in Normandy. The Allies took 50,000 prisoners and estimated they had destroyed 5,000 armored vehicles and tanks in the area. The German Army had lost 400,000 men in the campaign, and was in full retreat. They did not stop running until they reached the Vosges hills in the east and the canals east of Antwerp in the north.

The Invasion
of Southern France

Bernard Nalty

The invasion of southern France underwent several changes between concept and execution. President Roosevelt and his military leaders — notably Gen. George C. Marshall, and Gen. Dwight D. Eisenhower, who had commanded the Allied invasion of northwest Africa — believed in a knockout blow across the English Channel against the center of Germany's strength. In contrast, British Prime Minister Churchill and his advisors preferred to jab away at weak spots on the perimeter of Nazi-occupied Europe. After the conquest of North Africa, the Allies had to choose between the two strategies, a decision complicated by the fact that a battle-tested Anglo-American army stood on the shores of the Mediterranean, whereas the buildup in the United Kingdom had just begun. Although hard-pressed Soviet forces had checked the Nazi invaders at Stalingrad, the issue on the Eastern Front remained in doubt. The two western Allies could not ignore the danger to the Soviet Union, rein in their forces, and prepare for a cross-channel attack. Churchill's peripheral strategy, though it might delay the decisive blow from the west, would force Hitler to divert forces from the east and also sustain the momentum the Anglo-American Allies had gained in North Africa. Consequently, the Americans and British conquered Sicily, secured in August 1943, and invaded Italy in September.

In May 1943, before the western Allies invaded Sicily and Italy, the Anglo-American *Trident* conference in Washington committed the two nations to a cross-channel attack in the spring of the following year, but during the *Quadrant* meeting at Quebec in August, the British successfully resisted an American proposal to assign this operation, *Overlord*, an "overriding" priority. The possibility of

further peripheral jabs in Mediterranean area thus survived, and Churchill's strategy received a further boost when Josef Stalin, the Soviet dictator, indicated that he would accept a postponement of *Overlord* so that the western Allies could attack immediately in the Mediterranean or the Balkans. Stalin, however, changed his mind by the time he conferred with Roosevelt and Churchill at Tehran, Persia, in November 1943. The Red Army had defeated the Germans at Kursk in July of that year, recaptured Kharkov in August, and advanced westward. Stalin still wanted an Anglo-American invasion, but on the Channel coast of France, definitely not in the Balkans, where western troops might interfere with his plans to dominate the region after the war.

Operation *Anvil*

Stalin's endorsement of *Overlord* ensured that the western Allies would try for a knockout blow in France. The initial concept of operations there called for a pincers movement to crush German resistance. Simultaneously with *Overlord*, the cross-channel assault, the Allies would invade the French Riviera in Operation *Anvil*. Although he accepted *Overlord*, Churchill hoped to replace *Anvil* with an advance into the Balkans. He preferred to seize a beachhead in Yugoslavia, strike through the Ljubljana Gap, capture Vienna, and establish a British presence in the path of the Soviet juggernaut already gathering momentum far to the east. Britain, however, lacked the resources to undertake such a venture without American collaboration. While planning went ahead for *Overlord* and *Anvil*, Churchill won two American converts to his Balkan strategy — Lt. Gen. Mark W. Clark, commander of the Fifth Army in Italy, and Gen. Ira Eaker, who headed the Mediterranean Allied Air Forces — and arranged for one of his own commanders, Field Marshal Sir Henry Maitland Wilson, the Supreme Allied Commander, Mediterranean, to begin planning for a possible thrust across the Adriatic.

While Churchill looked to the Balkans, Allied planners in London realized they could not muster enough landing craft to invade Normandy and the Riviera at the same time. The Allies decided to launch *Overlord* early in June, knowing they could not shift

Left: The Allied invasion of southern France was a less ambitious undertaking than *Overlord* and faced a less capable defense, but was still a major and fairly risky undertaking that involved a corps of three US divisions later joined by a four-division French corps.

Above: On July 31, men of the US 3rd Infantry Division prepare to board their amphibious vessels in the harbor of Bagnoli, in the Formia area of Italy. This exercise paved the way for *Dragoon*, a landing that led to an impressively successful drive up the Rhône River.

Above: Seen on the flagship USS *Catoctin* on its way to southern France are commanders including (left top right) Brig. Gen. G.P. Saville, Lt. Gen. A.M. Patch, Vice Adm. Kent Hewitt, Sec. of the Navy James Forrestal, and Rear Adm. A.G. Lemonnier of the Marine National.

Below: Much of the southern French operation passed with minimal German resistance, and this view of the sea front of the famous Riviera resort of Nice, looking toward the German headquarters in the town, reveals beach defenses but no damage.

the necessary amphibious shipping to the Mediterranean before mid-August. Although the delay gave Churchill another chance to argue for the Balkan alternative, his eloquence could not overcome strategic and geographic reality. Ill-served by ports, highways, and railroads, the Ljubljana Gap wound through mountains where a defender could readily contain the Allied advance, as had happened in Italy, in an area too far to the east to support the post-*Overlord* liberation of France. In contrast, *Anvil*, even though delayed, could attract German strength from elsewhere in France. Moreover, the Riviera beaches provided access to two generally parallel routes to northeastern France or Germany. The invasion force might advance up the Rhône Valley to Lyon and then continue to Nancy or pass through the Belfort Gap to the Rhine and Germany, depending on Allied progress eastward from Normandy, or follow the Route Napoléon from Cannes, by way of Grenoble, to Lyon, thence to Nancy or the Belfort Gap. *Anvil* had other advantages over a Balkan operation, among them: the opportunity to use the Free (Fighting) French troops now fighting in Italy for the liberation of their homeland; a chance to take advantage of the French FFI, the Resistance — strong in southern France; and access to the ports of Marseilles and Toulon as conduits for supplies and reinforcements. The American arguments in favor of *Anvil* prevailed; the operation, redesignated *Dragoon* because the original name might have been compromised, would go ahead despite predictions of disaster from Churchill. Indeed, the Prime Minister's opposition gave rise to the legend that he insisted on the new name of *Dragoon* because he had been dragooned into going along with the plan.

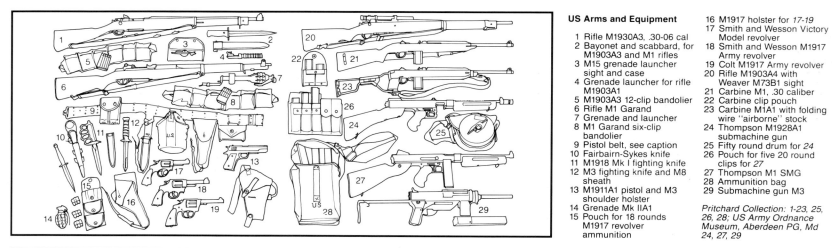

US Arms and Equipment

1 Rifle M1930A3, .30-06 cal
2 Bayonet and scabbard, for M1903A3 and M1 rifles
3 M15 grenade launcher sight and case
4 Grenade launcher for rifle M1903A1
5 M1903A3 12-clip bandolier
6 Rifle M1 Garand
7 Grenade and launcher
8 M1 Garand six-clip bandolier
9 Pistol belt, see caption
10 Fairbairn-Sykes knife
11 M1918 Mk I fighting knife
12 M3 fighting knife and M8 sheath
13 M1911A1 pistol and M3 shoulder holster
14 Grenade Mk IIA1
15 Pouch for 18 rounds M1917 revolver ammunition
16 M1917 holster for 17-19
17 Smith and Wesson Victory Model revolver
18 Smith and Wesson M1917 Army revolver
19 Colt M1917 Army revolver
20 Rifle M1903A4 with Weaver M73B1 sight
21 Carbine M1, .30 caliber
22 Carbine clip pouch
23 Carbine M1A1 with folding wire "airborne" stock
24 Thompson M1928A1 submachine gun
25 Fifty round drum for 24
26 Pouch for five 20 round clips for 27
27 Thompson M1 SMG
28 Ammunition bag
29 Submachine gun M3

Pritchard Collection: 1-23, 25, 26, 28; US Army Ordnance Museum, Aberdeen PG, Md 24, 27, 29

The US Ordnance adopted the M1 Garand (*6*) on January 9, 1936, and deliveries began in late 1937. The vast firepower advantage of a semi-automatic rifle was obvious, and production accelerated with Winchester supplementing production by the Springfield Armory. By the end of the war over four million Garands had been produced. Gen. Patton called the M1 "the greatest battle implement ever devised." The Carbine M1 was adopted on October 22, 1941. Developed in very short time, over six million were produced, manufactured by ten prime contractors. Item *7* features a grenade Mk IIA1 with grenade projector adapter M1A2 and grenade launcher M7. The M1936 pistol belt (*9*) features the M1942 first aid pouch, M1916 hip holster, M1910 canteen, modified and M1918 web magazine pocket.

Aware that an invasion was drawing near, Field Marshal Rommel, responsible for the defense of France, inspected the Mediterranean coast in May 1944 and found a shockingly thin shell of coastal fortifications backed by a fairly sizable mobile force. The task of shoring up the beach defenses that Rommel found so weak fell to two veteran officers, Generaloberst Johannes von Blaskowitz and General der Infanterie Friedrich Wiese. Blaskowitz, a thoroughly competent soldier whose zeal for the offensive and for the Nazi cause Hitler sometimes doubted, commanded Army Group G, which stood guard over the entire region from the Pyrenees to the Italian border. Wiese led the

Nineteenth Army, the principal combat force in southern France. They assigned the highest priority to the coastal fortifications, dispatching some 14,000 laborers — members of the Todt Organization, supplemented by French civilians impressed into the work force — to build almost 600 camouflaged gun positions covering likely invasion beaches. Some of the steel-reinforced concrete structures resembled bath houses or waterfront cafes. Inland of the beaches, level areas where gliders or paratroops might be expected to land sprouted stakes of Rommel's asparagus, supplemented by heavy wire strung among trees and poles to trip the gliders.

The defenses of the beaches and the inland obstacles grew more formidable, but after the invasion of Normandy, troop strength declined as Rommel shifted forces northward. By August 15, D-Day for *Dragoon*, Wiese's Nineteenth Army had one division at Toulon, the former French naval base, another at the port of Marseilles, a third near the Riviera beaches, and four other combat divisions and one reserve division between the Rhône River and the Spanish border. Finally, the 11th Panzer Division, commanded by Generaloberst Wend von Wietersheim, had refitted after fighting in the Soviet Union and was moving from Bordeaux on the west coast toward the mouth of the Rhône. Some 30,000 troops stood guard on the Riviera, with another 200,000 within easy reach.

While the Germans improved their fortifications along the Riviera, planning for *Dragoon* neared completion. Vice Adm. H. Kent Hewitt, USN, commanded the Western Naval Task Force, which would conduct the preliminary naval bombardment and land the assault force. The US Seventh Army, commanded by Lt. Gen. Alexander M. "Sandy" Patch, Jr., who had fought the Japanese on Guadalcanal, faced the task of seizing three beachheads along 45 miles (72km) of coastline from the Golfe de Napoule, southwest of Cannes, to the Baie de Cavalaire, southwest of St. Tropez. Three American divisions in Italy underwent hurried training on the Salerno beaches, where one of them, the 36th Infantry Division, had stormed ashore in September 1943, and another, the 45th Infantry Division, in reserve initially, had taken part in the subsequent fighting. The other, the 3rd Infantry Division, had landed in northwest Africa, Sicily, and in January 1944 at Anzio in Italy.

The *Dragoon* plan called for major landings over the *Camel* beaches at Fréjus in the north, the *Delta* beaches near Ste. Maxime in the center, and the *Alpha* beaches between St. Tropez and Cavalaire in the south. The *Camel* Force under Rear Adm. Don P. Moon, USN, a veteran of *Utah* Beach in *Overlord*, had the assignment of landing Maj. Gen. John E. Dahlquist's 36th Infantry Division. Rear Adm. Frank J. Lowry, USN, a participant in the Anzio invasion, commanded the *Delta* Force, carrying the 45th Infantry Division under Maj. Gen. William W. Eagles. Rear Adm. Bertram J. Rodgers, USN, and his *Alpha* Force would put ashore John W. "Iron Mike" O'Daniel's 3rd Infantry Division. The three assault divisions, plus their supporting units comprised the US VI Corps, under Lt. Gen. Lucian K. Truscott, Jr., who, while commanding the 3rd Infantry Division, had trained his men in the Truscott Trot, a forced march that in eight hours covered 30 miles (48km) instead of the usual 20 miles (32km). Subsidiary landings on Truscott's flanks would distract the defenders and capture coastal defenses. In advance of the assault, 41 eleven-man underwater demolition teams would clear lanes to the various beaches.

Throughout the planning process, French representatives, headed by Col. Jean L. Pettit, tried to insert Army B, commanded by Général d'Armée Jean de Lattre de Tassigny, into the *Dragoon* assault force with the mission of seizing a beachhead of its own. Patch,

Above: Weapons dropped or made by the French Resistance. This group includes delayed-action explosives and incendiary devices. Of note are the incendiary matches and the home-made fragmentation grenade. *Museum of the Liberation, Paris*

Below: British-made Resistance "case" radio. This "S" type portable radio in its civilian case was dropped onto Epaney, Normandy, on the night of September 17, 1943. It includes instructions and original batteries. *Museum of the Liberation, Paris*

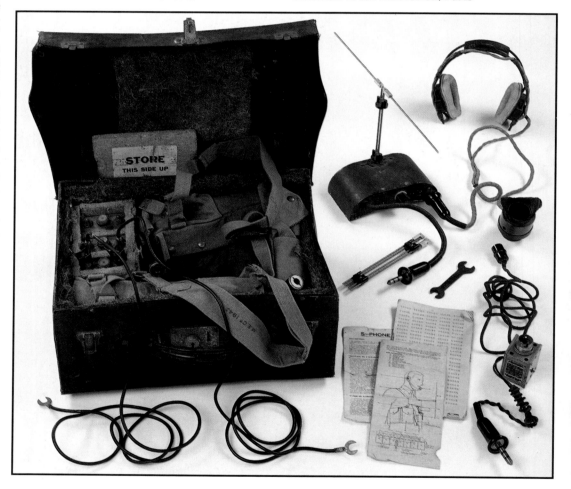

however, lacked the amphibious shipping and supporting aircraft to oblige, even if de Lattre's force had been fully trained to make assault landings, which it was not. As a result, French Army B would follow the Americans ashore and function as a component of Patch's Seventh Army. The first French troops ashore, II Corps of de Lattre's army, would land in the wake of O'Daniel's 3rd Infantry Division and seize Toulon and Marseilles; I Corps would not see action until early September.

Air power formed a critical element of Operation *Dragoon*. After heavy bombers of the American 15th Air Force, which normally hit industrial targets from southern Germany to Romania, had hammered the coastal

defenses, squadrons of the Mediterranean Allied Air Forces and carrier aircraft would join Brig. Gen. Gordon P. Saville's XII Tactical Air Command in supporting the operation. During the assault, fighter-bombers supporting *Dragoon* got their orders from controllers in the command ship USS *Catoctin*, who monitored air traffic, issued air raid warnings, and backed up the radar-equipped LST that directed the fighter defenses. Once VI Corps had established a beachhead, Saville's airmen would support the advance inland.

Dragoon, like *Overlord*, called for pre-dawn airborne landings beyond the invasion beaches to cut off reinforcements and confuse the defenders. Preparations for the airborne attack typified the hectic effort to

Top: A canister drop is made over occupied France by B-17s. Above: A metal drop canister and the remains of its parachute. This was used to deliver weapons to a beleaguered Maquis unit in March 1944.
Museum of the Liberation, Paris

Below: Three FFI fighters bring in a wounded German prisoner somewhere in southern France. These youngsters show just how "irregular" many of the Resistance forces were — and why the Germans often treated them as no more than criminals.

SUPREME HEADQUARTERS ALLIED EXPEDITIONARY FORCE

Office of Assistant Chief of Staff, G-2

WEEKLY INTELLIGENCE SUMMARY No. 19

Week Ending July 29, 1944

PART 1/F.

FILE G-2 MAIN *Cbel.*

MISCELLANEOUS

THE SITUATION IN THE LIMOGES AREA

The savagery of the Germans at **ORADOUR** is inexplicable. An SS detachment arrived at ten in the morning of 10 June. It was market day, and many people from **LIMOGES** had gone there to get supplies. There was also a great number of children sent there for their vacation — a total of about twelve hundred persons. On the pretext of searching for clandestine munitions depots, the SS commander had all the men shut up in two or three barns, and all the women and children in the church. The abandoned village was then pillaged.

At two o'clock, first, the houses, and then the barns, were set on fire. The Germans machine-gunned all who attempted to escape. At five o'clock, the church was set on fire. Here again machine guns were used. One woman only managed to escape. The German general commanding at **LIMOGES** acknowledged before the Prefect that this act dishonored his country. He permitted the bishop and the Prefect to visit the ruins and authorized a funeral service at the cathedral.

In the face of these barbarous acts, the whole region trembles. The peasants hide in the woods, and scouts signal the arrival of any German vehicles. The country experiences at one and the same time the violence of the enemy, of the Maquis, and of the Milice [fascist militia]. There is no longer any legal authority. The Prefect is powerless. A wild anger has seized the terrorized people. The fate of **LIMOGES** is very similar to that of all the cities in the center of **FRANCE**. The only comfort in this frightful situation is to be found in the intense patriotism of these people, in their hope for prompt deliverance, and in the reaction which is developing against all this violence. All hope for the constitution of the regular army and the reconstitution of a legitimate authority.

Courtesy of the Dwight D. Eisenhower Library

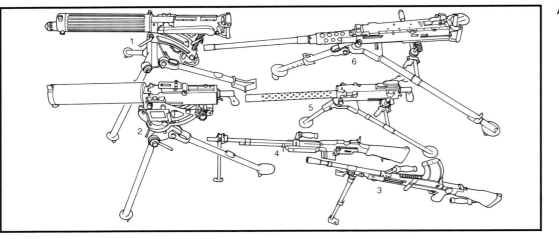

Allied Machineguns

1 British Vickers Mk I, medium, heavy machinegun and tripod. This .303 caliber weapon is belt fed and watercooled

2 US Browning M1917A1 light machinegun on M1917A1 tripod. This .30 caliber weapon was manufactured by Colt, New England Westinghouse, and Remington. This belt fed, water-cooled version was adopted in 1936

3 British Bren light machinegun, .303 caliber. This gas operated air-cooled, clip-fed weapon was developed from the Czech ZB 26 light machinegun. It was adopted in 1938

4 US Browning automatic rifle (BAR) M1918A2, .30 caliber. Introduced in 1918 this gas operated, air-cooled, clip fed arm was capable of firing at both semi and full automatic

5 US Browning light machinegun, M1919. This air-cooled, belt-fed .30 caliber arm was the basic company support weapon, and was used also used extensively on vehicles

6 US Browning heavy machinegun, .50 caliber. This air-cooled, belt-fed weapon was developed in the 1930s. Designed primarily as an anti-aircraft weapon.

US Army Ordnance Museum, Aberdeen PG, Md

The British Vickers Mk I (*1*) was made with both smooth and corrugated water jackets. The jacket held a total of 7 pints (.5l). To reduce water loss, a condenser tube and water container were used. The Vickers had a fire-rate of 500 rounds per minute. The Bren gun (*6*) was operated by a crew of two. The ammunition clips held 28-30 rounds which were fired at a rate of 500 rounds per minute. Though manufactured at Enfield, England in the beginning, over half of those used in World War II were produced in Canada — as is this example, made by Inglis.

launch *Dragoon*. Assigned to carry the airborne troops into battle, the American 1st Provisional Troop Carrier Division, led by Brig. Gen. Paul L. Williams, had to borrow 416 C-47s, their crews, and 225 glider pilots from units in the United Kingdom. Maj. Gen. Robert T. Frederick assembled his 1st Airborne Task Force, which would board the transports and gliders, from the airborne units available in the theater. Short of a dozen staff officers, he obtained them from the 13th Airborne Division, still training in the United States. Frederick's command consisted of one American parachute infantry regiment, a British parachute brigade group, and four American battalions — two of parachute

infantry, one of parachute field artillery, and one of glider infantry. Some of the fragile gliders would carry volunteers from line infantry units like the Japanese-American 442nd Infantry. Airborne troops began hurried training after the fall of Rome on June 4, two days before *Overlord*, but the available aircraft and crews did not permit more than a handful of men at a time to make practice jumps.

The rapidly approaching deadline of August 15 also complicated the training of the amphibious forces. Three American heavy cruisers and three old battleships, plus the French battleship *Lorraine* and the British *Ramillies*, joined Adm. Hewitt's naval forces,

while nine carriers, seven from the Royal Navy, prepared to help land-based aircraft in maintaining control of the skies over the Riviera beaches. After a disappointing rehearsal by his *Camel* Force, Adm. Moon decided that the amphibious forces could not be ready in time. He urged Hewitt to postpone D-Day, but the naval commander, even if he had shared Moon's concerns could scarcely have delayed the impending invasion. Hewitt tried to reassure his subordinate, on the verge of nervous collapse after the strain of *Overlord*, and thought he had succeeded, but on the morning of August 5, Moon killed himself, a victim of the intense pressure generated by two successive amphibious

OPERATION *DRAGOON*
Designated assault areas:
Alpha, Delta, Camel
Assault sectors: *Alpha Red, Alpha Yellow;
Delta Red, Delta Green, Delta Yellow, Delta
Blue; Camel Green, Camel Blue.*
Assault Divisions:
US 3rd Infantry, US 45th Infantry,
US 36th Infantry: US VI Corps.
Plus 1st Airborne Task Force.
H-Hour 08:00 all areas.

Planning for the Allied landings in the
Provence region of France began in the North
African city of Algiers in January 1944. The
invasion was to be undertaken by US Seventh
Army and French Army B. They would be
transported by US Eighth Fleet, and supported
by the US Twelfth Army Air Force. In overall
command of the operation's initial stages was
the Supreme Allied Commander
Mediterranean, Field Marshal Sir Henry
Maitland Wilson. Once established in France
to a satisfactory degree, command would then
pass to Gen. Eisenhower and SHAEF.
   The objectives of *Dragoon* were the major
French ports of Marseilles and Toulon, and an

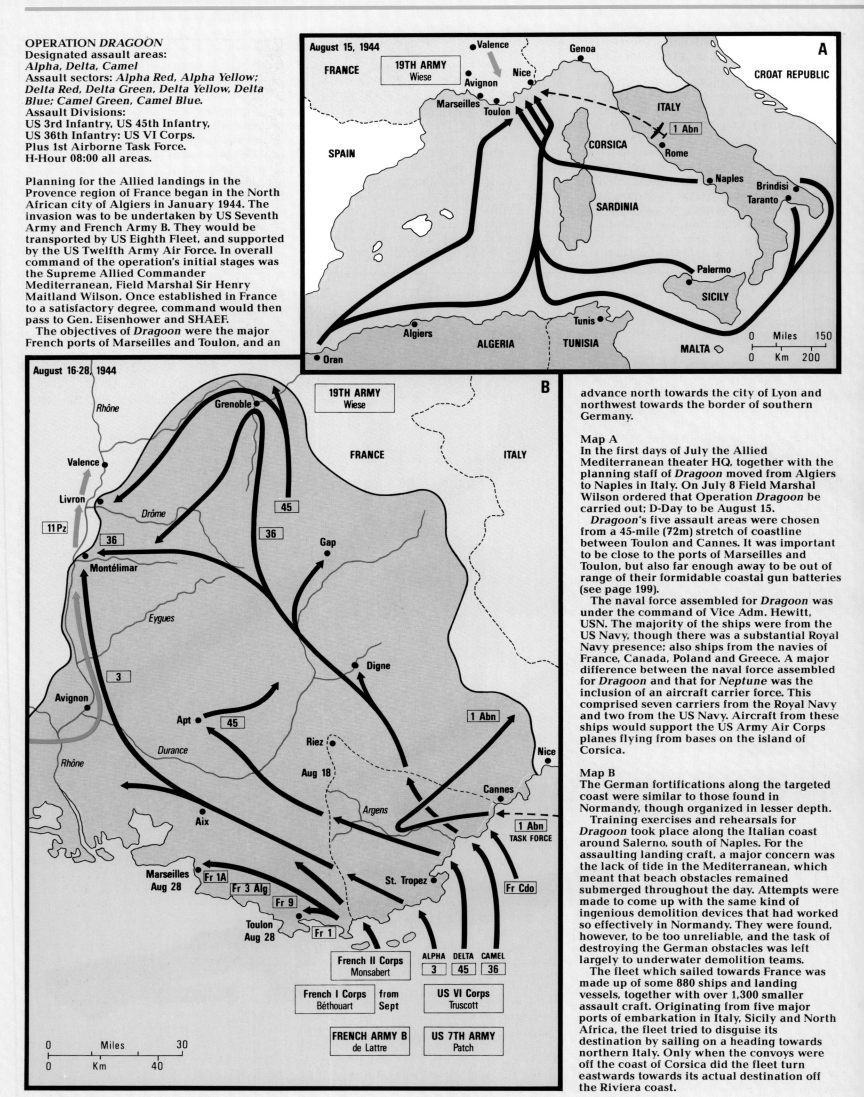

advance north towards the city of Lyon and
northwest towards the border of southern
Germany.

Map A
In the first days of July the Allied
Mediterranean theater HQ, together with the
planning staff of *Dragoon* moved from Algiers
to Naples in Italy. On July 8 Field Marshal
Wilson ordered that Operation *Dragoon* be
carried out; D-Day to be August 15.
   Dragoon's five assault areas were chosen
from a 45-mile (72m) stretch of coastline
between Toulon and Cannes. It was important
to be close to the ports of Marseilles and
Toulon, but also far enough away to be out of
range of their formidable coastal gun batteries
(see page 199).
   The naval force assembled for *Dragoon* was
under the command of Vice Adm. Hewitt,
USN. The majority of the ships were from the
US Navy, though there was a substantial Royal
Navy presence; also ships from the navies of
France, Canada, Poland and Greece. A major
difference between the naval force assembled
for *Dragoon* and that for *Neptune* was the
inclusion of an aircraft carrier force. This
comprised seven carriers from the Royal Navy
and two from the US Navy. Aircraft from these
ships would support the US Army Air Corps
planes flying from bases on the island of
Corsica.

Map B
The German fortifications along the targeted
coast were similar to those found in
Normandy, though organized in lesser depth.
   Training exercises and rehearsals for
Dragoon took place along the Italian coast
around Salerno, south of Naples. For the
assaulting landing craft, a major concern was
the lack of tide in the Mediterranean, which
meant that beach obstacles remained
submerged throughout the day. Attempts were
made to come up with the same kind of
ingenious demolition devices that had worked
so effectively in Normandy. They were found,
however, to be too unreliable, and the task of
destroying the German obstacles was left
largely to underwater demolition teams.
   The fleet which sailed towards France was
made up of some 880 ships and landing
vessels, together with over 1,300 smaller
assault craft. Originating from five major
ports of embarkation in Italy, Sicily and North
Africa, the fleet tried to disguise its
destination by sailing on a heading towards
northern Italy. Only when the convoys were
off the coast of Corsica did the fleet turn
eastwards towards its actual destination off
the Riviera coast.

operations. Another American, Rear Adm. Spencer S. Lewis, took over the *Camel* Force. In the aftermath of Moon's suicide, Churchill, still fascinated with the Ljubljana Gap, argued one last time for canceling *Dragoon*, but Eisenhower would not hear of it.

Although pressed for time and resources, the planners of *Dragoon* benefited from excellent intelligence. Indeed, Allied intelligence officers maintained a huge map that covered the Riviera coast from Cannes to Toulon, showing bunkers, artillery positions and their fields of fire, entrenchments, obstacles to airborne and amphibious landings, and in some instances the number of German defenders at a particular place and the names of their officers. Aerial photography revealed much about the defenses, but *Ultra* provided an even clearer insight into plans as well as troop dispositions. The results of the *Ultra* intercepts went to special liaison units reporting to commanders like Patch. Many of the details about names, numbers, and individual strongpoints came from the Resistance, which also engaged in sabotage and harassment, its activity sustained and coordinated by the Special Operations Executive (SOE) in London.

The SOE arranged to drop supplies to the FFI, which included such disparate elements of the Resistance as Communists loyal to Moscow and conservative followers of Charles de Gaulle. In the south of France, the Resistance sabotaged coastal guns, crippling two of the 340 mm weapons taken from the French battleship *La Provence* at Toulon and mounted ashore, and ambushed road and rail traffic. Lt. Col. Francis C. A. Cammaerts, a British officer of the SOE, who had parachuted into France, coordinated, albeit loosely, the activity of some 10,000 irregulars, lightly armed but able to materialize suddenly, make deadly use of explosives or automatic weapons, and then vanish into the countryside.

A series of successful ambushes, the Normandy landings, and a premature call for an armed uprising issued by mistake from de Gaulle's headquarters in London encouraged bolder action that had tragic consequences. On June 10, 1944, four days after *Overlord* began, de Gaulle's staff realized the wrong message had gone out and, too late, issued orders to revert to guerrilla warfare. Already, Resistance forces near the village of Oradour-sur-Glane in southwestern France were attacking the 2nd SS Panzer Division, ''Das Reich'' as it deployed to help defend Normandy. As an example to those who dared resist, German soldiers of this Waffen-SS division herded the populace of Oradour into buildings, opened fire through the wooden walls, and set the structures ablaze. A few people escaped, but 642 men, women and children perished in the village that afternoon.

On the Vercors, an elevated plateau stretching from Grenoble southward to Die, the Resistance forces, protected by the surrounding mountains and encouraged by a supply drop from American aircraft, celebrated Bastille Day, July 14, as their day of liberation, but freedom lasted little more than a week. On July 21, the Germans attacked with aircraft and armor, rapidly overwhelming

Above: A paratrooper of the 1st Airborne Task Force departs from his Douglas C-47 transport. The force dropped near Draguignan to secure the inland road between Fréjus and Aix-en-Provence, and was relieved by the US 36th Division moving from St. Raphael.

Above: Allied troops push toward a luxury hotel after their unopposed landing at St. Pierre on August 15. The landings suffered only 183 men killed and wounded, together with another 49 non-battle casualties. Movement inland quickly followed.

Above: DUKW amphibious trucks come ashore on *Alpha Red* beach near Cavalaire on August 18 with a military policeman (right) overseeing operations. The DUKW was a simple way to move supplies straight from transports anchored offshore to areas behind the fighting men.

the lightly-armed irregulars. The Waffen-SS troops who spearheaded the assault burned entire villages, slaughtered the inhabitants, and tracked down and executed many of the surviving members of the Resistance. Those who escaped the Nazi vengeance fled into the forest to await the Allied invasion of the Mediterranean coast.

The *Dragoon* Landings

Dragoon began on August 15 with an airborne assault. While a handful of aircraft jettisoned hundreds of dummy parachutists into the early morning darkness west of Toulon to confuse the defenders, 396 C-47s, launched from ten different airfields in Italy, thundered toward the fog-shrouded vineyards and meadows near the town of le Muy, where the first stick of paratroopers jumped at 04:30. The low-lying fog proved disconcerting to the parachutists, some of whom cast aside weapons and equipment under the impression they were coming down at sea, and it may also have contributed

to a navigational error that dropped one battalion more than 20 miles (32km) from the assigned drop zone. Save for this one unit, the vanguard of the 1st Airborne Task Force landed as planned.

Almost five hours later, the first of the gliders arrived near le Muy. En route, while over the Mediterranean, a tow rope parted, but the glider pilot ditched his Waco CG-4 near one of the lifeguard ships posted along the route, and all on board the aircraft survived. Shortly afterward, the right wing of another glider snapped off; the craft rolled sharply, broke the tow rope, and disintegrated, sending men and equipment tumbling into the sea. This time no-one survived. At 09:20, the first of the 71 remaining gliders hurtled out of the sky, plunging to earth at speeds approaching 90 miles (125km) per hour to deliver troops, jeeps, artillery pieces, and anti-tank guns. Some of the gliders slammed into trees or man made obstacles, even though the earlier wave of parachutists had thinned the crop of Rommel's asparagus. As dusk approached, another 332 gliders landed, so that at day's end some 9,000 American and British airborne soldiers, 221 jeeps, 213 artillery pieces, and miscellaneous other weapons and items of equipment stood ready to attack the Germans at le Muy. Thus far, airborne casualties totaled 434 killed and 292 injured.

Between the time the dummy parachutists plunged earthward and the real paratroopers arrived, Allied amphibious forces undertook a series of operations in preparation for the three main landings. On the left of the invasion beaches, a few vessels, trailing radar-reflecting balloons to multiply their numbers, created the illusion of a seaborne assault in conjunction with the airborne demonstration near Toulon. On the opposite flank, Lt. Cdr. Douglas Fairbanks, Jr., the hero of many an adventure film, landed a team of French commandos to cut the highway that hugged the coast. The commandos came ashore in an undetected minefield, causing explosions that drew German fire; the landing force then scrambled back into the boats, which Allied aircraft mistakenly strafed. The enemy captured the surviving commandos, who swam ashore, but within 24 hours, assault troops of the 36th Infantry Division freed the prisoners.

To the left of the invasion beaches, while French commandos cut the road to Toulon, the 1st Special Service Force, made up of Canadians and Americans, attacked the Iles

Above: On August 16, troops of Gen. Jean de Lattre de Tassigny's French II Corps started to land as the second component of Lt. Gen. Alexander M. Patch's US Seventh Army, and passed through the US VI Corps before moving west along the coast to Marseilles.

d'Hyères to silence German guns that dominated the *Alpha* beaches. Early on the morning of D-Day, the force overran the batteries and discovered only dummy weapons. Elsewhere on the islands, this so-called "Devil's Brigade," commanded by Col. Edwin A. Walker, overcame stiff resistance with the help of naval gunfire, including 15-inch salvoes from HMS *Ramillies*, and seized Port Cros for landing supplies.

The minefields and obstacles off the Riviera beaches presented a challenge to the planners of *Dragoon*, who sent minesweepers as close to shore as the depth of water would permit and followed up with explosives-laden, radio-controlled boats designed to blast lanes for the assault craft. Underwater demolition teams dealt with the least accessible of the obstacles, many of them booby-trapped with mines.

While the battleships, cruisers, and destroyers bombarded the German defenses, rocket-firing landing craft accompanied the assault waves along the cleared lanes. The

3rd Infantry Division seized the *Alpha* beaches, where aerial and naval bombardment had neutralized the strong defenses, and the 45th Infantry Division benefited from the most powerful of the gunfire support flotillas — built around the American battleships *Texas* and *Nevada* — in rapidly overrunning the *Delta* beachhead. On the *Camel* beaches, the 36th Infantry Division encountered formidable minefields and, off *Camel Red* Beach, savage enemy fire that not even repeated shelling by the battleship USS *Arkansas* could suppress. As H-Hour for storming *Camel Red* approached, Adm. Lewis, Moon's replacement, diverted the assault force to *Camel Green*, where it landed in the wake of other elements of Dahlquist's division.

On August 16, D + 1, the Allies consolidated their grip on the Riviera beachhead. As on the previous day, Gen. Dahlquist's 36th Infantry Division, which wore the T patch of the Texas National Guard, had the hardest fight, attacking *Camel Red* from the flank to avoid an anti-tank barrier disguised as a row of beachfront houses. Meanwhile, the airborne force captured its assigned objectives. British and American paratroops and American glider infantry took le Muy, and the American 551st Parachute Infantry Battalion, assisted by irregulars of the Resistance, captured Draguignan, freed the French guerrillas held there, and made prisoners of Generalleutnant Ludwig Bieringer, a corps commander, and his staff. Late in the afternoon, the battalion that had parachuted far from its intended drop zone — the 3rd Battalion, 517th Parachute Infantry, under Lt. Col. Melvin Zais — rejoined its regiment and helped push the enemy beyond les Arcs. At dusk, tanks from the beachhead made contact with the airborne force, and the invasion entered a new phase.

The buildup of the Seventh Army proceeded rapidly. By midnight on August 17, more than 86,500 American and French troops

BEACH MASTER CP

BEACH MASTER NAVY C.P.

had landed, along with 12,500 vehicles and 46,100 tons of cargo. During the month, 380,000 men crossed the *Dragoon* beaches, as did 69,000 vehicles, 306,000 tons of supplies, and 18,000 tons of fuel. As Patch's forces gained strength, Truscott's VI Corps set out in pursuit of the retreating Germans, and the French II Corps attacked Toulon and Marseilles.

Patch, in planning to exploit the beachhead, had three powerful advantages: *Ultra*, aerial domination, and the French Resistance. Of these, *Ultra* proved the most important, for it revealed Blaskowitz's intentions. On August 17, the German commander received orders to withdraw his mobile forces, leaving the garrison troops to hold Toulon and Marseilles for as long as possible. Bletchley Park decoded the message on the 18th, and by the 20th, Patch had received the information and, without indicating the true source, passed it to his subordinate commanders. Once *Ultra* had revealed that von Blaskowitz would withdraw, Patch pursued with his most mobile forces — the three infantry divisions of Truscott's VI Corps. The Seventh Army commander sent Frederick's airborne task force, which had fewer vehicles available than the "leg" divisions, to liberate Cannes and Nice and then secure the eastern flank, even though *Ultra* revealed no immediate threat from the German divisions in northern Italy.

The Allies controlled the skies over the invasion beaches, and only briefly could the Luftwaffe challenge this mastery. Between August 16 and 18, the Germans launched 141 sorties by Junkers Ju 88 and Dornier Do 217 bombers, some of the latter carrying glider bombs, and rushed fighters to the area. Aerial attacks sank an LST, and in the fading twilight of August 18, five Ju 88s bombed the command ship USS *Catoctin*, killing six and wounding 42 but causing only minor damage. After this parting shot, the Luftwaffe withdrew its squadrons from southern France.

Below: The Germans used French naval guns to defend Marseilles from seaward attack, but the decisive blows were struck from east and north by two of the lightly armed infantry divisions of the French II Corps and the German garrison soon capitulated.

For ten days after the landings, Saville's light and medium bombers and fighter-bombers tried to destroy the bridges across the Durance and Rhône rivers in the hope of isolating von Wietersheim's 11th Panzer Division from von Blaskowitz's main body. The Germans succeeded, however, in massing the available bridging equipment and bringing the armored troops across both streams. Von Wietersheim could shuttle his tanks between Route N7 on the eastern bank of the Rhône and the Route Napoléon, as the American threat dictated and the road network permitted. Patch soon realized that he needed the bridges to pursue the Germans almost as desperately as von Blaskowitz. After August 25, therefore, Allied airmen spared the bridges on which Patch depended to conduct and supply the pursuit, concentrating instead on strafing road and rail traffic. Reflecting the important change in priorities, Saville claimed the destruction of 1,400 vehicles, 30 locomotives and 263 railroad cars between August 23 and 29.

Above: Before their capitulation in Marseilles on August 28, the Germans sought to deny the Allies use of this great port for as long as possible, and scuttled ships in difficult positions. This is the steamer *Cap Corse* lying on the bottom in the harbor entrance.

The Resistance, including survivors of the disaster on the Vercors, gave Patch another advantage by providing him a source of both firepower and intelligence. The exploits of these men and women ranged from reporting German movements to ambushing retreating columns. On one occasion, Christine Granville, a Polish-born agent dispatched to southern France by the SOE, singlehandedly prevented the Germans from using an important pass through the mountains near Digne. Scrambling alone up steep and heavily forested slopes, she called out to the Polish conscripts in their own language and persuaded them to desert to the Resistance.

The Liberation of Toulon and Marseilles

While the pursuit of von Blaskowitz got under way, fighting raged at Toulon and Marseilles. The II Corps of de Lattre's army followed O'Daniel's 3rd Infantry Division ashore on August 16 and advanced on the two ports, expecting to capture them in 40 days. Toulon presented a formidable challenge to the French, lightly armed by American standards. Three fortified heights barred the way, backed up by minefields, barbed wire, trenches, and pillboxes. French shock troops scaled the hills and routed the defenders with flamethrowers and fire from rifles and mortars. By August 23, the attackers had captured the three objectives and begun probing Toulon itself, where some 1,800 Germans, commanded by Adm. Heinrich Rufus, manned the fortifications that dominated the harbor. The undamaged pair of 340mm guns taken from the battleship *La Provence* formed the backbone of the harbor defenses, which exchanged salvoes with an Allied fleet that included *Lorraine*, a sister ship of *La Provence*, and two other battleships, USS *Nevada*

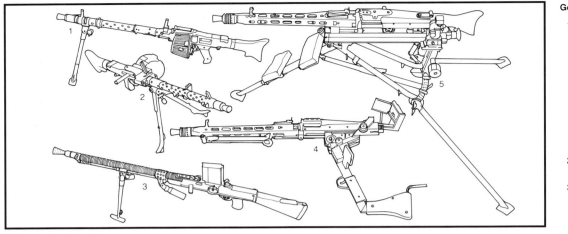

German Machineguns

1 Machinegun Model 1934/41 Maschinengewehr 34/41, (MG34) 7.92 caliber, with bipod in forward (assault) position and basket drum (Gurttrommel 34) containing a 50 round belt of ammunition. Production of the MG34 continued until 1945, concurrent with the later, heavier, MG42 (4). Note the shorter barrel and barrel jacket containing 50 round belt

2 MG34 with bipod in rear (defensive) position and 50 round drum attached

3 Czech ZB 26 (Maschinengewehr 26(t), 7.92mm caliber, with 20 round detachable magazine. This is the weapon on which the British Bren gun was based (see page 194). Note the Czech manufacturer's name and ''BRNO'' on the side

4 MG42, 7.92mm caliber with special periscope optics, stock and trigger group, allowing the gunner to operate the weapon from a concealed defensive position such as a trench. This is a very rare specimen

5 MG42, 7.92mm caliber with high-quality Zielfernrohr 40 optical sight, as used in the heavy machinegun role, mounted on a tripod (Lafette 42)

US Army Ordnance Museum, Aberdeen PG, Md

and HMS *Ramillies*. The hammering of the fortifications took a toll among the German guns, enabling the attacking warships to steam past the batteries on August 26 and enter Toulon harbor. Acknowledging the futility of further resistance, Rufus promptly agreed to surrender; he formally capitulated on August 28.

Instead of seizing Toulon before attacking Marseilles, the French II Corps moved simultaneously against both ports. Marseilles lacked Toulon's powerful hilltop defenses, and the Resistance provided information on the minefields and batteries the Germans had prepared. With the hour of liberation apparently at hand, the FFI inside Marseilles

attacked German strongpoints, which proved too rugged for the irregulars. A call went out for help, and II Corps responded. With the assistance of air strikes and naval gunfire, French troops overran the enemy defenses, sometimes in a building-by-building struggle. After brief negotiations, the Marseilles garrison surrendered, also on August 28.

While one corps of de Lattre's Army B seized the ports to which Eisenhower attached such importance — the French I Corps had not yet landed — Truscott set out to trap the German forces withdrawing northward. Von Blaskowitz had two first-rate divisions to screen this risky maneuver, the 388th Infantry Division and the 11th Panzer Division.

The armored unit had reorganized and refitted after serving in the Soviet Union, where its mobility earned it the nickname "Ghost Division." Again and again, the Ghost Division had materialized at the critical moment on the Eastern Front, and it would continue to do so as Army Group G retreated.

Truscott planned to harry and delay the German retreat toward the Belfort Gap so that the 36th Infantry Division, spearheaded by Brig. Gen. Frederick B. Butler's Provisional Armored Group, known as Task Force Butler, could speed northward up the Route Napoléon in the direction of Grenoble. The Resistance might be able to seal the Rhône Valley; if not, Butler could veer westward to

Left: The German defense of southern France was considerably less determined than that of Normandy, and large numbers of prisoners were taken. These Germans are being marched through Toulon to the dock for embarkation.

sever Route N7 on the river's east bank. Butler's objective would be the narrow gorge at Montélimar, through which road and river passed. While O'Daniel's 3rd Infantry Division, advancing at a Truscott Trot, pursued the Germans up Route N7, Butler led the 36th Infantry Division up the Route Napoléon and established a blocking position at the Gap. On August 20, when he realized that the FFI could not contain the retreating Germans, Truscott ordered Butler to head west, generally along the Drôme River valley, to cut Route N7 and slam shut the so-called Montélimar Gate. En route, Butler established a series of outposts to protect the road he had followed.

Battle for the Montélimar Gate

Elsewhere in the VI Corps zone, the rest of Dahlquist's 36th Infantry Division spread itself thin, capturing Grenoble on August 22 and holding the town until relieved by a regiment from the 45th Infantry Division, replacing the elements of Task Force Butler on the Drôme River outpost line, and reinforcing Butler's thrust toward the Rhône. Meanwhile, the 45th Infantry Division crossed the Durance River, mopped up east of Avignon, and advanced northward on the right flank of O'Daniel's division. If the Texas Division could seize and hold the high ground dominating Montélimar, Truscott could destroy Army Group G.

Task Force Butler — consisting of one battalion each of tanks, field artillery, and infantry, plus a reconnaissance squadron, and companies of tank destroyers and engineers — reached Route N7 late in the afternoon of August 21, but reinforcements from the parent division lagged behind, delayed by the threat of a German counterattack in the vicinity of Grenoble. Until additional troops arrived, Task Force Butler could only dig in and establish a roadblock north of Montélimar; the German force in the town proved too strong for Butler to dislodge, but help was on the way, following the same route the task force had used. During the night infantry and artillery units from the 36th Infantry Division joined Butler, and the gunners laid their 105mm howitzers to shell German road traffic on both banks of the Rhône.

The battle for the Montélimar Gate became a race between Dahlquist's infantry division and von Wietersheim's Ghost Division, and the Panzer unit got there first with the heaviest firepower. Despite a scourging from American artillery, the Germans held Montélimar, and from the town they could fight their way up Route N7 or take advantage of the roads that converge in the town to outflank Task Force Butler. Actually, they did both, with tanks leading each of the attacks. Dahlquist recognized that his divisional spearhead, Task Force Butler could be bypassed and cut off, so he jury-rigged a defensive line generally along the Roubion river, using troops that otherwise might have helped block Route N7. German armor crashed through the Roubion position on the night of August 25-26, even as the bulk of the 11th Panzer Division held open the Montélimar Gate.

To close the highway north of Montélimar, Dahlquist's Texans had to hold a dominant ridge line that rose some 300ft (91m) above the river valley. On August 25, Dahlquist reported from his command post near Grenoble, where an expected counterattack had yet to materialize, that his troops held the critical ridge, passing along information he had received from subordinates there. When he arrived on the scene, however, he discovered that his men held the wrong objective; the officers there had mistaken one ridge for another. The key terrain remained in German hands long enough for von Blaskowitz to escape. Although Army Group G survived to fight another day, it would do so without some 2,000 or more trucks, 80 artillery pieces, and five railroad guns destroyed at Montélimar by air strikes and artillery fire or overrun by Truscott's soldiers.

Furious at Dahlquist's erroneous report, Truscott's first impulse was to relieve the division commander, who realized all too well the consequences of the failure, but the corps commander relented. He accepted Dahlquist's explanation that hard-pressed subordinates had made an honest mistake at a time when he was distracted by the possible danger from the direction of Grenoble and the real threat to his supply line when the Germans broke through the makeshift Roubion line.

Dahlquist may have remained in command because Truscott realized that a shortage of ammunition prevented the Texas Division

Below: As the Germans flooded north along the road and rail lines paralleling the Rhône River, they were decimated by marauding US tactical warplanes. This scene, south of Montélimar, shows a convoy and train, the latter with a 280-mm gun, after being strafed.

from using its field artillery to deadliest effect, and in the US Army of World War II artillery proved the most effective of weapons. True, a concentration fired by the 133rd Field Artillery Battalion savaged a 55-car railroad train on the west bank of the Rhône, but Dahlquist's gunners had to prioritize targets to make the best use of a dwindling ammunition supply. Truscott, moreover, was carefully doling out gasoline, which hampered the movement of trucks carrying shells, and troops throughout VI Corps subsisted for a time on two-thirds rations. The crisis in logistics resulted from the distance that truck convoys had to travel in avoiding bridges that American airmen or German demolition teams had dropped into stream beds. Whether influenced by the supply shortage or not, Truscott kept Dahlquist in command, though he could easily have turned to Gen. Frederick of the 1st Airborne Task Force, who took over the 45th Infantry Division later in the war.

Once von Blaskowitz had skillfully extricated his forces through the Montélimar Gate, Truscott looked ahead to a new objective, Lyon, which he assigned to Dahlquist and the 36th Infantry Division. While the 45th Infantry Division under Eagles, cut the escape route eastward from Lyon, the 3rd Infantry Division would mop up around Montélimar, and the II Corps of de Lattre's army, the victor at Toulon and Marseilles, would advance on the west bank of the Rhône. The French I Corps was to close the gap between VI Corps and the Swiss border and provide security for Patch's right flank.

Eagles and his 45th Infantry Division, wearing the Thunderbird shoulder patch of the Oklahoma National Guard, moved swiftly to sever the roads east of Lyon, but on September 1, von Wietersheim's tanks pushed past a key strongpoint at Meximieux on the Lyon-Geneva highway. Meanwhile, Dahlquist's Texans reached the hills overlooking Lyon only to learn from documents captured by the Resistance that the Germans intended to abandon the city. After reconnaissance patrols verified the enemy's departure, the

36th Infantry Division waited on the outskirts so that the French II Corps could formally liberate the city.

Although the Germans had eluded them at Montélimar and again at Lyon, Patch and Truscott still hoped to trap Blaskowitz short of the Belfort Gap. The pursuit resumed with VI Corps in the center, the French II Corps on the left, and the French I Corps moving up on the right. The 11th Panzer Division succeeded in holding the Thunderbird Division at bay, but the 177th Cavalry Reconnaissance Squadron — a part of Task Force Butler until that organization disbanded on August 30 — got ahead of the Germans and set up a

Below: The liberation of French cities and towns was inevitably followed by retaliation against collaborators both known and suspected. Here French Resistance fighters herd away a crowd of collaborators rounded up in Lyon.

Above: After Lyon had been liberated, there was sporadic German resistance for a short time after this. Here French troops and Resistance fighters (FFI) fire across the Rhône River at German snipers occupying the city hospital.

roadblock at Bourg-en-Bresse on September 3, the same day that French troops took possession of Lyon. As had happened at Montélimar and Meximieux, the forces mobile enough to outpace the Germans lacked the firepower to stop them. Elements of von Wietersheim's Ghost Division all but destroyed the cavalry squadron, though suffering heavy casualties in doing so.

Blaskowitz next chose to fight a delaying action at Besançon to gain time for the final withdrawal through the Belfort Gap. Fortified in succession by Romans, the French monarchy, and finally the republic, Besançon seemed an ideal place to slow the American pursuit, and some 3,000 German troops massed there. On September 7, after a two-day fight, O'Daniel's 3rd Infantry Division captured the city, but the pursuit rapidly lost momentum. While O'Daniel's troops struggled for control of Besançon, the 45th Infantry Division became involved in a prolonged slugging match, as German resistance grew fiercer.

On the left of VI Corps, the French II Corps advanced from Lyon, liberating Dijon on September 10 and taking tens of thousands of prisoners, mostly second-line troops, East European volunteers like the battalion of Ukrainians that killed its officers and went over to the Allies. The best of the German units facing the French corps retreated in good order and conducted a stubborn defense of Langres that put an end to the pursuit in that region. On September 12, however, de Lattre's force made contact near Dijon with advance elements of Maj. Gen. Leclerc's French Armored Division, which had fought its way from Normandy. The Allies thus established a single front from the English Channel to Switzerland as they closed in on Germany.

Pursuit to the Seine

11

Roger Cirillo

The Strategic Setting

Cobra began the end of the Normandy campaign. When Bradley turned his *Cobra* breakthrough into a breakout, rushing his forces southward, he began the second phase of the *Overlord* plan, introducing new forces and changing the command structure. The activation of the US 12th Army Group on August 1, gave Bradley a field command equal to Montgomery's 21st Army Group and brought Lt. Gen. George S. Patton's Third Army into the field. Though Monty would retain temporary "coordinating authority" over both Army Groups then totaling some 38 divisions, American commanders eagerly awaited the day Eisenhower's SHAEF headquarters established itself on the continent, enabling Ike to assume control of the Allied armies.

The original forecast of operations designated Brittany and its key ports, St. Malo, Brest, and St. Nazaire plus the Quiberon Bay area, as Bradley's objective. Along with the entire area from the Brittany Peninsula to the perimeter formed by the River Loire in the south, and the Seine outside Paris in the north, this area constituted the American sector of the crucial "lodgment" required to begin the liberation of Western Europe. With 21st Army Group taking up the area from their boundary west of the Seine outside Paris to Le Havre, the planners forecast that the entire "lodgment area" would be occupied by D+90.

While the Allies paused to build up forces, the US 12th Army Group would switch to using Brittany's sea ports when available, to deploy America's armies directly from across the Atlantic. Then the 21st Army Group would take over Cherbourg for its supplies and then capture the Channel ports along the coast to mount the long drive towards Germany.

Cobra's success promised a change to that concept. With the German front collapsing without an established defense in depth, the total defeat of the German armies in the west appeared possible. Attacking east, the American First, British Second, and Canadian First Armies ground up the German main defense head on, while Bradley activated Patton's Third Army to take command of the forces breaking out of the Normandy perimeter both to seize Brittany and to position itself for its move towards the Seine.

Hitler's defense had surprised the Allies. Their estimates indicated that the Germans would fight on successive defense lines rather than attempting to form a tight cordon close to the water's edge. Though the defenders had held the attackers for 40 days in an area they had hoped to have captured within the first nine, fighting forward on a

Left: **Cheerful French civilians line the road as US forces roll through their town in pursuit of the retreating Germans. Allied forces were treated with the utmost liberality by the French, and this was at times an impediment to rapid advance.**

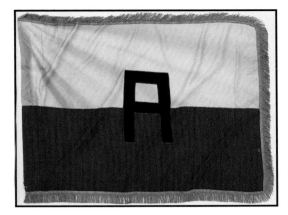

Above: The flag of the US Third Army. "Lucky," as it was codenamed by its commander Gen. Patton became operational on August 1, 1944. The insignia derives from its occupation duties after World War I. *Patton Museum of Cavalry and Armor*

solid line had been costly. Heavy losses and the necessity to match the growing Allied force stripped the Germans of reserves, thus preventing any shift to subsequent defense lines on favorable terrain or major river lines, while off-balancing their force, leaving most German armor in the east between Bayeux and Caen. When Bradley broke out, German forces weren't positioned to both hold the line and eliminate the breakthrough.

Breaking the ground deadlock would eventually reveal that there was a significant long-term effect for the Allies in failing to gain the ground marked on 21st Army Group's phase line map, beyond the perception of being slow or being behind schedule (see map page 27). The effect was a predictable shortfall in logistical support.

The Allied armies were limited in stockpiling supplies in their rear areas, which were being filled by reinforcing units. Bradley's sudden success created a problem. As divisions quickly advanced, the long-term forward "dumping" of supplies behind the lines became impossible, with all available transportation being used to supply the rapidly-moving forces. Trucks brought food,

ammunition, and most critically gasoline, directly to fighting units. Every mile forward doubled the distances for the supply vehicles. Every new division committed added hundreds of tons to the supplies.

Patton's Command

The VIII Corps' drive through Avranches was taken over by Patton, who now commanded nine of Bradley's 21 divisions. The 12th Army Group's first battle directive ordered Patton to drive south to take the area between Rennes and Fougères and then turn westward to take St. Malo, Quiberon Bay, Brest, and clear the Brittany Peninsula.

The plan was bold. Rennes was 25 miles (40km) south of VIII Corps' lead elements; it was nearly 90 miles (144km) to the peninsula's base and a further 135 miles (216km) to the western tip. Patton would have to race his divisions through the narrow gap at Avranches, and then form a rapidly expanding front, deploying his divisions towards

Above: An M-10 tank destroyer goes into action around St. Lô. M-10 units were organized into Tank Destroyer Groups within army corps. Seven groups served in Normandy (Nos. 1-7). The first group to arrive was the 3rd, which landed on June 8.

every point of the compass to overrun the peninsula and trap the defenders while ensuring his northern, eastern, and southern flanks were not counterattacked.

Patton was ideal for the job. His genius was in seizing the moment. His boldness and skill in operational maneuver, particularly pursuit, was unmatched by anyone in the Allied camp. Holding open a narrow movement corridor through Avranches as his divisions moved south, Patton planned to introduce three new corps into the battle behind Middleton's veteran VIII. First to follow would be Haislip's XV, and eventually Cook's XII, and Walker's XX, which initially were held back in reserve. Coming south through Avranches, the follow-on corps would begin pushing outward both to the south and east.

First into the peninsula's neck were his two armored divisions. Maj. Gen. John "P" Wood's 4th Armored reached Rennes' outskirts the first day and rapidly encircled the city, while Robert W. Gerow's 6th Armored moved to the North towards St. Malo and west towards Brest. The 79th and 8th Divisions

Left: An M-3 Stuart tank passes a knocked out Panther on its way to Brittany. Below: The flag of the US 2nd Armored Division. The division landed on June 9, and later took part in the American counterattack around Mortain. *Patton Museum of Cavalry and Armor*

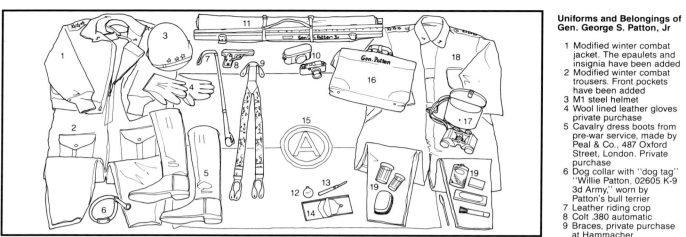

Uniforms and Belongings of Gen. George S. Patton, Jr

1 Modified winter combat jacket. The epaulets and insignia have been added
2 Modified winter combat trousers. Front pockets have been added
3 M1 steel helmet
4 Wool lined leather gloves private purchase
5 Cavalry dress boots from pre-war service, made by Peal & Co., 487 Oxford Street, London. Private purchase
6 Dog collar with ''dog tag'' ''Willie Patton, 02605 K-9 3d Army,'' worn by Patton's bull terrier
7 Leather riding crop
8 Colt .380 automatic
9 Braces, private purchase at Hammacher

Schlemmer, New York
10 German Leica camera and case marked: ''Ernst Leitz, Wetzlar''
11 Folding cot — ''Komfort Kot'' — made by the Byer Mfg. Co., Orono, ME
12 Abercrombie & Fitch, alarm, pocket watch, private purchase
13 Pocket knife
14 Wallet, embossed, made by Mark Cross, London
15 Flag of Third Army
16 Leather brief case
17 Binoculars with case, marked: Patton, 15th Cav
18 Modified herring bone twill work suit. Epaulets and insignia added
19 Selection of private purchase toiletries

Patton Museum of Cavalry and Armor, Fort Knox, KY

moved southeast and south to seal the peninsula.

Tension was high and the early command scuffles were predictable. Bradley had engineered his breakout with careful planning. His deputy and successor at First Army, Hodges, and the VIII Corps commander, Middleton, were methodical, professional infantrymen.

Bradley intentionally kept Third Army out of the attack, waiting instead to hand off the battle after the breakthrough when the pursuit began, wishing, his aide's diary explains, to maintain "finger tip control." Within hours, Bradley showed his ire at Patton's tactics.

The methodical Bradley chased after Patton whom he wrongly believed to have ignored orders to protect the vital corridor. Soon afterwards, Patton chastised Middleton for being too slow and concerned with flanks, and for temporarily stopping Gerow's advance. With Haislip's XV Corps finishing its passage, Bradley still gripped control like an army commander, ordering Patton to form a front facing east from the corridor's mouth down to Rennes, before developing operations towards Brest.

Patton pushed Middleton west; Haislip formed the flank protection by moving eastward. Patton had seven divisions committed within two days, with individual columns

moving rapidly under wide-ranging air cover provided by the XIX Tactical Air Command as the only flank protection.

As Patton's force began its drive against an enemy unable to form any cohesive front throughout Third Army's area, decisive opportunity presented itself. Eisenhower, Montgomery, and Bradley all independently stared at their maps and concluded the same: the German flank for their entire Army Group lay wide open. Montgomery and his planners decided earlier that the campaign should be modified to send a single corps westward, which he confirmed with orders on the morning of August 1. Ike's periodic appreciation to the Combined Chiefs now spoke of using

minimum forces in Brittany and pressing their advantage eastward. Bradley soon agreed.

Brittany no longer held significant forces and didn't require Patton's entire force for its capture; Patton would therefore drive east and north encircling the Germans using XV, XII, and XX Corps. For both army groups Montgomery defined the focus: "the main business lies east."

Other considerations intruded. Hitler's attempts to cobble together a last counterthrust loomed in *Ultra*'s decrypts, but initially German capability and intent didn't betray the location. Hitler wanted a counteroffensive to split the breakout corridor at Avranches to restore the Normandy front. While von Kluge scraped together forces to counterattack, army commanders Crerar, Dempsey, Hodges, and Patton struggled with tactical control of a fast developing situation.

By August 7 Patton had wheeled three corps towards the Seine. Brittany, meanwhile, had been completely overrun. But with the essential ports holding out and under siege, four of Patton's divisions, including his best armored formations, the 4th and 6th Armored, were out of the pursuit eastward. Wood, whose 4th Armored had just finished road-marching throughout the peninsula, making impressive gains against no opposition, railed at his corps commander:" . . . we're winning the war the wrong way, we ought to be going towards Paris."

With Hodges's First Army grinding ahead and Patton's three maneuvering corps heading both east to the Seine and south towards the Loire, Bradley looked at the narrow neck connecting First and Third Armies.

Above: Seen on the move toward Brest on August 18 as part of Maj. Gen. Troy H. Middleton's US VIII Corps effort in northern Brittany is this 155-mm Gun M1, affectionately called the "Long Tom" for its great range and high level of accuracy.

Worried about a counterthrust cutting across Patton's lines of communications at Avranches, he correctly forecast what intelligence later predicted, an attack designed to drive to the sea and split the Allied line.

Patton, too, looked briefly to his north at the hinge that connected his army with the main front. With his army aiming towards Le Mans and beyond, he had uncharacteristically held out three divisions from the battle, his diary noting "a secret source" predicting an attack from Mortain to Avranches.

The Mortain attack (Operation *Lüttich*) sealed the fate of France. Von Kluge's force was too small to effect an immediate decision and with American forces poised to block their advance and attack their flank, the pattern for German defeat was set. Bradley snatched one of Patton's three uncommitted divisions to hold Mortain's southern flank,

THE MORTAIN COUNTERATTACK
Known to the Germans as Operation *Lüttich*, this was the attempt by the Fifth Panzer Army to break out westwards, take Avranches and cut the narrow corridor which connected the US First and Third Armies. For the first time in the campaign, most of the German Panzer divisions were assembled in the American sector, facing east. The Fifth Panzer Army, though hurriedly assembled, comprised the 1st SS ("Leibstandarte Adolf Hitler"), 2nd SS ("Das Reich"), and 9th SS ("Hohenstaufen") Panzer Divisions, together with the 2nd and 116th Panzer Divisions, plus a Kampfgruppe of the 17th SS Panzer Grenadier Division ("Götz von Berlichingen"). To face the American armor, in all the Fifth Panzer Army contained between 200 and 250 tanks.

The attack began on August 7 under the cover of heavy fog. The Germans made rapid progress in the first hours, the 2nd Panzer Division making over 7 miles (11km) in the area of Mortain, bringing it to within 13 miles (20km) of Avranches and success. Elsewhere the advance was slower. To the north the 166th Panzers were checked by the US VII Corps, while in the south, 1st and 2nd SS Panzers were meeting spirited resistance from the US 30th Division.

On August 8, the weather changed, the fog lifted, and the cover enjoyed by the Germans disappeared. Allied tactical aircraft once again filled the skies, and the Fifth Panzer Army became a sitting target for the Allies' overwhelming air power. It still attempted to push westward, but by now the balance of the battle had swung against it. For the next three days, over 100 German tanks and vehicles were destroyed, and by August 12 Mortain was being evacuated and the Panzer divisions were pulling back east.

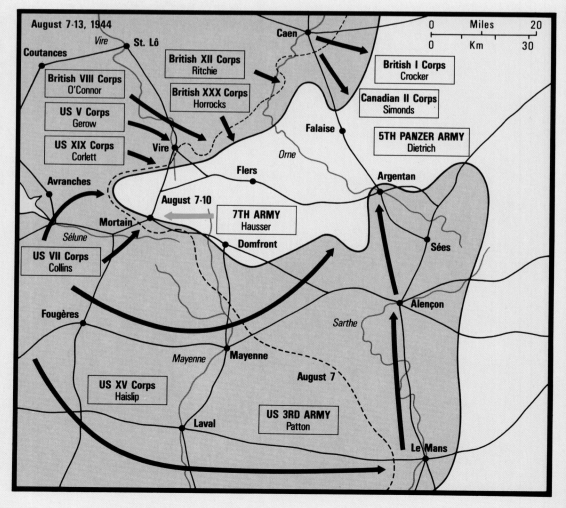

while the remaining two moved east with Patton whose forces were moving to the Seine.

Von Kluge's Mortain failure sparked differing solutions from Allied commanders each seeing battlefield opportunities to defeat the enemy. Montgomery looked to the Seine and beyond, seeing Patton as the right flank moving on Paris while paratroops blocked the escape between Chartres and Orléans.

While fending off the Mortain counterattack, Bradley sought immediate battlefield destruction of the enemy, planning a short envelopment to encircle the German Seventh Army at Falaise if Monty would send one of his armies south. Patton already had been converted to Wood's view, which a week before he had called "bull headed." He wanted a deeper drive towards Chartres or Dreux to ensure entrapping the Germans nearer the Seine, not the immediate turn to the north that Bradley directed for Haislip's XV Corps.

Bradley's Falaise encirclement was never consummated, but Patton didn't brood long over being held near Argentan and from closing the Falaise gap. He soon convinced Bradley to widen Third Army's move to the east, with the XX Corps moving towards Chartres, and the XII towards Orléans, while a temporary headquarters held the Argentan shoulder with three divisions and Haislip's XV Corps with two divisions moved east to Dreux. Despite the coordination problems of switching divisions from corps to corps or rapidly changing axes of advance, Patton kept his forces moving to overrun terrain before the Germans could form a defense on it.

While the rest of Third Army continued east, Middleton's VIII Corps continued its Brittany campaigning. Though the peninsula was generally under Middleton's control, the critical port objectives were still under siege. After more than two weeks, the peninsula held five of Patton's dozen divisions, a force that would remain constant through the end of the month. The capture of the ports proved disappointing. St. Malo held out until August 17, Brest to September 19, and Lorient and St. Nazaire managed to hold out until the war's end.

Third Army sent its divisions in four directions in its first two weeks of operations: west to capture the entire Brittany Peninsula and besiege its hold-out port fortresses, south to reach the Loire running west from St. Nazaire to northeast of Tours, east past Le Mans and Alençon, and around to the north to Argentan. In 15 days, Patton had filled out the planners' lines from the D + 20 line to approximately the D + 60 line. Third Army now held down Brittany as planned, plus a significant area originally designated for First Army's operations.

From a personal perspective, the night of August 15 brought personal vindication for one Allied general. With the blue arrows of Third Army marking the most impressive gains on SHAEF's maps, the world was finally told whose army was "touring France." Patton, whose presence was kept secret to account for his alleged command of the Calais invasion as part of the *Bodyguard* deception, was announced as commanding the army racing towards the Seine, Paris, and Germany. Patton was again in the news, not

Above: Seen at a field conference are three of the campaign's senior commanders, from left to right Lt. Gen. George S. Patton of the US Third Army, Lt. Gen. Omar N. Bradley of the US 12th Army Group and Gen. Sir Bernard Montgomery of the 21st Army Group.

Below: Gen. Patton's pistols. Top: Colt .45 single action revolver, with non-factory engraving and initialed ivory grips. Bottom: Smith and Wesson .357 Magnum revolver with initialed ivory grips; sent to Patton in 1935. *Patton Museum of Cavalry and Armor*

as the general slapping a soldier or politically embarrassing his country, but as the spearhead of the pursuit across France. The Third Army commander was proving what German intelligence had long since decided, that Patton was the most formidable field commander in the Allied camp.

While the newspaper maps showed sketches of Allied arrows moving across France, command decisions had to be made. Montgomery did send Crerar's Canadian First Army south to link with Hodges as Bradley desired. His real interest, however, appeared to be in a wider envelopment to destroy the Germans trapped in front of the bridgeless Seine, possibly an explanation for his lack of detailed interest in Crerar's linkup with Bradley's Army Group at Argentan. The wider focus caused Monty to send Dempsey east, while wanting Patton's forces to continue a wide envelopment south of Paris.

With von Kluge's forces trying to escape, issues appeared to distract the command. Churchill raised the first, again arguing against the impending invasion of southern France at the expense of the Mediterranean campaign. Neither Eisenhower nor Roosevelt would hear of it, and the subsequent landing not only added an indefensible front to Germany's problems, it added the significant port of Marseilles, which would eventually support an entire Allied army group holding down the southern German front.

The second was a new plan of campaign. Montgomery now called for an operational maneuver outstripping Bradley's battle plan. By mid-August, Monty introduced a new concept for campaigning beyond the Seine. While the plan percolated and the generals conferred, the eyes of the world turned towards the capital of France.

The Freedom of Paris
With the Germans encircled at Falaise and Third Army in full cry and about to cross the Seine, Paris loomed as a major strategic problem. The Press, the French populace, the Germans, and probably every soldier in the Allied armies thought the invasion was aimed to liberate Paris, the symbolic heart of France.

In fact the opposite was true. The planners had wanted a firm campaign win and logistical buildup before taking the city, and had carefully declared the "lodgment area" to the east of the Seine. Now, with the D + 90 line on the Seine no longer an objective but something to be ignored in passing, Patton's rampaging columns made the city appear within reach.

To the Allies, the mathematics of supply spelled out the problem. The planners believed that Paris would consume at least 4,000 tons of supplies daily, roughly three days marching and fighting supply for an army. The rapid moves of Patton's pursuit plus the advances of the other three armies, strained the logistical system. To Bradley, the Siegfried Line was reachable with a week's more campaigning; moving on Paris could end that.

French feelings were understandable. For more than 1,500 days, Parisians had borne the shame, terror, and despair, that had come with occupation at the hands of the Germans. More than 1,500 times, a battalion of troops

led by a military band had circled the Arc de Triomphe and marched down the Champs Elysées to the Place de la Concorde.

For them, and for all of France, the success of the invasion meant not destroying the German army in the field; it meant freeing the city of Paris. Events would show that the French people, not the Allied command, would decide when and how Paris would be freed.

On August 10, French railwaymen launched a strike calling for wages and better food in Paris; the first real strike of the occupation. The Metro stopped and gas and electric power became sporadic within the city. Three days later, the Germans began disarming Paris's 20,000 policemen. To counter this move, police resistance groups decided to strike, calling upon policemen to put aside their uniforms and retain their weapons. When word leaked to the Germans, the city's Resistance factions met issuing a proclamation telling the police to stand with the Resistance or be considered traitors and collaborators: "The hour of liberation has come."

What had begun on August 10 grew, and inevitably the Germans reacted. When shots were fired, SS elements responded quickly. Thirty-five French youths were machine-gunned on the night of the 16th at the Carrefour des Cascades, and the city's new commandant, Lt. Gen. Dietrich von Choltitz, received orders confirming Hitler's intent to destroy Paris. Firing was heard near the Gare du Nord and the Gare de l'Est on the 17th. The city that had made popular uprisings famous was now on the verge of another.

Resistance elements within the city prepared to seize the city. To the Resistance, freeing the City of Light meant freeing France. To the competing political factions — the Communists, Gaullists, and others, it also meant establishing an invaluable power base within liberated and postwar France. Charles de Gaulle's headquarters in Algiers sent word on August 11 outlining a plan for seizing government buildings by his supporters with the regular FFI occupying less symbolic structures.

Gen. Jacques Chaban-Delmas arrived in Paris with directions from FFI chief, Gen. Pierre Koenig, in London ordering a halt to uprising plans, at least until the Allies were outside the city's gates when de Gaulle's plan

Above: US infantry dash across a street against a backdrop of bursting white phosphorus shells as they drive German snipers from positions in the strongly built stone houses of the port city of Brest, which was secured by September 19.

could be implemented. Chaban-Delmas, however, was too late and could only send a message to London that the city was on the verge of insurrection.

The Germans prepared to meet an Allied attack and didn't wish to engage in stopping insurrections. Hitler, however, had decided that Paris would not fall into Allied hands unscathed. City commandant von Choltitz had first received orders to destroy Paris's significant industrial capabilities, the city's 45 bridges over the Seine, and eventually, her monuments. The list of buildings mined for demolition could replicate the best tourist guide. Only lack of orders from von Choltitz prevented the destruction from beginning.

When the rail strike began, some political prisoners were evacuated from prisons, most to die later in Buchenwald or Ravensbruck, although the 1,500 Jews scheduled for a predawn move from one prison found their transporting buses had been sabotaged and they had been granted a short reprieve. With the Allies close by, Vichy officials suddenly disappeared. It was inevitable that shots would be fired. When German soldiers were ambushed, the German commander threatened to retaliate by razing whole city blocks and killing inhabitants in reprisal.

The Swedish Consul Gen. Raoul Nordling met von Choltitz hoping to alleviate the inevitable destruction. He struck a deal freeing the remaining political prisoners based on a five to one exchange of Germans to Frenchmen, both sides ignoring the fact that the French prisoners would be released immediately, while the Germans would be released in the future.

Von Choltitz seemed content to meet, negotiate, and attempt to defuse the inevitable. For a veteran of the Eastern Front who had participated in Sevastopol's destruction, he appeared remarkably slow to follow his orders. Two weeks earlier, Warsaw's populace had risen and the Germans had rushed eight fresh divisions to reduce resistance house by house. The battle still raged there. Von Choltitz clearly didn't want that sort of battle with his enemy so close.

THE THIRD ARMY ATTACK INTO BRITTANY
Map A

The success of Operation *Cobra* totally exposed the flank of the German Army in Normandy. By August 1, when Third Army became operational, it became clear that most of Patton's corps could be switched from their original tasks of capturing the Brittany ports to the west, to the encirclement of the Germans, and a rapid extension of the Allies' lodgment area south to the Loire, and east towards the Seine. For this reason the Brittany operations and the capture of its deep-water ports were to be tackled by only one corps — Middleton's VIII.

By August 3, VIII Corps led by the 4th and 6th Armored Divisions had pushed through Avranches and was attacking Rennes. After another three days the whole of the Brittany Peninsula had been overrun and the ports of St. Malo, Brest, Lorient and St. Nazaire were under siege.

The rapid advances to the east, however, made the capture of these ports a lower priority than had been originally envisaged. The sieges were conducted using regular aerial bombardments, and offensive operations tried to avoid heavy losses to ground troops. As it turned out, this method of attack was entirely justified. Brest, for example, was found to be so heavily damaged on liberation that it was never used by the Allies.

THE PURSUIT TO THE SEINE
Map B

As Brittany was being overrun, Patton's other three corps, the XII, XV and XX, began their attack across France. His exploitation of the situation was masterful. After weeks of bitter fighting in Normandy, the German forces west of the Seine were mostly facing north and west. To the south and east where they lacked an organized defense in-depth, there was the space and the opportunity to take the

campaign by the throat and drive for the Seine. Patton saw his chance and took it.

The first attacks went east and south to secure the flank of his operations in Brittany. On August 8 Le Mans was taken, by the 12th Alençon had fallen. To the south, Nantes and the Loire River were reached by the 13th. The XV Corps at Alençon was then ordered north to Argentan to secure the southern edge of the Falaise Pocket. Though the pocket was not completely sealed at this point, XV Corps was in an ideal position to swing northeast across the path of Hodges's First Army to cut off the Germans' line of retreat. By August 19 XV Corps had completed this maneuver, had reached Mantes Gassicourt and had established a bridgehead over the Seine northwest of Paris.

Meanwhile, to the right of XV Corps, XX Corps had reached Chartres by August 16, and was driving towards Fontainebleau. On Third Army's southern flank, XII Corps was pushing along the north bank of the Loire. The city of Orléans was liberated on August 16, and with the 4th Armored Division (which had been transfered from VIII Corps on August 13) once again in the vanguard, the town of Troyes was captured on August 26.

By the end of August, and within a month of becoming operational, Patton's Third Army had reached the much-vaunted D + 90 mark on the planners' projected "phase lines" and was ready to continue the momentum of its advance beyond the Seine towards the Meuse, and from there to the French/German border.

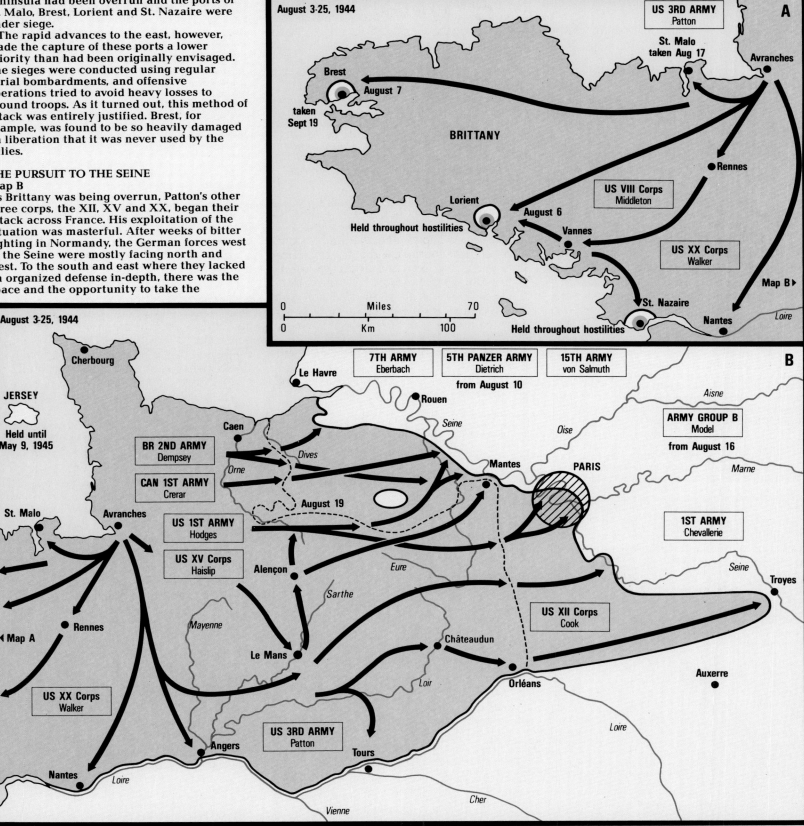

Unwittingly, von Kluge's replacement, Field Marshal Model, helped the French cause when he gave the city commandant permission to delay destroying the Seine River bridges, when von Choltitz reasoned that beginning any destruction at that time would further inflame the populace and hamper his efforts for defense.

On August 19, the Resistance planned to rise under the leadership of the French Communist, Henri Tanguy, whose nom de guerre was "Colonel Rol." Alexandre Parodi, heading the Gaullist Resistance group, learned of the Communist plan and decided to seize the Préfecture de Police near Notre Dame with striking policemen before the Communists could act. Other factions soon joined.

Two thousand police in civilian clothes assembled at the Préfecture, near Notre Dame, hoisting the Tricolor and singing the Marseillaise. Soon they took the Palais de Justice nearby, converting the connecting Boulevard du Palais into a fire-swept zone when German tanks and troops appeared.

The Hôtel de Ville fell the next day (August 20) and while Nordling worked to gain a truce, the Germans withdrew into strongholds in the city's center, leaving only to patrol with tanks and masses of infantry. Nordling met von Choltitz on the 20th, obtaining for the Resistance fighters combatant status and recognition from the Germans. Von Choltitz also agreed that the Préfecture and Hôtel de Ville could remain occupied if the FFI would not attack German strongholds.

Neither the Resistance leaders nor elements of the German forces such as the SS wanted such an agreement. Despite efforts both to publicize the truce and limit bloodshed, sporadic firing continued. Resistance leaders met on the 21st and decided to denounce the truce the following day. Rather than Nordling's truce, the famous cry "Aux Barricades" resounded.

In the Latin Quarter and to a lesser extent in other parts of the city uncontrolled by the Germans, hundreds of barricades appeared. Torn up street stones, trees, overturned carts and automobiles soon blocked streets and were manned by street fighters sporting homemade armbands, World War I poilu headgear or occasionally, German helmets.

The first battles set the tone. Tanks machinegunned windows or occasionally fired armor-piercing shot, but no high explosive rounds were used. The Germans never pressed attacks. Resistants used small arms, Molotov cocktails, and captured

THE LIBERATION OF PARIS
Maps A and B

On August 23, the decision was made to send Maj. Gen. Leclerc's 2nd French Armored Division into Paris. Twenty miles (32km) outside the city, Leclerc divided his attack force into three armored columns on a front 17 miles (27km) wide. The main thrust of his advance would come from a combat command under Col. Pierre Billotte which was to strike from the south.

The battle began on August 24, but the French ran into stiff German opposition. By nightfall Leclerc's forces were still 10 miles (16km) outside Paris. Knowing that it would take him another day to enter the city, and not knowing the situation of the besieged resistants, Leclerc ordered a small armored detachment of three tanks and six half-tracks under Capt. Raymond Dronne to infiltrate itself into the city. Under cover of darkness, Dronne's command drove up the Avenue d'Italie and was established in the Préfecture de Police by midnight.

The next day Leclerc's columns began to converge on the center of the city. Relying on speed and surprise and without the help of reserves, their objectives were the city's major centers and von Choltitz's headquarters at Hôtel Meurice on the Rue de Rivoli.

To the west, a combat command under Lt. Col. Paul de Langlade made its way north of the Seine to the Arc de Triomphe and the Champs Elysées. As planned, Billotte's command entered the city from the south, driving up the Boulevard St. Michel, to link up with Dronne's small detachment on the Ile de la Cité. It then turned left to meet up with Langlade's column on the Champs Elysées. Meanwhile another column from the south had split and was heading towards the Eiffel Tower and the Quai d'Orsay.

By mid-afternoon on the 25th, units from Billotte's column, under the command of Maj. Jean de la Horie were attacking von Choltitz's headquarters. After a sharp firefight, the French made their way inside and found von Choltitz and his staff ready to surrender. At 15:00 von Choltitz, escorted by La Horie was driven to Préfecture de Police where Leclerc and the leaders of the Paris Resistance waited to accept the surrender of the German garrison.

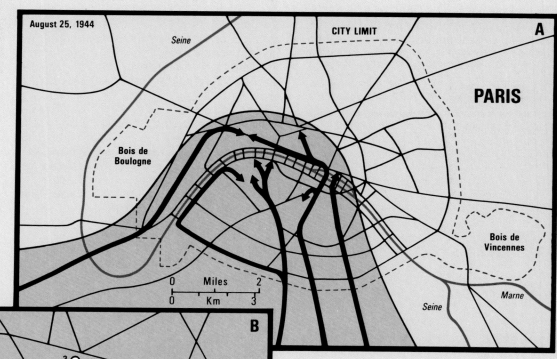

August 25, 1944 · Seine · CITY LIMIT · A · PARIS · Bois de Boulogne · Bois de Vincennes · Seine · Marne · Miles 0 2 · Km 0 3

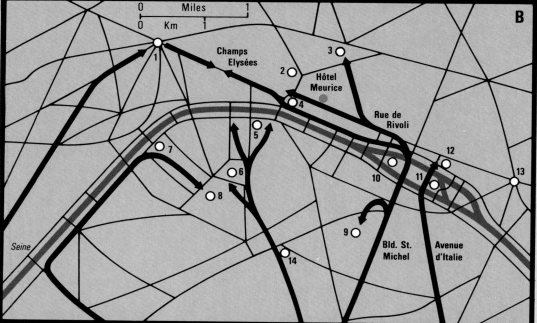

B · Miles 0 1 · Km 0 1 · Champs Elysées · Hôtel Meurice · Rue de Rivoli · Bld. St. Michel · Avenue d'Italie · Seine

KEY
The numbers on the map correspond to some of the major locations in the story of Paris's liberation. Note that von Choltitz's headquarters at Hôtel Meurice is identified with a green dot.

1 Place de l'Etoile (Arc de Triomphe)
2 Ministère de la Marine
3 Théâtre de l'Opéra
4 Place de la Concorde
5 Quai d'Orsay
6 Hôtel des Invalides
7 Eiffel Tower
8 Ecole Militaire
9 Palais du Luxembourg
10 Préfecture de Police
11 Ile de la Cité and
   Notre Dame Cathedral
12 Hôtel de Ville
13 Place de la Bastille
   (Leclerc's Headquarters)
14 Gare Montparnasse

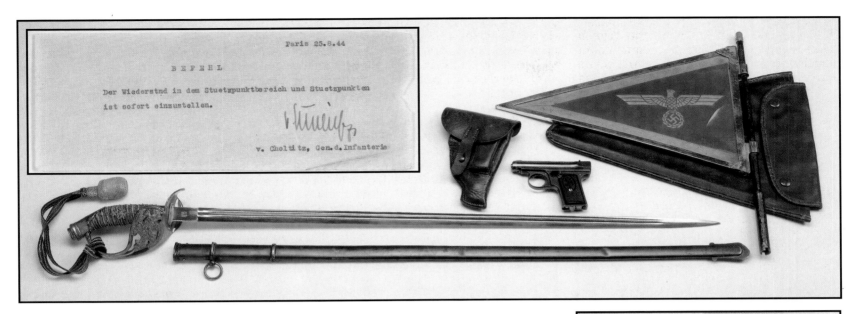

machineguns. Soft-skinned vehicles by the score were destroyed the first day, after which tanks became the primary accompanying vehicle for German troops. The French took prisoners; SS elements within the city shot theirs.

In ordering the city's defense, Hitler's orders were clear. "Paris must not fall into the hands of the enemy, or, if it does, he must find there nothing but a field of ruins." Von Choltitz's garrison had some 22,000 troops including an estimated 50 tanks. Another division was promised to make Fortress Paris a costly objective for the Allies to take.

By August 22, Paris was an open battlefield with three dozen miniature war zones. Emissaries to both Patton and Bradley pleaded for immediate assistance. Late on the 22nd, Eisenhower ordered Bradley to move on Paris. If von Choltitz decided to fight the Resistance with the tanks and aircraft he had available, thousands would die and the city would be ravaged.

Some German elements did fight. The Grand Palais was set ablaze by incendiary rounds on the 23rd and by nightfall, the 500th Parisian fell in battle. Fighting increased. Resistants seized the mairies, the borough halls that represented local government. Several were now attacked by machine gunning tanks. By the 24th, three-quarters of the city seemed occupied by freedom fighters with the inner city still a German stronghold.

Eisenhower had already directed that the 2nd French Armored Division under Maj. Gen. Philippe Leclerc would be the first

Above: Mementoes of Gen. von Choltitz. Von Choltitz's 1889 Prussian Infantry Officer's sword and scabbard. M1913 J.P. Sauer u. Sohn, 7.64mm pistol and holster. The general's vehicle pennant. Inset: one of the orders signed by the general commanding German strongpoints in Paris to surrender.
Museum of the Liberation, Paris

Allied division to enter Paris when that day came. Previously directed north from Patton's command to Hodges's to facilitate that move, Leclerc now had the orders he had waited for. Leclerc sent a Piper Cub aircraft to fly low over the Préfecture to drop a message to the police occupying the building, "Hold on. We are coming."

Seeing Leclerc's initial concentration as a confused start by the French, V Corps commander Leonard Gerow asked Bradley for permission to send his US 4th Infantry Division, which had landed on *Utah*, to join the rush to Paris. Bradley's reply reflected his chagrin at Allied politics ruining his advance, "To hell with prestige, tell the 4th to slam on in and take the liberation."

Leclerc's march was not unopposed. His three armored combat commands lost 40 tanks and selfpropelled guns, more than a hundred other vehicles, and over 300 men during their first day's advance to the city.

Below: The smoke from bursting shells rises over the rooftops of Paris. Hitler had ordered that Paris be held at all costs or reduced to rubble, but the German garrison put up only a sporadic resistance and then surrendered before the city had suffered very much.

Above: Gen. von Choltitz signs one of the documents ordering German strongpoints to surrender. At about 16:00 von Choltitz had been driven to Gare Montparnasse from his HQ through aggressive crowds of Parisians. Here he signed at least ten of these documents.

While he reorganized for the next day's advance, Leclerc infiltrated a small armored force into the city on the night of the 24th. With the column of three tanks and six halftracks wending its way to the Hôtel de Ville, church bells announced their arrival at 21:22 hours. Von Choltitz reportedly called Army Group B Headquarters, and holding the phone at arm's length for Model's chief of staff to hear, told him that the bells of Paris were telling the city that the Allies had arrived.

Early on the 25th, Leclerc's 2nd Armored and Barton's 4th Infantry Divisions made their final push. Leclerc's Fighting French entered from the west and south, amid hysterical crowds and occasional gunfire. Maj. Gen. Barton's veteran 4th came in from the south to clear the eastern part of the city.

By 10:00 hours, both divisions were in the city where only strong points remained as pockets of German resistance. Despite some street fighting, von Choltitz appeared to do nothing to inspire the city's defense. No orders were given to fire the demolitions. When Hitler received news that the Allies had entered Paris he raged. The negative reply to his question, "Is Paris burning?" marked von Choltitz as a criminal in his own army but made him the unacknowledged savior of Paris.

Von Choltitz signed documents surrendering the city to Maj. Gen. Leclerc and then

jointly to Leclerc and the Resistance. By noon on August 25 Tricolors flew over the Eiffel Tower and then Napoleon's Arc. Approximately 10,000 Germans were taken, along with three dozen tanks. Approximately a thousand freedom fighters died, and over 1,500 were wounded.

Charles de Gaulle entered the city on August 26, to proclaim his government without Allied sponsorship. That night, German bombers droned overhead attempting to do what von Choltitz refused to do: destroy Paris. Five hundred houses burned and 50 dead and 500 injured were added to the war's toll. It was the worst raid suffered during the war.

Left: Gen. Charles de Gaulle, the Free French leader, is seen at Gare Montparnasse in Paris with two of his senior army commanders, Maj.Gen. Philippe Leclerc and Gen. Alphonse Juin. It was Leclerc who had had the honor of liberating the city.

Above: As senior German officers of both the army and air force were rounded up after the liberation of Paris on August 26, they were lodged for safekeeping at the Hôtel Majestic, previously a German military headquarters in the Paris area.

Below: Men of 28th Infantry Division parade triumphantly along the Champs Elysées on August 29. The parade helped to persuade the nervous inhabitants of the French capital that there were sizeable Allied forces in the region.

On August 27 Eisenhower and Bradley arrived in the city, and on August 29, the US 28th Division made a triumphal march through Paris, both to soothe French fears and to position itself for battle outside the city the next day. For Paris, the nightmare was over. For the men of the 28th marching towards battles in the Hurtgen, the Ardennes, and the Colmar Pocket, the nightmare would continue.

The Strategic Argument

Allied intelligence reports reflected the euphoria that seemed to fill the Allied command. France was rapidly being overrun. The invasion of southern France had succeeded and Marseilles was in Allied hands. The Luftwaffe appeared to be shot out of the sky and only made intermittent appearances over German cities, not over the battlefields. SHAEF's estimate for the week ending August 19 summed up what many commanders believed true: "The enemy has lost the war and the defeat of Seven(th) Army and Panzer-gruppe West will hasten the end."

But how would it end? Eisenhower approved a general campaign plan shortly before the Normandy landings, based on a gradual advance to the Seine, a strong buildup, and a series of major actions that would bring the Allied forces to the German border by D + 330, linking up with the Allied forces in southern France, and clearing France, Holland, Belgium, and Luxembourg.

Four avenues existed for entering Germany: Flanders, Maubeuge-Liège-Aachen, the Ardennes, and Metz-Saarbrücken. The SHAEF "broad front" plan called for advancing on all four, with the main Allied attack being made north of the Ardennes through Aachen, and with a secondary effort going towards the Saar through Metz.

Forces would shift to meet opportunities and concentrate for major attacks, but the intent was to keep the entire front active. When the German Army was destroyed west of the Rhine, a massive double envelopment of the Ruhr would end the war. Using available resources, freeing allies, and tying in with an ongoing aerial campaign against Germany's economy and population, it was a sound plan. The generals closest to the battlefield, however, developed other plans.

Before the Falaise battle played out, Montogmery designed a campaign plan, which if it could not end the war, at least would restructure strategy for 1944. Briefing Bradley on August 17, he mistakenly believed that his American counterpart was still willing to follow his lead.

Montgomery's campaign plan focused on the final *Overlord* objective, the industrial Ruhr, and used all the Allied armies in France, which would go through Belgium entering Germany north of the Ardennes. He planned to keep both Army Groups together, his own 21st clearing the Channel coast, Flanders, and seizing Antwerp, while Bradley's 12th Army Group moved on the prime invasion route into the Ruhr: the Liège-Aachen-Cologne avenue of approach.

Montgomery's plan was attractive because if it succeeded, it would clear the coast of the V-2 rocket sites, obtain the Channel ports and Antwerp to solve the logistics problem, and place the Allies at the front door of Germany's industry and population.

Montgomery, however, tied the plan to the issue of command. He demanded total ground command for himself, which the Americans found both irritating and unsupportable as Montgomery began to cannibalize some divisions to replace losses in others. With up to four American divisions arriving monthly, and the planned final American force outnumbering the total British and Canadian divisions by four to one, the Americans no longer saw a need to serve under Montgomery.

Monty's stock had fallen in many circles, and the American public demanded a change, a feeling also universally held by American generals in Europe. US Chief of Staff, Gen. Marshall, urged Eisenhower to take control. When Eisenhower assumed the ground command at the end of August, Bradley, whose Army Group already was larger than Montgomery's own, would be fully independent.

By August 20, Bradley's planners published his "Operation Plan Normandy To The Rhine." His succinct mission statement defied Monty's ideas: "Twelfth Army Group upon completion of present operation will regroup and resume its advance to the northeast in zone, cross the SEINE, encircle PARIS, and continue the advance to seize the crossings of the RHINE River from STRASBOURG to MAINZ inclusive."

Eisenhower sought to define the next objectives before assuming the ground command in September by meeting Bradley on August 19, and then Montgomery and Bradley separately on the 23rd. Ike still accepted the "broad front" plan advanced in

May as the most reasonable course of action for the Allies and with it, granting priority to the Liège-Aachen-Cologne approach with a secondary advance through the Metz approach towards the Saar.

Additionally, he followed the logic of both the size and importance of the avenues of approach, plus their logistical supportability in giving priorities to the Army Groups. Eisenhower ordered Montgomery to take Brussels and Antwerp while clearing the Channel ports along the way. Realizing this would require both Montgomery's armies, he authorized Montgomery to "coordinate" Hodges's First Army's advance to cover his left, Hodges therefore to go to Aachen.

Though this decision kept Hodges under Bradley's command and gave Bradley responsibility for the key avenue of approach to Germany, Bradley viewed the decision as losing an army to Montgomery, and attempted to get Eisenhower to limit Montgomery's "coordinating" to a single corps, calling Montgomery "cautious."

As theater commander, Eisenhower realized that any future plans rode on logistics. He therefore directed Bradley to clear the Brittany ports, his real lifeline until Antwerp and Marseilles could be fully developed and the European rail net rebuilt. Eisenhower authorized Bradley to buildup east of Paris, which Bradley interpreted as tacit approval to continue Patton's advance. But in every guidance message to the army groups or summary to the Combined Chiefs, nowhere did Eisenhower place a priority on Patton's lunge to the Saar as anything but behind Montgomery's clearing the Channel coast and taking Antwerp and Bradley's opening the Brittany ports.

Eisenhower's decision was hotly decried by both his Army Group commanders, each believing that victory was within grasp if all the priorities for advance were to be given to his Army Group. The loudest protests came from the army commander on what Eisenhower, essentially, had designated the least decisive avenue of approach for the immediate future.

Patton fumed, claiming that given the gas and supplies, he could be in Germany with his Third Army in ten days. With one corps tied to capturing the Brittany ports, his other three corps mustered only seven divisions, which even if they made the Rhine at Mannheim, would suddenly find themselves stranded without gas, and minus the airfields needed to maintain essential close air support. Finally, Mannheim is about 175 miles (280km) south of the Ruhr and double that distance from Berlin.

Patton's plan of attack held a problem which summarized the drawback of every offensive plan advanced during that late August. Momentum was admirable, but a decisive-sized force able to fight the remainder of the German Army in a critical area with adequate supplies was a necessity, not a toehold or a force stranded from its own supplies.

The Allied front was too large for the forces available, even when logistically supported. This fact explains why Eisenhower's original plans concentrated forces in the north, leaving the southern flank thinly held. Until the Channel ports, Brittany ports, or Antwerp opened to ease the logistics problem, and rail and pipe lines were built to carry the required tonnages, supporting unlimited advances on all fronts was not possible.

Below: Uniform jacket and personal equipment of Gen. Omar N. Bradley. Including from the left: an inscribed canvas map case with leather handle; leather paratroop boots; German binoculars and case, marked "C.P. Goerz, Berlin, 6x30, Maringtruder." The case has a compass in the lid and is also marked "Goerz, Berlin." M1936 pistol belt, holster and first aid pouch; M1911 Springfield pistol, .45 caliber; B-10 type leather jacket manufactured by L.S.L. Garment Co.
US Army Military History Institute

Medical Supplies and Equipment

1 British nurse's field bag
2 British orderly's first aid haversack
3 Crutches from a British hospital in Bayeux
4 Package of American Red Cross bandages
5 Metal unit location sign: Canadian 77th Advanced Dressing Station
6 British first aid bag
7 American first aid kit
8-9 American bandages
10 American tourniquet
11 Insect bite ointment
12 Euflavine bandage
13 Canadian field dressing
14 American ammonia inhalant
15-16 American dressings
17 British first aid kit
18 American gas casualty kit

with No. 5 antigas ointment
19 Scissors and forceps
20 Bandage and box
21 Petroleum ointment
22-23 German portable field respirator and case
24 German first aid kit
25 German metal splints
26 German oxygen bottle
27-28 Salve and wadding
29 German field surgery saddle bag
30 German first aid box for vehicles
31 Urine Test kit
32-35 Contents of *30*
36 Limb sling and packet
37 German bandages
38 German antiseptic
39 Roll of plaster
40 Detoxification kit and detoxification cream
41 Bottle of Rivanol tablets

Memorial Museum, Bayeux

The race to the Rhine, however, was still not over. Montgomery strained to drag every mile of advance before the predicted gasoline famine halted his forces.

Not able to move with "40 divisions," Montgomery still aimed to have a bridgehead across the Rhine before the German defense solidified, which would require a future river crossing to be an over-water assault approaching a miniature invasion. Spurred on by increasingly optimistic intelligence reports, Montgomery among others, might have hoped that with the Allies at the front door, perhaps German resolve would crumble as it did in 1918, sparing Britain another war winter.

Nor was Bradley convinced he should curb his advance to support Monty's left. He gave Patton equal gasoline rations and directed one of First Army's corps south to maintain linkage with Patton and to support Third Army's advance.

The advance continued with September promising ground gains for perhaps two weeks — gains which could complete France and Belgium's liberation while tightening the grip on Hitler's borders. With no apparent operational decision obtainable, Eisenhower approved Montgomery's thrust to the Rhine, but realistically did not see the move as being able to topple Germany or even reach Berlin.

Yet Monty's Rhine thrust did serve critical needs that Bradley's favored Saar line of operations neglected. Most importantly, it would end the immediate V-weapon threat to England, a threat that if turned against her ports instead of her cities could have severely curbed Allied supplies and disrupted the Allies' logistics.

Antwerp was a key and an obvious objective, but if 21st Army Group were to continue beyond, the Netherlands could be freed and the entire German Fifteenth Army could be bagged like the Seventh had been at Falaise. In the fall of 1944, geography, logistics, and politics ensured that Montgomery's advance would be supported.

The Final Days of August

While Monty was discussing his new campaign plan with Bradley on August 17, Patton was pushing reconnaissance east of Orléans and Dreux, which fell the day before. Three divisions were attached to First Army to close the Falaise Gap, but within the shift, Patton acquired two more divisions for his Brittany reduction. He pushed Haislip's XV Corps to the northeast to seize crossings on the Seine as part of the wide envelopment to interdict any German withdrawals from the Falaise area.

Within a day he had forces on the Seine and by the 19th, while Eisenhower and Bradley met, Patton had a bridgehead at Mantes Gassicourt northwest of Paris. First Army and the Canadians closed the ''Gap'' on the 20th at Chambois. XII Corps, now commanded by Manton S. Eddy who replaced the ill Gen. Cook, added Seine bridgeheads to Patton's eastern drive.

Patton, whose success spurred Bradley to propose a two-army advance to Metz and Germany by the 12th Army Group, proposed two alternative plans to his boss.

''Plan A'' would swing Third Army north pivoting on the Seine to take the enemy's rear east of the Seine and in front of the other three Allied armies; ''Plan B'' sent Third Army east to Germany and the Rhine.

Having already sold Eisenhower on an advance to the Saar, Bradley immediately rejected Plan A. Patton's orders, however, included the statement, ''. . . be prepared to change direction and execute Plan A on

Above: Men of the US 11th Infantry Regiment, 5th Infantry Division, XX Corps pass through Chartres on August 19 as part of the large, fast-moving sweep undertaken by Lt. Gen. George S. Patton's US Third Army to reach the line of the Seine River upstream of Paris.

Army order.'' That order never came.

The Seine was the point of no return in the ''great argument.'' Plan B ended the last chance at an even-handed approach to a ''single thrust.'' Had Patton swung north, Eisenhower could still have modified the thrust to send Patton towards Aachen from the south, and the full body of two army groups towards the Ruhr, with Eisenhower in command.

But with Patton racing east, every day made Eisenhower's ''broad front'' decision more irreversible. Montgomery continued to argue for his plan but now demanded Patton's halt, an unfortunately necessary requirement to consolidate logistical support behind his own advance. Refusing to abandon his plan, Ike

permitted Patton's advance and held firm against Montgomery's demand for total ground command.

By August 25 when Paris surrendered to Leclerc, Patton's six divisions were angled to the southeast from Paris all along the Seine with ''P'' Wood's 4th Armored characteristically 30 miles (48km) further out in front at the city of Troyes. He still had five divisions in Brittany and, despite having lost XV Corps to First Army as the result of closing the ''Gap,'' Patton still looked east towards Germany.

His columns were being fed, fueled and rearmed by the ''Red Ball Express,'' an ad hoc grouping of more than 130 truck companies, making up to a 600-mile (960km) round trip to carry essential supplies direct to the advancing divisions.

Bradley stopped Third Army for a day in accordance with Eisenhower's priorities to build up, but then unleashed Patton who was determined to drain his tanks and trucks of gas going east and then continue his army's advance on foot. Mesmerized by getting his two corps on the Rhine, Patton headed for the World War I battlefields where he had first commanded tanks in battle.

August's final days brought further spectacular successes, seemingly belying predictions of a future halt in operations. Montgomery's British and Canadian forces, whose hard-bought advances against the bulk of the German armor in the west brought them to the Seine about a week after Hodges's and Patton's armies, now readied their grand advance. They began crossing the Seine as part of the general Allied attack on the 26th. Dempsey's British Second Army with Horrocks's XXX Corps in the lead began its pursuit to the Belgian-Dutch border, and within days would match Patton's best time by covering 250 miles (400km) in six days, freeing Brussels by September 3.

Below: Taken on August 17, Orléans was the most important city to fall to the US XII Corps, the right-hand formation of the US Third Army, during its sweeping dash through northern central France just to the north of the Loire River.

Above: German machinegunners try to impede the work of US Army engineers as they ferry vehicles across the Seine River near Montereau on August 25. A new stage in the defeat of Germany was about to begin with a four-army Allied offensive from the Seine to the Rhine.

Crerar's Canadians moved to take the vital Channel ports. Hodges's First Army pivoted on Paris with "Lightning Joe" Collins's US VII Corps racing north encircling a further 25,000 Germans in the "Mons Gap."

When Eisenhower took command of the Allied Force on September 1, 21st Army Group's 14 divisions had a bridgehead on the Somme and within ten days would overrun the Channel coast; investing the key ports, freeing Brussels, capturing Antwerp, and would be sitting on the Dutch border.

Hodges's First Army raced 100 miles (160km) to the Belgian border and by the time logistics stopped Monty, most of Belgium and all of Luxembourg would be liberated, and patrols would be probing across into Germany. First Army prepared to attack the Siegfried Line, using Collins's VII Corps in the Aachen corridor. Patton crossed the Meuse at Verdun by the 1st, and with only six divisions pressed rapidly east reaching the Mosel from Metz to Nancy. But even Patton could be stopped by a supply famine.

Finally, logistics halted the general advance while limited attacks tried to strain forward. Eisenhower's four armies were no longer tightly joined presenting a powerful front, but holding a front of approximately 300 miles (480km). By September 10, the pursuit was over, and the war in northwest Europe entered an entirely new stage.

Normandy: The Final Account

Overlord's objectives were met on August 24 — D+79 — when the line outlining the "lodgment area" was reached, although historians normally consider Eisenhower's assumption of command on September 1 as the logical end of the campaign.

By September, the Allies had suffered nearly 210,000 casualties, including almost 37,000 dead. Thirty-eight Allied divisions were on the continent facing 51 German "divisions" whose actual combat strength SHAEF computed at 33 divisions. German losses have been variously estimated between 400,000 and 500,000, with at least 1,500 tanks and 3,500 guns destroyed.

With an Allied force rapidly growing to eight divisions moving up from southern France, most of France was free. Belgium, Luxembourg, and the Netherlands were days away from freedom for some of their populations. The war, however, was far from over. Neither Holland nor France would be totally freed until the end of the Rhineland campaign the following spring. Luxembourg and Belgium would be liberated and then fought over again during the bloody Ardennes campaign in December and January.

Normandy, however, was the essential starting-point on the road to liberation. The "Second Front" long awaited by the Soviets and the "Cross-Channel Attack" that was the center piece of America's direct approach strategy to destroy Hitler, spelt doom for the Third Reich.

Neither the strategic bombing offensive that contributed so much, the essential efforts of the Allied navies and merchant marine, nor the valiant campaigns fought in the Mediterranean, North Africa, nor even the Eastern Front, could have brought victory by 1945 without *Overlord*. Within a year of the invasion, Nazi Germany was smashed, and Western Europe was free.

History's judgements on *Overlord*, its contributions, and its personalities will long continue. Historical research never ends; each generation seems to have the need to reevaluate and assess in the light of its values. Perhaps *Overlord's* epitaph should follow the symbolism represented on the shoulder sleeve insignia of the Supreme Headquarters Allied Expeditionary Force.

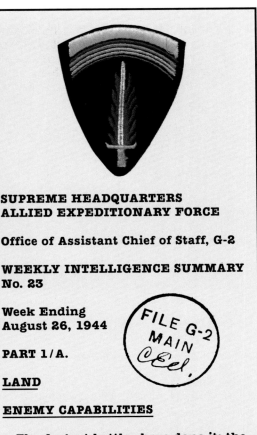

The insignia featured a crusader's sword of liberation representing avenging justice to break Nazi power in Europe, on a sable shield representing the oppression that had fallen over Europe. Atop the shield is a rainbow representing the colors of the Allied national flags, under an azure field representing the peace and tranquility that the United Nations would attempt to restore to Europe's people.

The accomplishments of the Allied Force that marched, flew, or sailed under SHAEF's command matched in deeds what the symbolism of SHAEF's insignia represented. So many years after the event, history has to record that SHAEF's objectives were met.

Bibliography

Adleman, Robert H, and George Walton. "The Champagne Campaign." Boston, 1969.
Adleman, Robert H. "The Devil's Brigade." Philadelphia, 1966.
Ambrose, Stephen E. "Pegasus Bridge." London, 1984.
Ambrose, Stephen E. "The Supreme Commander: The War Years of General Dwight D. Eisenhower." London, 1971.
Barker, Thomas M. "The Ljubljana Gap Strategy: Alternative to Anvil/Dragoon or Fantasy" Journal of Military History, vol LVI, Jan. 1992. pp 57-85.
Barnett, Correlli. "The Audit of War." London, 1986.
Beck, Alfred M., Abe Bortz, Charles W. Lynch, Lida Mayo, and Ralph F. Weld. "The United States Army in World War Two; The Technical Services; The Corps of Engineers: The War Against Germany." Washington, D.C., 1985.
Belchem, David. "Victory in Normandy." London, 1981
Belfield, Eversley, and H. Essame. "The Battle for Normandy." London, 1965.
Bennett, Ralph. "Ultra and the Mediterranean Strategy." New York, 1989.
Bennett, Ralph. "Ultra in the West: The Normandy Campaign of 1944-1945." New York, 1979.
Blumenson, Martin. "Breakout and Pursuit." Washington, D.C., 1961 & 1984.
Blumenson, Martin, ed. "The Patton Papers" vol II. 1940-1945. Boston, 1974.
Bond, Brian. "War and Society in Europe, 1870-1970." London, 1984.
Boyd, Carl. "Hitler's Japanese Confidant: General Oshima Hiroshi and Magic Intelligence, 1941-1945." Kansas, 1993.
Bradley, Omar. "A Soldier's Story." New York, 1951.
Bradley, Omar, and Clay Blair "A General's Life." London, 1983.
Breur, William B. "Operation Dragoon: The Allied Invasion of Southern France." Novato, 1987.
Bryant, Arthur. "Triumph in the West: A History of the War years Based on the Diaries of Field Marshall Lord Alanbrooke, Commander of the Imperial General Staff." New York, 1959.
Bryant, Arthur. "The Turn of the Tide." London, 1957.
Butcher, Harry C. "Three Years with Eisenhower." London, 1946.
Butler, Roland M., ed. "History of the Second World War." 6 vols. London, 1957-1986.
Calder, Angus. "The People's War." London, 1969.
Calvocoressi, Peter, Guy Wint, and John Pritchard. "Total War." London, 1990.
Carter, Worrall Reed, and Elmer Ellsworth Duvall. "Ships, Salvage, and the Sinews of War: The Story of Fleet Logistics afloat in the Atlantic and Mediterranean Waters During World War Two." Washington, D.C., 1954.
Cline, Ray S. "Washington Command Post: The Operations Division." Washington, D.C., 1951.
Collins, J. Lawton. "Lightning Joe." Baton Rouge, 1979.
Creveld, Martin van. "Supplying War." London, 1977.
Creveld, Martin van. "Fighting Power: German and United States Army Performance, 1939-1945." London, 1983.
Crookenden, Napier. "Drop Zone Normandy." London, 1976.
Delvin, Gerard M. "Paratrooper!; The Saga of the United States Army and Marine Parachute and Glider Combat Troops During World War Two." New York, 1979.
Eisenhower, Dwight D. "Crusade in Europe." New York, 1948.
Ellis, John, "Brute Force: Allied Strategy and Tactics in the Second World War." New York, 1990.
Ellis, Lionel F. "Victory in the West." 2 vols. London, 1962.
Feis, Herbert. "Churchill, Roosevelt, Stalin: The War They Waged and the Peace They Sought." Princeton, 1967.
Florentin, E. "Battle of the Falaise Gap." London, 1965.
Fraser, David. "Alanbrooke." London, 1982.
Greenfield, Kent Roberts. "American Strategy in World War Two: A Reconsideration." Baltimore, 1963.
Hale, Edwin R.W., and John Frayn Turner. "The Yanks are Coming." New York, 1983.
Hammerton, J.C. "Achtung Minen." Lewes, 1991.
Harrison, Gordon. "Cross-Channel Attacks; United States Army in World War Two: The European Theatre of Operations." Washington, D.C., 1951.
Hartcup, Guy. "Code Name Mulberry." London, 1977.
Hastings, Max. "Overlord, D-Day and the Battle for Normandy 1944." London, 1984.
Haswell, Jock. "The Intelligence and Deception of the D-Day Landings." London, 1979.
Higgens, Trumbull. "Soft Underbelly: The Anglo-American Controversy over the Italian campaign, 1939-1945." New York, 1968.
Higgens, Trumbull. "Winston Churchill, and the Second Front, 1940-1943." New York, 1957.
Hinsley, F.H. "British Intelligence in the Second World War." vol. III. London, 1988.
Historical Section, Seventh United States Army. "Report of Operations: The Seventh United States Army in France and Germany 1944-1945." 2 vols. Nashville, 1988.
How, J.J. "Normandy: The British Breakout." London, 1981.
Howard, Michael. "British Intelligence in the Second World War." vol. V. London, 1990.
Howard, Michael. "The Continental Commitment: The Dilemma of British Defence Policy in the Era of the Two World Wars." London, 1972.
Howard, Michael. "The Mediterranean Strategy in the Second World War." New York, 1968.
Huston, James A. "The Sinews of War: Army Logistics 1775-1953." Washington, D.C., 1966.
Irving, David. "The War Between the Generals." London, 1981.
Keegan, John. "Six Armies in Normandy." London, 1981.
Kirkpatrick, Charles E. "An Unknown Future and a Doubtful Present: Writing the Victory Plan of 1941." Washington, D.C., 1990.

Larrabee, Eric. "Commander in Chief: Franklin Delano Roosevelt, his Lieutenants, and Their War." London, 1988.
Leighton, Richard M., and Robert W. Coakley. "Global Logistics and Strategy, 1940-1943." Washington, D.C., 1955.
Leighton, Richard M. "Overlord Versus the Mediterranean at the Cairo-Teheran Conferences." Kent Roberts Greenfield, ed. "Command Decisions." Washington, D.C., Reprint 1984.
Lewin, Ronald. "Churchill as Warlord." New York, 1982.
Lewin, Ronald. "Montgomery as Military Commander." London, 1968.
Liddell-Hart, Basil H. "The Other Side of the Hill." London, 1986.
Lindsay, O. ed. "A Guards General." London, 1986.
Macrea, R. Stuart. "Winston Churchill's Toyshop." Kineton, 1971.
Masson, Madeline. "Christine: A Search for Christine Granville." London, 1975
Matloff, Maurice. "The Anvil Decision: Crossroads of Strategy" Kent Roberts Greenfield, ed. "Command Decisions." Washington, D.C., Reprint 1984.
Matloff, Maurice. "Strategic Planning for Coalition Warfare, 1943-1944." Washington, D.C., 1959.
Matloff, Maurice, and Edwin S. Snell. "Strategic Planning for Coalition Warfare. 1941-1942." Washington, D.C., 1953.
Maule, Henry G. "'Caen." London, 1976.
McKee, Alexander. Caen: Anvil of Victory." London, 1965.
Miller, Robert A. "August 1944: The Campaign for France." Novato, 1988.
Montgomery, Bernard L. "Normandy to the Baltic." Boston, 1948.
Montgomery, Bernard L. "The Memoirs of Field Marshal, The Viscount Montgomery of Alamein, K.G." Cleveland, 1958
Morison, Samuel Eliot. "History of United States Naval Operations in World War Two." vol. XI, "The Invasion of France and Germany, 1944-1945." Boston. 1964
Morison, Samuel Eliot. "The Two Ocean War: A Short History of the United States Navy in the Second World War." Boston, 1963.
Neaman, W.L. "Making The Peace, 1941-1945: The Diplomacy of Wartime Conferences." Washington, D.C., 1950.
Norman, A. "Operation Overlord." Greenwood, 1982.
Patton, George S. "War As I Knew It." Boston, 1948.
Pelling, Henry. "Britain and The Second World War." London, 1970.
Pemberton, A.L. "The Development of Artillery Tactics and Equipment, 1939-1945." London, 1950.
Pogue, Forrest C. "George C. Marshall: Ordeal and Hope, 1939-1942." New York, 1965.
Pogue, Forrest C. "George C. Marshall: Originator of Victory, 1943-1945." New York, 1973.
Pogue, Forrest C. "The Supreme Command." Washington, D.C., 1954.
Popper, M. "Heaven and Hell." New York.
Roberts, P. "From the Desert to the Baltic." London, 1987.
Roskill, S.W. "The War at Sea, 1939-1945", vol. III, "The Offensive", part II, "1st June 1944-14th August 1945." London, 1961.
Ruppenthal, Roland G. "Logistical Support of the Armies", vol I. Washington, D.C., 1953.
Ryan, Cornelius, "The Longest Day." New York, 1960.
Scarfe, Norman. "Assault Division." London, 1947.
Schoenbrun, David. "Soldiers of the Night: The Story of the French Resistance." New York, 1980.
Schofield, Brian B. "Operation Neptune." Annapolis, 1974.
Simpson, Albert F. "The Invasion of Southern France" Wesley Frank Craven and James Lea Cate. "The Army Air Forces in World War Two" vol. III, "Europe: Argument to, V.E. Day, January 1944-May 1945." Chicago, 1951.
Stacey, C.P. "The Victory Campaign." Ottawa, 1960.
Stoler, Mark. "The Politics of the Second Front: American Military Planning and Diplomacy in Coalition Warfare, 1941-1943." Westport, 1977.
Thornton, Willis. "The Liberation of Paris." New York, 1962.
Truscott, Lucian K, Jr., "Command Missions: A Personal Story." New York, 1951.
Turner, John Frayn, and Robert Jackson. "Destination Berchtesgaden: The Story of the United States Seventh Army." New York, 1975.
Tute, Warren, John Costello, and Terry Hughes. "D-Day." London, 1974.
United States Army, Center of Military History. "Omaha Beachhead." Washington, D.C., 1980.
United States Army, Center of Military History. "Utah Beach to Cherbourg." Washington, D.C., 1980.
United States Army, Center of Military History. "St. Lô." Washington, D.C., 1984.
Watson, Mark S. "Chief of Staff: Prewar Plans and Preparations." Washington, D.C., 1950.
Weigley, Russell. "The American Way of War: A History of United States Military Strategy and Policy." New York, 1973.
Weigley, Russell. "Eisenhower's Lieutenants: The Campaign of France and Germany, 1944-1945." Bloomington, 1981.
Wilmot, Chester. "The Struggle for Europe." London, 1952.
Wilson, Theodore A. "The First Summit: Roosevelt and Churchill at Placentia Bay, 1941." Lawrence, rev. ed., 1991.
Wilt, Alan F. "The French Riviera Campaign of August 1944." Carbondale, 1981.

CAPTION AND KEY SOURCES

Black, Robert W. "Rangers in World War Two." New York, 1992.
Barnett, Correlli. "Engage the Enemy More Closely, The Royal Navy in the Second World War." London, 1991.
Benamou, Jean-Pierre. "Normandy 1944, An Illustrated Field-Guide." Bayeux, 1982.
Benamou, Jean-Pierre, Georges Bernage, and R. Grenneville. "Invasion Journal Pictorial, 6th June-22nd August 1944." Bayeux, 1991.
Collins Larry, and Dominique Lapierre. "Is Paris Burning?." London, 1991
Davis, Brian L. "Badges and Insignia of the Third Reich, 1933-1945." London, 1992.
Davies, Howard P. "British Parachute Forces — 1940-1945." London, 1974.
Desquesnes, Remy. "The Canadians to Europe's Rescue." Caen, 1992.
Fletcher, David. "Vanguard of Victory, The 79th Armoured Division." London, 1984.
Fosten, D.S.V. and R.J. Marrion, "Waffen SS., Its Uniforms, Insignia and Equipment 1938-1945." London, 1972.
Hamilton, Nigel. "Monty. Vol. 2, Master of the Battlefield 1942-1944." London, 1987.
Hinsley, Harry, and C.A.G. Simkens. "British Intelligence in the Second World War. Vol. 4." London, 1990.
Holt, Tony and Valmai. "The Visitor's Guide to Normandy Landing Beaches." Ashbourne, 1990.
Joslen, H.F. "Orders of Battle — Second World War 1939-1945." London, 1990.
Lefèvre, Eric. "Panzers in Normandy, Then and Now." London, 1983.
Lovat, Lord. "March Past — A Memoir by —." London, 1978.
Lyndhurst, Joe (Chief Consultant). "Military Collectables." London, 1983.
Messenger, Charles. "World War Two, Chronological Atlas." London, 1989.
Mollo, Andrew. "The Armed Forces of World War Two. Uniforms, Insignia and Originisation." New York, 1987.
Myatt, Frederick. "Modern Small Arms." London, 1978.
Polish Air Force Association. "Destiny Can Wait." Nashville, 1988.
Rosignoli, Guido. "Badges and Insignia of World War Two — Air Force, Naval, Marine." London, 1980.
Stanton, Shelby L. "Order of Battle, U.S. Army World War Two." Novato, 1984.
Terraine, John. "The Right of the Line, The Royal Air Force in the European War, 1939-1945." London, 1988.
Warner, Philip. "The D-Day Landings." London, 1990.
Weeks, John. "Airborne equipment, A History of its Development." Newton Abbott, 1976.
Wilkinson, Frederick. "Badges of the British Army, 1820 to the Present." London, 1980.
Wood, Alan. "History of the World's Glider Forces." Wellingborough, 1990.

Acknowledgments

LIST OF MUSEUMS
The artifacts featured in this book can be found in the following museums:

Airborne Museum
50480 Ste. Mère-Eglise, Normandy
France
Open: February to mid-November
Closed mid-December to mid-January
Open Saturdays and Sundays for the
remainder of the year

D-Day Museum, Portsmouth
Clarence Esplanade
Southsea, Hampshire PO5 3NT
England
Open: All year, 10:30 — 5:30

Dwight D. Eisenhower Library and Museum
Abilene, Kansas 67410
USA
Open: 9:00 — 4:45 Daily
Summer Hours May 29 — August 14
8:00 — 5:45

5th Regiment Armory
Maryland National Guard
29th Division Street
Baltimore, Maryland
USA
Open: 2nd and 4th Sunday of the month
2:00 — 4:00, or by appointment

Memorial Museum of the Battle of Normandy
Boulevard Fabian Ware
14400 Bayeux, Normandy
France
Open: June, July, August, 9:30 — 5:00
March 1 to May 31, September and
October, 10:00 — 12:30; 2:00 — 6:30
November 1 to February 28,
10:30 — 12:30; 2:00 — 6:00

The Military History Shop, Inc.
Kennett Square, Pennsylvania
USA
Open: Monday, Thursday, Friday
11:00 — 6:00, Saturday 10:00 — 3:00
Closed Tuesday, Wednesday, Sunday

Milwaukee Public Museum
800 W. Wells Street
Milwaukee, Wisconsin
USA
Open: All year, 9:00 — 5:00

Museum of the D-Day Landings
14117 Arromanches, Normandy
France
Open: All year

Museum of the Order of the Liberation
(Liberation Museum)
Hôtel National des Invalides
51 bis, Boulevard Latour-Maubourg
75007 Paris
France
Open: 2:00 — 5:00 except Sundays

Pegasus Bridge Museum
10 Avenue du Commandant Kieffer
14970 Bénouville, Normandy
France
Open: March — October

Patton Museum of Cavalry and Armor
Fort Knox, Kentucky 40121-0208
USA
Open: Monday — Friday 9:00 — 4:30
Saturday — Sunday 10:00 — 4:30

Royal Marines Museum
RM Barracks
Eastney, Portsmouth
Hampshire PO4 9PX
England
Open: September-Easter, 10:00 — 4:30;
Summer, 10:00 — 5:30

The Sikorski Museum
20 Princes Gate, London SW7 1QA
England
Open: Monday — Friday, 2:00 — 4:00

US Army Military History Institute
Carlisle Barracks, Pennsylvania
USA
Open: Monday — Friday, 8:00 — 4:30

US Army Ordnance Museum
Aberdeen Proving Ground
Aberdeen, Maryland 21005-5201
USA
Open: Tuesday — Saturday 10:00 — 4:45
Closed Sunday and Monday

West Point Museum
United States Military Academy
West Point, New York 10996
USA
Open: All year, 10:30 — 4:15

TOURS
Expert guided tours to the D-Day landing beaches and Normandy battlefields can be booked through:

Major & Mrs Holt's Battlefield Tours Ltd
15 Market Street, Sandwich
Kent CT13 9DA
England
Tel: 0304 612248
Fax: 0304 614930

INSTITUTIONAL COLLECTIONS

Airborne Museum, Ste. Mère-Eglise
Jean d'Aignaux, President
Pierre Galin, Vice President
Auguste Foche, Treasurer
Phillipe Jutras, Curator
Annick Hamel, Museum Technician

D-Day Museum, Portsmouth
Stephen Brooks, Curator

Dwight D. Eisenhower Library and Museum
John E. Wickman, Director
Dennis H.J. Medina, Curator
Marion M. Kamm, Registrar
Gary W. Holman, Exhibit Specialist

5th Regiment Armory,
Maryland National Guard
Col. Ernest M. Snyder (Ret.d), Records
    Management and Support Officer
Joseph Balkoski, Historian

Memorial Museum of the Battle of Normandy
Dr Jean-Pierre Benamou, Curator
The Friends of the Memorial Museum

Milwaukee Public Museum
H. Michael Madaus, Assistant Curator
    of History
John B. Lundstrom, Assistant Curator
    of History
Claudia Jacobsen, Registrar

Museum of the D-Day Landings
Jean Noël, Curator

Museum of the Order of the Liberation
Catherine Horel, Curator

Pegasus Bridge Museum
Marc Jacquinot, Curator

Patton Museum of Cavalry and Armor
John Purdy, Director
Charles R. Lemons, Curator

Royal Marines Museum
Col. K.N. Wilkins, Curator
Ed Bartholomew, Photographic
    Librarian

The Sikorski Museum
Krzysztof Barbarski, Curator

US Army Military History Institute
Michael J. Winey, Curator
Randy Hackenburg, Assistant Curator

US Army Ordnance Museum
William F. Atwater, Ph.D., Director
Roger A. Godin, Curator
Armando E. Framarini, Museum
    Specialist
James Broome, Armorer
Lesley M. LeRoy, Administrative
    Assistant

West Point Museum
Michael E. Moss, Director
Robert W. Fisch, Curator of Arms
Michael J. McAfee, Curator of
    Uniforms and History
Walter J. Nock, Museum
    Specialist/Conservator

PRIVATE COLLECTIONS
Dale E. Biever, Boyertown, Pa.
Allan D. Cors, McLean, Virginia
George J. Fistrovich, Winterthur, Del.
Eugene C. Gibson, Jr., Ambler, Pa.
Howard O. Hendricks, Gibsonville, N.C.
William A. LePard, Ardmore, Pa.
Henri G. Levaufre, Périers, France
Joseph A. McFalls, Malvern, Pa.
Russ A. Pritchard, Bryn Mawr, Pa.
Tony Stamatelos, Cambridge, Mass.
Melvin J. Strunk, Abilene, Kansas

PICTURE CREDITS
t, Top   bc, Bottom center
tl, Top left   l, Left
tr, Top right   r, Right
tc, Top center   c, Center
b, Bottom   cl, Center left
bl, Bottom left   cr, Center right
br, Bottom right

Front Cover, National Archives, Washington, DC, (NA); 6/7, Bundesarchiv, Koblenz, (BA); 8, Salamander Books Ltd.; 9, (tr) NA, (bl) Imperial War Museum, London, (IWM); 12 (tr) IWM, (bl) NA; 13, Association of American Railroads; 14, (both) IWM; 15, (both) Smithsonian Institution, National Air & Space Museum, Washington, DC, (NASM); 18, (tr) IWM; 19, (bl) NA; 20, IWM; 21, (bl) NA; 26, (bl) IWM; 27, (br) IWM; 29, (tr) D-Day Museum, Portsmouth, Hampshire, (DDM), (tl & c) NA, (cl,bl,bc &br) IWM; 35, (cr & bl) IWM; 36, (bl) IWM, (bc & br) Royal Armoured Corps Tank Museum, Bovington, Dorset; 37, (b & inset) Dwight D. Eisenhower Library, Abilene, Kansas (DEL); 38, (all) IWM; 40, BA; 41, (tl) IWM, (tr) Fistrovich Collection; 46, (tl) NA, (bl) BA; 47, (tl & cl) BA; 48, (t,br & bl) NA; 49 (t) DDM, (cr) IWM, (cl,bl,bc & br) NA; 54, (tr) BA; 55, (tl) NA, (bl) BA; 56, (tr & br) NA; 57, (both) BA; 58, (bl) IWM; 59, (both) BA; 64, (tr NA; 65, (tl) NA; 66, (bl) IWM; 67, (tl, bl, br & tcr) IWM, (remainder) Royal Marines Museum, Southsea, Hampshire, (RRM); 69, (br) IWM; 71, (t & c) National Meteorological Library, Bracknell, Berkshire; 72, (bl) IWM, 76, (bl) DDM, 80, BA; 81, (tr) NA; 82, (both) NA; 84, (br) NA; 85, (bl) NA; 88, (bl) NA;92, (bl) NA; 93, (both) NA; 94, (b) IWM; 95, (t,cl & bl) NA; 96, (tr & cl) National Archives of Canada, Ottawa, Ontario, (NAC); 97 (br) IWM; 98, (bl) Airborne Forces Museum, Aldershot, Hampshire (AFM); 99, (tr) AFM, (cl & cr) IWM; 102, (cr & b) IWM; 103, (bl) IWM; 106, (tr) NAC, (br) IWM; 107, (bl) NAC; 108 (both) NAC; 19, (tr & tl) IWM, (b) NAC; 110, (tr) DDM, (cl & bl) IWM; 112, (tr) RRM, (cr & br) IWM; 113, (bl) IWM; 115, (br) NA; 116, (tr & cl) IWM, (b) NA; 118, (tr & bl) IWM, (br) BA; 119, (tl) IWM, (cl) BA, (bl) NA, (br) DEL; 120, (tl) IWM; 123, (tr) IWM; 128, (tr) NAC, (b) NA; 129, (tr) IWM, (bl) BA; 130, RAF Museum, Hendon, London, (RAF); 131, (t) DDM, (cr) RAF, (br) IWM; 135, (t) NASM, 136, (tr) NASM, (cl) IWM; 137, (bl) NASM, 139, (inset) BA; 140, (t) DEL; 141, (cr) BA, (bl) IWM, (br) DEL; 143, (inset) IWM; 144, (both) via Alfred Price; 145, (tl) Messerschmitt Archiv, (cl) IWM, (bc) NA; 148, (tr) NASM, (cr & br) NA, (bl) RAF, (cl) IWM; 149, (tl) Clarence Simonson; 151, (tr) Doon Campbell; 155, (tr) IWM; 160, (tr) IWM, (bl) BA; 161, (tr) IWM, (br) BA; 164, (all) BA; 165, (tr,br &bl) BA; 166, (tr) NAC, (inset) IWM; 167, (bl) IWM; 170, (tr) BA, (bl) NA; 171, (tr) NA; 172, BA; 173, (tr) NA, (bl) BA; 177, (tr & bl) NA; 180, (bl) BA; 182, (tr) NA, (cr & br) NAC; 183, (tl) NAC, (bl) BA; 187, (all) The Polish Institute & Sikorski Museum, London; 188, Constance Stuart Larrabee, Chestertown, Maryland; 189, (all) NA; 193, (tl) IWM; (bl) NA; 197, (all) NA; 198, (both) NA; 199,(both) NA; 202, (both) NA; 203, (both) NA; 204, NA; 205, (tr & bl) NA; 208, (tr) NA; 209, (tr) IWM; 210, IWM; 213, (cr) IWM, (bl) NA; 214, (tl) IWM, (cl & bl) NA; 218, (both) NA; 219, (tl) NA; 220, Memorial Museum, Bayeux; 221, Patton Museum of Cavalry and Armor; 222, 224, Levaufre Collection.

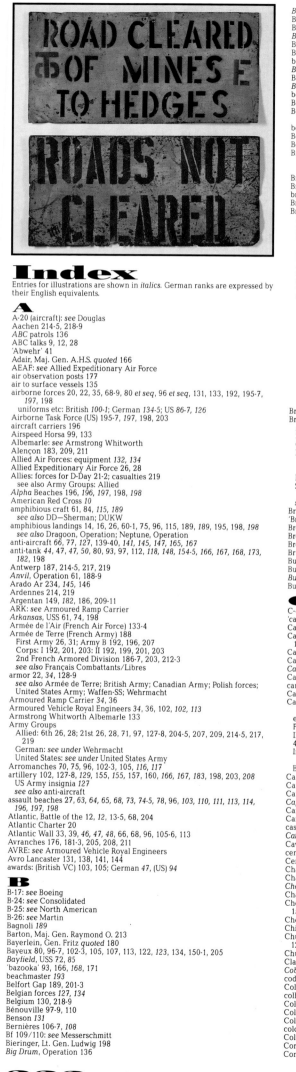

Index

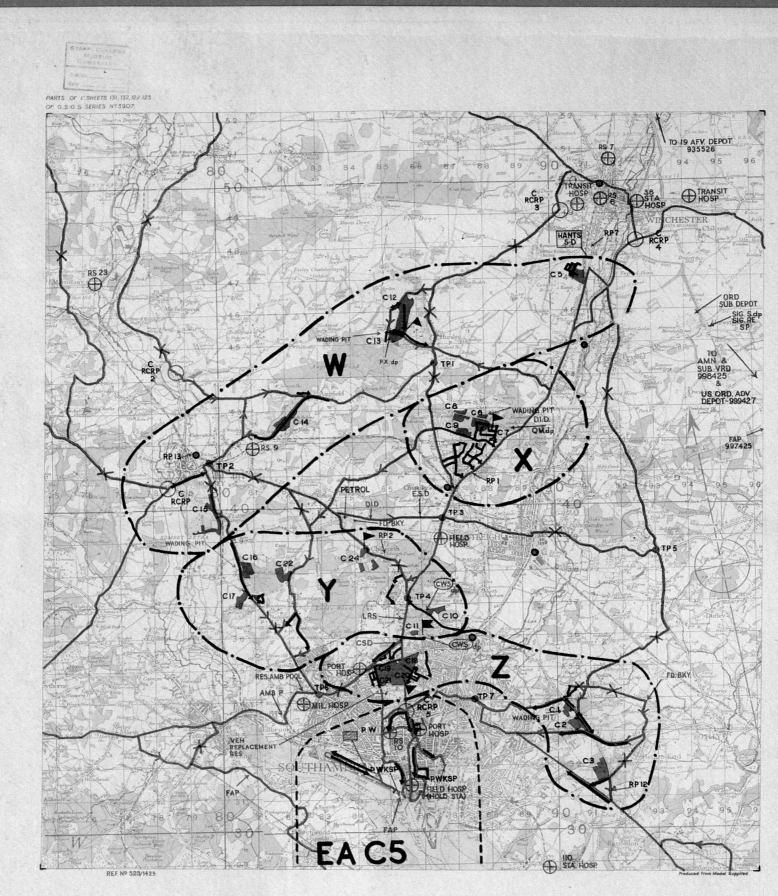

W

C12

WADING PIT   C13

PX dp

TP1

C8   C6

C9   C7   WADING PIT
                   D.I.D.
                   QM dp

X

W

RS 23

C
RCRP
2

C14

RP 13   RS 9

TP2

C
RCRP

C15

WADING PIT

PETROL
D.I.D.

FD. BKY.

RP 2

FIELD
HOSP

TP 3

RP 1

TP 5

C16

C22

C24

Y

C17

CWS
d

TP 4   C10

LRS   C11

CSD   CWS dp

Z

FD. BKY.

PORT
HOSP   C19   C18
              RCRP C20
TP6

RES. AMB POOL

AMB P

MIL. HOSP

P W   RS
             10

VEH
REPLACEMENT
RES.

SOUTHAMPTON

P WKSP   P WKSP
                FIELD HOSP
                (HOLD. STA)

RCRP
5   PORT
           HOSP

WADING PIT   C1
                    C2

C3

RP 12

FAP

FAP

FAP

EA C5

110
STA HOSP

C
RCRP
3

TRANSIT
HOSP

RS 7

TO 19 AFV. DEPOT
935526

RS 6

38
STA
HOSP

TRANSIT
HOSP

WINCHESTER

HANTS
S.D   RP 7   RCRP
                           4

C 5

ORD
SUB DEPOT
SIG. S dp
SIG. RE
S P

TO
AMN &
SUB VRD
998425
&
US ORD. ADV
DEPOT-999427

FAP
997425

REF. Nº 523/1425

Scale: One Inch to One Statute Mile = 1/63360

Scale of Kilometres